Gambling, the State and Society in Thailand, c.1800–1945

During the nineteenth century there was a huge increase in the level and types of gambling in Thailand. Taxes on gambling became a major source of state revenue, with the government establishing state-run lotteries and casinos in the first half of the twentieth century. Nevertheless, over the same period, a strong anti-gambling discourse emerged within the Thai elite, which sought to regulate gambling through a series of increasingly restrictive and punitive laws. By the mid-twentieth century, most forms of gambling had been made illegal, a situation that persists until today. This historical study, based on a wide variety of Thai- and English-language archival sources including government reports, legal cases and newspapers, places the criminalization of gambling in Thailand in the broader context of the country's socio-economic transformation and the modernization of the Thai state. Particular attention is paid to how state institutions, such as the police and judiciary, and different sections of Thai society shaped and subverted the law to advance their own interests. Finally, the book compares the Thai government's policies on gambling with those on opium use and prostitution, placing the latter in the context of an international clampdown on vice in the early twentieth century.

James A. Warren is a lecturer in the Social Science Division of Mahidol University International College, Thailand.

Routledge studies in the modern history of Asia

1 **The Police in Occupation Japan**
Control, corruption and resistance to reform
Christopher Aldous

2 **Chinese Workers**
A new history
Jackie Sheehan

3 **The Aftermath of Partition in South Asia**
Tai Yong Tan and Gyanesh Kudaisya

4 **The Australia–Japan Political Alignment**
1952 to the present
Alan Rix

5 **Japan and Singapore in the World Economy**
Japan's economic advance into Singapore, 1870–1965
Shimizu Hiroshi and Hirakawa Hitoshi

6 **The Triads as Business**
Yiu Kong Chu

7 **Contemporary Taiwanese Cultural Nationalism**
A-chin Hsiau

8 **Religion and Nationalism in India**
The case of the Punjab
Harnik Deol

9 **Japanese Industrialisation**
Historical and cultural perspectives
Ian Inkster

10 **War and Nationalism in China**
1925–45
Hans J. van de Ven

11 **Hong Kong in Transition**
One country, two systems
Edited by Robert Ash, Peter Ferdinand, Brian Hook and Robin Porter

12 **Japan's Postwar Economic Recovery and Anglo-Japanese Relations, 1948–62**
Noriko Yokoi

13 **Japanese Army Stragglers and Memories of the War in Japan, 1950–75**
Beatrice Trefalt

14 **Ending the Vietnam War**
The Vietnamese communists' perspective
Ang Cheng Guan

15 **The Development of the Japanese Nursing Profession**
Adopting and adapting Western influences
Aya Takahashi

16 **Women's Suffrage in Asia**
Gender nationalism and democracy
Louise Edwards and Mina Roces

17 **The Anglo-Japanese Alliance, 1902–22**
Phillips Payson O'Brien

18 **The United States and Cambodia, 1870–1969**
From curiosity to confrontation
Kenton Clymer

19 **Capitalist Restructuring and the Pacific Rim**
Ravi Arvind Palat

20 **The United States and Cambodia, 1969–2000**
A troubled relationship
Kenton Clymer

21 **British Business in Post-Colonial Malaysia, 1957–70**
'Neo-colonialism' or 'disengagement'?
Nicholas J. White

22 **The Rise and Decline of Thai Absolutism**
Kullada Kesboonchoo Mead

23 **Russian Views of Japan, 1792–1913**
An anthology of travel writing
David N. Wells

24 **The Internment of Western Civilians under the Japanese, 1941–45**
A patchwork of internment
Bernice Archer

25 **The British Empire and Tibet 1900–1922**
Wendy Palace

26 **Nationalism in Southeast Asia**
If the people are with us
Nicholas Tarling

27 **Women, Work and the Japanese Economic Miracle**
The case of the cotton textile industry, 1945–75
Helen Macnaughtan

28 **A Colonial Economy in Crisis**
Burma's rice cultivators and the world depression of the 1930s
Ian Brown

29 **A Vietnamese Royal Exile in Japan**
Prince Cuong De (1882–1951)
Tran My-Van

30 **Corruption and Good Governance in Asia**
Nicholas Tarling

31 **US–China Cold War Collaboration, 1971–89**
S. Mahmud Ali

32 **Rural Economic Development in Japan**
From the nineteenth century to the Pacific War
Penelope Francks

33 **Colonial Armies in Southeast Asia**
Edited by Karl Hack and Tobias Rettig

34 **Intra-Asian Trade and the World Market**
A. J. H. Latham and Heita Kawakatsu

35 **Japanese–German Relations, 1895–1945**
War, diplomacy and public opinion
Edited by Christian W. Spang and Rolf-Harald Wippich

36 **Britain's Imperial Cornerstone in China**
The Chinese maritime customs service, 1854–1949
Donna Brunero

37 **Colonial Cambodia's 'Bad Frenchmen'**
The rise of French rule and the life of Thomas Caraman, 1840–87
Gregor Muller

38 **Japanese–American Civilian Prisoner Exchanges and Detention Camps, 1941–45**
Bruce Elleman

39 **Regionalism in Southeast Asia**
Nicholas Tarling

40 **Changing Visions of East Asia, 1943–93**
Transformations and continuities
R. B. Smith, edited by Chad J. Mitcham

41 **Christian Heretics in Late Imperial China**
Christian inculturation and state control, 1720–1850
Lars P. Laamann

42 **Beijing – A Concise History**
Stephen G. Haw

43 **The Impact of the Russo-Japanese War**
Edited by Rotem Kowner

44 **Business–Government Relations in Prewar Japan**
Peter von Staden

45 **India's Princely States**
People, princes and colonialism
Edited by Waltraud Ernst and Biswamoy Pati

46 **Rethinking Gandhi and Nonviolent Relationality**
Global perspectives
Edited by Debjani Ganguly and John Docker

47 **The Quest for Gentility in China**
Negotiations beyond gender and class
Edited by Daria Berg and Chloë Starr

48 **Forgotten Captives in Japanese Occupied Asia**
Edited by Kevin Blackburn and Karl Hack

49 **Japanese Diplomacy in the 1950s**
From isolation to integration
Edited by Iokibe Makoto, Caroline Rose, Tomaru Junko and John Weste

50 **The Limits of British Colonial Control in South Asia**
Spaces of disorder in the Indian Ocean region
Edited by Ashwini Tambe and Harald Fischer-Tiné

51 **On The Borders of State Power**
Frontiers in the greater Mekong sub-region
Edited by Martin Gainsborough

52 **Pre-Communist Indochina**
R. B. Smith, edited by Beryl Williams

53 **Communist Indochina**
R. B. Smith, edited by Beryl Williams

54 **Port Cities in Asia and Europe**
Edited by Arndt Graf and Chua Beng Huat

55 **Moscow and the Emergence of Communist Power in China, 1925–30**
The Nanchang Rising and the birth of the Red Army
Bruce A. Elleman

56 **Colonialism, Violence and Muslims in Southeast Asia**
The Maria Hertogh controversy and its aftermath
Syed Muhd Khairudin Aljunied

57 **Japanese and Hong Kong Film Industries**
Understanding the origins of East Asian film networks
Kinnia Shuk-ting

58 **Provincial Life and the Military in Imperial Japan**
The phantom samurai
Stewart Lone

59 **Southeast Asia and the Vietnam War**
Ang Cheng Guan

60 **Southeast Asia and the Great Powers**
Nicholas Tarling

61 **The Cold War and National Assertion in Southeast Asia**
Britain, the United States and Burma, 1948–62
Matthew Foley

62 **The International History of East Asia, 1900–1968**
Trade, ideology and the quest for order
Edited by Antony Best

63 **Journalism and Politics in Indonesia**
A critical biography of Mochtar Lubis (1922–2004) as editor and author
David T. Hill

64 **Atrocity and American Military Justice in Southeast Asia**
Trial by army
Louise Barnett

65 **The Japanese Occupation of Borneo, 1941–45**
Ooi Keat Gin

66 **National Pasts in Europe and East Asia**
P. W. Preston

67 **Modern China's Ethnic Frontiers**
A journey to the West
Hsiao-ting Lin

68 **New Perspectives on the History and Historiography of Southeast Asia**
Continuing explorations
Michael Aung-Thwin and Kenneth R. Hall

69 **Food Culture in Colonial Asia**
A taste of empire
Cecilia Leong-Salobir

70 **China's Political Economy in Modern Times**
Changes and economic consequences, 1800–2000
Kent Deng

71 **Science, Public Health and the State in Modern Asia**
Edited by Liping Bu, Darwin Stapleton and Ka-che Yip

72 **Russo-Japanese Relations, 1905–17**
From enemies to allies
Peter Berton

73 **Reforming Public Health in Occupied Japan, 1945–52**
Alien prescriptions?
Christopher Aldous and Akihito Suzuki

74 **Trans-Colonial Modernities in South Asia**
Edited by Michael S. Dodson and Brian A. Hatcher

75 **The Evolution of the Japanese Developmental State**
Institutions locked in by ideas
Hironori Sasada

76 **Status and Security in Southeast Asian States**
Nicholas Tarling

77 **Lee Kuan Yew's Strategic Thought**
Ang Cheng Guan

78 **Government, Imperialism and Nationalism in China**
The maritime customs service and its Chinese staff
Chihyun Chang

79 **China and Japan in the Russian Imagination, 1685–1922**
To the ends of the orient
Susanna Soojung Lim

80 **Chinese Complaint Systems**
Natural resistance
Qiang Fang

81 **Martial Arts and the Body Politic in Meiji Japan**
Denis Gainty

82 **Gambling, the State and Society in Thailand, c.1800–1945**
James A. Warren

83 **Post-war Borneo, 1945–50**
Nationalism, empire and state-building
Ooi Keat Gin

Gambling, the State and Society in Thailand, c.1800–1945

James A. Warren

LONDON AND NEW YORK

First published 2013
by Routledge

Published 2014 by Routledge

2 Park Square, Milton Park, Abingdon, Oxfordshire OX14 4RN

Simultaneously published in the USA and Canada
by Routledge
711 Third Avenue, New York, NY 10017

Routledge is an imprint of the Taylor and Francis Group, an informa business

First issued in paperback 2015

© 2013 James A. Warren

The right of James A. Warren to be identified as author of this work has been asserted by him in accordance with the Copyright, Designs and Patents Act 1988.

All rights reserved. No part of this book may be reprinted or reproduced or utilised in any form or by any electronic, mechanical, or other means, now known or hereafter invented, including photocopying and recording, or in any information storage or retrieval system, without permission in writing from the publishers.

Trademark notice: Product or corporate names may be trademarks or registered trademarks, and are used only for identification and explanation without intent to infringe.

British Library Cataloguing in Publication Data
A catalogue record for this book is available from the British Library

Library of Congress Cataloging in Publication Data
Warren, James A.
Gambling, the state and society in Thailand, c. 1800–1945 / James A. Warren.
p. cm. – (Routledge studies in the modern history of Asia; 82)
Includes bibliographical references and index.
1. Gambling – Thailand – History. I. Title. II. Series: Routledge studies in the modern history of Asia (2005); 82.
HV6722.T5W37 2013
363.4'209593 – dc23   2012039547

ISBN 978-0-415-53634-9 (hbk)
ISBN 978-1-138-95636-0 (pbk)
ISBN 978-0-203-55210-0 (ebk)

Typeset in Times New Roman
by Cenveo Publisher Services

For my parents

Contents

List of illustrations and table xii
Acknowledgements xiii
Explanatory notes xv
Abbreviations xvii

Introduction 1

1 Gambling and socio-economic change in nineteenth-century Siam 14

2 Games, dens and players: gambling in nineteenth-century Thai society 27

3 Gambling revenue and the creation of the modern Thai nation-state 44

4 The Thai elite, anti-gambling and lawmaking 68

5 The police and enforcement 90

6 The judiciary, punishment and the prison 105

7 The press and the Bangkok middle class 118

8 Buddhism, the Sangha and the silent majority 137

9 The criminalization of vice: gambling policy in comparative perspective 149

Conclusion 173

Notes 188
Bibliography 227
Index 241

Illustrations and table

Figures

2.1	Equipment for playing *po pan*	30
2.2	Temple mural of a cockfight	37
7.1	Cartoon from *Bangkok kanmuang*, 15 September 1923	128
7.2	Cartoon from *Kro lek*, 30 November 1924	129
7.3	Cartoon from *Kro lek*, 11 January 1925	130

Table

1	Number of cases of homicide, gang robbery and robbery between 1909/10 and 1919/20	176

Acknowledgements

This book started life as my PhD dissertation, 'Gambling, the State and Society in Siam, c.1880–1945', which was completed at the School of Oriental and African Studies, University of London, under the supervision of Professor Ian Brown. He has been an inspiring teacher and I am deeply grateful for his guidance, insight and continuing support of my work. Special thanks go to my Thai-language teachers at SOAS, Dr David Smyth and Walaiporn Tantikanangkul, for guiding me through my initial forays into reading Thai sources and for their help in deciphering handwriting and some near illegible documents. I would also like to thank Professors Dhiravat na Pombejra and Piyanart Bunnag for their advice and assistance while I was conducting archival research in Thailand. Mention is also due to the staff of the National Archives in Bangkok for making the archives a pleasant environment in which to work. My fieldwork in Thailand was partially funded by grants from the University of London Central Research Fund and the SOAS Scholarships Committee. I also received a generous scholarship from the Harold Hyam Wingate Foundation for the writing up of the dissertation, for which I am very grateful.

Additional research and the task of revising the dissertation into this hopefully more readable study was undertaken while I was a postdoctoral fellow in the Department of History at the National University of Singapore. I would like to thank Professors Albert Lau and Bruce Lockhart in particular for their help and support during my fellowship. The suggestions of my PhD examiners, Professor John Sidel and Dr Roger Munting, provided an invaluable base for revising the dissertation for publication. I am also grateful to Dr Michael Montesano for reading and commenting on some of the draft chapters, and to Dr Stefan Hell for providing me with a copy of his dissertation and sharing his ideas on the influence of the League of Nations upon Thai government policies. Naturally, all opinions and errors in this study remain my own.

I would also like to acknowledge the assistance of John Peter Andersson and Gudrun Salevid in providing the image of the equipment for playing *po pan*, Dr Gerhard Jaiser and Diethard Ande at White Lotus Press (www.thailine.com/lotus) for the temple mural image and Dr Matthew Copeland for the Thai newspaper cartoons in Chapter 7.

Over the years, numerous other people have generously offered their thoughts and help. My particular thanks go to Rajeswary Brown and Rachel Harrison for their encouragement of my academic endeavours, Tomas Larsson for his companionship in the archives, Peter Smith for his efforts in helping to promote this book, Chatnopdol Aksornsawad and Antika Preeyanon for their warm hospitality in Bangkok, Peter Sowden at Routledge for his interest in this project and help in bringing it to fruition and, most of all, Michelle Tan for her friendship.

Finally, words cannot express my gratitude to my parents, Rosemary and Peter Warren. Without their love and support, none of this would have been possible. This book is dedicated to them.

Explanatory notes

Transcription

Thai names and words have been transcribed using the 'General System of Phonetic Transcription of Thai Characters into Roman' as set out in the Royal Institute, *Romanization Guide for Thai Script*, Bangkok, 1982. Following this system, diacritics have not been employed. Proper names of well-known people have been spelt according to the preference of that person, where known, or according to common usage: for instance, Vajiravudh instead of Wachirawut, and Devawongse rather than Thewawong. Official spelling has been used for all place names.

Names, ranks and titles

Following convention, Thai people are referred to by their first name and this is how they are listed in the Bibliography. Various titles are used for royalty and these indicate the generational descent of a particular member of the royal family. Under the absolute monarchy, members of the royal family that entered government service were also granted a rank. In this study, the children and grandchildren of kings have been referred to simply as princes or princesses. Until the absolute monarchy was abolished in 1932, bureaucrats and military officers were granted the following ranks in ascending order: *khun, luang, phra, phraya, chaophraya* and, very rarely, *somdet chaophraya*. Individuals were also given a title, which was commonly used in place of their actual name, and this is how they are referred to in the text. For example, Pan Sukhum is referred to as Chaophraya Yomarat. Many retained these titles as surnames following the 1932 coup, most notably Luang Phibun Songkhram (Plaek Khittasangka).

Until 1939, Thailand was known as Siam. In the text, the country is referred to by the name which was in use at the particular time being discussed. The terms Siamese and Thai have been used more interchangeably, however.

Dates and periods

During the period covered by this study, two different dating systems were used: the Bangkok Era (*rattanakosin sok*, abbreviated to R. S.) and the Buddhist Era (B. E.). The former ran from the founding of Bangkok in 1782. In 1911, it was replaced by the Buddhist Era, which is 543 years ahead of the Western calendar. Traditionally, the Thai year ran from 1 April to 31 March. Therefore, the year R. S. 111 was equivalent to 1 April 1892 to 31 March 1893 and in the text is written as 1892/3. Similarly, February B. E. 2478 (1935/6) was February 1936. In B. E. 2483 (1940), the start of the year was changed to 1 January, meaning that particular year was only nine months long (from 1 April 1940 to 31 December 1940).

The reigns of each of the nine kings in the present dynasty (the Chakri dynasty) are numbered according to where a particular king comes in the dynastic sequence. As in other studies of modern Thai history, the reign of Rama III is thus sometimes referred to in the text as the Third Reign and that of King Chulalongkorn as the Fifth Reign, for instance.

Currency

The Thai currency unit is called the baht but was sometimes referred to as the tical by foreigners during the period covered by this study. For much of the nineteenth century, the baht was valued at eight to the pound sterling. From the 1880s until the Second World War, its value fluctuated at around 11 to the pound.

Abbreviations

Thai archival documents

B	*Bettalet* (miscellaneous)
K Kh	*Samnakngan setthakit kankhlang* (Office of the Financial Adviser)
Kh	*Krasuang phrakhlang mahasombat* (Ministry of Finance)
KhPh	*Khamphiphaksa* (Legal judgments)
KS	*Krasuang kasettrathikan* (Ministry of Agriculture)
M	*Krasuang mahatthai* (Ministry of the Interior)
MT	*Krasuang mahatthai* (Ministry of the Interior)
N	*Krasuang nakhonban* (Ministry of Local Government)
NA	National Archives of Thailand
R	*Ratchakan ti* ... (the ... Reign)
RL	*Ratchanulekanukan* (Royal Secretariat)
SR	*Samnak nayok-ratthamontri* (Office of the Prime Minister's Secretariat)
Y	*Krasuang yuttitham* (Ministry of Justice)

Published sources

BTWM	*Bangkok Times Weekly Mail*
PKPS	Sathian Laiyalak et al. (comps), *Prachum kotmai pracham sok* [Collected Laws in Chronological Order], Bangkok: Daily Mail Press, Nitiwet, 1935+, 70 vols.
RFAB	Thailand, Ministry of Finance, *Report of the Financial Adviser upon the Budget of the Kingdom of Siam*, 1902+.
RPAB	*Report on the Police Administration of Bangkok Town, Suburbs and Railway District* (title varies), 1899+.
SY	Thailand, Ministry of Finance, Department of Commerce and Statistics (name varies), *Statistical Yearbook of the Kingdom of Siam/Thailand* (title varies), 1916+.

Introduction

'Gambling places were allowed at one time,' Phloi said. 'Then they were banned and if you got caught you could be sent to jail. Now they're back to being legal and respectable again. Why, Khun Luang? What's the reason for the change? Which government was right, or wrong?'

'The world turns and turns, Mae Phloi. The pendulum swings. Let us enjoy our roast duck.'

Kukrit Pramoj, *Four Reigns*[1]

It is World War Two Thailand and Phloi, the heroine of Kukrit Pramoj's historical novel *Four Reigns* (*Si phaen-din*), is in her twilight years. Born in 1882 to a wealthy nobleman and his minor wife, she has led a sheltered existence; her life revolving first around the Inner City of the Grand Palace, where she was sent at the age of ten, and then, once married to an up-and-coming palace official, her family and home. Nevertheless, Phloi has witnessed a bewildering array of events that have transformed the traditional, semi-feudal kingdom of Siam into the modernizing, nation-state of Thailand: the reigns of four successive monarchs, as indicated by the novel's title; the 1893 Paknam crisis in which France sent gunboats up the Chaophraya River to Bangkok in order to force the Siamese government into surrendering its claims to the territory of present-day Laos; the much-celebrated administrative, fiscal and legal reforms of King Chulalongkorn (r. 1868–1910), who is widely credited with securing Siam's independence and laying the foundations of the modern Thai state; the controversial reign of King Vajiravudh (r. 1910–25), during which her husband, Prem, rose to prominence within the court; Siam's entry into the First World War on the side of the Allies in 1917, and the sending of an expeditionary force to France; the impact of the worldwide economic depression of the early 1930s; the 1932 coup by a handful of military and civilian officials, including one of Phloi's sons, who overthrew the last absolute monarch, King Prajadhipok (r. 1925–35) and established a constitutional democracy; the 1933 failed royalist revolt led by Prince Boworadet, in which another of her sons took part and was imprisoned for many years as a result; the military's subsequent usurpation of political power under the strongman, Luang Phibun Songkhram; the country's change of name from Siam to Thailand in 1939; the war with French Indochina in 1940–41 that resulted in the regaining of the 'lost' territories in Laos and Cambodia; the alliance with Japan that quickly turned into an occupation; and, most recently, Thailand's 1942 declaration of war against Great Britain and the United States, leading to the Allied bombing raids on Bangkok that destroyed Phloi's home. Throughout her life, Phloi has born such misfortunes with good grace and Buddhist stoicism. Indeed, she is 'the embodiment of those ideal, genteel values most Thais still hold dear'.[2] However, Phloi has only a limited understanding of what has gone on around her, of which her bemusement at the about-turns in government policy on gambling is a good illustration. But her reaction is also understandable, for government attitudes towards gambling had continually shifted throughout her lifetime and were often contradictory and hypocritical.

Until the late nineteenth century, public gambling houses could be found throughout Siam. These were run by tax farmers, mostly Chinese, who paid the government substantial sums for the right. Indeed, the revenue they provided was crucial in funding Chulalongkorn's reforms. Nevertheless, in 1887 that king initiated a policy of gradually closing the gambling houses – a policy, it will be argued, that was motivated by a mix of humanitarian and social concerns, a need to enhance the population's productivity, and a desire to show the West that the leadership of Siam was enlightened and civilized. Due to financial constraints, however, the gambling houses were not completely abolished until the reign of Vajiravudh. In their absence, people turned to other forms of gambling: betting on horse racing and billiards were the crazes of the 1920s, for instance, but Thai and Chinese games also remained popular. All of these were regulated by a series of increasingly restrictive and punitive laws, culminating in the Gambling Act B. E. 2478, which was issued in 1936 and is still in force today. During the 1930s, the first state lotteries were started and they also remain a feature of present-day Thailand. To ensure their success, other organizations were prohibited from issuing their own lotteries. In short, the state established a monopoly on the provision of large-scale gambling activities. As part of this policy, the government experimented with state-owned casinos, the first opening in the South in 1939 and others in Bangkok during the closing stages of the war. All were short-lived; the last were closed in 1945 and the experiment abandoned. It is from one of the Bangkok casinos that Phloi's brother, Phoem, has just returned triumphantly, his winnings having purchased the roast duck the siblings are enjoying in the opening quotation. His answer to her questions is based on the Buddhist tenet that everything is impermanent. It also implies that as societies evolve, so too do attitudes towards gambling. Jan McMillen sums up this process in more technical terms: 'Periodic reformulations of the relation between gambling and society have been related to culturally and historically accepted definitions of what gambling is, influenced by fluctuating conceptions of morality which reflect prevailing social and political-economic conditions'.[3] The about-turns and shifts in the Siamese government's attitudes and policies towards gambling were intimately linked with those era-defining events witnessed by Phloi. Charting the swing of the pendulum is the purpose of this study.

Definitions of gambling

The first question that needs to be addressed is: what is gambling? There is no straightforward answer. The crux of the problem is that gambling is 'virtually a universal phenomenon in human societies', occurring 'in nearly all cultures and in every period of time'.[4] This leads McMillen to observe that:

> Despite its apparent universality, the concept of gambling has no intrinsic meaning; rather, its meaning always depends on the socio-historical context in which it occurs. The perception and experience of gambling vary significantly – in its history, its organisation and its meanings – according to different types of gambling, the various groups involved, and the particular society within which the gambling takes place.[5]

In a modern, capitalist context, gambling is usually defined in terms of a financial transaction. Roger Munting offers the following definition from the 1978 Rothschild Committee report: 'Gambling consists of an agreement between parties with respect to an unascertained outcome that, depending on the outcome, there will be a redistribution of advantage (usually but not always monetary) among those parties'.[6] This uncertain outcome might be decided by the skill of the parties, by pure chance, or by a combination of the two. In Thai, the word for gambling is *kanphanan*. A survey of Thai legal commentaries, encyclopaedias and dictionaries on the term *kanphanan* indicates that in a contemporary context its meaning is essentially the same as the definition given above. These sources make it explicit that both parties involved in the transaction must have a chance of both winning and losing.[7] For example, offering someone a prize for doing well in their exams before they have sat those exams is not gambling because the examinee can only gain, while the other person can only lose.

In the past, however, the Thai state's perception of what constituted gambling was broader and more nebulous than the preceding definition. None of the four principal gambling laws issued in the period covered by this study, nor the Civil and Commercial Code, contains an explicit and precise definition. While reviewing the draft of one of these laws in 1928, the Minister of Justice alluded to the reasons behind this omission by noting that the word 'gambling' was particularly difficult to explain.[8] Rather than define gambling, the Thai state preferred to identify the media through which people gambled. In many cases, the act of gambling and the means of doing it were virtually synonymous.[9] Perhaps the best example of this was the Gambling Revenue Act R. S. 120, which stated that, for the purposes of this particular law, gambling meant engaging in any of the games or activities listed in the accompanying regulations for property of value.[10] Each of the main gambling laws split the most common forms of gambling into two broad groups: those that were totally prohibited and those that were permitted subject to licence, initially from the tax farmers and later from the state. These groups included contests determined by varying degrees of skill – cockfighting, boat races, pitching coins, and some card games, for instance – and others based on chance – dice games, various forms of lotteries, and such like. Some of these activities might not usually be considered gambling in a Western context: for example, target shooting and throwing hoops over prizes, seemingly innocuous activities usually found at fairgrounds, consistently appeared in gambling legislation.[11] Clearly, the Thai government's historical conception of gambling diverges from the modern, Western-derived one. Accordingly, this study will cover all those games and activities that the Thai government considered to be gambling.

The criminality of gambling

Before considering why gambling or, more accurately, certain forms of gambling are criminalized, it is worth examining what crime is. Like some of its practitioners, crime as a concept is a slippery and shady character, and notoriously difficult to pin down.[12] It is generally recognized that crime is not a fixed category but rather a social construct that is both culturally and temporally relative. Honour killings, for instance, have been tolerated by many cultures; in some countries, they remain so today, but in others, such killings are now considered criminal acts. Conceptions of criminality are thus dependent on the political, economic, social and cultural context in which they arise. As societies evolve, then so too do attitudes towards certain actions and modes of behaviour. In a modern context, and at the most basic, essential level of definition, a crime is any action or form of behaviour that is proscribed by law. Indeed, some would say that crime is a product of the law; it cannot exist independently.[13] This is not the place for an in-depth discussion of these issues. It suffices to note that criminalization and lawmaking are merely two terms for opposite sides of the same coin. Any study of criminal behaviour must therefore examine the process by which the laws governing that behaviour came into being.

The definition of crime can be refined further: crimes are acts proscribed by law because the state perceives them to be injurious to individuals and the wider society. Gambling is often described as a 'victimless' crime, a term that disguises the potential damage that might arise from unrestricted indulgence. For instance, the gambler's habit might lead them into debt and destitution; this has ramifications for not only the gambler and their dependents but also for the community in which they live. To feed their family or perhaps just their habit, the gambler might turn to crimes such as theft or fraud. The modern state thus has two justifications for criminalizing gambling: first, it has a duty to protect people from self-harm, and second, it is responsible for the prevention of crime.[14]

The social origins of criminal law – in other words, how criminal behaviour is determined and defined – has long been a subject of debate among criminologists and social historians. One dominant argument is that crimes are acts that threaten the interests and values of powerful groups within society. In short, laws are made by elites in the interests of elites. This interpretation is termed conflict theory. On the other hand, an older and more traditional view holds that crimes are acts which transgress universal norms of conduct. Criminal law is thus the embodiment of a moral consensus within a particular society. This is termed the functional or, more commonly, consensus theory of crime.[15] Rather than seeing them as two contending models it is better to consider them as the opposite ends of a sliding scale, with specific crimes falling somewhere between the two. In their 1970s study of crime and civil strife in four cities – London, Stockholm, Sydney, and Calcutta – during the nineteenth and early twentieth centuries, Ted Robert Gurr, Peter Grabosky and Richard Hula sought to overcome the then perceived dichotomy between these two interpretations. They found that the crimes on which there was the greatest degree of consensus in all four societies were those against the person – principally, murder and assault – and crimes of acquisition.[16] Along with other studies, theirs also indicated that activities such as drug-taking and gambling fall towards the conflict end of the spectrum: the large number of people that continue to take part in these activities once they are criminalized shows there is a lack of consensus.[17]

Moreover, in their attempt to delineate the precise role of political elites in defining criminality, Gurr et al. highlight the various influences and latent constraints to which elites are subject. Firstly, as members of a particular society, elites share certain values and beliefs, but not necessarily all, with other members, which they are expected to uphold and adhere to. Elites also have to contend with the concerns of those institutions responsible for the maintenance of law and order, namely, the police, the judiciary and the penal administration. Bureaucratic inertia, indifference and even resistance can also act as powerful constraints. Lastly, there may be external pressure for change from the press, special interest groups, and the general public. Gurr et al. conclude that 'it is too simplistic to maintain that changing policies of public order are merely manifestations of an elite's class interests or narrow desire to retain power'.[18] Laws may be made by elites but they are moulded for and by society. To fully understand why some acts are criminalized it is thus necessary to examine the attitudes and perceptions of all the various social groups, not just the governing elite.

In his work on the shifting attitudes towards off-course betting on horse races in England and Wales between the 1890s and the 1930s, David Dixon also stresses the need to broaden the scope of inquiry in lawmaking studies; it is not enough to focus solely on the enactment of criminal legislation by senior legislatures. Firstly, attention must also be paid to the role of subordinate lawmakers and the judiciary who, through court decisions, 'contribute crucially to the process out of which statutory enactments are produced'.[19] Secondly, the subsequent processes of enforcement, interpretation, and implementation also need to be examined. Just because a law was promulgated does not mean it was enforced. Moreover, the judiciary might interpret the law in a way that is at odds with the original intentions of the lawmakers. To sum up, Dixon asserts that: 'Law-making has to be seen not as a single event, but as a *process* in which groups and individuals interact, in which the meanings of legislative initiatives change, in which ideologies and commitments vary and shift'.[20]

This study incorporates all these theoretical guidelines and methodological concerns in order to present a comprehensive account of the development of the Thai state's attitudes and policies towards gambling. It examines the emergence of a strong anti-gambling discourse among the Thai elite and the accompanying gambling legislation, which had effectively criminalized most forms of popular gambling by 1945. Attention is also given to how the criminalization process was shaped by various state institutions, particularly the police and judiciary, and segments of Thai society, such as the Buddhist monkhood (the Sangha) and the nascent Bangkok middle class of the 1920s, to advance their own political and economic interests. Besides providing insights into how laws are made and criminal behaviour defined in a modern Asian context, such an approach has many benefits for the development of Thai historiography.

Gambling and Thai historiography

The late nineteenth and early twentieth centuries were a critical period in Thai history for it was during this time that the political, economic and social contours of present-day Thailand began to come into focus. In the nineteenth century, Siam underwent a number of broad socio-economic changes, brought about by mass Chinese immigration and the expanding European imperial presence in the region, which laid the foundations for the modern Thai state. Faced with the threat of colonialism, the Thai elite of the mid-nineteenth century sought to accommodate Western ambitions in mainland South-East Asia through signing a series of so-called 'unequal' treaties with the European powers and the US, starting with Britain in 1855. Under the provisions of these treaties, customs duties were fixed and extraterritorial rights granted to all Western subjects, including Asian nationals of colonized countries. Siam's fiscal and judicial sovereignty were heavily compromised, while its economy was opened to the demands and rigours of the global market. Significantly, the traditional system of manpower control that formed the basis of state power was gradually eroded, leading to the decline of the nobility and the emergence of a peasantry free from the bonds of indentured labour. These factors helped stimulate the growth of agricultural production and a monetized market economy in the country, resulting in its integration into the world capitalist economic system as a primary producer. Furthermore, the colonial threat provided the motivation for a comprehensive restructuring of the administrative, financial and judicial systems along Western lines in the latter part of the century, making the theoretically absolute monarchy into a reality. At the same time, the Bangkok-based absolutist state became locked in a race for control of surrounding territories with the British and the French. Although the Thai government was forced into conceding its claims to sovereignty over Laos to the French in the 1890s and the northern Malay sultanates to the British in the 1900s, it was able to gain an unprecedented degree of control over the core of the kingdom and its peripheries, such as Patani. By the end of Chulalongkorn's reign, the borders of present-day Thailand had been set and its independence secured.

The Bangkok absolutist state was only a transitional phenomenon, however, that gave way to a Thai nation-state in the first half of the twentieth century. In order to legitimize Bangkok's direct rule over its former tributaries, the absolute monarchy attempted to forge a Thai national identity of which it was the focal point and the guarantor. Furthermore, the rationalized administrative apparatus of the state required educated bureaucrats: at first, these consisted of the offspring of the old provincial ruling families but as the functions and depth of the state expanded, commoners began to fill the lower echelons of the civil service. Education was thus used to instil notions of a common Thai identity based on a holy trinity of the Thai nation, Buddhism and loyalty to the throne. However, in the early twentieth century, a popular nationalism slowly emerged in opposition to this official nationalism. During Vajiravudh's reign, bureaucrat commoners and other members of a nascent Bangkok-based middle class grew increasingly frustrated with the economic mismanagement of the absolutist regime and its monopoly on political power. This came to a head following the onset of the worldwide economic depression in the early 1930s: in 1932, the self-styled People's Party (*Khana ratsadon*), composed of disgruntled military officers and low-level civilian bureaucrats, overthrew the absolute monarchy and established a constitutional monarchy with a partially elected assembly in its place. The work of nation-building continued apace, though the new regime attempted to displace loyalty to the monarchy with loyalty to the constitution. Under the rule of the military strongman Phibun, an admirer of the fascist regimes in Germany, Italy and Japan, Thai nationalism reached a fever pitch, represented most obviously by the change in the country's name, from Siam to Thailand, in 1939. Demands for the restoration of the 'lost' territories in French Indochina led Thailand to enter the Second World War on the side of the Axis powers, though the alliance with Japan effectively became an occupation. By the end of the war, the civilian faction in the government had gained the upper hand and concerted diplomatic negotiations ensured that Thailand was treated as an enemy-occupied country.

Conventional historiography on this period has long suffered from a number of innate and largely unquestioned assumptions that have limited the boundaries of historical inquiry.[21] These stem from the fact that Siam was never directly colonized; as such, the country is deemed to be unique within South-East Asia and, indeed, most of the non-Western world. Unsurprisingly, this supposed uniqueness has served to limit comparative studies. Moreover, Siam's avoidance of direct colonization is generally attributed to the benevolent and farsighted leadership of its absolute monarchs, the exemplar being King Chulalongkorn. Siam's kings have thus been enshrined as heroic, modernizing nationalists: symbols of Thai ingenuity and independence. This royalist interpretation remains the paradigm of Thai historiography, largely due to the reverence in which the current monarch, King Bhumibol Adulyadej, is held, the moral authority he wields, and his symbolic power as a unifying figure. This master narrative was also reinforced and legitimated by the work of numerous Western scholars, such as David Wyatt and Walter Vella, during the 1960s and 1970s.[22] Imbued with the anti-colonial sentiments and pro-indigenous sympathies common among South-East Asianists at the time, these scholars uncritically adopted the established monarchs-as-nationalists narrative.[23] Moreover, they showed an inclination towards the 'Great Man' theory of history, their studies focusing almost exclusively on the reigns or policies of a particular king.[24] The net effect is that Siam's absolute monarchs have been given an overwhelming centrality within Thai historiography – making it little more than hagiography, at times – and are commonly depicted as the sole agents of change, at the expense of other Thai institutions and social groups.

This conventional, royalist historiography has not gone unchallenged, however. During the 1950s and again in the 1970s, Thai Marxists highlighted Siam's loss of economic sovereignty and the absolute monarchy's collusion with foreign economic interests to argue that those kings 'modernized' the state only so far as it allowed them to consolidate their power, and in so doing they condemned the country to a semi-colonial status and economic backwardness.[25] Rather than being an enlightened institution acting for the greater good of the incipient Thai nation, the absolute monarchy is portrayed as self-serving, exploitative and oppressive. Furthermore, these scholars challenged the centrality of Siam's kings within the historical narrative by concentrating on class struggle and socio-economic factors as the determinants of change. However, like the royalist scholars before them, the Thai Marxists tended to ignore the mass population; the common man appears in the historical narrative only as the subject of changes imposed from on high or without.

More recently, a number of studies have turned the spotlight upon other Thai actors. Matthew Copeland and Nakkharin Mektrairat, for instance, have both focused upon the growing disaffection and frustration with the absolutist social order among the urban middle class in the decades before the 1932 coup.[26] Shifting attention away from the political arena, Scot Barmé has highlighted how this middle class began to wield an increasing influence over Thai socio-cultural life and acted as agents of modernity.[27] In her study of the legal reform process that led to the promulgation of Siam's modern law codes in the early twentieth century, meanwhile, Tamara Loos has drawn attention to the transnational character of this process and the previously underestimated role of foreign legal advisers.[28] Moreover, in detailing how Vajiravudh and Prajadhipok both wished to abolish the practice of polygamy but were prevented from doing so due to the entrenched opposition of other members of the Thai elite, she reveals that, rather than being omnipotent, the absolute monarchy was just one powerful actor among others.[29]

Similarly, the notion of Thai exceptionalism has been challenged by studies that explore the relationship between the country, colonialism and modernity: with turn-of-the-twentieth-century Siam on the one hand as a semi-colony of the European powers, especially Britain, and on the other as a colonizing power itself, finally bringing some of its former tributaries such as Patani under its direct control.[30] Evidence of Siam's semi-coloniality lies in the economic dominance of European and Chinese enterprises in the country, and the juridical hierarchy created by extraterritoriality which protected both Westerners and their colonized Asian subjects from supposedly 'uncivilized' Thai law.[31] The imperial nature of the Thai state, meanwhile, is illustrated by the way in which the reformed administration adopted the techniques and technologies of colonialism – the co-option of local elites, for instance, the expansion of communications infrastructure or the mapping of borders – to assert its sovereignty over territories in which previously it had only been symbolic.[32] Perhaps the best elucidation of Siam's split identity is Loos' study of family law in the kingdom. Based on the colonial notion that a society's cultural authenticity lay in the family and religion, the Thai government copied British initiatives in Malaya and established Islamic courts in its newly acquired southern Malay provinces in order to preserve local customs. According to Loos, the Thai elite considered this region to be 'a showcase for Siam's colonial modernity'.[33] At the same time, Thai officials and foreign legal advisers sought to use the same logic of cultural authenticity to protect the 'traditional' Thai institution of polygamy from domestic and foreign criticism. But in failing to accept monogamy as the legal standard of marriage – one of the criteria by which a society's level of modernity was measured by the West – until 1935, the Thai elite inadvertently delayed the removal of extraterritoriality. In the case of Siam, the dichotomy of colonized versus independent is thus a false one. Loos concludes that: 'Looking at Siam's political trajectory from the perspective of family law demonstrates that Siam was independent at the same time it was colonized and colonizing'.[34]

This present study builds on these insights in order to broaden the scope of Thai historiography. Firstly, by using the methodological framework of criminalization/lawmaking studies outlined in the previous section, it illustrates how the Thai government's legislation and policies on gambling were the result of a complex interaction between the political elite, the state institutions responsible for enforcing, implementing and interpreting the law, and the mass population. Examining the lawmaking process also uncovers some of the relationships underpinning Thai society: between the centralizing Bangkok state and its agents, for instance, or between government officials and the common people. Additionally, studying the various forms of gambling that fell in and out of fashion has much to reveal about changes in both elite and popular tastes, and conceptions of leisure. Indeed, gambling is a prism through which the light of historical inquiry can be shone in order to illuminate various facets of a particular society. Secondly, focusing on a universal aspect of human behaviour, namely gambling, provides a convenient starting point for comparisons between Thailand and other Asian countries. As Chapter 5 will show, for instance, the problems posed by extraterritoriality to the enforcement of the kingdom's gambling laws were remarkably similar to those faced by the Chinese police force in Shanghai in the 1920s and 1930s.

Just as importantly, by detailing the process that culminated in the 1936 gambling law and the state lotteries, both of which remain in place today, this study provides a much needed historical perspective on the Thai government's present stance on gambling. Apart from a few tightly regulated exceptions such as betting on horse racing, most forms of gambling are, to all intents and purposes, illegal. Needless to say, however, illicit gambling operations are rife throughout the country, nurturing organized crime and depriving the regular economy of capital. Consequently, proposals for relaxing the gambling laws so that the government might profit from gambling taxation are regularly touted but these invariably meet with fierce opposition.[35] In short, gambling remains a prominent and highly divisive issue in twenty-first century Thailand. However, there are only a few studies that examine the historical background of gambling in the country. Giving some indication of how important the absolute monarchy thought the gambling issue was, Prince Damrong Rachanuphap, a half-brother of Chulalongkorn and the so-called 'father of Thai history', wrote a detailed account of the gambling dens and the *huai* lottery not long after their abolition.[36] In his position as the Minister of the Interior from 1892 to 1915, Damrong was a key architect of the administrative reforms of the Thai state. He was also president of an Anti-Gambling League, set up to press for the abolition of the gambling tax farms.[37] As Chapters 3 and 4 will show, Damrong played a decisive role in shaping the absolute monarchy's policy on gambling, often suggesting particular initiatives and overseeing the drafting of new legislation. His study of the gambling tax farms is very much a reflection of his multiple roles as a member of the royal family, former government minister, dedicated recorder of the past, and anti-gambler. It is largely descriptive and little attention is paid to the socio-economic contexts in which the gambling tax farms first emerged and were later abolished. For Damrong, the only virtue of the gambling houses and the *huai* lottery was that they were a highly effective and convenient means of indirect taxation, providing the state with revenue for administrative purposes without unduly burdening the population. As for their disadvantages, these were numerous: it sufficed to say that unfettered gambling impoverished people and corrupted their character.[38] His study thereby justifies both the existence of the gambling tax farms and their abolition; it can thus be seen as dynastic propaganda. By emphasizing the amount of revenue the government sacrificed in abolishing these tax farms, Damrong propagates the image of an altruistic and enlightened absolute monarchy.[39] Besides Damrong's work, there are two Thai-language master's theses that examine gambling in nineteenth and early twentieth-century Siam: the first examining the Thai government's policy towards the gambling tax farms from a predominantly financial perspective and the more recent looking exclusively at the socio-cultural role of the Chinese gambling dens in Thai society.[40] Neither study, however, pays much attention to forms of gambling such as cockfighting and card playing that took place outside the dens. Nor do they consider developments in gambling and policy following the abolition of the dens in the late 1910s in any depth. Of all the English-language studies on modern Thai history, only Ian Brown's *The Creation of the Modern Ministry of Finance in Siam, 1885–1910* deals with the government's gambling policy in detail.[41] As with the two master's theses, this covers only the period up to the abolition of the gambling tax farms, however. A perusal of the more general histories of Thailand, meanwhile, finds countless fleeting references to the economic, social and criminal dimensions of gambling.[42] Like furtive underground gambling operations, the subject of gambling has been lurking in the shadows of Thai history for some time. This study brings it into the light.

Overview of the study

Chapter 1 details the broad socio-economic changes Siam underwent during the nineteenth century and argues that these were responsible for a boom in the level of gambling. It is also argued that the spread of gambling was not merely a reflection of the commercialization and monetization of the Siamese economy but, more crucially, a driving factor in these processes. Chapter 2 describes the various games of chance – Thai, Chinese and Western – that were popular during the nineteenth and early twentieth centuries, and how they were managed under the tax farming system. It also details how all sections of Thai society participated in gambling and examines their reasons for doing so. Chapter 3 explores the relationship between the taxation of gambling as a source of state revenue and the emergence of the modern Thai nation-state, arguing that gambling revenue was crucial in funding the administrative reforms of Chulalongkorn that established the absolutist state and the nation-building programmes of both Vajiravudh and the post-1932 constitutional regime. Despite the importance of gambling revenue for the state, however, the Thai government began to progressively limit the scope for legal gambling from the last decades of the nineteenth century. Chapter 4 examines their motivations and rationale for doing so, and how the elite anti-gambling discourse was related to Western conceptions of progress, modernity and civilization. It then details how this discourse was translated into actual legislation and examines some of the inconsistencies that emerged in attempts to balance the demands of human nature and the introduction of Western forms of gambling. Chapter 5 shifts attention to the police force and how its attempts at enforcing the gambling laws were hindered by various exogenous obstacles and institutional weaknesses. The first part of Chapter 6 focuses on how the judiciary tried and sentenced gambling offenders. Special attention is paid to the way members of the elite were disciplined for their involvement in illegal gambling. The second part of this chapter then follows the convicted gambling offender into the kingdom's prisons in order to examine the impact of the penal system on the government's anti-gambling policy. Chapter 7 describes how gambling and its control became a hotly debated topic in the pages of the popular press from the 1910s on, focusing on the manner in which the Bangkok middle class appropriated the anti-gambling discourse of the Thai elite and used it to attack the existing absolutist social order. The first part of Chapter 8 explores the influence of Buddhism and the monkhood upon attitudes towards gambling. This is followed by an examination of popular attitudes towards gambling and resistance to government policy. Lastly, Chapter 9 examines the development of the Thai government's policies on prostitution and opium use, moving from taxation and tolerance at the start of the twentieth century to eventual prohibition in the second half of the century. These processes are then compared with the criminalization of gambling in order to determine why the government seemed to prioritize regulating gambling over restricting the other two activities.

A note on sources

A wide variety of sources have been used in this study, the majority of which are in Thai and are held in the National Archives of Thailand in Bangkok. These archival materials include correspondence between the king and his ministers; reports of ministerial and cabinet meetings; the annual reports of the Bangkok police department and the Ministry of Justice; files from the foreign Financial Advisers; anonymous letters, usually complaining of illegal activities or the corrupt practices of government officials, from members of the public to the administration; and newspaper clippings collected by the government.

Special mention should be made of some important published collections of official documents used in this study. All the legislation referred to comes from *Prachum kotmai pracham sok* [Collected Laws in Chronological Order], compiled by Sathian Laiyalak and others, and which, as the name suggests, reproduces all Thailand's laws since the beginning of the Bangkok era in 1782.[43] A large number of Supreme Court (*san dika*) rulings on gambling cases have been drawn from the annual legal journal *Thammasan* that was published from 1917/18 onwards. Lastly, the records of the meetings of the National Assembly, established following the 1932 coup, have also been employed.[44]

These archival materials and official documents have been supplemented by the memoirs of prominent Thais, such as the noted scholar Phraya Anuman Rajadhon (1888–1969), and the accounts of Western visitors and residents in Siam.[45] One final important source is the English-language *Bangkok Times Weekly Mail*, a summary of the news from the six previous daily editions of the *Bangkok Times* that was distributed overseas. Both versions of the paper often carried translations of government announcements and of articles from the Thai-language press.

1 Gambling and socio-economic change in nineteenth-century Siam

Gambling has long been a feature of Thai society, just as it has elsewhere in the world. Some forms, such as betting on cockfights and boat races, are no doubt indigenous, while others, such as dominoes and cards, were brought to Siam by foreign traders and immigrants, particularly those from China. In his comprehensive account of Siam in the late seventeenth century, Simon de la Loubère noted the Thai passion for gambling on cockfighting and *saka* (the Thai version of backgammon) and speculated that the latter had been introduced by the Portuguese.[1] Since he makes no mention of the Chinese game of fan-tan (called *thua* in Thai), one of the most popular gambling activities in nineteenth-century Siam, it would seem it did not become widespread until after La Loubère's visit. Similarly, it was probably only in the very late seventeenth or early eighteenth centuries that the first institutionalized forms of gambling appeared, in the guise of state-sponsored gambling houses for the Chinese community in the capital city of Ayutthaya.[2]

In the early nineteenth century there was a marked increase in the level of gambling, as more people started to gamble more often on an increasing variety of games. It was during this period, for example, that the game of *po pan* and the *huai* lottery were introduced from China; both quickly became popular among the people of Siam. This boom in gambling was the result of a series of broad socio-economic changes which were set in motion by the destruction of Ayutthaya by the Burmese in 1767 and which played a fundamental role in the subsequent reconstruction of the Siamese state in the decades that followed. These changes transformed Thai society and laid the foundations for the creation of the modern Thai state in the late nineteenth century. An examination of these factors behind the spread of gambling – specifically, mass Chinese immigration, the expansion of the agrarian frontier and the growth of international trade – forms the core of this chapter. In the latter part, attention is also given to the role gambling played in the monetization of the Thai economy.

The socio-economic transformation of Siam and the spread of gambling

From the seventeenth century onwards, Western visitors to Siam were quick to comment upon the Thai's perceived penchant for gambling and the problems that this caused.[3] During the 1830s and 1840s, however, Western missionaries, many of whom had resided in Bangkok for some time, discerned a substantial increase in the level of gambling in the capital. Dr Dan Beach Bradley, for instance, noted that it 'is the reigning passion of the Chinese, and is rapidly enlisting the heart and soul of the Siamese'.[4] Such observations were usually accompanied by moralistic sermons on the pernicious effects of unfettered gambling and were part of broader concerns about a perceived increase in licentious behaviour, particularly drunkenness.[5] Although these missionaries may have been prone to exaggeration, it seems that their fears were not totally unfounded. With regards to gambling, while walking through the capital in 1836, one missionary observed:

> a long row of new bamboo buildings erected, amounting I should imagine to 100 habitations. These, I was informed, are all rented as gambling and lottery shops at 30 ticals [baht] per annum each. [...] All the tenements which were completed seemed to be well occupied.[6]

The most concrete manifestation of this explosion in vice was, however, the rapid growth in state revenue from tax farms on gambling and alcohol. Around the start of the nineteenth century, gambling provided the state with an annual income of about 20,000 baht; by the 1850s this had risen to over 200,000 baht a year.[7]

The first large-scale gambling houses, in Thai *bonbia*, were established in Ayutthaya by the government sometime in the late seventeenth or early eighteenth centuries. These establishments specialized in games of Chinese origin, specifically fan-tan and a modified Thai form called *kamtat*. Initially, the Siamese government did not intend them to generate revenue but, rather, to provide Chinese traders with a regulated outlet for gambling, while preventing Thais from taking part. Unsurprisingly, this prohibition proved ineffective and the government subsequently removed the ban against Thais gambling in the dens, with a consequent rise in revenue. Realizing there were profits to be made from such places, entrepreneurs then began to submit bids for monopoly rights for gambling houses in particular areas.[8] Damrong dates the appearance of these gambling house tax farms to sometime between 1688 and 1732.[9] State-run gambling dens (*bon luang*) coexisted with ones managed by tax farmers (*bon phukkhat*) into the early Bangkok era.[10] Traditional Thai gambling activities, meanwhile, do not appear to have been taxed or regulated.

Following the fall of Ayutthaya, King Taksin (r. 1767–82) and Rama I (r. 1782–1809) sought to restore the Siamese state and revive the economy through promoting trade with China and encouraging Chinese immigration.[11] Both had extensive Chinese familial connections and considerable trading experience, which they used to establish royal monopolies on certain import and export goods in alliance with members of the nobility and Chinese merchants. These two groups were also encouraged to engage in private trading enterprises as the king stood to profit from the various taxes and fees related to trade. This focus on trade was given further impetus by the state's need for cash to hire wage labourers for infrastructure construction and skilled tasks such as shipbuilding. The destruction of Ayutthaya had left the country depopulated and had severely disrupted the traditional system of manpower control, under which all commoners (*phrai*) were required to be registered with a patron (*nai*) through whom they provided the state with a fixed period of labour every year. In the early Bangkok period, however, the Siamese elite preferred to hire Chinese immigrants, who lay outside the traditional manpower system, for public works and use conscripted commoners for military purposes. Chinese trade, capital, expertise and labour were thus essential to the revival of the Siamese state and economy. Given this importance, Kanchana argues that the gambling houses were re-established in order to encourage Chinese immigration.[12] From its inception, the reconstructed Siamese state was therefore directly involved in promoting gambling, though not purely for revenue purposes.

In turn, the growth in foreign trade stimulated the production of cash crops – first sugarcane, pepper and tobacco, then later rice – and manufactured goods such as cloth, tin utensils and dyes for export. Initially, these activities were confined to the immigrant Chinese communities but they were gradually taken up by the other inhabitants of Siam. Thai cultivators began to sell their agricultural surplus to Chinese merchants in return for cash. With the Chinese in the vanguard, a market economy slowly emerged, first in Bangkok and then in the provinces. As Hong Lysa has highlighted, by the mid-1820s, the level of economic activity in Siam was large enough to support an extensive system of internal revenue collection.[13] Well aware of this development, Rama III (r. 1824–51), himself a successful merchant while a prince, withdrew from active engagement in trade and terminated most of the royal monopolies shortly after coming to the throne. Rather than exploiting foreign trade directly, the state shifted to exploiting internal production and consumption. Tax farming was now to be the basis of state revenue. In addition to a host of new tax farms on products such as salt, attap and cotton, the *huai* lottery farm, covering Bangkok, was established and the number of gambling house farms increased. Moreover, all the government-run gambling dens were closed and replaced with tax farming ones.[14] The boom in gambling was thus a reflection of a flourishing market economy, for all these forms of gambling were dependent upon the ready availability of cash.

Concomitantly, these economic developments further weakened the state's ability to extract forced labour, a fact reflected in the series of increasingly desperate registration drives and other enforcement measures that were conducted well into the second half of the nineteenth century.[15] As a result of the expanding agrarian frontier and the increasing penetration of the cash economy, Thai commoners were able to escape their corvée labour obligations, either through evasion or the payment of a commutation tax. By mid-century, this tax was the single largest item of state income.[16] Moreover, the state had totally abandoned the use of conscripted labour for major public works such as canal digging, importing Chinese coolie labour instead. This trend towards freer labour was encouraged by those elements of the Siamese elite that stood to profit from taxes on trade and the production of cash crops. The value of Thai commoners to the state now lay in their role as producers (and consumers) rather than corvée labourers.[17] Consequently, the duration of their labour obligations were progressively reduced: from six months at the start of the Bangkok era to four, then to three and finally one month in the 1850s. Corvée labour was finally abolished in 1899. These socio-economic transformations have an important bearing on the spread of gambling: indicating that increasing numbers of Siamese commoners had both the cash and free time to indulge, while the growing Chinese community meant a greater demand for gambling facilities.

Nevertheless, the changing material circumstances of the Siamese population cannot account for the boom in gambling alone. The efflorescence of economic activity also had a profound effect upon people's thinking. One of Thailand's leading historians, Nidhi Eoseewong, has famously remarked how the Thai elite's involvement in foreign trade in the early Bangkok era made them 'more bourgeois, in the sense that the main foundations of their power came to rest on commerce. Their worldview, tastes, and preferences became like those of the bourgeoisies in other places and eras.'[18] There were many aspects to this bourgeois-ification but the most crucial for the spread of gambling was the shifting qualifications for determining people's position in the social order. Whereas during the Ayutthaya era one's status in Thai society had been defined largely by blood and rank, in the commercial milieu of the first half of the nineteenth century, one's wealth became increasingly important. Extravagant displays of wealth through the consumption of luxury goods, some of which had previously been reserved for royalty, thus became a way for members of the traditional Thai elite to reaffirm their status and a means for newcomers, mostly successful Chinese entrepreneurs, to assert theirs. Moreover, their mercantile activities meant they had access to the latest luxury items from overseas, which in turn fed a desire for the new and innovative.[19] The penchant for gambling among both these elite groups of the early Bangkok era can thus be seen as another form of conspicuous consumption.[20] Tellingly, even Rama III was said to gamble by proxy.[21] Here it is revealing to note that there was a similar explosion in gambling in seventeenth-century Europe that also coincided with the emergence of a mercantile society. As Gerda Reith comments:

Increased affluence allowed greater participation in games previously played only by the very rich, but more important were new notions of making money and the parallel between the dynamic of commercial development and that of games of chance. The growth of a money economy created a standardized, universal measure of value, and as such, its place in gambling was central. The universal equivalent in a capitalist economy became the universal wager in games of chance.[22]

It was this enterprising, risk-taking mercantile milieu that stimulated the development of probability theory and statistics, which were later tested at the gaming table.[23] Within early nineteenth-century Siam, meanwhile, it led to a greater 'rationality' in the commercial enterprises of the Thai elite: manifested in the development of more detailed accounting methods, the move away from using Chinese junks to higher-capacity, Western-style sloops, and the establishment of long-term business ventures such as sugarcane plantations.[24] In such a context, it is easy to imagine how minds attuned to the maximization of profits and the minimization of risk in trading activities would be comfortable with calculating the odds of winning, and placing their stakes accordingly, in gambling games. Thus, the boom in gambling in Siam can be seen as symbolic of the kingdom's economic transition towards capitalism.

Just as crucial as all the factors outlined above, however, were the attitudes and policies of the early Bangkok government, which actively encouraged gambling through the establishment of further tax farms upon it. The decline of the China trade in the 1840s, partly due to that country's defeat in the Opium War with Great Britain, and consequent drop in revenues, hastened the growth of tax farming. Farms were imposed on a greater number of everyday items, including sugar and utensils such as pots, increasing people's tax burden and, in the case of sugar, leading to a reduction in manufacture. Combined, these trends had a negative impact upon the Siamese economy, which was exacerbated by a series of natural disasters. All this brought greater hardship to the general population, leading B. J. Terwiel to suggest that the oft-commented upon increases in alcohol abuse and gambling at the time were due to people seeking temporary refuge from the harsh economic reality.[25]

King Mongkut (r. 1851–68) continued the expansion of tax farming, most notably, establishing a farm on opium and another on various forms of Thai gambling, including cockfighting and fish fighting, in the first years of his reign. At the same time, there was increasing pressure from the British for greater trading concessions. Aware of Britain's growing power in the region and convinced of the benefits to be derived from free trade, Mongkut and younger members of the Bunnag family, his closest supporters in the nobility, pushed for accommodation with the British, finally concluding the Bowring Treaty in 1855. Further such unequal treaties were subsequently signed with other European powers and the US, marking the re-orientation of the Siamese economy towards the West. Import duties were fixed at three per cent and limits were placed on export duties. Most remaining trade monopolies were abolished, except for those on opium and guns. Crucially, in surrendering its fiscal autonomy in exchange for some temporary respite from the threat of imperialism, the Siamese state became increasingly dependent upon tax farming for its revenue. The opening up of the economy, meanwhile, reinforced those socio-economic trends outlined above – the move towards freer labour, rising levels of Chinese immigration, the creation of a market economy – and, most significantly, acted as a spur to the widespread cultivation of rice for export. Siam's new role within the world economy was to be a primary producer. By the time Chulalongkorn became king in 1868, tax farming had become the mainstay of state finances, and of all the various farms none were more lucrative than those on gambling. Revenue from these made up about one-fifth of the total derived from tax farming.[26] As Chapter 3 will illustrate, this income was vital in funding Chulalongkorn's reforms of the Thai state in the late nineteenth and early twentieth centuries.

Chinese immigration and the spread of gambling

As should already be apparent, the gambling boom in Siam was intimately linked with the steady growth of the Chinese immigrant population during the nineteenth century. Most obviously, all the games conducted within the gambling houses, along with the *huai* lottery, were of Chinese origin. Before examining this dynamic, however, it is necessary to outline just who these Chinese immigrants were and what they were doing in Siam.[27] Throughout the nineteenth century, they consisted, overwhelmingly, of single young men – Cantonese, Hakka, Hainanese, Hokkien or Teochiu – from the south-eastern coastal provinces of China, particularly Guangdong and Fujian. Most of the early arrivals were involved in the trade between Siam and China, with some becoming successful entrepreneurs and developing close associations with the Thai elite. Some, especially the Teochiu, acquired official positions and became tax farmers, intermarrying with and assimilating themselves into the upper levels of Siamese society. The poverty and social unrest that wracked southern China from the 1830s on acted as a further spur to migration, with increasing numbers coming to Siam, and elsewhere in South-East Asia, to seek their fortunes before returning home. In the 1820s and 1830s, there were between 6,000 and 8,000 arriving a year, of which about half returned to China within a few years.[28] The advent of the steamship in East Asia in the 1860s and the establishment of regular direct services between China's southern ports and Bangkok in the 1880s gave further impetus to this trend. The annual net inflow increased from just over 3,000 in the 1820s to around 7,000 in the 1870s and 15,000 by 1900.[29] Initially, many worked as coolie labour in the capital: in the ports, in the rice mills or on construction projects.

Others settled on the outskirts of the city where they cultivated agricultural produce for the market. Steadily, these immigrants spread into the provinces, and towns such as Nakhon Chaisi in the Central Plains and Phuket in the South became Chinese in essence. The more successful established their own businesses, as shopkeepers, traders, factory owners or middlemen in the rice trade; while the less fortunate continued to work as labourers, in rubber and pepper plantations, for instance, or in the tin mines of the peninsula. By the turn of the twentieth century, G. William Skinner estimates that there were roughly 600,000 Chinese residents in Siam, of whom 200,000 lived in Bangkok.[30] Most significantly, they totally dominated the economic activity of the country.

The Chinese grouped together into self-help associations (*angyi*), based on dialect and clan ties, that had a wide range of functions, including labour union, welfare provider, and protection racket.[31] These groups were also involved in running gambling dens, smuggling opium and distilling alcoholic spirits. Their involvement in such illicit activities, along with the fact that they were well armed, led the government and Westerners to view them with suspicion as sinister 'secret societies'. From the 1870s on, a shortage of labour gave these organizations considerable bargaining power and they often brought Bangkok and the southern tin-mining towns to a halt through strikes. Similarly, disputes between rival groups sometimes led to riots which had to be put down by government force. Many of the heads of these societies were also tax farmers – particularly those dealing with gambling, opium and liquor – and, unsurprisingly, they used their organizations to secure their monopolies through intimidation. As the state became increasingly dependent upon the revenue from the vice farms in the second half of the nineteenth century, the influence of these tax farmers and secret societies grew. Initially, the government sought to control the *angyi* through co-opting the leadership and patronage. By the late nineteenth century, though, it had resorted to suppression: in 1897, a Secret Societies Act was passed that required the registration of all such associations, and a special Chinese branch was established within the reorganized Bangkok police force. Nevertheless, the secret societies remained a powerful political and social force well into the twentieth century.

Realizing their importance to the economic development of the kingdom, the Thai government allowed the Chinese to travel freely in the country and absolved them of corvée labour obligations, levying a triennial head tax upon them instead. As already noted, Kanchana argues that the government let them gamble as they did back home as a further inducement to settle.[32] The number of gambling houses in Siam thus grew in tandem with the Chinese population. Unsurprisingly, areas with a large number of gambling houses, such as Sampheng district in Bangkok, tended to be those with a sizeable Chinese community. At first, the government tried to prevent the local population from gambling in these places but, once this proved futile, separate dens for the Chinese and the Thais were created, probably in the early 1830s.³³ This was a damage limitation exercise; Thai dens were subject to stricter regulation in order to discourage excessive gambling. For instance, the amount of cash that could be advanced to gamblers in Thai dens was dictated by their financial standing, whereas there were no such limits in Chinese ones.³⁴ According to Damrong, this ethnic separation was maintained until the mid-1880s.³⁵ In reality, however, it must have been nigh on impossible to prevent Thais from entering Chinese dens. Thus, by allowing the Chinese to gamble as they were accustomed to, the state inadvertently encouraged gambling amongst the local population.

Throughout the existence of the gambling houses and the *huai*, the Chinese made up the majority of customers. Although this assertion is hard to quantify accurately, there are numerous indications to support it. For example, the tax farm for Chinese dens invariably attracted greater bids than its Thai counterpart covering the same area. Additionally, those in areas where there was a high concentration of Chinese – Bangkok, Songkhla, and Ratchaburi, for instance – commanded a higher price than those in other parts of the country.³⁶ Rather than correlating with the relative size of the total population, Terwiel asserts that the price of a farm reflected the size of the Chinese community in that particular locale.³⁷ Furthermore, in 1916, Chaophraya Yomarat (Pan Sukhum), then Minister of Local Government, estimated that 75 per cent of the gambling houses' clientele – except during Thai festivals – was Chinese and that they also made up 50 per cent of the *huai* lottery's custom.³⁸ Indeed, all the tax farms on vice – opium, gambling and alcohol – were based on Chinese consumption, primarily that of coolie labourers. Far from the societal restraints of home and family, and engaged in long days of back-breaking work, it is easy to see why so many sought respite in gambling, opium and alcohol.³⁹ For the Thai state, this was a convenient means to tax and control this essential but transient labour force. Direct taxation on the Chinese, specifically the triennial poll tax, was kept deliberately low to encourage immigration: from 1828 until it was abolished in 1909 it was fixed at 4.25 baht.⁴⁰ Therefore, the freedom to gamble was not merely just another lure but a highly effective mechanism for the indirect taxation of the Chinese. Skinner captures this exploitative aspect of the vice tax farms as follows: 'while the country depended on Chinese virtues for the expansion of commerce and industry, the government relied on Chinese vices for the expansion of public revenue'.⁴¹ Moreover, the majority of these immigrants originally came to Siam with the hope of acquiring enough money to set themselves up back home. Encouraging them to gamble depleted their savings, prevented them returning and helped keep remittances to China low.⁴²

The exploitation of the Chinese coolie's gambling habit was most blatant in the southern tin-mining regions around the towns of Phuket, Ranong and Nakhon Si Thammarat. Until the twentieth century, the tin-mining industry was a virtual Chinese monopoly: the workforce consisted of Chinese labourers and the mine owners were invariably Chinese too.

Along with the tin-mining tax farm, these entrepreneurs commonly held the other major farms – on the import tax, opium, alcohol, and gambling – and were often appointed by Bangkok as the local provincial governors.[43] The mines were organized around the *kongsi* system whereby the miners were provided with all their necessities on site: food, opium, liquor, and housing. But while their wages were relatively high, to compensate for the harsh conditions, they managed to save little. Indeed, the whole system was predicated on the mining magnate recouping as much of his workers' wages as possible through their consumption habits. Miners were often advanced part of their wages; come payday sometimes they might not be left with anything, having already blown it all on booze and gambling.[44] In the 1890s, it was estimated that the government received 40 per cent of the earnings of all the miners in Phuket indirectly through these tax farms.[45] Suehiro Akira even goes so far as to suggest that this was the main reason Chinese capital was not active in introducing new technology into tin mining for, although machinery would have saved on labour costs and raised productivity, it would also have reduced the manpower requirements and, consequently, the profits of gambling, liquor and opium dens attached to the *kongsi*.[46] Indeed, these tax farms were often the only way of making the whole operation a viable endeavour for the mine owner.[47] A comparable situation existed in the Federated Malay States where Chinese capitalists used gambling to encourage indebtedness and thereby hold onto their workforce.[48] To sum up, the Thai state's promotion of gambling was a means of attracting Chinese labour, taxing it, and restricting its movements.

Gambling and the monetization of the economy

So far it has been argued that the upsurge in gambling was a result of the socio-economic developments of the nineteenth century. However, the gambling boom was not just a symptom of these transformations but, more importantly, it was also a key factor in the monetization of the economy. The extent of the cash economy in nineteenth-century Siam is poorly understood by historians and difficult to determine accurately, though it is clear that it lagged behind the growth of the market economy.[49] As Nidhi highlights, the limited volume of currency in circulation during the early Bangkok period constrained the expansion of the market economy and retarded the development of capitalism, although on the positive side it did keep the price of domestically produced goods low and made them competitive in the world market.[50] This section will argue that the activity of gambling helped keep currency in circulation, while the tax farms on gambling also performed some vital economic and financial functions.

In the first half of the nineteenth century, the main currency in the core of the kingdom was the silver baht or tical, which was popularly known as the bullet coin among Westerners on account of its shape.[51] This came in various denominations, including two-baht coins, a quarter (a *salung*), and an eighth (a *fuang*), though denominations other than the one-baht coin were less common.[52] As in many other countries, cowrie shells (in Thai *bia*) were used for small purchases: 800 were normally equivalent to one *fuang*. However, this exchange rate fluctuated depending on the quantity of cowries available on the market, reaching as low as 1,200 to the *fuang* in the 1850s.[53] This devaluation caused great hardship for much of the population, with the cost of a meal doubling from 50 to 100 cowries.[54] While there were items, such as the betel leaf, which could be purchased for just a single shell, large numbers of cowries were required for most transactions, making them a cumbersome and time-consuming medium of exchange.[55] Clearly, there was insufficient coinage of a suitable denomination for everyday purchases, while cowries were too unwieldy and of unreliable value. Moreover, the manufacture of bullet money was slow, inefficient and unable to keep pace with demand.[56] Unsurprisingly, goods and products, including rice, continued to be bartered into the second half of the century, especially in the remoter parts of the kingdom and its tributaries.[57] By 1850, though, it can reasonably be concluded that a cash economy existed throughout the Central Plains and the upper part of the peninsula. This is most clearly shown by the increasing number of Thais who preferred to pay the commutation tax in lieu of their corvée labour obligations to the state.[58] Given the scarcity of hard currency though, it can be surmised that people wanted to hold onto their precious cash to pay this tax rather than spend it in the market, leading to hoarding. Such a situation was compounded by both the absence of banking facilities and widespread counterfeiting. It was imperative, therefore, that what currency there was be kept in circulation and the Thai government saw the promotion of gambling as a means of achieving this, perhaps the best illustration being the establishment of the *huai* lottery in Bangkok in the Third Reign. According to Damrong, during the early 1830s there was a drought that caused a serious rice shortage and, in turn, a scarcity of cash. A Chinese alcohol farmer called Chin Hong told the king that the people had buried their money and suggested starting a lottery so as to encourage them to dig it up. Rama III approved of the idea and Chin Hong established the *huai* in 1835.[59] Mongkut used the same justification for allowing the lottery to be set up in the town of Phetchaburi, which had prospered as a base of the sugar industry and from the booming rice trade, in 1865.[60] This latter lottery was short-lived, however; the government claimed it had impoverished the people and abolished it within a year.[61] Nevertheless, it can be argued that, for at least the first half of the nineteenth century, the Thai government saw the promotion of gambling as a way of encouraging the development of a cash economy.[62]

Helping currency circulate was not the only way in which gambling contributed to the growth of the Thai economy. The upsurge in foreign trade following the Bowring Treaty made the shortage of currency critical, forcing Mongkut to issue an act making foreign coins legal tender as a temporary solution in 1857. In 1860, a new mint began producing the first flat coins in silver, copper and tin to replace the bullet coins and cowries. People were reluctant to accept the new copper and tin coins, however, as their value was dependent on government guarantee rather than the actual value of the metal, and the old bullet ones remained in circulation long afterwards.[63] Once again, this distrust was exacerbated by the fact that these coins were easy to counterfeit. Indeed, counterfeiting was so acute that the government was forced to devalue these coins, further undermining people's trust in them.[64] Fortunately, the gambling houses provided another solution to this shortage of dependable currency. Within the dens, counters (*pi*) were used as substitutes for cash in order to facilitate play, just like the chips used in modern-day casinos. These counters were made from numerous materials – most commonly, glass, porcelain, or brass – and came in a variety of shapes: some round or octagonal, for instance, others in the form of a butterfly or star. Most were engraved with the name of the gambling house in Chinese characters and all bore their value in both Chinese and Thai figures.[65] Sometime in the second quarter of the nineteenth century these counters began to be used as small change; Damrong postulates this practice started with gamblers using them to buy food or beverages in stalls outside the gambling houses, where they could easily be exchanged for cash by the stallholder.[66] Given the scarcity of coinage of reliable value, they became a common means of exchange and by the 1860s they were certainly in use in Bangkok and the major towns of the North.[67] While in Raheng, a major staging post on the river route between Bangkok and Chiang Mai, Adolf Bastian noted that they 'were accepted by almost everybody without too many difficulties', while, 'The actual money of Siam [...] was seen very infrequently'.[68] Some idea of the utility of these counters is given in his later description of the town of Kamphaeng Phet, where they were not accepted as legal tender and, consequently, there was no form of small change:

> A smaller coin than 2 *annas* was not available, and people wanting to buy something below this price had to wait until the need for something else justified spending such an amount, or they had to combine with other buyers and work out whose share was what. Occasionally, cups of rice could be used to complete an exchange.[69]

Clearly, this would have discouraged trade and other transactions, limiting the growth of the economy.

During the first decade or so of Chulalongkorn's reign, gambling counters became the de facto currency in large parts of the kingdom. People's faith in the Thai state's currency was further shaken in the first year of the reign when a currency panic, stemming from fears that the issue of any new flat coins would render those of the Fourth Reign void, forced the government to offer to exchange the old copper and tin coins for their face value in silver for a period of 15 days, after which the exchange rate was reduced.[70] In these circumstances many people might have decided that their local gambling farmer's counters were a more reliable currency than that of the state. Later, as the price of tin and copper on the world market rose above the face value of the kingdom's tin and copper coinage, speculators began to melt down these coins for export abroad. Consequently, the reliance on counters became more pronounced and even received official sanction.[71] Each of the gambling house tax farms produced their own counters, which were legal tender only in the respective district and for the duration of the tax farmer's monopoly. At the end of their tenure, the tax farmer would announce a period, usually 15 days, during which people could redeem their counters for cash, after which they were void.[72] If the tax farmer suspected there were counterfeit tokens in circulation, he might also announce such a recall before issuing a new set. This gave rise to a huge variety of counters, with estimates of the number of different sets ranging from 890 to over 2,000.[73] In short, the gambling houses were now effectively the central banks for their district, issuing their very own money. Obviously, this system was problematic for the government as it was a huge delegation of state authority and ripe for abuse by the tax farmer. Once the government mint was able to produce specie in sufficient quantity, the issue of counters was prohibited in 1875.[74] Nevertheless, gambling counters remained in circulation long afterwards.[75] Moreover, tax farmers in the North and Northeast continued to issue counters into the 1880s and this suggests that their use as currency was still endorsed by the Thai government in up-country areas where official specie remained scarce.[76]

Besides providing a temporary currency, the gambling houses performed a number of other important functions in the Thai economy right through to their eventual demise in the first two decades of the twentieth century. Like the *huai* lottery but on a far wider scale, the dens encouraged the circulation of currency. Indeed, it is particularly telling that, when newly minted coins were sent to the governor of Ratchaburi in the 1870s, he was instructed to hand them over to the gambling house tax farmer for general distribution.[77] Some idea of the amount of specie that passed through the dens is given by the incidence of bent or dented coins. Unlike the old bullet coins, the new flat *salung* and *fuang* coins issued in the Fourth and Fifth Reigns could not be hooked or pushed easily with the croupier's bamboo rake so the den managers punched them into bowls or bent them for convenience's sake.[78] Estimates of the number of such deformed coins in circulation around the turn of the twentieth century range from two-thirds of the total to almost all.[79] This is not just testimony to the effectiveness of the gambling houses in circulating cash but also to the sheer level of gambling in Siam at the time.

With their large reserves of cash or, at least, easy access to it, the gambling houses also acted as sources of credit to local people. In a 1902 report on rural farming, the Director of the Land Registration Department, W. A. Graham, described these tax farmers as the banks of the rural population, condemning them for not just exploiting people's love of gambling but also for squeezing interest on loans out of them.[80] Since interest rates commonly ranged between 30 and 50 per cent, sometimes reaching as high as 80 per cent, this criticism is not unfounded.[81] Moreover, given the scarcity of hard currency for much of the nineteenth century, it is easy to imagine how some people might have had no other option but to approach these tax farmers for a loan. Nevertheless, Graham was correct in highlighting the vital role the gambling house tax farms played in local economies. In the absence of any domestic banks until the first decade of the twentieth century, they were the financial institutions of their day: issuing their own currencies and providing loans.[82]

To sum up, the spread of gambling throughout Siam during the nineteenth century was a symptom of the wide-ranging socio-economic transformations the country underwent. Of all these changes, perhaps the most important in this respect was the growth of the Chinese population. For its part, the Thai government was willing to let Chinese immigrants gamble as they wished in order to promote settlement, while also taxing them indirectly. By endorsing Chinese gambling, however, the government inadvertently encouraged the local population to gamble as well. As a result, state revenue from the taxation of gambling grew significantly, becoming a major item of income by the 1850s. For much of the century, though, the economic functions of gambling and the tax farms on it were of more importance as they hastened the monetization of the Thai economy. In a situation where the volume of specie was limited, the counters used by the gambling houses served as a temporary form of small change that bridged the gap between the old bullet coins and the new, flat coin and paper-based currency. More generally, gambling was the heartbeat of the nineteenth century economy, pumping the life-blood of cash through the kingdom's circulatory system. But gambling did not have only an important economic role in nineteenth-century Siam. As Chapter 2 will show, gambling became a central feature of Thai social life during this period, with the Chinese games played in the gambling houses being the most popular.

2 Games, dens and players
Gambling in nineteenth-century Thai society

Through the course of the nineteenth century, gambling and the institutions that grew up around its provision came to play a significant role in not only the economy but Thai society as a whole. The socio-economic changes outlined in Chapter 1 made visiting a gambling house or placing a bet on the *huai* lottery an affordable and accessible endeavour for increasing numbers of people. Indeed, gambling was perhaps the main form of entertainment for the majority of Siam's population from the mid-nineteenth century until long into the twentieth century. While the dream of winning big was certainly a motivating factor, the thrill and sociability of gambling were just as important, if not more so. Given gambling's centrality within Thai social life, this chapter will focus upon the games commonly played and the organizations responsible for their operation and management. Of course, these underwent numerous changes during this period; what follows is a rough snapshot of them in the late nineteenth century, before the Thai government embarked on its attempts to restrict gambling. Consideration is also given to who exactly played the various games and their reasons for doing so.

The gambling houses

As noted in Chapter 1, the gambling houses were places where certain Chinese games, principally fan-tan and *po pan*, were played. The holder of the tax farm enjoyed the total monopoly over the operation of such establishments within his district (*khwaeng*): upcountry, one province, city or town constituted one district, while Bangkok was divided into many such areas.[1] Nobody could play these particular games elsewhere without the tax farmer's permission. Until tighter regulations were imposed on the gambling farms in the late 1880s, the tax farmer could open as many dens as he wanted but establishing too many would have undermined his profits. Rather than build new dens every time the holder of the farm changed, the incoming farmer would 'inherit' those of his predecessor. These were either staffed with the farmer's own personnel or, more commonly, sublet out to another, who might manage that den for many years.[2]

Evocative descriptions of the gambling houses abound. Indeed, for the contemporary Westerner, no trip to Siam was complete without a visit to a den.[3] A number of Thais also recorded their impressions for posterity.[4] In Bangkok, the locations of the dens mirrored the city's growth outward from the core of Rattanakosin Island.[5] The first gambling houses were undoubtedly established in the Chinese quarter of Sampheng. During the first half of the nineteenth century, the majority of these, and those in other parts of the city, were found in large houseboats upon the river or canals, clustered around piers and markets such as that at Tha Tian. As Bangkok expanded away from the river and began its gradual transformation into a land-based city in the latter part of the century, increasing numbers of dens sprung up along newly built roads such as Charoen Krung. Most were extremely basic in design; little more than large bamboo sheds with roofs of nipa-palm leaves and earthen floors.[6] One Westerner in 1870s Bangkok claimed: 'you can scarcely go in any direction five minutes without coming to a gambling shed or gambling floating house'.[7] This was no exaggeration; in 1887, on the eve of the first wave of den closures, there were officially over 400 in the capital, 126 of which were described as large.[8] Following the initial closures between 1888 and 1892, the remaining 16 dens were transferred to permanent, state-owned premises that were rented to the tax farmer. Phraya Anuman describes a typical such den as:

> a large tile-roofed hall, without any ceiling and with cement walls. The front wall was lower in height and topped with an iron grill. Such a building normally had two or three entrances with pots of *saladai* [a cactus-like shrub] hanging in the doorway.[9]

These were located away from the city's major roads and waterways in order to discourage passers-by from entering.[10] As for the provinces, it was claimed that gambling houses could be found in every village.[11] It is difficult to pinpoint an exact figure, though, because the only available statistics are for the number of provincial dens closed between 1896 and 1906, and in some areas no figure was given. Nevertheless, Kanchana estimates that there were at least 243 by 1898.[12] The announcement of closures for that year suggests these were concentrated in the Central Plains, although it seems most large provincial towns had at least one den.[13]

Three games were commonly played in the gambling houses: fan-tan, called *thua yai* in Thai or just *thua*; *po pan*; and *po kam*.[14] They were known collectively as *thua po* and, discarding cheating, were games of pure chance. Placing a bet was conducted on the same principle for all three games, and each was played on one of the many mats that covered the floors of the dens. They differed only in the equipment used. Each mat was divided into four quarters by a large cross, like the letter X. The four openings, or 'gates' (*pratu*), formed by the cross were the points on which to bet. The opening directly in front of the dealer represented the number four and was called *khrop*, meaning 'complete'. Going clockwise from the dealer in ascending order were the numbers one to three. This arrangement was well known and there was no need for the gates to be marked.

There were various ways of placing a bet and the winner would receive between one and three times their stake, in addition to their stake, depending on the odds of winning, losing or 'drawing'. These variants were designed to keep players interested. *O* was the most straightforward method: if the gambler's number came up, they won three times their stake. Other methods were a little more complex since there was the added possibility of neither winning nor losing, in Thai gambling parlance, *chao*. For instance, if *meng* was used, the player would receive only the amount of their stake if correct. However, should one of the adjacent numbers come up, then they would neither win nor lose and their stake would be returned. In other words, they had the same chance, one in four, of winning or losing. Players would indicate how they were betting either by placing a card in or between the four 'gates' marked on the mat or by positioning their stakes in these areas. Most dens required a minimum stake for *thua* and *po pan*, ensuring these games tended to be played by the well-off.[15] Once a round of play had finished, croupiers moved the players' stakes and any winnings dexterously across the playing mats with long bamboo rakes. In addition to receiving all the losing stakes, the house levied a ten per cent commission on all winnings.[16]

Thua was the game on which the big money was won and lost, and most gambling houses ran only one circle. The large circular mat on which it was played formed the focal point of the establishment. The dealer would take between 100 and 200 cowrie shells and heap them in a pile in front of him. He would then count out the cowries in sets of four. The remainder was the winning number; if the final set was complete, *khrop*, then four was the winner. A good indication of how deeply fan-tan permeated Thai social life is given by the fact that this method of counting out cowries has entered popular vocabulary, with the phrase *chaeng si bia*, literally 'to explain to the extent of four cowries', meaning 'to explain in full detail'.[17] *Po kam* was conducted on similar lines: a smaller amount of cowries were used and these were covered with a bowl, with the players only getting a brief, tantalizing glimpse of the pile as a basis for placing their bets. Since there was no minimum stake this was the most popular game and there would be as many circles as demand warranted. Unsurprisingly, there was some cheating at both games. W. A. R. Wood, a former British consul in Siam, implies that the dealers were adept at secreting cowries so that the result would be the most amenable for the house.[18]

Po pan was played with a cube, each side of which was half red and half white. Before play, the dealer and the players would agree which of the colours would be the winner; they usually chose white. The dealer would place this cube in a brass rectangular box consisting of two parts, the larger of which slid over the other to conceal the cube (see Figure 2.1). The brass

30 *Games, dens and players*

Figure 2.1 Equipment for playing *po pan* (photograph by Gudrun Salevid).

box was placed in the centre of the cross on the mat and then spun by the dealer. After all bets had been placed, the dealer removed the outer box to reveal the top face of the cube. The winning 'gate' was that facing the agreed colour. As with the other games, the house and the players might try to cheat: the latter, for instance, might take advantage of a diversion, staged or otherwise, to lift off the cover and sneak a look at the cube.[19]

As mentioned in Chapter 1, the clientele was predominantly male Chinese labourers but large numbers of Thai men and women, of all classes, could also be found inside, along with members of other ethnic groups. Parents often visited the dens with their children in tow and mothers might be seen breastfeeding their babies.[20] At any time of day, there might be someone gambling therein: housewives on their way to market in the morning, for instance, or rickshaw-pullers escaping the harshness of the midday sun.[21] The busiest times, though, were the late afternoon, evening and throughout the night. By the end of the nineteenth century, attendance at the 13 gambling houses in the heart of the capital averaged between 300 and 400 people a den per night, with the lowest being for the one in Bangrak at 150 to 160 and the highest that at Samsen with between 700 and 800.[22] Since sleeping mats and cooked food were available on site players need never leave, and sometimes play might have continued until sunrise.[23]

Being open around the clock made the dens a perfect hangout for a jobless underclass of male beggars, opium addicts, thieves, and toughs, collectively known as the 'ghosts of the gambling houses' (*kia-kui* or *phuak kui*, a term of Chinese origin).[24] The dens gave them plentiful opportunities for crime: picking the pockets of a gambler absorbed in the game or jumping some unlucky winner on their way home and relieving them of their winnings.[25] Moreover, this environment was also a fertile recruiting ground for bandit gangs, whose ill-gotten gains would invariably be blown on gambling, opium and liquor.[26] Unlicensed prostitutes could also be found soliciting inside or out. In short, a criminal underworld revolved around the gambling houses.

Gambling was not the only attraction. Theatrical and musical performances – Chinese operas (*ngiu*), Thai classical dramas (*lakhon*), folk comedies (*likay*), and shadow-puppet shows – were staged in dens throughout the country in order to entice people inside.[27] As Anuman highlights, the gambling houses, along with the lottery hall, were the entertainment hotspots of their day.[28] This aspect of the dens is rightly emphasized by Nuttaya, who highlights the significant role the government played in the transformation of the gambling houses into entertainment centres through the gradual elimination of other dens and the construction of permanent ones with accompanying stages and kitchens.[29] With the closure of the provincial gambling houses and the gradual extension of the rail network from around the turn of the twentieth century, large numbers of people descended on Bangkok during public holidays to seek fun and a possible fortune in the capital's dens.[30] The gambling houses were the first manifestation of the leisure industry in Thailand.

Within the immediate vicinity of the gambling houses there were various 'support industries': food and liquor stalls, tobacco and betel-nut vendors, opium dens, brothels, and pawnshops, all looking to draw on the crowds coming to gamble or watch a show. The dens thus helped nurture commercial enterprises and often became the focal point of local communities. Indeed, the relationship between the gambling houses and pawnshops was almost symbiotic. Players down on their luck would pawn their jewellery, ornaments, furniture, and even their clothes, before returning to gamble once more.[31] Moreover, pawnshops commonly received stolen property, enabling thieves to easily acquire funds for gambling.[32] The depth of this relationship is illustrated by the impact of the 1901 Pawnbrokers Act, which required all pawnshops to be licensed, all forfeited pledges to be examined by the police before sale, and the owner to report any items that appeared on a list of stolen property published daily by the Police Special Branch.[33] Its immediate effect was the closure of all 432 pawnshops in Bangkok as the proprietors initially refused to comply with the regulations. The profits of the gambling house and opium farmers were hit so severely that they agitated, unsuccessfully, for the law to be repealed.[34] As for the consequent reduction in crime, Eric St John Lawson, commissioner of the Bangkok police force, observed that:

The very large body of snatch thieves found themselves in the awful predicament of either having to do some work or else give up gambling and opium. They chose the lesser of two evils and a large number of coolies appeared, as if by magic, and the novel sight of Siamese coolies working in the streets was seen.[35]

With their profits down, the gambling houses then started to receive stolen property and other goods in pawn; some den managers even ended up being convicted under the Pawnbrokers Act.[36] When licensed pawnshops opened later that year, crime returned to more regular levels but with the pawnshops now acting as instruments of detection.

The combination of alcohol, opium, gambling, prostitution and pawnshops created a locus of criminality. But this was not merely limited to theft and robbery. The ready availability of alcohol combined with frustration at gaming losses and the practice of going around armed created a highly volatile atmosphere. Arguments over some perceived slight or allegations of cheating sometimes ended in murder.[37] After blaming the high number of murders in the Bangkok area in the year 1904/5 on this deadly combination of gambling and drinking, Lawson expounded on the connection as follows:

> Drinking, like opium eating and smoking, is getting worse and worse every year. A large percentage of the drunkards either murder someone or get murdered. The majority of the opium smokers and eaters become robbers and thieves. The original main cause, however, is the gambling house. The gambler nearly always drinks or smokes opium. How much these three vices depend on each other is clearly shewn by the fact that when the gambling houses at Pacret [Pak Kret], Nontaburi and Paklat were closed on April 1st, nearly all the drinking shops and opium shops at those places closed up because there was not enough business to be done.[38]

The British officers that headed the Bangkok police force in the early twentieth century clearly believed that the gambling houses were a prime cause of crime and this subsequently became the orthodox view among Siamese officers as well.[39] The perceived link between gambling and crime as a component of the elite anti-gambling discourse will be examined in greater depth in Chapter 4.

The gambling houses were not only breeding grounds for crime, however; given the large amounts of cash on site they also made an attractive target for criminals. Tax farmers frequently complained to the government about the unwelcome attentions of Chinese secret societies and Thai hoodlums.[40] Employees and punters were harassed and sometimes violently assaulted. In August 1899, for example, a den manager was stabbed in the head.[41]

One tactic of these gangs was to hurl bricks and stones into the dens, and then, in the ensuing disturbance, seize the cash from the mats and rob the customers.[42] Alternatively, fires were lit inside to provoke chaos. Some of these incidents were probably attempts at extortion by Chinese secret societies. The tax farmers would then hire their own gangs for protection, leading to vicious turf wars between rival groups.[43] To counter this, the government issued regulations in the early 1890s requiring police officers to be stationed in every den to maintain order.[44] However, this only created further problems. Primarily, it placed an additional burden upon an already undermanned and overstretched police force. In the late 1890s, the British head of the force repeatedly asked for extra men to supervise the dens.[45] The shortage of police is also attested to by the gambling house farmers who requested more men, sometimes complaining that there were none assigned to their dens in the first place.[46] Even if there was a police presence it was no guarantee against fights or extortion. In at least one case, off-duty police caused trouble and their on-duty colleagues were reluctant to intervene and make arrests.[47] On occasion, the police might even have been in cahoots with the gangs of troublemakers.[48] More seriously, bandit gangs also staged raids on gambling dens in remote areas.[49] One particularly bloody example occurred in May 1902 when 36 bandits raided the Samrong gambling house to the south of Bangkok in broad daylight. About 100 shots were fired, leaving nine dead and six seriously wounded. The gang made off with over 4,000 baht in cash and then plundered the homes of eight Chinese living in the area.[50] This sparked a major investigation: the culprits were eventually brought to justice and some publicly executed.[51] Clearly, the gambling houses nurtured crime. This alone was a compelling reason for their abolition.

The closure of the last five dens in Bangkok in 1917 marked the end of a long-established feature of Thai life. The neighbourhoods in which they had stood became deserted overnight and the businesses associated with them packed up and moved on.[52] However, there is little to suggest these closures had much impact upon the incidence of gambling. Indeed, people had had plenty of time to accustom themselves to the fact that the dens' days were numbered, for the government had announced its intention to close them all over ten years earlier. As had happened in the provinces, card dens sprang up rapidly throughout the capital as enterprising individuals sought to capitalize on the sudden gap in the market.[53] Underground dens offering *thua po* also proliferated, providing work for some of the dealers and croupiers of the departed gambling houses.[54] Just as significantly, new forms of mass entertainment were also appearing within the capital. People had been flocking to the cinema, for instance, ever since the first permanent one was established in 1905.[55] The former Bangrak gambling house even found a new lease of life as the Phatthana Chai cinema, while two others were transformed into theatres.[56] Life went on and so did the gambling.

The *huai* lottery

As detailed in Chapter 1, the *huai* lottery was established during the Third Reign in order to stimulate the circulation of currency, as well as furnish the Thai state with additional revenue.[57] It was played with 34 letters of the Thai alphabet; hence, it was called *huai ko kho*, literally the ABC lottery. Each letter had a name based on that of a famous character from Chinese legend and was represented pictorially by both this individual and an animal that suggested their former birth-state. Stories about these personages were immortalized in verse during the late nineteenth century. The fact that these were highly popular and that adults and children alike could remember all the letters by name is evidence of how the *huai* pervaded Thai life. Winners stood to gain 30 times their original stake, with one-thirtieth being claimed by the operators as commission. The odds were not as good as those in the gambling dens but the potential prize made an attractive inducement. As B. O. Cartwright noted, by picking a winner just once in 10 or 20 times or by staking on 10 or 20 letters and winning on one, people could expect to make some profit.[58]

For the greater part of its existence, the *huai* lottery was limited to Bangkok and its immediate environs.[59] It was part of the Bangkok gambling house farm until the early 1870s, when Chulalongkorn made it a single, distinct farm so as to increase state revenue.[60] At first there was only one draw a day but, when it was seen how profitable the founder Chin Hong's operation was, a rival *huai* was set up, with a draw in the evening. This was short-lived, however, and the two draws were subsequently made part of the same farm. The administration of the lottery was organized like a three-tiered pyramid. At the apex was the lottery farmer, whose centre of operations was the lottery hall, located, from the 1870s on, inside the city walls at Pratu Samyot. Here he had about 200 staff working directly for him.[61] The next tier consisted of the district managers. Bangkok and its suburbs were divided into 38 districts (*khwaeng*), each with its own office. There were two kinds of district, inner and outer, the classification being based on its distance from the lottery hall. The inner districts were responsible for sending the daily stakes to the lottery hall, for which they received a commission. Any winnings were paid with cash from the lottery hall. The outer districts, meanwhile, held onto the stakes they received but had to pay any winnings themselves. At the base of the pyramid were the lottery clerks, who were essentially subcontractors of the district managers. These clerks could be found, sat behind their stalls waiting to receive people's stakes, throughout the city. In 1873, it was estimated that there were over 1,000 in Bangkok.[62] They took their places when the afternoon markets opened, around 4 pm, so that they might catch the market traffic. Punters would tell the clerks the letter or letters they had chosen for the morning and/or evening draw and how they wished their stake to be placed. There were several ways of staking. For instance, with the *hu* method players would re-stake the winnings, or part of, from the morning letter on another letter for the evening draw. Doing the double was highly profitable: Cartwright recalls winning 155 baht 56 atts on an original stake of just 12 atts.[63] The clerk would provide the punter with a stamped receipt specifying the date and details of their stake. He then made two records of the bet, one for himself and the other for the lottery hall. The latter account was called the *bai phoi*. Around 10 pm, the clerks sent the *bai phoi* to the district offices, where the accounts were then compiled. The inner districts then submitted the *bai phoi* to the lottery hall, where the draw took place. The morning letter was drawn around 1 am and the evening one around 4 am. After each announcement, runners were sent out to tell the district offices and clerks the result. If the punters were not awoken by the sound of the runner shouting out the letter, then they could easily learn the result the following day from the board hanging next to the clerk's stall.

Perhaps the most curious aspect of the *huai* was that the winning letter was not selected randomly; the lottery farmer chose the morning letter before any of that day's bets had been made, placed a wooden tile bearing that letter in a bag and then hung it up in the lottery hall. His decision was made after consulting the *bai phoi* for the previous week to see which letters had been heavily backed recently, hoping this might indicate which ones people were likely to back that day and thus be avoided. The evening letter was chosen after the farmer had examined the winning *bai phoi* for the morning draw. In this sense, the farmer was playing the game as well. Regular lottery gamblers, meanwhile, had various methods for getting into the farmer's mindset: keeping records of the results and then trying to discern any particular patterns, such as how many days would pass before the farmer would draw the same letter.[64] This was actively encouraged; all the lottery clerks had a record board showing all the recent results hanging near their stall. Moreover, the 34 letters were divided into six groups according to the Chinese personage associated with them for this very purpose; on the days when the farmer made merit at the temple, it was believed he would draw one of the six letters in the *phra* (holy men) group, for instance.[65] The *huai* was thus a battle of wits between the farmer and the hardcore punters, with each trying to guess which letter the other might back. Indeed, when Damrong asked one lottery farmer why he did not draw a letter at random he was told that, if they were to do so, these players would lose interest and the amount staked would fall.[66] It would seem that the lottery farmers had ample opportunities for fraud but the historical record is surprisingly quiet on this. While the farmer may always have been trying to fix the result in his favour, it can be surmised that corrupt practices were kept in check by the fear of being exposed and the disastrous loss of custom that might result. Of course, whichever letter the farmer chose, someone was bound to win.

There were a host of less systematic means of predicting the *huai*. People were constantly on the lookout for lucky omens – a gesture from a holy man, a strange marking on an ancient tree or a dream – as an indication of the winning letter. Offerings were made and rituals performed. Many monks, willingly or not, acquired reputations as great tipsters.[67] Indeed, there was a whole lottery-tips industry made up of astrologers and fortune-tellers, magic potions and books of formulas.[68] Part of the lottery's popularity was no doubt due to the way in which it appealed to people's superstitious beliefs and sense of fate. It is also easy to imagine market places buzzing with speculation about that day's winning letter.

Unlike the gambling houses, which had low-class and criminal associations, the *huai* had universal appeal and was played by all sections of Bangkok society.[69] According to Damrong, its popularity amongst the higher classes was partly due to the fact they could play it anonymously by getting another to place a stake for them.[70] In the early 1870s, the most common stake was one baht – though the wealthy might bet as much as 50 baht or more – and the daily receipts of the lottery hall were apparently between 4,000 and 4,800 baht.[71] By the latter years of the *huai*'s existence this had risen to about 40,000 baht a day, out of which the lottery farmer would usually pay out around 10,000 baht.[72] As with the gambling houses, the increase in lottery takings was partly due to the construction of a rail network into the provinces – the north-eastern line to Nakhon Ratchasima was completed in 1900, for instance – which enabled people to come to Bangkok occasionally to place a stake.[73] The most popular time of year for this was the end of Buddhist Lent in October: in 1904 passenger demand was so great that additional trains had to be put on.[74] Huge crowds would gather outside the lottery hall to await the draw, and food and drink stalls would do a brisk trade. The total amount staked at this time reached as much as 140,000 baht a day, though the farmer might have had to pay out large sums.[75] Clearly, much like the gambling houses, the *huai* was an integral part of Siamese life.

Cockfights, cards and kites

Besides those discussed so far, there was a plethora of other activities on which people in Siam gambled. During the 1850s, a tax farm on 17 games – including cock, bird and fish fighting; a number of card and dice games; and various types of racing involving boats, horses and ox-carts – was established, covering Bangkok, the Central Plains and the lower north. The farmer was entitled to a commission on all stakes on these games but, as with the other farms, he might sublet his monopoly rights on a district-by-district basis.[76] Compared to the gambling house and lottery farms, though, the revenue provided by this farm was negligible.[77] Rather than see its creation as a revenue raising measure, it is thus more tempting to view it as an attempt to regulate, and thereby control, the boom in gambling outlined in Chapter 1. It seems that similar farms were later set up to cover other gambling activities on an ad-hoc, regional basis. During the Fourth

Reign at least, these farms were usually held by the same tax farmer that controlled the gambling houses in a given region.[78] The two separate types of gambling farm were merged by 1891 at the latest.[79]

Animal fights, along with the obligatory betting, were immensely popular with men throughout the country; perhaps none more so than cockfighting, the quintessential pastime of the Thai farmer (see Figure 2.2). Indeed, the prohibition against cockfighting that was in force for much of the first half of the nineteenth century was widely flouted.[80] During his sojourn in the north-eastern town of Phimai in the 1880s, Étienne Aymonier spent some time observing how the fights were conducted:

> In the shade of tall trees, a perimeter of trellised bamboo, knee high, enclosed a battlefield three to four meters in diameter. A kind of water clock, a punctured metal cup slowly sinking in a basin of water, served to indicate the duration of each round. Some fifteen bamboo stakes threaded together and pulled out of the ground one by one after each round indicated how many rounds it took one cock [to] put the other out of the fight. A small rattle announced the beginning as well as the end of a fight.[81]

Figure 2.2 Temple mural of a cockfight (photograph by Gerhard Jaiser, source: Gerhard Jaiser, *Thai Mural Painting, Volume 2: Society, Preservation and Subjects*, Bangkok: White Lotus, 2010, Plate 35c).

Fights were held every day; the day he arrived there were about ten spectators only and the local tax farmer, waiting to collect his commission.[82] Considering the popularity of cockfighting in the entire South-East Asian region, Anthony Reid highlights how this was due to 'the close identification of the rooster with the male ego'.[83] Cockfighting and the associated wagers thereby acted as a status signifier. Drawing on the work of Clifford Geertz, he concludes:

> The apparently frenzied betting was motivated not so much by the hope of big winnings as by identification with the kin group, faction, or village of the cock's owner. The cockfight was therefore a vivid dramatization both of the solidarity of the vertically organized group and of the hostilities generated in its endless status competition with other groups.[84]

A similar argument could be advanced for bullfighting, which was unique to the South. Two bulls were set upon each other, butting and shoving until one was driven off. A particular curiosity for the Westerner was the Siamese fighting fish, which are so pugnacious they are known to attack their own reflections. Other such contests involved rams, buffalo, birds and various insects such as stag beetles, cockchafers and crickets. Perhaps the most cruel and bizarre, though, was tortoise racing, which involved smearing some resinous, flammable substance on the poor animals' shells and then igniting it to incite them to greater speeds.[85]

There was also much betting on contests involving human skill and strength such as Thai boxing (*muai thai*) and boat races. Anything was fair game. While in Chiang Mai in the early 1880s, Carl Bock witnessed a trial by water, held to resolve a dispute between two officials over the ownership of some slaves. Two men were chosen to represent the disputants; whoever remained under water the longest would be the winner. Predictably, there was much betting amongst the spectators who lined the riverbank.[86] Even an activity as innocuous as kite flying provided opportunities for gambling, with people betting on the outcome of dogfights.[87] This was largely a Bangkok phenomenon: from the 1890s onwards, contests were held on the Sanam Luang field near the Grand Palace. These attracted large numbers of people, including members of the aristocracy, and the sport enjoyed the patronage of the king.[88]

Playing cards, and the games associated with them, were apparently introduced into Siam from China during the Third Reign.[89] These cards were then adapted to suit Thai playing styles and became known as *phai phong thai* or just *phai tong*. A pack consisted of 120 cards numbered one to ten and divided into three suits with four of each number.[90] Cards became a favourite pastime and a factory for producing them was established in Bangkok.[91] With the opening of the country to Western trade in the second half of the nineteenth century came Western cards and games.

Collectively these were called *phai pok*, the second word probably being derived from the word poker.[92]

Bets were also placed on board games such as *saka*, which was similar to backgammon, dice games such as *hi-lo* and *si ngao lak*, and games using dominoes, called *phai to tem* in Thai. A range of other games, such as *mai mun* (a Thai version of roulette) and *nam tao* (matching pictures on dice with those on a board), were played at the assorted festivals and fairs that punctuated the year, perhaps the most famous of which was that at the Golden Mount in Bangkok.[93] Usually these games were played for prizes rather than cash. As the following chapters will show, new games and forms of gambling were constantly springing up, while others fell out of fashion. In the early part of the Fifth Reign, for instance, the Chinese introduced the game *huai chap yi-ki*, a type of lottery played with 12 cards. Gambling house farmers asked that it be included in their monopolies but Chulalongkorn refused and the game was prohibited.[94]

The players

Every section of Siamese society gambled: from princes to slaves, Chinese merchants to coolies, government officials to farmers and monks to children. Moreover, it seems that men and women gambled equally. For Western contemporaries, it was *the* Siamese vice.[95] Given their imperial or proselytizing ambitions, they may have had reasons for exaggeration but, as this chapter and Chapter 1 have shown, gambling was a pervasive feature of Thai life. Moreover, as Chapter 4 will show, the Thai elite also shared this view. Its ubiquity is graphically represented by the numerous depictions of people gambling in temple murals. The 'rationalist' outlook of the early Bangkok elite discussed in Chapter 1 fed a greater interest in realism in artistic expression. Scenes from everyday life thus became a feature of nineteenth-century temple murals and gambling was a natural topic.[96] These murals also provided some subtle social commentary. For instance, among the mostly Thai spectators at the cockfight in Figure 2.2, there is a solitary Chinese man, with his hair tied in a queue, clasping an opium pipe.

If the country suffered from a gambling mania, as Westerners and the Thai elite both claimed, then how can it be explained? The attraction of certain games has already been mentioned but it is worthwhile considering some more general reasons. Before examining why people gambled, it is necessary to consider how gambling became so engrained in Thai society. Here, a quick look at the involvement of the Thai aristocracy and children is particularly revealing. As argued in Chapter 1, gambling acted as a status signifier for both the traditional political elite and the new commercial one during the early Bangkok period. This did not go unchallenged, however. Rama I, for instance, increased the penalty for government officials playing *thua po*: offenders were to be whipped 90 times, reduced to the status of a commoner, and tattooed upon their forehead.[97] Mongkut, meanwhile, attempted to prohibit gambling within royal palaces after there had been a serious theft, supposedly motivated by gambling debts.[98] A key reason for such laws was the government's awareness of how gambling by these privileged members of society set a bad example to the lower classes.[99] Judging by various reports, however, these prohibitions were generally ignored.[100] Indeed, the aristocracy were usually the first to engage in new forms of gambling that then filtered down to the rest of Thai society: Rama III, for instance, was said to have played cards with his favourite grandchild.[101] What is most interesting, though, is how various residents of different status gambled together within the royal palaces. In 1893, for example, two concubines of the king (*chao chom*) were caught playing *thua* with four household slaves in the Bang Pa-In palace. One of the women justified their behaviour by explaining that because the slaves often sneaked out to gamble during the night, they thought it preferable to let them gamble within the palace.[102] The Thai elite thus acted as one of the main means of transmission for new forms of gambling and through their participation sanctioned play among the lower classes.

Western observers often commented on how the gambling passion was instilled in the Thais from a young age.[103] There were many opportunities to learn the mechanics of gambling. Children could commonly be seen playing *yot lum* – a game similar to marbles played with coins that also doubled as the stakes – in the streets.[104] Within the gambling houses, meanwhile it was: 'no uncommon thing to see little creatures of seven or eight years old [...] joining, with all the zest imaginable, in "backing" the luck of older gamblers'.[105] Some of these were runaways who subsisted through fetching drinks or snacks and scavenging for coins under the floors of the dens.[106] Others were merely accompanying their parents. More sinisterly, unscrupulous characters cheated children out of their cash and jewellery by using card tricks and such like.[107] In short, children grew up in an environment where gambling was pervasive and their participation in it encouraged.[108] It is unsurprising, therefore, that Chulalongkorn's first efforts to wean people off gambling were aimed at the young. In the mid-1870s, three Acts were passed prohibiting adults from gambling with children and which encouraged parents to prevent their children from playing games that might lead to more hardcore forms of gambling.[109]

Turning to the question of why people in Siam gambled, it is clear that monetary gain, while important, was not the main reason. Damrong, for instance, thought that people gambled more for fun (*sanuk*) than for money.[110] Western visitors took a similar view: 'In the gambling-houses of this phlegmatic people neither party – the banker nor those that play – seem to care a whit whether they win or lose; only let them enjoy their excitement, and that seems to satisfy even the unfortunate'.[111] This indifference to winning or losing is a common feature among all gamblers: money is the *means* through which people play, rather than its goal, and gives their involvement value, thereby generating the excitement they crave.[112]

Kanchana also emphasizes this leisure aspect, arguing that as a primarily agrarian society, the majority of the population had large amounts of free time, some four to seven months a year, between harvesting and planting; free time that would be spent gambling.[113] Here the absence of other types of leisure activity needs to be emphasized: as Western contemporaries noted the only rival attraction to the gambling dens or cockpits for the majority of the population throughout the nineteenth century was the theatre.[114] Of course, the only places likely to be staging *likay* or *ngiu* performances in rural areas, if not in Bangkok as well, were the gambling houses. With all its thrills and spills, gambling was thus an escape from the tedium and hardship of day-to-day life.[115] Indeed, as Reith highlights, one of the distinctive features of gambling is its 'separateness', meaning that it is 'a self-contained realm of activity [...] with its own rules and conventions and within which the gamblers' orientation to the everyday world is altered'.[116] The lure of this 'separateness' will become more apparent below.

Gambling in Siam also had an important social function. It was, and indeed remains, an integral part of the various ceremonies and festivals that measure the rhythm of life. For instance, parents often sought permission from the tax farmer for *thua po* to be played at their child's topknot shaving ceremony.[117] Similarly, cards might be played at funeral wakes.[118] In his study of these 'funeral casinos' in present-day Thailand, Alan Klima highlights how gambling is offered in order to attract large numbers of people to keep the deceased's spirit company.[119] A similar logic can be applied to other life ceremonies and festivals. Indeed, one justification for the numerous gaming stalls at most temple fairs, in blatant breach of Buddhist doctrine, was that nobody would come if no gambling was offered.[120] In this sense, gambling had an integrative function, nurturing a sense of community at various levels. This was most apparent during the three main festivals of the year: Chinese New Year, Thai New Year and Songkran.[121] These were occasions when taboos were lifted and licence given for indulgence; significantly, they were also the only times when people could gamble freely without the permission of the tax farmer.[122] Naturally, people took full advantage of this dispensation, gathering in houses and shops or in the streets throughout the country to gamble unrestrainedly.[123]

Besides sociability, the need for excitement and the hope of wealth, there are a number of 'deeper' reasons why people gamble. Numerous scholars have observed that what is at stake in many forms of gambling, especially though not exclusively in contests and games involving some degree of skill, is not really money but status, respect and face.[124] In Chapter 1, for instance, it was argued that gambling by the Thai political elite and the Chinese commercial one was a form of conspicuous consumption: it enabled both groups to display their wealth and either confirm or assert their status by showing indifference to large gambling losses. Similarly, gambling provides opportunities for displays of character: to show how one acts when under pressure and faced with loss. Within Thai society, a premium is placed on remaining cool-headed (*chai yen*) in high-pressure situations, gambling is thus a way of illustrating this trait. In other words, one can lose large amounts of money through gambling but gain prestige and respect in return. Moreover, gambling is also an arena for what Erving Goffman called 'character contests', whereby one can symbolically challenge another's character or place in a status hierarchy by betting against them.[125] In this sense, gambling's 'separateness' allows rivals to let off steam in a safe and unthreatening manner outside the usual constraints of society. Lastly, gambling has the capacity to negate completely any inherent or acquired advantages one person has over another since luck is blind to merit, skill and status alike. Indeed, for Reith, the 'absolute democracy' of games of chance is part of their 'unique appeal'.[126] In the case of the two royal concubines gambling in the palace with their slaves mentioned earlier, the slaves had as good a chance of winning at *thua* as their higher-ranking hosts. Gambling thus offered an escape from the stratified nature of Thai society: a chance for people of different status to interact with each other, albeit briefly, as equals.[127]

In seeking to explain why people in Siam gambled, it is also worth reversing the question to consider: why not? Gambling is often condemned as an irrational activity because it is a form of unproductive expenditure: it wastes both time and money that could be better spent or invested elsewhere.[128] However, the underlying assumption here is that capital accumulation is a universal feature of human societies but this is by no means so. Indeed, so long as one has enough for basic welfare, why save? While there may have been a tradition of capital accumulation within the Chinese immigrant communities in Siam, this was not the case among the rural Thai population. Thai attitudes towards money are vividly illustrated in the following folktale:

> The king on his travels asked a peasant what he did with his surplus. 'Your majesty, all the money I am able to save, after paying the expenses of our frugal household, I divide into four parts. The first part I bury in the ground; the second part I use to pay my creditors; the third part I fling into the river; and the fourth and last part I give to my enemy'. The king sent his retinue away and asked him to specify. The peasant answered: 'The money I bury in the ground is the money I spend on alms and in making merit. The money I give to my creditors is what it costs me to keep my father and mother, to whom I owe everything that I have. The money I fling into the river is the money I spend on gambling and drink and opium; and the money I give to my enemy is the money I give to my wife'. The answers pleased the King, except that he protested that a man's wife was not his 'enemy'.[129]

As Ruth Benedict highlights, the peasant did not consider saving any of his surplus for purchasing animals, tools and suchlike; although some of the money given to his wife might have constituted savings in the form of jewellery. Benedict goes on to claim that '"burying in the ground" and "throwing in the river" are folk designations of where money *should* go'.[130] In other words, gambling was a legitimate use of one's capital. It should also be noted that there were three major factors that militated against capital accumulation. First, one needs cash in order to save and, as noted in Chapter 1, the volume of currency in circulation in pre-twentieth-century Siam was limited. Second, and related to the first point, even if they did manage to acquire some money there was nowhere, given the complete absence of banking facilities in rural areas until long into the twentieth century, to keep it safely, besides burying it.[131] Third, the income of the rural cultivator was intermittent and came in large chunks; principally, once they had sold their crop following the harvest. In his study of working-class gambling in Britain around the turn of the twentieth century, R. McKibbin notes that it was an irregularity of income, combined with other factors, that created 'a rhythm of debt and credit of which gambling was to become an intrinsic part'.[132] Under these circumstances, he argues that betting by the working class can be seen as a 'rational' activity.[133] Such an analysis also seems pertinent to the rural Thai population.

Rather than see the prevalence of gambling in Siam/Thailand as stemming from some cultural disposition towards gambling, this chapter and Chapter 1 have argued that it was the result of a conjunction of socio-economic factors from the mid-nineteenth century onwards, which marked the country's transition towards capitalist modernity. Increasing prosperity through integration into the world economy meant greater numbers of people could afford to gamble, which was one of the few, if not the only, form of entertainment readily available to most of the population. As such the gambling houses and other establishments providing gaming opportunities became a distinctive feature of nineteenth-century Thai life. The significance of gambling in the modern history of Thailand is not just limited to the economic and social sphere, however; as Chapter 3 will show, the revenue from gambling played a vital role in the construction of the modern Thai nation-state.

3 Gambling revenue and the creation of the modern Thai nation-state

Gambling has been used as a revenue source by states and other institutions all over the world at different points in time. The attractions are clear. Activities which involve gambling, such as betting on contests or lotteries, are relatively easy to organize. The organizers then stand to profit directly from the proceeds or, particularly in the case of governments, indirectly from commission or tax. Due to the grip gambling has upon human passions and purse strings, its financial exploitation can be highly lucrative. During the seventeenth and eighteenth centuries, for instance, the English government regularly issued lotteries to facilitate loans. After almost two centuries of anti-gambling legislation, the British government instituted the National Lottery in the late twentieth century to raise funds for 'good causes' such as arts, sports and heritage. In Asia, meanwhile, the Singapore government allowed two operators to establish casinos in the republic in 2010 in order to boost tourism and tax revenues.[1] The use of gambling for revenue purposes in Thailand is not out of the ordinary, therefore. This chapter will argue that the promotion and taxation of certain forms of gambling played a crucial role in the transformation of the semi-feudal Siamese kingdom into the modern nation-state of Thailand.

Prior to Chulalongkorn's administrative reforms in the late nineteenth century, the Bangkok-based Thai state had direct control only over the capital and its immediate environs. Beyond this core, it governed the provinces of the kingdom through negotiations and alliances with local rulers, most of whom had hereditary control over their fiefdoms. On the kingdom's peripheries were a number of tributary states – the northern Thai kingdoms clustered around Chiang Mai, the Lao kingdoms of Luang Prabang and Vientiane, and the Malay sultanates in the South – in which the Bangkok state's authority was largely symbolic. Moreover, within the central administration the power of the king was severely constrained by that of the Bangkok noble families. Indeed, by the mid-nineteenth century, the Bunnags were the de facto rulers of the kingdom. However, the Western imperial threat, combined with the socio-economic changes outlined in Chapter 1, gave the Siamese state both the pretext and the resources to establish direct control over its peripheries. These factors also helped tilt the balance of power between the monarch and the nobles firmly in favour of the former. During the early nineteenth century, the revenue base of the Siamese state shifted from customs duties and trade monopolies to taxes on production and consumption. Siam's gradual integration into the global economic system as a primary producer of rice, teak and tin, combined with increasing Chinese immigration, further broadened the state's revenue base, of which gambling taxation became a major component. In the latter part of the nineteenth century, this formed the foundations for administrative reforms modelled on colonial forms of governance that established the centralized Thai absolutist state. Just as importantly, both the absolute monarchy under Vajiravudh and the post-1932 constitutional governments used lotteries to fund nation-building programmes and promote a common Thai identity in order to shore up support for their respective regimes.

Tax farms and gambling in nineteenth-century Siam

Tax farming is a system of revenue collection that has been used by states across all continents and throughout history.[2] It was a compromise on the part of the state in that it delegated its sovereign powers of tax collection on a range of products and services to private operators in exchange for a certain fixed rent, which in theory was greater than that which the state could collect on its own. The allocation of tax farms was determined by auction, with the monopoly rights going to the highest bidder. For their part, tax farmers were granted certain powers and privileges to help them run their monopolies and meet their obligations, effectively making them quasi-state officials. Crucially, they got to keep all the income over and above what they had promised to the state. Although rather crude, the attractions of tax farming for the state are obvious: it entailed little expenditure, if any, on its part but provided a certain level of income. It was up to the tax farmers to ensure they ran an efficient and profitable collection system. Moreover, competition from other tax farmers meant that the state could expect bids for the monopoly to increase if it proved profitable. As Hong Lysa has highlighted: 'The automatic escalation of state revenue in proportion to the profitability of the farm was the cornerstone of the dynamics of the tax farming system'.[3] This was the theory, at least. But as the first part of this chapter will show, there were some inherent contradictions in the system that bred instability and would ultimately lead the state to assume responsibility itself for tax collection.

As mentioned in Chapter 1, by the mid-nineteenth century the Siamese state had become dependent on tax farming for the greater part of its revenue. This was due to the restrictions on custom duties and land taxes imposed by the unequal treaties that had deprived the state of alternative sources of income. Additionally, the state had neither the administrative apparatus nor the knowledge to collect taxes on its own. Tax farming thus provided a relatively stable source of income at a critical period in the formation of the modern Thai state, funding Chulalongkorn's administrative reforms of the late nineteenth and early twentieth centuries, which laid the foundations of absolutism and safeguarded Siam from the colonial threat.[4] According to Damrong, the particular beauty of the gambling tax farms was that they were the most effective means of extracting revenue from the population without provoking discontent; people gambled of their own free will and, should they lose everything, they were likely to blame themselves or misfortune rather than the gambling houses or the *huai* lottery.[5] Moreover, the numerous gambling farms were not plagued by the instability associated with the larger opium farms.[6] Indeed, their relative stability probably accounts for the fact that they were among the last tax farms to be abolished in Siam.

The tax farming system was constantly evolving throughout the nineteenth century; the following section describes the system roughly as it existed at the start of Chulalongkorn's reign.[7] Geographically, Bangkok-controlled tax farms covered all the major towns as far north as Uttaradit, to Nakhon Ratchasima in the east, and to Songkhla in the South.[8] Tax farmers normally held the monopoly rights for three years and would pay the amount they had pledged to the government in periodic instalments. If they fell behind in these payments, though, the farm might be put up for re-auction. As a precaution against tax farmers defaulting, they were required to have a guarantor who might cover their debts to the government. The auctions and payments for particular tax farms were supervised by various government departments, which would retain the revenue received for their own purposes. For much of the second half of the nineteenth century, key departments such as the *Kalahom* (military affairs), which supervised the opium farm, were under the control of the Bunnag family, who used the revenue from the tax farms administered by these departments to build up their powerbase at the expense of the monarch.

Chinese entrepreneurs made up the overwhelming majority of gambling tax farmers, with Thais only occasionally securing the monopolies.[9] This dominance is usually attributed to the fact that only the Chinese had the financial resources, knowledge, and organizational capabilities to run these large farms.[10] Many who held the gambling farms during the mid-nineteenth century had made their fortunes earlier in the junk trade. Some were also heads of the numerous Chinese secret societies, using their organizations to intimidate potential rivals from placing higher bids when their monopolies came up for renewal.[11] Crucially, they had cultivated close connections with the Thai elite since the boom in the junk trade at the start of the Bangkok era, ties later cemented by intermarriage and joint business ventures. Indeed, the patronage of members of the royal and noble families could be crucial in ensuring one submitted the winning bid. Tax farming was, in essence, an alliance between Chinese economic might and Thai political authority.

All tax farmers were given an official title with a minimum of 400 *sakdina* marks, making them lesser nobility, and a range of special powers to help facilitate their operations. Indicating the importance of gambling revenue to the state, gambling house and lottery farmers were sometimes granted as many as 800 *sakdina* marks.[12] Amongst other privileges, they had the right to arrest any illegal gamblers within their jurisdiction and receive any fines incurred once the case had been tried.[13] Some had their own jails where debtors could be confined in chains until their debt was cleared.[14] Moreover, to enforce and protect their monopolies, these tax farmers employed their own networks of spies and private armies of toughs.[15] As Howard Dick observes of tax farming in general, 'the state delegated not only the collection of taxes but also its powers of coercion'.[16] Gambling tax farmers thus enjoyed a high level of autonomy; their farm was essentially their personal fiefdom to administer as they wished. While this power may have been necessary for the farm to run effectively, it also gave the tax farmer the opportunity to abuse his position for personal gain to the detriment of the Siamese state and population. Discussing the gambling farms in the Federated Malay States, John Butcher highlights how colonial officials justified their existence on the grounds that they were the most effective means of restricting gambling because 'it was in the farmer's interests to prevent any gambling taking place except with his permission, the implication being that he would seldom if ever allow gambling except in the known gambling houses since this would undermine his profits'.[17] It is possible to discern a similar logic to the gambling farms in Siam but, in both cases, the reality was rather different. Gambling farmers were only too willing to tolerate illicit gambling so long as they received a cut of the profits, and they even ran games prohibited by the state themselves.[18] Sometimes people conspired with the gambling farmer to set up an illegal game: once many people had gathered, the farmer would turn up to arrest them. The organizer and the farmer would then split the money the latter received in fines.[19]

As noted earlier, the revenue from tax farming should have, in theory, provided the state with a guaranteed level of income that steadily rose. This was not always the case, however. There were two principal reasons for this: first, the inability or unwillingness of tax farmers to pay the full auction price of their monopoly, and second, the domination of tax farms by certain individuals and syndicates. Although an agent of the state, the tax farmer was first and foremost a private entrepreneur and, consequently, would try to maximize his income at the state's expense.[20] Citing problems such as a decline in custom because of a bad harvest, the unwelcome attentions of rival Chinese secret societies or the failure of subcontractors to make their payments, gambling tax farmers would either request a reduction in the sum of each instalment or just ask for a deferral and go into debt to the government.[21] This problem of incomplete payment was intensified by the fierce competition involved in securing a farm. Overestimating the potential profits or just being determined to beat all other competitors might lead a prospective farmer to submit a bid he could not possibly honour.[22] When a farmer asked for a reduction in the monopoly price or merely fell behind in his payments, the government might decide to put the farm up for re-auction. However, the value of the farm would be significantly reduced, especially if the farmer had defaulted because of external problems. In some cases there might be no others willing, or able, to place a bid and the original farmer would end up retaining his farm at a reduced price while still being in debt to the state. Of course, when the gambling farmers profited from their operations they rarely raised their bids for the following year but as soon as they were in danger of making a loss they were quick to ask the government to help share the responsibility.

More seriously, the monopolization of tax farms by syndicates undermined the very basis of the system, namely that state revenue would increase in proportion to the profitability of the farms. As Hong emphasizes, however, this was dependent on the free play of market forces, a prerequisite that was in short supply by the end of the Fourth Reign.[23] With the backing of Chinese secret societies, provincial authorities or a powerful patron within the court, tax farmers were able to subvert the bidding process and retain their monopoly at the original price for many years. Intimidation might also be used to ensure there were no rival bids. Syndicates were formed in which control of the gambling farms was rotated amongst members, with the bidding price stagnating or even falling. In 1855, for instance, the revenue from the gambling farm on animal fights and other games dropped from 16,000 baht to 13,600, where it remained until at least 1868.[24] This problem was compounded by a shortage of potential tax farmers with the capital and organizational capabilities to run the gambling and lottery farms. Unlike tax farms that were based on people's production, these two required large amounts of capital to cover operational costs and losses. A limited pool of competitors meant the state had to rely on certain individuals they might not otherwise have chosen.

To sum up, although tax farming provided the state with a fairly reliable and regular source of income, the machinations of the tax farmers ensured that the system never worked to its full potential. Revenue was always being drained away from the state into the pockets of the tax farmers. For much of the nineteenth century, this was a price the Siamese state was willing to pay. Indeed, while it lacked the resources to collect taxes for itself, the balance of power lay with the tax farmers. In the late nineteenth century, however, the balance began to tilt in favour of the Siamese state.

Gambling revenue and the creation of the Thai absolutist state

When Chulalongkorn came to the throne in 1868 at the age of 15 the monarchy was in a weak position vis-à-vis the Bangkok noble families, and the Bunnags in particular. The head of the Bunnag family, Somdet Chaophraya

Si Suriyawong (Chuang Bunnag), had been appointed regent until Chulalongkorn came of age, making him the most powerful man in the kingdom. He consolidated the position of his family further by transferring the supervision of numerous tax farms from crown offices to departments under Bunnag control. During the Regency period (1868–73), royal revenues fell from 4.8 million baht a year to just 1.6 million.[25] Chulalongkorn's first priority in his struggle for supremacy against the nobility, therefore, was to seize control of revenue supervision. In 1870, he assumed direct control over several important farms, including that covering the gambling houses and *huai* lottery in Bangkok. Changes were implemented to maximize the crown's income from this source: the *huai* lottery was made into a separate tax farm and the original Bangkok gambling house farm was divided into 20 districts, each of which was put up for auction as an individual farm.[26] These smaller monopolies could be secured for much smaller bids than the former farm that had covered the entire city, thereby broadening the pool of potential gambling house farmers and encouraging greater competition. It also encouraged the rapid proliferation of dens within Bangkok.[27] By 1874, the crown was receiving 880,000 baht a year from these remodelled Bangkok gambling and lottery farms.[28] On a broader scale, Chulalongkorn established the Finance Office (*Ho Ratsadakonphiphat*) in 1873 as a centralized agency to supervise all the tax farms.[29] This was the first crucial step in rationalizing the tax farming system. New regulations concerning the auction procedure and the method of payment were implemented in order to minimize the leakage of revenue to the nobles and tax farmers. For instance, to ensure the state received the money due, newly appointed farmers were required to pay a deposit of three monthly instalments in advance, with the rest of the bid being paid in monthly instalments. Moreover, the term of appointment was reduced to just one year, at the end of which the incumbent could continue to hold the farm so long as they had not fallen into debt to the government and there were no others who wished to take it on.

These initiatives and other reforms enacted during the same period provoked a conservative backlash, however, that led to the Front Palace Incident in late 1874 and early 1875. After staging what seemed to be an attempted coup, Prince Wichaichan, the Second King and a client of the former regent Suriyawong, sought refuge in the British Consulate. Faced with the threat of possible foreign intervention in the affairs of the kingdom, Chulalongkorn only managed to defuse the situation by putting his fiscal reforms on hold. Nevertheless, while the greater proportion of the kingdom's revenue remained under the control of the Bunnags and other noble families, he had managed to secure sufficient revenues to win supporters and implement less controversial reforms in areas such as education and defence.[30] It was not until the mid-1880s, however, that Chulalongkorn was in a sufficiently strong political position to restart his modernization programme. By this time, Suriyawong and other key figures of the old order had passed away and the king was able to start appointing his brothers and half-brothers as heads of the government ministries and departments.

Under the stewardship of Prince Narathip Praphanphong, the Finance Office and, from 1892 onwards, the Ministry of Finance assumed control of all the kingdom's tax farms and began replacing those on commodities with direct collection by government officials. Specific measures were also taken to increase the efficiency of the three main farms: the liquor, opium and gambling monopolies. With regard to the latter, between 1888 and 1892, the number of gambling houses in Bangkok was reduced from over 400 to 16, each of which was made into an individual farm.[31] But, while making its commitment to restricting gambling clear, the government had no intention of closing all the capital's dens in the immediate future. Rather, this first wave of closures should be seen as part of a concerted effort to rationalize the gambling tax farms and maximize their revenue. In correspondence with the king, Narathip had identified 16 as the optimum number of dens and noted that their abolition would be impossible while there were no alternative revenue sources.[32] Along with the closures, comprehensive regulations, combining new and existing rules, were issued for both the gambling houses and the *huai* lottery.[33] These included the fixing of opening hours from 7 am to 12 am and the requirement that police officers be stationed in every den to maintain order. By assuming greater responsibility for the security of the gambling houses and the farmer's monopoly, the government hoped to lessen complaints and requests for reductions in payments due to one problem or another.

These initial closures and attendant regulations had a number of effects. Most obviously, concentrating the capital's legal gambling facilities in 16 establishments ensured these places enjoyed a massive boom in custom. Indeed, as Nuttaya emphasizes, these gambling houses were transformed into the entertainment centres of their day, not only attracting the patrons of the closed dens but other people who might have come to enjoy a theatrical performance, visit the brothel next door or smoke opium in an adjacent shop.[34] Naturally, increased custom meant greater profits for the tax farmers, leading to higher bids for the gambling houses at auction time. Between 1874/5 and 1893/4, for instance, the price of the Saphan Han den quadrupled, while that for the one at Khlong Bangkok Yai almost doubled.[35] Combined with the reduction in the number of farms, this led to many tax farmers being priced out of the market and the concomitant rise of certain groups and syndicates that were able to monopolize particular dens for many years. Chin Tan Khai Ho and his associates, for example, controlled the Ban Tawai gambling house almost continuously between 1894/5 and 1909/10, when it was finally closed.[36] The shrinking pool of potential farmers also magnified the government's dependence on those remaining, meaning they could exert pressure on the government to annul certain regulations that impacted too heavily upon their profits. Perhaps the best example of this was the compromise over opening hours. Although all the Bangkok gambling houses were supposed to close at midnight, this was widely ignored. When Police Commissioner Lawson successfully prosecuted one proprietor for violating the regulations in 1902, two gambling house farmers petitioned the Ministry of Finance for redress. With his eye firmly on the balance sheet, Prince Mahit Ratchaharithai, Minister of Finance from August 1896 to May 1906, argued that the regulations were an unnecessary hindrance for the tax farmers and did little to prevent excessive gambling. Despite the commissioner's claims that the all-night gambling dens were hangouts for criminals and that there would be less crime in the city if the closing time was enforced, the fiscal side of the government prevailed.[37] The regulations were amended, enabling the Minister of Finance to issue special permits for extended opening hours 'in order to meet the entertainment needs of the public'.[38] As was often the case, concerns about law and order were trumped by revenue considerations.

Despite the growing influence of certain tax farmers and syndicates, however, the real winner was the Thai state. Although there are no consistent figures for the revenue from the Bangkok gambling houses before 1892, it appears that the state's revenue was not affected adversely.[39] More significantly, between 1892/3 and 1896/7 when there were no further closures or significant changes to the gambling farms, revenue from the dens rose from 1.8 million baht to 2.9 million.[40] When combined with the proceeds from the *huai* lottery, opium and liquor farms, this amounted to around half the government's total revenue.[41] The rationalization of these tax farms swelled the state's income and provided the financial basis for Chulalongkorn to implement the wide-ranging administrative, fiscal and judicial reforms that secured his political supremacy and his kingdom's independence. The era of the absolutist state was ushered in with the formal inauguration of cabinet-style government, dominated by Chulalongkorn's brothers and half-brothers, in April 1892. Functionally-differentiated ministries with salaried officials were established, the most important, in the short term, being the Ministry of the Interior. In 1893, Damrong, as head of this ministry, began to implement the *thesaphiban* system of administration throughout Siam, gradually bringing the peripheries under the direct control of Bangkok. Under this system, the kingdom's provinces and its former tributaries were grouped together into administrative units called *monthon*, each of which was supervised by a Bangkok-appointed commissioner. The Ministry of the Interior was the vanguard of the Thai state's administrative push into outlying areas and, since it was usually the first ministry with personnel on the ground, it often assumed the duties of other ministries, including that of revenue collection.[42] The irony, of course, is that by providing the Thai state with the funds to create a strong centralized bureaucracy that could collect its own taxes, tax farming rendered itself obsolete.[43] In the short term, however, the revenue from the gambling and other vice farms became indispensable as state revenue and expenditure expanded in tandem.[44] Finding an adequate replacement thus became the primary factor in determining the pace of further gambling den closures.

With the expansion of the Bangkok state's control throughout Siam, the government was able to implement a similar policy of rationalization and progressive closures for the provincial gambling houses. Between 1898 and 1903, all the dens in *monthons* Nakhon Si Thammarat and Chumphon in the South and another 122 in the rest of the country were closed.[45] As with the initial closures in the capital, the Minister of Finance was working on the principle that fewer gambling house farms would mean greater competition among the tax farmers and higher bids for the remaining dens. Increased auction prices would thus offset the revenue losses incurred by closure.[46] As before, this actually resulted in a substantial increase in government income. Revenue from the gambling house farms rose from 2.9 million baht in 1896/7 to a peak of 6.8 million in 1904/5.[47] Yet Mahit was well aware that this balancing act could not be maintained indefinitely: sooner or later a tipping point would be reached whereby there would not be enough gambling houses, whatever their auction price, to cover the shortfall from further closures. Consequently, he brought den closures to a halt in 1904 so the government might concentrate on finding alternative revenue sources to compensate for the eventual abolition of all the kingdom's gambling houses.[48]

The growing administrative strength of the state was signalled by the promulgation of the Gambling Revenue Act R. S. 120 in March 1902. Under the provisions of this law, the government assumed responsibility for the licensing of all forms of gambling, apart from the Chinese games played in the dens and the *huai*, from the gambling house farmers.[49] Recognizing that games and methods of gambling varied from region to region, there were separate regulations for Greater Bangkok, the inner *monthons* that constituted the core of the kingdom, and *monthon* Phayap, which consisted of the northern provinces centred on Chiang Mai.[50] There were few significant differences in these regulations, though, and all three worked on the same principles, listing games that were forbidden and those that were permitted subject to licence. The way in which the legality of games was determined will be discussed in Chapter 4; for now, it should be mentioned that licensed games were divided into three classes. Class 1 covered games that involved large congregations of people, such as cockfighting, and which could only be conducted in certain licensed venues. Class 2 might be termed 'fairground games' since it included activities such as target shooting, throwing rings over prizes, and raffles. These could be played, with a permit, only during important festivals and other special occasions. Lastly, Class 3 games could be played anywhere and at any time once a permit had been obtained; this included all card games and some dice, board and domino ones. In keeping with tradition, they could be played without licence during the Chinese New Year, Thai New Year and Songkran periods.

It is important to note that the revenue from licence fees was minor when compared to that from the den and lottery farms; indeed, the government never intended this revenue item to replace those farms. During the first decade of government licensing, revenue from permits averaged just under 600,000 baht a year, rising to a high of 770,373 baht in 1906/7 when all the provincial gambling houses were closed.[51] Although this was due to large increases in the licence fees for many popular games, and cards in particular, it was not a cynical move by the government to capitalize on the gap in the market resulting from the provincial closures. Instead, as asserted by Damrong, the rise in permit prices was designed to deter people from gambling, a claim supported by the fact that when the increase in fees is taken into consideration, the figure for licensing revenue for 1906/7 indicates a sharp decline in the actual number of permits issued compared to the previous year.[52] Rather than being a revenue-raising device, the 1902 Act was more a means of control.

Just as significantly, the gradual enactment of the law in Siam's peripheries during the 1900s also acted as a mechanism for reinforcing the kingdom's administrative integration. For instance, in the semi-autonomous province of Nan and *monthon* Udon, both of which bordered on French Indochina, the law was enacted in 1907 to help alleviate outbreaks of banditry supposedly attributable to unregulated gambling.[53] The government no doubt feared that this banditry might destabilize these sensitive border regions and provoke intervention by France; the implementation of the gambling law was thus a security precaution. The 1902 Gambling Revenue Act can therefore be seen to mark the coming of age of the modern Thai state: it not only illustrated the state's capacity to manage and collect revenue on its own but its enactment throughout the kingdom also mirrored the process through which the geographical shape, or what Thongchai Winichakul has termed the 'geo-body', of present-day Thailand came into focus.[54]

The abolition of the gambling tax farms and the changing taxation basis of the Thai state

The 1902 gambling law's focus on management and restriction rather than revenue was consistent with government attempts to shift the taxation base away from indirect taxes to direct ones, particularly those based on the rice economy. In 1899, the corvée labour system was abolished and replaced with a capitation tax, the rate of which was based on the area's prosperity and fertility. Then, in 1900 Britain consented to a treaty revision which allowed the Thai government to increase the land tax to the same rate as that charged in Lower Burma. Unsurprisingly, when the government began to consider closing the gambling houses once and for all, raising both these taxes was seen as a way of replacing the revenue to be lost. Damrong's insistence that the dens in Bangkok should be closed at the same time as those in the provinces, else the capital would be swamped by an influx of criminals, meant that the estimated total revenue deficit to be made up amounted to approximately seven million baht a year.[55] After extensive discussions, the government initiated an ambitious three-year plan. In 1905/6, all dens where the revenue derived was less than 50,000 baht would be closed. This included five dens in Bangkok. All the remaining provincial dens would be abolished the following year. The revenue lost would be replaced by raising the land tax throughout the kingdom and increasing the capitation tax in *monthons* Nakhon Si Thammarat and Chumphon. Lastly, the government would enter into negotiations with the treaty powers over revising import duties and, provided these were successful, the capital's gambling dens would be closed in 1907/8.[56]

Following Damrong's advice, the government announced the broad outline of its plan and the rationale behind it in advance.[57] There were two target audiences: the population of Siam and the Western treaty powers. By carefully outlining the economic benefits of abolition alongside the consequent increases in taxation, the notification can be seen as an appeal for understanding from the local population. The closing of the provincial gambling houses thereby became both a pretext and a justification for increasing direct taxation, amplifying the power of the central state and reducing its dependence on tax farming. Furthermore, this statement of intent was designed to convince the West that the Thai government was determined to rid the country of gambling. By emphasizing the potential benefits to the Thai economy and, in turn, foreign trade, the government sought to use the abolition of the Bangkok gambling houses as leverage to revise some of the provisions of the unequal treaties and regain a degree of fiscal sovereignty. This was a win–win situation, for if the treaty powers refused then the Thai government could claim it had done all it could to restrict gambling and the continued existence of the dens was due to their intransigence.[58] In other words, the government was trying to use its essential weakness as a bargaining chip to increase its power. This approach does seem unduly optimistic, though. As long as the treaty powers continued to benefit from low customs duties, they were unlikely to agree to a rise. It is more instructive to view the government's announcement as a symbolic act, designed to counter criticism, both at home and from overseas, about its reliance on gambling revenue.

The two-year closure of the provincial dens went ahead as planned. Once the government realized that each of the treaty powers would require a more significant quid pro quo for the revision of customs tariffs, however, it put the closure of the Bangkok dens on hold.[59] As expected, gambling revenue dropped by about 3 million baht, from the high of 6.8 million in 1904/5 to 3.6 million in 1906/7, but this was easily covered by the revenue from the revised land tax, which almost doubled.[60] Proceeds from the capitation tax also grew and, by the end of the decade, these two direct taxes accounted for 20 to 25 per cent of total government revenue.[61]

In contrast, the combined revenue from the dens and the lottery dropped to just over ten per cent and remained around this level until the farms' demise in the late 1910s.[62] Significantly, the burden of taxation had been transferred somewhat from the Chinese labour force to the Thai peasantry. Indeed, the Chinese were not required to pay the annual capitation tax until 1910.

The closure of the provincial gambling houses had a number of effects. Most significantly, it made Bangkok the gambling centre of Siam, with country folk travelling to the capital by train every holiday period to try their luck.[63] Patrons of the closed dens, meanwhile, transferred their custom to the 11 remaining ones. Combined, these factors drove up the potential profits and, in the short term, the auction prices of the gambling houses and the lottery. Many of the provincial tax farmers that had operated alone found themselves priced out of the market. Furthermore, the established Bangkok syndicates were able to divert the capital they had used to bid for the closed dens into their bids for the remaining ones, thereby cementing their control over the monopolies. Consequently, the auction prices of 8 of the 11 dens dropped in 1908/9, leading to a fall in total gambling house revenue from 3.5 million baht to 3 million.[64] Nevertheless, the government was able to break the syndicates by further reducing the number of Bangkok dens from 11 to 5 between 1910/11 and 1912/13.[65] This made dividing the dens between all the syndicate members unfeasible and raised the stakes of failing to secure one of the monopolies significantly, stimulating greater competition. However, while there was a brief increase in the auction prices of the dens in 1914/15, bids the following year fell. Prince Chanthaburi, the Minister of Finance from 1908 to 1923, gave several reasons for this decline such as the fall in the price of rice due to the war in Europe but, most significantly, noted that those tax farmers who had received the monopolies the previous year had lost money.[66] The intense competition had made escalating bids unsustainable.

When the end came, it came quickly. In February 1916, Chanthaburi presented King Vajiravudh with an ambitious plan to abolish the *huai* lottery and the gambling houses within three years. Rather than introducing new taxes or attempting renegotiations of import duties, the loss of revenue was to be made good through the use of treasury reserves and by economizing in government expenditure. The treasury had been strengthened by budget surpluses totalling nearly 20 million baht for the years 1913/14 and 1914/15, and part of this sum was to be used to cover the shortfall incurred by abolition. Natural increases in other sources of government revenue, combined with frugality on the part of all government ministries, would then, it was hoped, help state finances return to balance within five years.[67] Vajiravudh approved of the scheme, only requesting that all the dens be closed a year earlier, in 1917/18, so as to coincide with the festivities celebrating his thirty-sixth birthday and completion of his third life-cycle.[68] This suggests the Thai elite considered abolition to be, in part, a question of image and prestige. Indeed, for Chanthaburi, curtailing the government's dependence on gambling revenue, and the accompanying criticisms, seems to have been just as important as limiting the population's gambling habits.[69] These considerations will be examined in detail in Chapter 4. For now it suffices to say that, by renouncing gambling as a key component of state income, the Thai government sought to show the 'civilized' West that it was a responsible, enlightened administration which deserved to have its fiscal sovereignty restored.

The *huai* lottery was abolished on 1 April 1916 and the last of the gambling houses were closed a year later, marking the end of the kingdom's major tax farms. Not only had they provided a significant proportion of the revenue that funded Chulalongkorn's state-building programme from the late 1880s onwards but they also helped ease the subsequent transition from a predominantly indirect taxation system reliant on tax farming to a more diverse and direct one based on government collection in the 1900s and 1910s. It is important to note, though, that the abolition of the gambling tax farms was not just about dismantling the last vestiges of an archaic system: the *huai* lottery and the games of *thua po* were forbidden at the same time, indicating that the Thai government found these activities undesirable in themselves.[70] The rationale behind these prohibitions will be examined in Chapter 4.

Winter Fairs and Wild Tiger lotteries: gambling in the twilight of absolutism

Despite supposedly rejecting gambling as a major revenue provider, within just a few years of the abolition of the gambling tax farms the absolute monarchy began to promote Western-style lotteries and other forms of gambling in order to raise money for prestige development projects. The origins of this apparent u-turn in government policy lie in the numerous lotteries established by the kingdom's resident European communities during the First World War in aid of their respective countries' Red Cross organizations. The legality of such lotteries was debatable. Technically, all lotteries were categorized as Class 2 gambling under the 1902 law, meaning they could be conducted, subject to licence, only on special occasions. Tickets for them could be sold only on those particular days.[71] Nevertheless, these restrictions seem to have been ignored in the case of the Red Cross lotteries; indeed, their very success would have depended on tickets being available for purchase over a long period of time. Understandably, the Thai government was none too happy about this situation as it conflicted with its restrictionist policy. On the advice of Prince Devawongse, the long-standing Minister of Foreign Affairs, these lotteries were allowed to go ahead, however.[72] This should be seen in the context of the Thai government's efforts to build up goodwill among the European powers for the eventual renegotiation of the unequal treaties. To this end, it abandoned its policy of neutrality and entered the war on the side of the Allies in July 1917.

The Red Cross lotteries had a profound impact upon the government's gambling policy. Most fundamentally, they re-legitimized the use of gambling as a revenue provider: the Thai elite had to concede that exploiting people's gaming instincts for charitable causes was acceptable under certain circumstances. Furthermore, they set a precedent for similar lotteries organized by Thais. In 1918, lotteries were established in *monthons* Ratchaburi and Phuket in order to raise money for the expeditionary force to France and the Siamese Red Cross. The Ministry of Finance initially objected to these lotteries but, when it was revealed that the local authorities had already granted permission and many of the tickets had already been sold, it was forced to consent, for otherwise the local authorities would have been liable for the losses incurred by cancellation. Nevertheless, Chanthaburi felt it necessary to have some principles for regulating these lotteries: 'permission should only be given to people of reliable financial standing in proportion to the total value of the tickets, and that the persons who issue them must do so without any profits to themselves'.[73] Additionally, not less than a quarter of the proceeds from the sale of tickets was to be set aside for the charity or the Siamese government. Finally, Chanthaburi considered this special dispensation to run lotteries to be only a temporary wartime measure.[74] Other members of the Thai elite had different ideas, however.

In the first half of the 1920s, large-scale lotteries became a regular occurrence in Siam. This was partly due to the funding requirements of the king's personal paramilitary unit, the Wild Tiger Corps (*Sua pa*). Vajiravudh had created the Wild Tigers at the start of his reign as an instrument for promoting loyalty to the throne, fostering Thai nationalism and instilling a sense of unity among civil servants. Since it received no allowance in the state budget, the corps was dependent primarily on royal grants and membership fees for funding. This placed a heavy strain upon the Privy Purse, already depleted by Vajiravudh's extravagant whims and taste for luxury.[75] Equipping the force with guns and ammunition meant the Wild Tigers also incurred significant debts.[76]

The economic crisis that beset the Thai state in the immediate post-war period gave further impetus to the lottery trend. The rising price of silver and rice created a heavy demand for the baht, which although tied to gold, had a substantial silver content. A disastrous rice crop in 1919 then provoked a foreign-exchange crisis and a deficit in the country's balance of trade. The end result was a series of budget deficits, which were exacerbated by increases in the monarchy's expenditure. The government sought to alleviate the problem by reducing its ordinary expenditures, which formed the major part of its total expenditure. Minimal amounts went on capital expenditures, such as public works and development projects, which in the recent past had been funded largely by foreign loans. But in 1922 and 1924, the government was forced to float two foreign loans just to replenish the treasury's foreign currency reserves, which had been depleted during the crisis. Despite these belated attempts to resolve state finances, Vajiravudh continued to exceed his personal budget and by the end of his reign the treasury's reserve fund had almost been exhausted.[77] In short, the government had little capital for investment in projects, the development of a national air force in particular, that the absolute monarchy deemed essential for the welfare and security of the kingdom.[78]

Lotteries were an attractive solution to these funding problems. The first one appears to have been that organized by Chaophraya Yomarat in connection with a motor-racing meeting held at Sanam Luang in Bangkok during the Thai New Year of 1920. To raise money for the Wild Tigers, tickets of admission were sold in advance at one baht each, these then doubled up as a ticket for the lottery drawn on that day. Despite fierce opposition from the Minister of Finance, Yomarat received special permission from the king for his scheme.[79] Similar events, which came to feature aviation displays as well, were held in 1922 and 1923, with the value of the attendant lotteries rising to one million baht.[80] Over the same period, Phraya Nonthisen (Maek Siansewi), a royal favourite and the Chief of the Wild Tigers General Staff, also organized lotteries on behalf of the corps. Like the motor-racing ones, these had royal approval and thus were not subject to the restrictions of the 1902 law.[81] The first Wild Tiger lottery was issued in 1921 to raise money for the purchase of firearms.[82] Tickets for a second went on sale in late 1923 and it was hoped the draw would be held before April 1924. A million tickets were issued for each, and, besides the large first, second and third prizes, there were numerous smaller prizes. After expenses, it was hoped that the Wild Tigers would gain at least 300,000 baht from the second lottery.[83]

Other institutions and private groups also applied for permission to hold lotteries but most did not have the advantage of close contact with the king and were refused. In late 1919, for instance, one Nai Hong Heng and 42 others petitioned Vajiravudh for permission to conduct a three million baht lottery to raise funds for the lengthening and dredging of the Singhanat canal in Ayutthaya province. Although this scheme would have benefited many and encouraged trade at no expense to the government, Chanthaburi insisted it was against the law and permission was denied.[84] By selectively giving special dispensation for lotteries and effectively overriding the law, the absolute monarchy was making itself vulnerable to accusations of double standards and favouritism. What was more damaging, though, were the frequent scandals connected to these lotteries, the most infamous of which was that involving the second Wild Tiger lottery mentioned above.[85] When this lottery was finally drawn in January 1925, Phraya Nonthisen and some associates conspired to hold the winning tickets for 40-odd prizes; some of which they claimed there and then, while others were claimed later under false names. Suspicions of foul play were raised by a number of abnormalities; for instance, none of the tickets for the top three prizes were creased or soiled in any way. Despite a huge public outcry and a concerted campaign by local newspapers for a thorough inquiry, it was some six months before Vajiravudh ordered an investigation into the scandal. Although no accounts for the lottery were found (it was suspected they had been destroyed), the investigative committee found sufficient hints of wrongdoing for the case to be passed on to the Department of Public Prosecutions. Concomitantly, Phraya Nonthisen was declared persona non grata within the royal court. After a series of court cases spanning two years, Nonthisen and an accomplice were sentenced to 15 and 6 years' imprisonment respectively, and ordered to repay the 253,106 baht they had embezzled.[86]

Although public faith was severely shaken by this scandal, this did not curtail the absolutist regime's reliance on lotteries. Vajiravudh had set his heart upon holding a national exhibition, modelled on the annual Wembley Exhibition in England to mark the fifteenth year of his reign in November 1925. The Siamese Kingdom Exhibition was to be staged in Lumphini Park and would be a showcase for Thai art, agriculture and industry. It was also intended to promote economic development and increase awareness of the country, among both foreigners and Thais.[87] Indeed, Walter Vella argues that Vajiravudh hoped that, by bringing large numbers of people together in a glorification of the country, the exhibition would instil pride in the Thai nation.[88] Unfortunately, though, the government did not have the funds to complete the landscaping of the park, let alone cover the costs of the exhibition. Among other fundraising schemes, a two million baht lottery, that was optimistically hoped to produce 600,000 baht in profit, was issued.[89] Vajiravudh died shortly before the exhibition was scheduled to open, however, and his successor, King Prajadhipok, promptly cancelled it. Significantly, Vajiravudh's hope that the Siamese Kingdom Exhibition might instil nationalism suggests a more subtle purpose behind the frequent semi-official lotteries of the Sixth Reign. By appealing to people's love of gambling, the government used lotteries to excite interest in and encourage attendance at patriotic events in aid of national development projects. Furthermore, in purchasing a ticket, people would have been aware that they were one among many sharing the same dream of winning big and that, by supporting the lottery's cause, were participating directly in the life of the nation. In other words, these lotteries were promoting nation-building not only by raising funds for infrastructure projects but also by prompting the development of a Thai national consciousness.

A similar argument can also be advanced for the fundraising fairs and fetes, where gambling was a key attraction, that were staged regularly in Bangkok and the provinces during the 1920s. Foremost among these was the capital's annual Winter Fair, held for a week during January or February in one of the royal gardens to mark the cool season. Organized by the royal court in aid of the Wild Tigers and charities, it was the great social event of the year, attended by all levels of Bangkok society. As one travel guide to Bangkok noted, the fair was divided into two:

a popular and an aristocratic portion. In the former the Chinese dominate with their stalls, selling cheap toys, cakes and sweets. Besides this all sorts of popular amusements such as animal theatres, strong men, sorcerers, etc., are found here and the populace enjoys itself immensely. In the latter portion the stalls are nearly all kept by the ladies of high officials and well-to-do people and many beautiful articles of Siamese and Chinese workmanship are sold. One may witness performances of classical Siamese plays, hear plenty of good music and see exhibitions displaying the progress of the National Red Cross movement and the Royal State Railways, dance in the large dancing hall, and utilise one of the many restaurants.[90]

In addition to all these attractions, there were the ubiquitous gambling stalls. Most of the games on offer were of the Class 2 'fairground' variety: raffles for motorcars, wheels of fortune, fishing for prizes, target shooting and such like. During the 1920s, though, more serious forms of gaming, especially cards and dice games played for cash rather than prizes, became widespread. Although the legality of gambling for money at such occasions was ambiguous, it was guaranteed to draw in the crowds. Some idea of the extent of the gambling is given by the high price gaming operators were prepared to pay for their stalls: one entrepreneur even submitted a bid of one million baht for the sole rights to the gaming stalls at the 1925 fair.[91] Unsurprisingly, many commentators felt that the Winter Fair had become little more than an excuse for gambling; not for nothing was it known as the country's 'annual Monte Carlo'.[92]

Similar fairs were also staged in the provinces, though if anything, the emphasis was even more heavily on gambling. In 1923 and 1924, for instance, the Lord Lieutenant of *monthon* Ratchaburi held week-long fetes in Ratchaburi town, the first to raise money to build an airstrip and purchase aeroplanes and the second in aid of the Wild Tigers.[93] The rights to the gaming stalls were auctioned off on both occasions and, as with the Winter Fair, playing for cash was permitted. While these fairs were held ostensibly in the name of good causes, they were highly controversial. Local newspapers were full of horror stories detailing the fall-out from the unfettered gambling. Take, for instance, the wife of a soldier who hanged herself after losing more than 7,000 baht at the Winter Fair, or the naval officer who slit his throat, apparently also out of despair at his losses.[94] Press opinion on these events will be examined more deeply in Chapter 7. The general consensus, though, was that the facilities for public gambling at the fairs impoverished people and encouraged crime, just as the *huai* lottery and gambling houses had done. Moreover, the promotion of gambling was seen as symptomatic of the moral turpitude of the absolutist social order.

The legacy that Vajiravudh bequeathed to his successor, and the last of Siam's absolute monarchs, was an unenviable one. Upon his accession to the throne, Prajadhipok was immediately faced with a range of unresolved economic and social problems, not least of all the gambling issue. Scandals such as that surrounding the Wild Tiger lottery and the blatant contradictions in government policy had given critics of the absolute monarchy ample ammunition. Consequently, it was imperative that the government settle upon a consistent approach. The Winter Fairs were discontinued and, besides the Lumphini Park lottery which was already underway, the Seventh Reign government abandoned the use of gambling as a fundraising device. This was made possible by the restoration of financial stability in the late 1920s. In early 1926, the new king launched an economy drive to reduce government spending, which he led by example in cutting royal expenditures. By the late 1920s, state finances were on a sound basis once more; the government even managed to record budget surpluses. This was helped considerably by the successful revision of the unequal treaties, which allowed for a modest rise in import duties.

Unfortunately, it was not long before Siam began to feel the impact of the worldwide economic depression following the Wall Street Crash in 1929. Crop failures in May 1930 were swiftly followed by a slump in rice exports and, by early 1932, the price of rice had fallen to one-third of its 1930 value.[95] The economic crisis was exacerbated by the government's decision to remain on the gold standard when Britain abandoned it. The high foreign currency price of Siam's rice, compared to rice sold in currencies that had left the gold standard, made it uncompetitive. This led to a severe reduction in farmers' cash income and an inability to pay their taxes or debts. Consequently, there was a flood of petitions to the king calling for reductions in the capitation and land taxes to alleviate the economic distress. Moreover, a drop in imports and exports meant a fall in government revenue and, by early 1932, the need to cut state expenditures was painfully apparent. The government embarked upon another round of retrenchment more drastic than the last. Many government officials were dismissed or had their salaries cut. The bureaucracy was also burdened with a controversial salary tax. Criticisms of the absolutist regime neared a peak.

In mid-1932, at the lowest point of the crisis, the Siamese Red Cross requested permission to conduct a 500,000 baht lottery. This organization relied on donations from the public and the government for its income but these had dried up, and it had been unable to balance its budget. Income from the lottery was vital if it was to continue its operations. Although this was the first request for several years, both the king and the Minister of the Interior supported the proposal, arguing that the lottery would benefit public welfare and the government, which stood to receive 50,000 baht in tax under new regulations. A final decision was deferred to the next meeting of the Council of Ministers, scheduled for 27 June 1932.[96] But the Siamese Red Cross had to wait a little longer for their reply. On 24 June 1932, the People's Party staged a remarkably bloodless coup, bringing an end to the absolute monarchy and instituting a new age of constitutional government.

'The Monte Carlo of the Far East': gambling in the constitutional era

Under the direction of the People's Party but in active consultation with the king, a constitution that invested supreme authority in a partially elected National Assembly was drawn up. The permanent version of this constitution was proclaimed on 10 December 1932. Yet, despite the change in leadership and all its professed democratic ideals, real political change was slight. The People's Party was the real power in the country and it tried to halt any challenges to its authority by outlawing rival political parties. In other words, a small royal elite was merely replaced by an equally small elite composed of military officers, old-school bureaucrats and younger officials. Within this loose coalition, there was fierce jockeying for power during the initial years of the constitutional era. From this emerged two figures who were to play a central role in the politics of the 1930s and 1940s: Phibun Songkhram, head of the military faction, and Pridi Phanomyong, leader of the civilians. Both saw the promotion of certain types of gambling, and the suppression of others, as a means of developing the Thai nation-state and shaping Thai society to their divergent ideals. Economically, the new regime had the good fortune to come to power at the worst point of the depression. Recovery was rapid due, in part, to the decision to leave the gold standard. Exports began to grow almost immediately, as did the government's revenues. Indeed, despite all the upheaval, budget surpluses were the norm during the 1930s. Financial conservatism remained the guiding principle. Significantly, there was no radical change in gambling policy. As one contemporary observer put it, 'The constitutional regime inherited its predecessor's confusing and unrealistic attitude towards gambling, namely, that it was demoralizing if for private benefit but harmless if the State used the proceeds to finance public works'.[97] In this respect, it is telling that the People's Party gave approval to the Siamese Red Cross lottery within two months of coming to power.[98] However, the new regime was to go much further in promoting state-sponsored gambling than the absolute monarchy ever had.

From the outset, state-run lotteries were a key component of the government's plans for the economic development of the country. In early 1933, Pridi submitted his 'Outline Economic Plan' to the National Assembly. Influenced by European socialist thought, to which he had been exposed during his studies in Paris, this plan was an expression of Pridi's belief that the state should play a central role in fostering economic progress. Tucked in amongst proposals for the voluntary nationalization of all land and state-led industrialization was the suggestion for a national lottery, which Pridi justified by citing the use of lotteries on government bonds in France.[99] The more radical proposals in Pridi's plan caused a wave of controversy and sparked a political struggle, both within the People's Party and between the new regime and the displaced royalist one. From this, the military faction of the People's Party emerged as the dominant force. The plan was rejected, the Assembly suspended and Pridi sent into brief exile. Nevertheless, the idea of a state-run lottery was taken up with enthusiasm. Many European governments had recently lifted restrictions on lotteries – France, for instance, reintroduced government lotteries in 1933 – and this lent additional legitimacy to the Thai government's scheme. Moreover, previous experience had shown that if the state was not going to provide an outlet for gambling, other interests, legal or illegal, would take advantage of the gap in the market. These justifications will be explored more fully in Chapter 4.

The first state lottery was drawn on 8 April 1934 and the second four months later, on 17 August. Rather than having just a few large prizes, the government decided to have many smaller ones as well, in order to encourage sales and ensure a large number of winners.[100] Additionally, winning tickets for the second lottery were evenly distributed throughout the country; when the results were issued only two provinces did not have a winner.[101] Revenue from the first lottery was to be used to develop education and health care, while that from subsequent ones was meant to make good the shortfall incurred by the reduction in the rate of the capitation tax in 1934/5.[102] Crucially, to prevent competition and ensure that all tickets were sold, it was decided that other organizations would be prevented from issuing their own lotteries.[103] Thus, when the Siamese Red Cross, which was still experiencing financial difficulties, asked for permission to conduct another lottery, it was refused, though with the consolation that it might request a share of the proceeds from the state lottery.[104] Henceforth, lotteries were to be a monopoly of the state. Although there were a number of teething problems – delays in printing tickets, difficulties distributing them in the provinces, accusations of official negligence and suchlike – the lotteries proved to be highly popular among the population and profitable for the government.[105] Regular state lotteries thus became a permanent fixture, culminating in 1939 with the establishment of the Government Lottery Office to conduct monthly lotteries. These have continued to the present day, going twice monthly in 1989.

Besides the official state lottery, the new regime initiated another in 1933: the Constitution Celebration Lottery. The proceeds from this were to cover the costs of the countrywide festivities for Constitution Day on 10 December 1933. Any surplus would be used to distribute copies of the constitution.[106] But the Constitution Celebration Lottery did not only have a fundraising purpose. Having brought an end to monarchical absolutism, the People's Party used constitutionalism as the basis for rationalizing and legitimizing its rule. Moreover, it sought to displace the monarch as the central component in the pre-existing state ideology – the holy trinity of Nation, Religion, and King – that formed the bedrock of Thai identity and the unity of the Thai nation. A fourth element, the constitution, was now promoted as the guarantor of Thai independence and progress.[107] Making the constitution a focus of public loyalty was thus imperative for the new government. For most of the population, however, a constitution – in Thai, *ratthathammanun* – was an alien concept of which they had only a shaky understanding. Apparently, some even thought *ratthathammanun* was a relation of Phraya Phahon, the prime minister from June 1933 to September 1938.[108] During the Constitution Day celebrations, people were encouraged to make offerings to copies of the constitution, which was presented as a sacred entity to which even the king was subordinate.[109] By the mid-1930s, Constitution Day had become the premier national holiday, complete with beauty contests, musical concerts and parades. The attendant lotteries were also regular fixtures, serving to generate public interest in the event. Even the lottery tickets were an integral part of the strategy for familiarizing people with the constitution and sacralizing it. Each bore an image of the constitution resting on a pedestal, with rays of light emanating from it suggesting enlightenment.[110] Indeed, the political purpose behind the lottery was perhaps greater than the financial one.

One final type of lottery was also established in this period. In July 1934, the Cabinet gave the Ministry of the Interior permission to issue lotteries to help raise capital for the establishment of municipal authorities (*thesaban*) in every province.[111] Taking up some earlier proposals of Prajadhipok's for more representative government at the local level, the constitutional regime had issued the Municipality Act in 1933. This was intended to counteract the extreme centralization of power that had emerged during the absolutist era by giving people a greater say in the administration of their provinces. To support the country's 70-odd municipal governments, two types of municipal lottery were established: monthly ones of 200,000 baht a time in aid of particular provinces, the tickets of which could be sold only in that province; and countrywide ones to the value of one million baht that were issued every four months. Proceeds from this second type went into a central fund that was then shared among all the provinces for building municipal offices, provincial hospitals, schools, wells, and sports stadia.[112]

Within a few years of the 1932 coup, the constitutional government had established a range of state-run lotteries that formed an integral part of its plans for the economic, administrative and educational development of the country. The provision that winning tickets in the state lottery were evenly distributed throughout the country made this a truly national event. The structure of the municipal lotteries, meanwhile, emphasized the individuality of each province but as a unit within a greater national whole. Lastly, the Constitution Celebration lotteries served to raise public awareness of and, possibly, loyalty to the new pillar of state authority. In short, these state lotteries were tools for nation-building.

Another idea that gained currency in the government, business circles, and the press during the 1930s was the creation of Western-style casinos and the transformation of Siam into 'the Monte Carlo of the Far East'.[113] This was not the first time Monte Carlo had appeared in public discourse but it seems to have particularly excited popular imagination in the mid-1930s.

Indeed, as will be discussed in Chapter 4, the casino was identified as a symbol of modernity. Crucially, powerful elements within the new political elite saw casinos as a means for promoting economic development and tourism. In May 1934, for instance, the Ministry of Economic Affairs proposed establishing a public corporation, with the government as the majority shareholder, to manage a casino in the royal coastal resort of Hua Hin. It would also stage horse-racing meetings.[114]

It was not until Phibun became Prime Minister in December 1938 that the casino idea became reality, however. In April 1939, a royal decree was issued that laid down the framework for government-run casinos. It allowed for the playing of any games on the prohibited list within the premises, empowering the Minister of Finance to choose which games in particular and also to issue regulations prohibiting certain classes of people from entering. To deter the poorer sections of Thai society, entrance fees were set at no more than 20 baht a day; for foreigners who had the necessary identification it was just two baht.[115] On 3 May 1939, the first establishment was opened in Hua Hin. The opening was a grand affair, attended by senior government officials, members of the royal family and other notables. One of the inauguration speeches stated the rationale for casinos as follows:

> Though a Casino is a place for gambling, yet it is based on strict methods, quite different from the gambling houses of former times. This Casino has as its aim the promotion of tourist traffic, which is a means of attracting money from foreign parts in the country and at the same time it prevents the export of money.[116]

While it was generally acknowledged that the Hua Hin casino was not ideally placed to attract tourists, Pridi explained that it was an experiment, with the government planning to open further casinos in the South close to the border with Malaya.[117] During the first week, admission fees were kept low to attract customers but most of these appeared to be from Bangkok and there was a distinct lack of Westerners.[118] Indeed, the experiment seems to have been a failure. Not long after opening, the casino was closed temporarily, though it never seems to have reopened.[119]

In spite of this initial setback, the government did not abandon its casino project, opening one with 'real Monte Carlo settings and atmosphere' in Hat Yai in late 1939.[120] By locating the casino so close to Malaya, where gambling was restricted to horse racing, the government hoped to attract large numbers of Malayans, particularly Chinese. Besides encouraging tourism, the casino was intended to provide alternative revenue sources to replace that lost through the abolition of the land and capitation taxes.[121] This was part of Pridi's extensive tax reforms, manifested in the enactment of the country's first revenue code in March 1939, which attempted to shift the tax burden from the rice farmer onto business groups in pursuit of a more equitable society.[122] The Hat Yai casino had a promising start.

During January and February 1940, attendance was around 1,000 people a day, rising to 2,000 over the Chinese New Year. Most of the gamblers were Chinese labourers from the nearby tin and rubber plantations and Malays from across the border. Few Thais were present.[123] Moreover, between January and March, the casino recorded profits of between 90,000 and 100,000 baht per month; the expected profits for the year were one million baht. Nevertheless, from 1 April 1940 the casino was closed temporarily. According to Pridi, this was due to the war in Europe, which hampered the tourist trade and the flow of money into the country; the casino would be reopened once conditions returned to normal.[124] The *Bangkok Times*, meanwhile, attributed the closure to the fact that too many Thais, and not enough foreigners, frequented the casino.[125] As with the Hua Hin establishment, it seems never to have reopened.

The casino project was given one last roll of the dice during the final years of the Second World War. The first Khuang Aphaiwong government (1 August 1944 to 31 August 1945) opened casinos throughout Bangkok and in some provinces in order to 'tax' wartime profiteers. Again, these were supposed to be for the rich but in reality were open to all. Predictably, it was said that the casinos encouraged gambling and were responsible for greater hardship and poverty. Under mounting criticism from the press and the public, the government shut all the casinos on 10 June 1945.[126] Despite the revenue it provided, the casino experiment had been a failure, primarily because the government was unable to attract the 'right' clientele – whether foreign tourists or wealthy Thais – or to exclude the majority of the population that could ill afford to gamble. The Thai government's flirtation with casinos was over.

With the establishment of the various state lotteries and, despite its failure, the casino experiment, the Thai government's taxation and gambling policies had almost come full circle since the days of Chulalongkorn. Limited by the restrictions on custom duties imposed by the unequal treaties and lacking the administrative structure to collect its own taxes, the Thai government of the late nineteenth century relied on revenue from gambling and other vices to fund a programme of state-building that led to the creation of the absolutist state. Indeed, as was the case with the Western colonial states in South-East Asia, the taxation of vice formed the foundations of the modern state in Thailand. Similarly, the greater administrative depth of the state then enabled Chulalongkorn to start reducing its dependence on gambling revenue and shift the taxation basis from indirect to direct taxes. In the depressed economic climate of the early 1930s, meanwhile, the constitutional government partly reversed this process in order to alleviate the hardship being felt by the Thai population. State lotteries and casinos were established as indirect forms of taxation that supposedly targeted the well-off, enabling the government to first reduce and then abolish direct forms of taxation which fell heaviest upon the rural majority. These gambling enterprises also provided income for infrastructure and administrative schemes, such as the creation of municipal governments. But whereas Chulalongkorn had exploited the taxation of gambling for state-building purposes, the People's Party used the state lotteries more for nation-building in their attempt to transform absolutist Siam into constitutional Thailand. Regardless of these differences, though, gambling policy was an integral part of these elites' efforts to shape Thai society. As Chapter 4 will illustrate, this also involved the prohibition of certain forms of gambling that these elites found undesirable. In doing so, however, successive Thai governments ran the risk of seeming hypocritical and inconsistent. There was thus a need to reconcile the promotion of particular games for the benefit of the state with an avowedly anti-gambling policy. What should be clear from this chapter is that the financial fortunes and requirements of the state were invariably the main determining factor in the nature and extent of government gambling policy. Rather than saying that the Thai population was addicted to gambling, it is more accurate to say that the Thai state was addicted to gambling revenue.

4 The Thai elite, anti-gambling and lawmaking

The three preceding chapters have outlined the role of gambling in the economic development of Siam, the social life of the kingdom's inhabitants and the creation of the modern Thai nation-state, respectively. Despite gambling's importance in these developments, however, in the late 1880s the Fifth Reign government initiated an anti-gambling policy that involved progressively restricting legal outlets for state-sanctioned gambling and clamping down on unsanctioned activities. This policy was continued by both Chulalongkorn's successors and the constitutional regime that supplanted the absolute monarchy, resulting in the effective criminalization of most forms of popular gambling by 1945. The central theme of this chapter is how the anti-gambling policy and discourse arose from a complex array of factors closely related to Siam's encounter with colonialism in the nineteenth and early twentieth centuries. As contacts with the West increased and the British and French presence in mainland South-East Asia grew, the Thai elite of King Mongkut's generation onwards were exposed to, and absorbed, the Enlightenment concepts of scientific rationalism, progress and civilization.[1] In this process, they came to perceive Siam as occupying a mid-point on a sliding scale of civilizational achievement, with the West at the high end and 'barbarian' peoples, such as the hill-tribes of northern Siam, at the other. Being civilized, or *siwilai* as it was transliterated into Thai, was associated with Western practices and modes of conduct. Moreover, the Thai elite were acutely aware of how the imperial powers used these concepts to justify colonial intervention and thus felt it was imperative that the Thai people become more *siwilai*. As Thongchai Winichakul has highlighted, however, the 'quest for *siwilai*' was not just a defensive reaction to pre-empt colonization but also an attempt 'to attain and confirm the relative superiority of Siam' because 'as the traditional imperial power in the region, Siam was anxious about its position among modern nations'.[2] It was therefore a strategy for preserving both Thai independence and dignity, and also for asserting Thai supremacy over those peoples on Siam's peripheries. In this context, 'uncivilized' practices such as polygamy and slavery came under intense scrutiny and criticism from some sections of the elite. As this chapter will illustrate, the discourse of *siwilai* also had a profound influence upon government gambling policy. Certain gambling games, particularly traditional Thai ones such as cockfighting, were dubbed uncivilized. Conversely, new gambling activities introduced from the West, such as playing bridge and betting on horse races or billiards, were seen as *siwilai* and, consequently, desirable.

The case against gambling

There have long been proscriptions against gambling within Thai society. Most obviously, in Buddhism, gambling is one of four vices which lead to certain self-ruin and destruction; in Thai these are collectively known as *abaiyamuk*, which literally means 'the portals of hell'.[3] For the layperson, gambling is thus something to be avoided if one wishes to lead a life free of suffering. Apart from these religious condemnations, government edicts against gambling emphasized its social and economic costs. The first two Bangkok monarchs prohibited a number of games, including cockfighting and fish fighting, on the grounds that they were cruel to animals, against Buddhist precepts, and a cause of arguments and fraud. Of greater importance, though, was the growing popularity of these activities, cockfighting especially, which were drawing people away from the gambling houses, resulting in a drop in revenue.[4] In other words, the underlying rationale for prohibiting these games was financial: to ensure the dens had no competition. The early nineteenth-century Siamese state lacked the enforcement apparatus to make such a ban effective, however; the French Catholic missionary Monsignor Pallegoix, who travelled throughout the core of the kingdom in the 1830s and 1840s, noted that the prohibition on cockfighting was widely ignored.[5] Mongkut's decision to establish a tax farm on cockfighting and other popular games played outside the dens stemmed from the realization that it was better to regulate gambling, and in doing so derive some revenue from it, than to impose unenforceable laws.[6] Indeed, responding to criticisms that the Siamese government was promoting vice, Mongkut highlighted the failure of the British colonial authorities to successfully prohibit gambling in Singapore and Penang.[7] As this chapter will show, difficulties in enforcement continued to be a critical determinant of government policy.

Chulalongkorn was the first Thai monarch to have the administrative and financial resources to attempt to restrict gambling seriously. While the gambling dens were still in existence, protecting their profitability, and thereby safeguarding government revenue, remained a key reason for restricting some games. For example, following complaints from two Bangkok gambling house farmers about the widespread playing of the dice game *si ngao lak*, which could be conducted with a licence outside of their dens and was supposedly responsible for a drop in custom, the Minister of Finance reclassified the game in 1903 so that it could be played only on festive occasions.[8] However, such a rationale cannot account for the progressive closures of the gambling houses themselves or the abolition of the *huai* lottery. Clearly, Chulalongkorn and the elite of his generation found something undesirable in these activities and, more broadly, in the nature of gambling itself. Besides being a vice, gambling was more commonly referred to in laws and government correspondence as 'an evil thing' that led people to 'utter ruin'.[9] The metaphor of disease was also employed. Chaophraya Wongsanupraphat (M. R. W. Sathan Sanitwong), a prominent government minister during the early twentieth century, described gambling as 'this cancer which is eating into our bones'.[10] Similarly, when Prince Damrong assessed whether the gambling houses or the *huai* was more harmful, he compared the speed with which the two drove people into poverty: 'a loser in a gambling den was like a cholera patient, while the lottery addict was a tuberculosis patient. Both patients are bound to die, but one at a slower rate than the other'.[11] This disease had infected the Thai people, corrupting their morals and behaviour.[12] Its symptoms were crime, poverty and debt slavery.

In regard to crime, both the Thai elite and Westerners in government service considered gambling to be a prime cause of robbery, theft, banditry, plunder, and murder.[13] This was especially true among the British officials in charge of the Bangkok police force around the turn of the twentieth century, and formed part of a broader discourse of vice as a cause of crime. In his 1903/4 report, Commissioner Lawson drew a comparison between serious crime in Bangkok, Bombay, Calcutta and Rangoon:

> Bombay and Calcutta are larger than Bangkok, Rangoon much smaller. All four towns are otherwise very similar. All four are ports with a mixed and constantly changing population. It is therefore rather startling to find that in Bangkok more cases of serious crime were reported to the Police [5,510 cases] than in Bombay [4,053], and more than in Calcutta [2,504] and Rangoon [1,289] together.[14]

For Lawson, Bangkok's greater crime level was due to three factors: the gambling houses, the opium dens, and the drinking saloons, all of which were open around the clock. In contrast, the other three cities had no gambling houses, and opium and alcohol consumption were regulated more strictly. Combined, these three vices made Bangkok 'one of the most criminal places in the world'.[15] Similarly, the increase in crime in the mid-1910s – which brought the number of serious crimes in Bangkok town (as opposed to Bangkok province) to a comparable level to those in the whole of British Burma – was blamed on gambling and drinking.[16] However, when it came to making a causal connection between the two, only anecdotal evidence was cited. In 1907, for instance, there was an outbreak of banditry in the Central Plains. Damrong attributed this to migrant Lao farmhands from the Northeast who had gambled away all their savings and were unable to return home. With nowhere to live and no job, they had resorted to banditry.[17] Despite the lack of statistical information that might confirm such an assertion, the belief that unrestricted gambling was a threat to law and order had a significant effect upon government policy. For instance, in 1902 the government introduced a blanket ban on all forms of gambling in the volatile district of Mae Sot, in Trat province, bordering British Burma.[18] The implications of basing policy on general impressions rather than quantifiable evidence will be considered alongside the success of government gambling policy in the Conclusion.

Claims that gambling was responsible for much of the poverty throughout the country were based on similarly vague observations. In a 1903 government report, for instance, Phraya Sukhumnaiwinit (the future Chaophraya Yomarat) blamed the gambling dens for the impoverishment of the local population in parts of Suphanburi and Nakhon Chaisi provinces in the Central Plains, comparing the situation with that in *monthon* Nakhon Si Thammarat in the South, where all dens – except for those kept open exclusively for Chinese miners – had been closed and trade was thriving.[19] Needless to say, the report failed to consider other reasons for the poverty in the former areas or for the relative prosperity of the South. It was also widely held that impoverished gamblers sold themselves and their families into debt slavery.[20] In the 1890s, for instance, the British adviser H. Warrington Smyth attributed 'half the slavery' in the capital 'to the reckless love of gambling'.[21] In his 1907 doctoral thesis on agriculture in Siam, Prince Dilok Nabarath, one of Chulalongkorn's many sons, expounded upon the causal link between gambling and slavery as follows:

> According to old customs and traditions there were, as there are today, great feasts after the harvest time with gambling too and farmers often lost not only their cash money but also their farm-yard and all their possessions. Also, when farmers went with their crop on ships and boats to Bangkok and other great cities to sell it and they had completed their sales, they often went into gambling houses there and when they had lost their crops' proceeds they took, devoid of means, a loan against debt-serfdom. Often, they also immediately gambled away this loan in the gambling houses and piled up their debts with a new loan which they could no longer pay with their home and farm. Numerous Siamese have become debt slaves through gambling.[22]

This assessment is verified by the testimony of people who either sold their children into slavery or were sold by their parents or husbands.[23] Interestingly, when Chulalongkorn took the first step towards the gradual abolition of slavery by restricting the buying and selling of slaves in 1874, some people among the poorer sections of Thai society complained that they were no longer able to sell their children in order to pay off gambling debts and wondered when gambling might be prohibited.[24] This suggests that they felt gambling was a greater evil than debt slavery.

More importantly, it highlights how the ability to sell one's self or family acted as an economic safety net for the poor. As Thanet Aphornsuvan observes, the 'paradox of the Thai abolition of slavery' meant that for commoners, 'the end of "freedom to sell" children or wives spelt poverty and starvation for the family as a whole'.[25] Additionally, the slaves of some wealthy nobles might have enjoyed greater physical security and material comfort than some free commoners. This is not meant to suggest that Thai forms of slavery were 'benign' or 'attractive'; as Andrew Turton highlights, the numerous laws designed to protect slaves from the depredations of their owners indicates that physical and sexual abuse did occur.[26] Rather, it is to underscore the importance of slavery as an economic institution for large sections of pre-twentieth century Thai society. Crucially, the impetus for its abolition did not come from below; it came from the Thai elite, who were motivated by a similar rationale to that behind the restriction of gambling.

Gambling, material progress and the *siwilai*-zing mission

In the introduction to this chapter it was noted that the Thai elite of the mid-nineteenth century onwards absorbed the Western notions of progress, glossed in Thai as *khwam charoen*, and civilization (*siwilai*) as both a defensive reaction to the colonial threat and as part of their own colonial offensive against the peoples on Siam's peripheries. Western missionaries, envoys and other visitors were often highly critical of slavery and polygamy, citing their prevalence as evidence of Siam's 'uncivilized' state. The Thai elite were acutely sensitive to such criticisms, either seeking to defend and legitimize these practices, as in the case of polygamy, or adopting the Western viewpoint and restricting or abolishing them, as was done with slavery.[27] As already noted, the prevalence of gambling and the state's profiting from it had long been criticized by Western observers as well. The efforts to restrict gambling were, therefore, partly a response to such criticisms and were meant to illustrate the enlightened nature of the Thai government under Chulalongkorn and his successors. Commenting on the abolition of the gambling dens and the *huai* lottery, for instance, Prince Chanthaburi claimed this move 'placed the administrative reputation of the country on a still higher plane'.[28] Such efforts at restricting gambling were indeed successful in garnering praise from the West, affirming the country's place among civilized nations. Following the closure of the provincial dens in 1905, the US ambassador passed on the following message from American missionary groups: 'In taking this step the Government is bringing itself into line with the best reforms of modern Government and is doing what is not only right in itself but what is for the largest and most permanent interest of the Siamese people'.[29] Concerns about how gambling affected the country's image persisted throughout the period of this study. In November 1939, Phibun made a radio broadcast in which he urged people to refrain from gambling on the street. Not only did it have a deleterious effect upon the players but on the nation as well: foreign visitors might think Thailand was a country of inveterate gamblers and leave with an unfavourable impression.[30]

Peter Jackson has argued that this need to accommodate Western sensibilities led to the emergence of a distinctive form of Thai power in a Foucauldian sense, which he has styled the 'Thai regime of images'.[31] This is characterized by 'an intense concern to monitor and police surface effects, images, public behaviours, and representations combined with a relative disinterest in controlling the private domain of life'.[32] Although the regime of images emerged due to Siam's subordinate position vis-à-vis the Western imperial powers, it helped legitimize the rule of the absolute monarchy, in its role as the mediator of *siwilai*, both internationally and domestically. It also enabled the Thai elite to subject the population to 'a more intense form of state authority while representing this as a form of liberty, from the West, rather than as subjection to [a] new form of local tyranny'.[33] Following the 1932 revolution, the constitutional government deployed the regime of images in its battle for legitimacy against the deposed monarchy, which was portrayed as decadent and morally bankrupt. Attempts to police public behaviour reached a peak during the first Phibun government (December 1938 to August 1944), which launched a series of socio-cultural reforms designed to radically refashion Thai society and create a decisive break with the absolutist past. In regards to gambling, the regime of images manifested itself in concerns about the prevalence of particular gambling games. As suggested by Phibun's radio broadcast mentioned above, it was not so much the act of street gambling that worried the authorities but rather its public nature. Indeed, visibility seems to have been a determining factor in the legality of certain games; something that will be taken up later in the chapter. Nevertheless, there was more behind the restriction of gambling than simply keeping up appearances.

The concepts of *siwilai* and *khwam charoen* had strong connotations of material progress and economic development, with a society's level of civilization being determined by the nature of its economic system. Consequently, the traditional manpower system came to be seen as backward and barbaric: trade and taxation were the economic basis of a modern, civilized state's power.[34] As Barmé highlights: 'Given this particular formulation, such developments as the expansion in commodity production and increased trade with the West following the Bowring Treaty represented Siam's gradual progress along the path to civilization'.[35] In other words, being civilized meant integration into and production for the world economy. Consequently, the quest for *siwilai* gave further justification for and impetus to the reduction of labour controls. It made the abolition of slavery an economic imperative for those sections of the elite, specifically the faction led by the Bunnag family, who stood to profit from increased participation in the world economy. Kullada Kesboonchoo Mead claims that restricting gambling was part of this attack on slavery.³⁶ More fundamentally, however, it was a way of making Thai cultivators more effective producers by encouraging them to forgo 'wasteful' habits. Here it is particularly revealing that Chanthaburi likened the abolition of the dens and the *huai* to the abolition of slavery for it indicates how the elite saw these acts as part of a continuum in the freeing up of labour and, thus, milestones on the road to *siwilai*.³⁷ Moreover, the idea of progress also entailed a new awareness of the role of the state: it was now responsible for promoting economic development, particularly through trade, and for stamping out bad habits, such as gambling, that interfered with this.³⁸ This was also closely entwined with Damrong's redefinition of the nature of the Thai monarchy. Drawing on a supposed tradition of paternalistic leadership that had marked the thirteenth-century Thai kingdom of Sukhothai but had then been subsumed by the ideology of the *devaraja* or god-king during the Ayutthaya period, Damrong cast the king as a father figure, nurturing the well-being of his children: the people.³⁹ In restricting gambling, Chulalongkorn was demonstrating his paternal wisdom and concern.

A good summation of the anti-gambling discourse that emerged from these various influences was the preamble to the notification about the closure of the provincial gambling dens in 1905:

> People expend in gambling not only their own wealth but the wealth of others. They devote to gambling time during which they should be attending to their work. Under present conditions, large sums of money which come into the hands of the gambling farmers are sent out of the Kingdom. Gambling is also responsible for much of the crime that is committed. The abolition of gambling would, therefore, not only result in an improvement in the morals of the people and in increased industry, but money expended therein would remain in circulation within the country, thereby adding to the wealth of the community.⁴⁰

While mention is made of the social impact of gambling, the central concern is its effect upon the economy. Here the main issue was that of remittances. While gambling was thought to help limit the remittances of Chinese labourers, the super-profits from the gambling tax farms enabled the Chinese plutocrats that controlled them to remit even greater sums. As noted in the preamble above, this limited the amount of cash in circulation and prevented capital accumulation for investment in the kingdom. However, there are only sketchy estimates as to the total sums that might have been remitted: Chaophraya Yomarat placed it at 30 million baht in 1916, while the Financial Adviser Walter Williamson cited a figure of 26 million for 1912. The latter sought to downplay the significance of remittances by arguing that they amounted to only a fraction of Chinese earnings, the greater part of which were spent in the country. Furthermore, the problem was by no means unique to Siam.⁴¹ On the other hand, a fierce proponent of the view that the gambling farms fuelled remittances was F. H. Giles, head of the Provincial Revenue Department in the 1900s and the man thus charged with finding alternative revenue sources to the dens and *huai*. Based on the actual prices of the farms, he estimated the total profits of the farmers amounted to 1.5 million baht per year, of which he believed the major portion was remitted.[42] Whatever the actual amount and significance of remittances, the important point is that some parts of the Thai administration believed them to be a drain on the economy and this consequently had a direct impact upon the abolition of the gambling tax farms.

Just as importantly, restricting gambling was a fundamental part of the government's strategy to 'civilize' the Thai population. As already indicated, this was partly focused on disciplining the Thai cultivator into being an efficient participant in the world economy. Perhaps the most revealing example of this was a 1910 memorandum by Chaophraya Wongsanupraphat, in his role as Minister of Agriculture, on proposals to alleviate the economic distress caused by the recession in the country's rice economy during the second half of the 1900s. Although he identified a number of reasons for the recession – increases in the rate of land tax, the high exchange value of the baht, and the effects of conscription on rural families, for instance – he primarily blamed the farmers for their own hardship: 'With the gradual development of the gambling habit, all sense of saving and economising for bad times is practically gone. So that when the blow comes it will lay them prostrate'. He went on to conclude:

> In order that the people can thoroughly enter into the spirit of agriculture and commerce, it is most important that they must be weaned from the general thriftlessness, uneconomical habits, and the lack of sufficient energy in their work. All of which has been mostly brought about by long years of the gambling habit which is ingrained in their bones. This can only be done by abolishing gambling in all its forms.[43]

As Ian Brown has observed, this patronizing view of the Thai cultivator as indolent and irresponsible mirrored Western attitudes towards 'the native'.[44] For instance, J. G. D. Campbell, a British educational adviser to the Thai government at the turn of the twentieth century, described Thai people as 'probably among the laziest on the face of the earth, and laziness has become thoroughly ingrained in their disposition'.[45] In this respect, the similarities between Chulalongkorn's absolutist regime and colonial governments went beyond shared techniques of governance and administrative patterns: the Thai elite were engaged in a *siwilai*-zing mission of their very own.

This mission also involved forging a Thai national identity and moulding the population into citizens of the new nation-state. Many methods were employed in achieving this, not least of all the promotion of sport. While at school in England, Vajiravudh had been impressed by the fervour with which crowds of spectators cheered their football or cricket team and the camaraderie created by team sports. Encouraging sports in order to instil nationalism consequently became a signature policy of the Sixth Reign.[46] As part of this programme, the long-established custom of allowing people to gamble freely during the Chinese and Thai new years and the Songkran festival was cancelled by royal decree in October 1913.[47] According to the preamble, Songkran had traditionally been the time when people stopped work to make merit and take part in all manner of fun and games, of which sporting contests such as running and boat races were an integral part. This was designed to keep the male population fit and ready to fight in the region's periodic wars. No doubt there was some small-scale gambling on the outcome of these contests and, perhaps to encourage them, a moratorium on the collection of gambling taxes was declared. With the increase in Chinese immigration during the Third Reign, this was extended to the Chinese New Year as well. However, as the kingdom began to enjoy relative peace from the mid-nineteenth century on, there was less need to keep large numbers of men in readiness for war and, as the *Bangkok Times* put it, 'coincident with this the virility of the people began to find other and less praiseworthy outlets'.[48] By the Fifth Reign, the sports element of these festivities had almost disappeared as people devoted themselves to Chinese gambling games and cards. By cancelling the dispensation for free gambling and organizing athletics events in its place, Vajiravudh hoped to restore the 'warrior spirit' – dissipated by indulgence in gambling, drinking and opium smoking – in the Thai man.[49] The implication that this corruption was due to the malign influence of the Chinese is consistent with Vajiravudh's views; the strong racial element behind the suppression of gambling will be discussed in the following section.

The most contentious attack upon the gambling habits of the Thai male, however, was the prohibition on cock and fish fighting introduced by the Phibun government in July 1939.[50] This was part of a broader programme of socio-cultural reforms – exemplified by the State Conventions (*ratthaniyom*) issued between 1939 and 1942 – in which the regime attempted to radically refashion the Thai nation and its people.[51] Their purpose was to show that the country had left its royalist past behind and had entered the new age of the strong nation-state, a transformation potently signified by the change of name from Siam to Thailand on 24 June 1939. Phibun was acutely concerned about how Thailand and Thai society appeared in the eyes of Westerners. Dictating proper social etiquette, behaviour and dress were, therefore, fundamental aspects of his reform programme. In order to build a modern image for the country, certain Western modes of behaviour and dress – the wearing of hats and kissing one's wife before leaving for work are two of the more infamous examples – were officially encouraged, while some traditional Thai customs that were considered uncivilized – such as betel-nut chewing – were proscribed. Cockfighting and fish fighting were also targets of this policy. Given the popularity of these pursuits, prohibition was bound to cause resentment. In anticipation of this, perhaps, the Director-General of the Department of the Interior made a radio address in which he outlined the reasons for the ban.[52] Besides the standard criticisms that both activities were cruel to animals and that the free-flowing booze within the dens made them a hotbed of violence, the government justified its stance by highlighting their corrosive impact on family relationships and agricultural development. In order to build up its legitimacy, the constitutional regime had taken up the popular press' call for the promotion of women's rights and greater gender equality.[53] It had also initiated a campaign to improve the population's diet by encouraging people to cultivate kitchen gardens and raise poultry. The critique of cock and fish fighting was framed within these discourses. According to the broadcast, most men who raised cockerels or fish for these purposes were the heads of their households and neglected their families in favour of these animals, even considering the latter to be more important. Their wives had to bear the burden of making a living alone while the children were left to their own devices. Prohibition would redress the balance. With regard to the agricultural side, rearing cockerels or fish for fighting was of little economic benefit and the government urged these men to focus on more profitable forms of animal husbandry. What is clear from this and previous examples is that the restriction of gambling was mainly a means of disciplining and controlling the behaviour of common Thai men rather than that of women or immigrant male Chinese. The implications of this will become more apparent in the following section.

'A Chinese disease'

In Chapter 1 it was established that the boom in gambling in the nineteenth century was closely related to the growing Chinese immigrant population. This connection was not lost on Thai or Western contemporaries. Prince Dilok, for instance, attributed the prevalence of debt slavery partly to 'an age-old passionate gambling compulsion which has spread very widely these last years, i.e. since the immigration of numerous Chinese to Siam'.[54] To a certain extent, the restriction of gambling was a reflection of anti-Chinese sentiment and part of an attempt to curb their influence. Here it is worth reiterating the reasons why gambling was perceived to be a Chinese-related problem. First, the most popular games during the nineteenth and early twentieth centuries were those played in the gambling dens, namely *thua* and *po pan*, and the *huai* lottery, all of which were of Chinese origin. Second, Chinese men made up the majority of the clientele of the dens and the lottery. Third, the management and operation of the various gambling tax farms was dominated by Chinese entrepreneurs.

In regards to this last point, Kanchana argues that the abolition of the dens and the *huai* lottery were part of an attack upon the wealthy Chinese who, by the start of the twentieth century, were threatening to turn their economic might into political power.[55] During the early nineteenth century, these Chinese plutocrats had been dependent upon royal and noble patronage to secure the tax farms. As they diversified into other areas such as sugar processing, rice milling and banking in the late nineteenth century, however, they became less dependent upon the Thai elite. Moreover, the court was alarmed at how events in China, culminating in the overthrow of the Manchu dynasty in 1911, had politicized the Chinese population of Bangkok and fuelled a nascent overseas Chinese nationalism. In June 1910, Bangkok was plunged into chaos when Chinese workers went on a mass strike in protest against their increased tax burden following the imposition of the annual capitation tax upon them. The strike was organized by the secret societies and, as government investigations later revealed, a prominent Chinese tax farmer called Chin Hong, who held the monopoly for the *huai* and a Bangkok den. It left a marked impression upon Vajiravudh, who came to the throne shortly after, and later wrote an anti-Chinese tract titled *The Jews of the East*. The Sixth Reign government tried to curtail the growing influence of people such as Chin Hong by preventing any Chinese person from becoming a tax farmer. However, there were few non-Chinese individuals who had the necessary resources and personnel to administer the den and lottery farms. Kanchana claims it was this lack of alternatives that forced the government into abolishing the lottery in 1916.[56] But while this argument might illuminate some of the short-term precipitating factors behind abolition, it does not explain why the Thai government committed itself to the restriction of gambling from the late 1880s. Moreover, as mentioned above, these Chinese entrepreneurs had other, more secure sources of capital accumulation. Consequently, abolishing the tax farms was not guaranteed to reduce Chinese economic influence. Lastly, as Brown has highlighted, in the early twentieth century, the Thai elite was dependent upon Chinese capital for its own business ambitions and an attack upon the Chinese was not in its interests.[57] Rather than seeing the Thai government's anti-gambling policy as being part of an attempt to limit the economic power of the wealthy Chinese, it is more instructive to view it as a concern about the influence of Chinese cultural practices and gambling in particular.

The clearest expression of such concerns was the first announcement of gambling house closures from 1887. This identified the Chinese games of *thua po* as 'evils' that had led Thai people into gambling addiction, causing them to waste both their time and money. The dens were to be shut in order to eliminate these games.[58] Although there is no indication as to why *thua po* were so addictive or malign, it can be speculated that the Fifth Reign government wished to prohibit them largely because they were games of chance involving no skill whatsoever and people could lose large amounts of money in a very short time. Nevertheless, the way in which these games were compared unfavourably to indigenous Thai activities such as cockfighting and foot races suggests their Chinese-ness also made them undesirable. What is most striking about the announcement of closures, though, is the government's evident concern over Thai people playing these games, which is in sharp contrast to its attitude towards the Chinese. In fact, the need to continue providing the Chinese population with places to gamble was the stated justification for the gradual nature of the den closures:

> To forbid them [*thua po*] at once would upset the Chinese immigrants who have come to make their living in Siam under the protection of the King and are accustomed to playing their games of *thua po*. It follows from the King's kind disposition towards his subjects that he wishes, on the one hand, to prevent the Siamese from ruining themselves by gambling on *thua po* and, on the other, to avoid upsetting the Chinese immigrants.[59]

The implication was that the Chinese were unable to give up their gambling habit. Indeed, so great was their perceived love of gambling that Vajiravudh once described it as 'a disease ingrained deep in the blood of the Chinese'.[60] Thus, while the Thai government was responsible for preventing this 'disease' from infecting the Thai population, it had no such responsibility towards the Chinese migrants who were already beyond hope. Such an attitude is reminiscent of colonial depictions of and policies towards the Chinese throughout South-East Asia.[61] Typically, the Chinese were considered to be irredeemable and irreformable, unlike indigenous peoples such as the Malays and Thais who might be 'civilized' under the guidance of European rule.[62] Moreover, since the majority of the overseas Chinese were just 'sojourners' who intended to return home one day, colonial states had no moral duty to try to change their behaviour.[63] This provided a convenient excuse for the exploitation of the recreational habits of Chinese labourers in Siam and its colonized neighbours.

The need to cater for the Chinese was the stated reason for the reopening of gambling dens in the southern *monthons* of Nakhon Si Thammarat and Chumphon in 1902. The closure of all the dens in these areas four years previously had apparently caused unrest among the Chinese workforce employed in the tin mines. Gambling had been one of their few means of recreation; when this outlet was removed they had become reluctant to work and some had moved away from the region, resulting in a labour shortage. To resolve this situation, tax farmers were allowed to temporarily re-establish dens exclusively for adult Chinese males in those districts where mines were located. The still existing dens in *monthon* Phuket were also subject to this new regulation.[64] As such, the provision of gambling facilities was not just a strategy for luring this crucial workforce back but also a means of preventing them from leaving once more by encouraging indebtedness. It also enabled the Thai government to ignore the fact that the Chinese miners might have left to seek better conditions elsewhere. The discourse of Chinese irredeemability was employed to mask this exploitative aspect and justify the prolonged existence of the dens. This raises broader questions about the idea of gambling as a part of human nature and its implications for policy-making that will be addressed in the following section.

Human nature and *siwilai*-zed gambling

In Chapter 3 it was argued that the financial requirements of the Thai state were the critical factor in determining the government's stance on gambling at any particular time. Nevertheless, government policy was also tempered by the belief that indulgence in vice, and gambling especially, was a fundamental aspect of human behaviour. As such, it could never be eliminated entirely. In discussions over ways to counteract the anticipated upsurge in still legal forms of gambling following the closure of the provincial dens in the mid-1900s, for instance, Damrong observed that 'gambling is similar to opium addiction. Forcing people to stop it at once is more difficult than getting them to reduce it gradually'.[65] As predicted, there was an increase in card playing after the abolition of both the provincial and Bangkok gambling houses as people sought still legal mediums for gambling.[66] In the capital, card dens, packed with players day and night, sprung up along the streets.[67] Revenue from licence fees jumped from 715,901 baht in 1915/16 to 1,065,905 the following year and then almost doubled in 1917/18 to reach a high of 2,129,025 baht.[68] While these developments were unwelcome, the government realized on both occasions that an outright ban on card playing would be counterproductive. Chanthaburi concluded that: 'Even if it [card playing] is prohibited, people will do it illegally and the means of suppression are insufficient to deal with this effectively. Prohibition might do more harm than allowing play to continue under official supervision'.[69] This recognition of the irrepressibility of people's urge to gamble consequently legitimized the state's continued promotion of gambling, for if the state did not provide some legal outlet then others would. Asked to comment on the proposal for municipal lotteries in 1934, for instance, the Financial Adviser James Baxter noted his opposition to state-run lotteries in principle but then conceded that:

> Since it would, however, appear that the Siamese are ardent devotees of the Goddess of Chance and will not be denied access to Her shrine, public interest would seem to lie in the Cult being guided, controlled and exploited by the State.[70]

The need to accommodate Western interests also had a distinct influence upon gambling policy. As noted in Chapter 3, the Thai government felt unable to prevent European residents from organizing lotteries in aid of the Red Cross during the First World War. During the latter half of the Sixth Reign, the court and other members of the elite subsequently turned this Western endorsement of lotteries as valid fundraising devices to their own advantage, running lotteries in aid of various organizations such as the Wild Tiger Corps and the Siamese Red Cross. Although lotteries fell out of favour during the Seventh Reign, the government reconsidered its stance when, at the height of the worldwide economic depression in the early 1930s, the Siamese Red Cross applied for permission to run one in order to help it balance its books. Prince Boriphat gave weight to his approval by noting that a Royal Commission on Lotteries and Betting had recently been set up in Britain to consider relaxing the prohibition on lotteries in aid of public charities.[71] Pridi used a similar justification for his proposal for a state lottery in his 1933 'Outline Economic Plan':

> Concerning the organization of a lottery in this way, some Thai people are sensitive to criticism for promoting gambling. But please see the example in France where the *Credit National* bonds to raise money for rebuilding the country which had been destroyed in the war, were bonds of a type which also provided a lottery for the bondholders. In Britain itself there are horse racing courses and there are many British people who like horse racing. But we have no wish to go that far. We wish only for a lottery which people can play in small amounts but have an opportunity to make a lot of money.[72]

In short, if a particular form of gambling was acceptable in Europe, then it was acceptable in Siam.

Numerous other games and activities benefited from being associated with the West. Billiards, and the betting that accompanied it, was common in gentlemen's clubs, both Thai and Western, from at least the 1910s on.[73] Its popularity among the Thai elite was due, no doubt, to it being seen as a modern, sophisticated and *siwilai*-zed pursuit. Perhaps the best example of such an activity, however, was horse racing, which, true to its status as the 'sport of kings', enjoyed the patronage of the Thai royal family, with Chulalongkorn and his successors presenting a gold cup to be raced for annually.[74] Regular race meetings were held in Bangkok from the late nineteenth century onwards, first under the Gymkhana Club and then later the Royal Bangkok Sports Club (hereafter the RBSC). This was established by royal charter in 1901 and was given a lease of land on which it still stands today. Among its many purposes, the club was to 'promote horse breeding and to organise horse shows'.[75] Siamese ponies were generally used and the methods of betting included a tote, the bookmakers, and sweepstakes. At first, the government wanted to tax the club's gambling operations, which would also have required a special permit from the Ministry of Finance.[76] The club's president, A. E. Olarovsky, objected strongly to these proposals, however, reasoning that free permission for the tote and lotteries should be given because 'all over the world [they] are not considered gambling and are not subject to gambling laws'.[77] Moreover, he argued that, with the exception of France, no country taxed the tote and if the club were burdened with taxes in its infancy, it would be unable to function.[78] The government was swayed by these arguments: the club was granted a tax exemption for three years – although this does not seem to have been rescinded after that time – and betting on horse racing was not subject to any of the provisions of the 1902 gambling law.[79] The RBSC was later joined by the Royal Turf Club, which presumably enjoyed similar privileges. For the first two decades of the twentieth century, only upper-class Thais and Westerners seem to have attended the race meetings.[80] Lack of regulation meant that the two clubs were perfectly placed to take advantage of the abolition of the gambling tax farms, however. As will be shown in Chapter 7, the sudden rise in horse racing's popularity among other sections of Bangkok society in the early 1920s became a cause of alarm in the capital's burgeoning press.

The constitutional regime's project to establish casinos in the late 1930s was an important part of its attempts to remake the country's image. Indeed, there was much talk of turning Siam into 'the Monte Carlo of the Far East', which clearly indicates how casinos were associated with modernity and being *siwilai*.[81] Literate Thais were familiar with Monte Carlo and its casinos through their portrayal in essays, travelogues and M. C. Arkartdamkeung Rapheephat's 1929 hit novel, *The Circus of Life* (*Lakhon haeng chiwit*) in particular.[82] Although Arkart did not hold back in detailing the grim realities of the resort, the overall impression of Monte Carlo is of a sophisticated locale in which the rich and famous rub shoulders. The novel's protagonist, a Thai man called Wisoot who works as an overseas journalist, meets and interviews an array of luminaries, including Edgar Wallace, George Bernard Shaw and the American millionaire Vanderbilt.[83] While these people may have been unfamiliar to the average Thai reader, the name-dropping would have enhanced the glamorous image of Monte Carlo and its casinos. It should also be noted that the word 'casino' was adopted in Thai to refer to these establishments, clearly differentiating these establishments from the gambling dens of yesteryear and adding to their cachet. Indeed, casino became such a buzzword in the late 1930s and early 1940s that the noted Thai philologist Prince Wan Waithayakon recounted how he was often asked to explain the provenance of the term.[84]

Overall, while the discourse of *siwilai* condemned traditional Thai gambling activities such as cockfighting because they were barbaric throwbacks to the old Siam, it also condoned Western forms of gambling, principally lotteries and betting on the horses, as modern, *siwilai*-zed pursuits. Moreover, the regime of images can also be seen to be at work since the places where these latter activities took place – the casinos, clubs and racing grounds – were closed, exclusive, private spaces, whereas many of the un-*siwilai*-zed games were played in open, inclusive, public areas. Lastly, there was clearly a class dynamic at work as Western gambling games were mainly played among the Thai aristocracy and government officials as opposed to the Thai and Chinese games that were popular with the rural majority and the urban lower classes. A good illustration of how these factors enabled the government to turn a blind eye to gambling in certain circumstances occurred when an informer wrote to Vajiravudh's secretary in 1921 concerning the illicit gambling taking place in a teacher's social club.[85] Chaophraya Yomarat merely responded by urging the chairman of the club, Chaophraya Thammasakmontri, to be more careful in future. He justified this stance by arguing that, although gambling in members clubs was against the law, it was in reality quite normal and a custom all over the world. So long as it was for entertainment and relaxation, was conducted among members only, and the sums staked were not excessive, it was harmless. Additionally, since it was not possible to prohibit gambling in the clubs and hotels frequented by foreigners, it was inappropriate to take action against Siamese social clubs where gambling also went on.[86] Unsurprisingly, the Thai government's gambling policy often seemed contradictory and hypocritical. In September 1939, for instance, one MP questioned how the government could truly be committed to restricting gambling when it was opening casinos.[87] Such contradictions had a profound impact upon the success of government suppression efforts and created a zone of contestation in which the Bangkok middle class was able to challenge the authority of the absolute monarchy in the 1920s and early 1930s. These issues will be discussed in detail in Chapter 5 and Chapter 7, respectively. The last part of this chapter, meanwhile, will concentrate on how all the factors outlined above were translated into actual gambling legislation.

Gambling and the law

Between the late 1880s and 1945, successive Thai governments issued four main gambling Acts, along with a myriad of regulations, amendments and notices, through which they attempted to regulate and restrict gambling in the country. All four Acts were based on the same principle, specifying games that were totally prohibited and games that were permitted subject to licence. Broadly speaking, any gambling activity not mentioned in these laws was legal and could be done freely. Two of these laws were issued during the Fifth Reign: the Gambling Revenue Act R. S. 111 in April 1893 and the Gambling Revenue Act R. S. 120 in March 1902.[88] In terms of its format and purpose, the 1893 law can be considered Siam's first 'modern' gambling law. Unlike previous legislation that was issued on an ad hoc basis, it was an attempt to lay down a comprehensive system for the management of gambling by the relevant tax farms and their regulation by the state. As described in Chapter 3, the 1902 law dealt with the licensing of all games not part of the gambling house or *huai* lottery farms by the state. There was some overlap between these two Acts and together they formed the legislative basis for the control of gambling until 1930. By the late 1920s, it had become apparent that the existing legislation was ambiguous, deficient and out of date. Some members of the absolute monarchy also felt that these laws had been designed more with the regulation and protection of gambling revenue in mind rather than the actual restriction of gambling.[89] After two years of drafting, the Gambling Act B. E. 2473 and accompanying regulations were finally promulgated in September 1930, annulling all previous gambling legislation.[90] However, this law was replaced in January 1936 by the Gambling Act B. E. 2478.[91] This was little different from the 1930 law but, significantly, it included a provision that allowed for casinos, in which any games on the banned list could be played, and was thus designed to accommodate the interests of the new constitutional government. It is this 1936 law that remains in force today, though it has been periodically updated to cover new ways of gambling such as slot machines, which are forbidden, and mini-football tables and pinball machines, both of which require a licence.[92]

In many cases, it was clear why certain games were prohibited. For instance, the different ministerial regulations for specific parts of the kingdom issued under the 1902 law had three broad categories of banned games: first, games that were calculated to deceive the players, including three-stick trick (*mai sam an*) and its card equivalent; second, games in which the chances were disproportionately in favour of the banker, such as *huai chap yi-ki* (12 card lottery); and third, games which entailed cruelty to animals, such as cockfighting with spurs or making tortoises race by lighting fires on their shells.[93] However, there were some inconsistencies, as certain games might be prohibited in one region but permitted under licence in another.[94] This indicates that, while some games were prohibited clearly on moral grounds, the undesirability of other games was highly subjective. Perhaps the clearest statement of a single principle for determining the legal status of individual games came up in discussions on how to forestall the anticipated boom in gambling following the abolition of the dens in 1917: 'it is not until a particular game is *too frequently played*, or proves injurious to morals or public security, that it should be dealt with by law, either in the way of imposing the restriction of a licence, or by forbidding the game altogether'.[95] In other words, the legality of a game was partially determined by its popularity; when the playing of it reached epidemic levels, the government would take action.

It is here that the regime of images and the policing of public behaviour comes into play, for perhaps the only way of measuring a game's popularity was by its visibility: how much and where it was played. Government attitudes and policies towards card playing provide a good illustration of how this worked. As noted earlier in this chapter, there was a boom in card playing in Bangkok following the closure of the last gambling houses in 1917. People set up public card rooms throughout the city, levying commissions on players for the money they won. What seems to have particularly concerned Chanthaburi was that this went on openly and in a manner similar to the gambling in the recently closed dens. But, realizing the futility of trying to ban it outright, he chose to regulate the issuing of card licences more strictly.[96] Under the Gambling Revenue Amendment Act B. E. 2461, issued in April 1918, anyone applying for a permit for any Class 3 game (which included cards) had to satisfy the licensing officer that it was going to be played only for pleasure, not profit. Profit was defined as any money received by the licensee or another from any of the players, except as stakes on the game.[97] This essentially meant that playing at home or in a club *in private* was acceptable but playing in a card room *in public* was not. Card playing per se was not the problem; it was where it was done that needed to be controlled. This point is underlined by the fact that, under the 1930 Gambling Act, licences were no longer required to play cards for entertainment value among friends and family at home, or among members in a club, so long as the organizer or owner of the house received no commission.[98] That a particular game could be perfectly legal under certain conditions but illegal under others was a potent source of contradictions and confusion. Definitions of the term 'friend', for instance, were open to interpretation.[99] As Chapter 6 will illustrate, such ambiguities created problems when it came to trying illegal gambling cases in court.

The main problem in regard to gambling legislation was obsolescence: styles of gambling were constantly evolving as old games went out of favour and new ones became popular, meaning that the relevant laws rapidly became out of date. Discussing the promulgation of the 1902 law, for instance, Damrong observed that the 1893 law mentioned games that nobody played anymore and was totally inadequate for the day and age.[100] This was partly due to the vagaries of fashion – as already argued, some Western games became popular precisely because they were Western and, ergo, *siwilai* – but, more importantly, it was often a response to government policy. Following a clampdown on street gambling in the late 1920s, for instance, labourers and teenage boys simply turned to a variant of billiards, called billiard *ru*, to get their gambling fix.[101] Like an old, leaking ship, once one hole had been plugged another one would quickly appear. If these new games then became so widespread as to cause concern, the government would have to issue further Acts or Regulations to deal with them. Gambling legislation was essentially reactive, and this was because it was founded on the principle that all gambling was legal except for that proscribed by law. One solution to the obsolescence problem frequently touted, therefore, was to prohibit all forms of gambling except for those specified in the appropriate legislation.[102] On each occasion, however, this proposal was rejected as too radical and impractical. A common objection was that defining gambling was extremely difficult, and people might be imprisoned for something as innocuous as playing billiards for cigarettes or a beer. Perhaps the decisive factor, though, was that forbidding all forms of gambling was in direct opposition to established international (Western) legal principles.[103] Given the inherent problems in legislating against gambling, it is perhaps unsurprising that successive governments took an increasingly punitive and restrictive stance.

Over the course of this period, there was a steady increase in the penalties for illegal gambling, although whipping, in addition to fines, was still a potential punishment for playing certain banned games in the early 1890s.[104] This was discontinued under the 1893 law, however, which prescribed a range of fines that were determined by the severity of the offence. For example, the fine for playing a prohibited game was 2,000 baht compared with 200 baht for playing a permitted game without a licence. If the fine could not be paid, the guilty party was subject to terms of imprisonment with hard labour, the length of which was determined by the amount that was unpaid.[105] Penalties under the 1902 law, meanwhile, consisted of fines and/or prison sentences of up to six months.[106] As part of the pre-emptive measures designed to forestall the anticipated rise in other forms of gambling following the closure of the provincial dens, an amendment to this law was issued in March 1906 that increased the maximum fine for playing a permitted game without licence from 200 baht to 1,000 and for playing prohibited ones to 4,000 baht.[107] For the majority of offences, this remained the tariff until 1930 when the new Gambling Act was issued. Under this law, all offences carried a maximum sentence of two years or a fine of up to 5,000 baht or both.[108] Significantly, the 1936 Act introduced guaranteed jail sentences for the convicted organizers and bankers of prohibited games such as *po pan* and three-stick trick, with terms of between three months to three years *and* a fine ranging from 500 to 5,000 baht.[109] Finally, the third edition of this Act, issued in 1942, provided for heavier penalties for repeat offenders who were convicted of illegal gambling within three years of having served a sentence or paid a fine for a previous offence.[110] The progressively harsher penalties for illegal gambling are indicative of how successive governments adopted an increasingly hard line in an effort to deter would-be gamblers. But it also suggests this was in vain, for the threat of a large fine or a jail sentence was clearly an insufficient deterrent for large sections of the population. Nevertheless, it is important to remember that in most cases the stated tariff was the maximum punishment and the actual sentence was left up to the court. How the courts punished gambling offenders will be considered in Chapter 6, along with the impact of fines upon the convicted.

Besides these increasingly punitive penalties, there were other legislative measures that underline the seriousness with which the Thai government viewed the gambling problem and the difficulties it had in policing it. Among the most controversial examples were the provisions in Section 5 and 6 of the 1930 law, which read as follows:

Section 5: In the case of anyone who arranges for or promotes games which are usually considered to be gambling games, whether the stakes be money or other property, the law assumes that such person arranges such games to derive personal profit. And anyone who takes part in such games is assumed by the law to be gambling for money or other property.

Section 6: Any person found in the circle where there is being played a game that contravenes this Act, the Ministerial Regulations or the conditions of the license, is assumed to be taking part in the game. This Section does not apply to spectators of games at fairs, markets or other public places.[111]

As a contemporary commentary on the Act observed, these sections effectively reversed the established Western legal principle whereby the prosecution was responsible for proving the guilt of the defendant.[112] In other words, if the accused contested the prosecution's claim that they were gambling illegally, it was up to them to prove they were not. This was tantamount to a presumption of guilty until proven innocent and, from a Western legal point of view, highly dubious. Nevertheless, the inclusion of these sections, which were maintained in the 1936 law, was a reflection of the inherent difficulties in prosecuting illegal gambling cases successfully. It also highlights that although Western legal principles were important in shaping legislation, they were by no means decisive.

Compared to the absolute monarchy, the constitutional regime adopted a far more restrictive stance towards forms of gambling in which the state was not directly involved, namely the various state-run lotteries and the casinos. Indeed, for these enterprises to be successful, the government needed to ensure there was an enthusiastic market for them and that any competition, legal or illegal, was blunted. During the 1930s and early 1940s, there was a clampdown on many popular forms of gambling, including bookmaking at horse races and, as already mentioned, cockfighting.[113] In particular, gambling at festivals and temple fairs was brought under stricter control. Local authorities and temples had long allowed gambling at such events in order to raise money. However, a range of illegal practices had sprung up around these gambling operations: stallholders commonly altered the methods of play to make their games more appealing to the public, and got around restrictions on giving cash prizes by allowing winners to exchange the articles they won for money, or to use those prizes as future stakes. More seriously, individuals who had received the monopoly rights for the gaming stalls would auction them to others for large profits, in clear violation of the law.[114] All of these practices were on display at the Nakhon Pathom festival, an annual event held around the great Buddhist stupa in the town, in November 1934. As usual, the *Bangkok Times* attributed the large crowds to the opportunity to gamble.[115] The police were kept busy closing down gaming stalls that broke the law, eventually shutting them all; by which time it was estimated that over 20,000 people had entered the gambling enclosure. Despite the police action, both the stallholders and the monopolists were reported to have made healthy profits. Just days after this festival finished, the Ministry of the Interior issued regulations to stop these abuses. Permission for gambling games during festive occasions was suspended until the gambling law could be amended; only games of skill such as target-shooting or throwing hoops over prizes were to be allowed. Moreover, stallholders were to be vetted by licensing officials and required to pay a security, which would not be returned should they contravene the law or conditions of their permit.[116] These measures seem to have brought an end to large-scale gambling at some public events; indeed, the Nakhon Pathom festival the following year was marked by the complete absence of gambling.[117] Overall, the constitutional regime sought to criminalize all private profit-making from gambling and create a virtual state monopoly on the exploitation of gambling as a revenue provider. This monopoly was not just limited to the provision of gambling facilities, however.

One idea for controlling gambling that had often been mooted was imposing restrictions on the possession, production, and importation of gambling equipment.[118] Following the final, successful renegotiation during 1937 and 1938 of the unequal treaties and the consequent restoration of the country's fiscal and judicial sovereignty, the government finally implemented this idea when it issued the Playing Cards Act B. E. 2481 in March 1939. Under this law, the production, retail and import of playing cards was prohibited except under licence from the Excise Department.[119] As a result of the Act, Bangkok-based card manufacturers were forced to shut down and their printing presses were bought by the Excise Department. With a government investment of 180,000 baht, this department established its own printing house and began producing Thai, Chinese and Western cards in December 1939.[120] Overseas manufacturers, meanwhile, were allowed to import no more than 200,000 packs a year.[121] The production of playing cards was thereby transferred to government control and, just as with lotteries, the state assumed a virtual monopoly. As might be expected, there were various loopholes in the law and these were ruthlessly exploited.[122] Eventually, the Phibun government was forced to replace the existing Act with the Playing Cards Act B. E. 2486 in December 1943 in order to cement control over the import and sale of cards.[123] This law remains in force today and, consequently, all packs of cards, whether produced locally or imported, bear a government tax seal. The net effect of all this legislation was the criminalization of gambling that was done for private gain; the Thai state's right to exploit people's gambling habits was something to be guarded jealously.

While the anti-gambling discourse articulated by the Thai elite of the late nineteenth and early twentieth centuries still bore traces of Buddhist morality, it was framed predominantly by the concepts of *siwilai* and material progress. This meant that it was not an attack upon gambling per se but rather upon forms of gambling that the Thai government found uncivilized or impediments to economic development. Consequently, gambling activities such as cockfighting or the Chinese games of *thua po* were prohibited because they were relics of old Siam, whereas casinos and lotteries were promoted because they represented the *siwilai*-zed, modern nature of the Thai nation-state that the elite sought to build. The anti-gambling discourse was also a channel through which the absolutist state and its constitutional successor could exert its newly acquired power over the Thai population. The common Thai man, degraded by his indulgence in gambling, was a distinct target of restrictionist policies as the government attempted to discipline him into being a responsible, economically productive citizen. However, the blatant hypocrisy and inconsistencies in this anti-gambling policy created a space in which the authority of the absolute monarchy could be challenged. This will become more apparent over the course of the following chapters that consider, first, the ways in which the anti-gambling legislation was implemented and enforced on the ground by state officials and, second, the reactions of the Bangkok urban middle class and the rural majority.

5 The police and enforcement

Laws are meaningless if not enforced. This chapter will examine how those tasked with law enforcement implemented the government's gambling policy on the ground and the obstacles they faced in doing so. Professional police forces with the powers to investigate, arrest and prosecute lawbreakers are one of the hallmarks of the modern state. The modern Thai police force was established in the mid-nineteenth century but it shared detection and investigation duties with a number of other state and quasi-state officials, notably the tax farmers. As a result of Chulalongkorn's reforms and the demise of tax farming, however, the police became increasingly responsible for the suppression of illegal gambling. Indeed, it was they, more than any other state institution, that tested the viability of the restrictions on gambling outlined in Chapter 4 and ultimately determined the success or failure of particular policies. Consequently, the police acted as a feedback loop that shaped future initiatives.

Agents of enforcement

Before exploring how gambling legislation was enforced it is necessary to establish who was responsible for its enforcement. Until the 1890s, the suppression of illegal gambling was primarily the responsibility of the gambling tax farmers. As noted in Chapter 2, they had the power to investigate any cases of unsanctioned gambling within their district, arrest those involved, prosecute them, and then receive any fines imposed by the courts. To aid them in their suppression efforts, gambling tax farmers employed their own networks of spies and private armies of toughs. This delegation of responsibility by the state was due, in part, to the absence of a proper police force to deal with criminal offences until the latter half of the nineteenth century. It is thus necessary to outline briefly the development of Thai law enforcement.

During the early Bangkok period, there was no centralized police institution. Within the capital, each government department had its own quasi-police force that was responsible for its areas of interest, and incidents of public disorder were suppressed by palace guards. It was only in 1861 that King Mongkut saw the need for a dedicated police force for Bangkok, commissioning Captain Samuel Joseph Bird Ames, an Englishman and former ship's captain, to raise a body of men.[1] This force consisted mostly of Indians, Pathans and Sikhs in particular, who had served in the British Army or police in Singapore, and its main function was the maintenance of peace within Phra Nakhon district, the royal and administrative core of Bangkok. Initially, recruitment standards were almost non-existent but there were few Thai recruits, as police work was not perceived to be a worthwhile career. Indeed, the police were widely held in disregard by the city's inhabitants: Thais, Chinese and Westerners alike.[2] This situation persisted until the late 1890s, when there was a comprehensive reorganization of the Bangkok force under the guidance of Prince Naret Worarit, the Minister of Local Government from 1892 to 1907, who wished it to be modelled on the London Metropolitan Police Force, and A. J. A. Jardine, an Englishman who had served in the Burmese police force and was employed for this precise purpose. The numerous different forces in the city and its suburbs, including the Railway Police, were brought under the centralized authority of Jardine, in his position as the first Inspector General. A Chinese branch was also established to oversee all matters related to the city's Chinese community. Several other European officers were hired, not just for their experience but also in the belief that they were better able to deal with the Western consuls in Bangkok. Recruitment procedures were tightened, a training school established and pay increased, though initially these reforms appear to have had little effect in improving the quality of men.[3] Increasing numbers of Thais began to enlist: in 1902/3 the force consisted of 3,252 Thais, 8 Europeans, and 320 Indians.[4] The duties of the police force were also broadened from its peacekeeping function to encompass the detection, investigation and prosecution of criminal cases. Eric St John Lawson, who succeeded Jardine in 1902, initiated further reforms: setting up a Special Branch of detectives, based on the Criminal Investigation Division of the London Metropolitan Police, and introducing the use of finger-printing for identifying previous offenders. During the 1900s, such changes led to a gradual improvement in police efficiency and a perceived decrease in levels of crime.[5]

In the provinces, the maintenance of law and order was a minimal concern of the Bangkok government for much of the nineteenth century. The extent of Bangkok's involvement was to dispatch military expeditions only once banditry had become intolerable in a particular area.[6] When Chulalongkorn started to send out commissioners to oversee Siam's former tributaries and outer provinces in the 1870s, these commissioners often established local police forces under their direct control to maintain the peace. It was not until 1897, however, that a centralized force under the Ministry of the Interior, the Provincial Gendarmerie, was established, with Colonel G. Schau, a Dane, at its head. This force was formed along military lines and its primary duty was suppressing banditry.[7] With regard to petty crime, detection and suppression were essentially the responsibility of local communities and local officials such as the *nai amphoe* (district chief), *kamnan* (sub-district chief) and village headman, a state of affairs that persisted outside Bangkok into the 1920s, if not longer.

Following the first closures of the Bangkok gambling houses in the late 1880s and early 1890s, the powers of the gambling tax farmers were gradually qualified and limited as the state assumed greater responsibility for managing crime. For instance, the regulations for the gambling houses and *huai* lottery farm issued during this period required the tax farmers to be accompanied by either the district chief or the police when making arrests.[8] Over the same period, state officials were given greater responsibility for suppressing illicit gambling. The 1893 gambling law, for example, charged the Ministry of the Interior and inspectors within the Revenue Department, in addition to the tax farmer, with enforcing the Act.[9] Nevertheless, Jardine indicates that the gambling tax farmers detected and prosecuted the majority of gambling offences until the end of the nineteenth century at least.[10] The 1902 gambling law saw a further broadening of responsibility: all government officials down to the level of *kamnan* and village headman were charged with investigating and arresting cases of illegal gambling.[11] Thus, while the gambling and lottery farms remained in existence, enforcement duties were shared between the tax farmer and state officials. However, the limitations on the tax farmer's authority made them unduly dependent upon the state for the protection of their monopolies, an interest that was not always shared by officials. In July 1899, for instance, the gambling house farmer for Khlong Kret district in Nonthaburi complained to the Ministry of Finance that people were playing *thua po* and cards without his permission and the local authorities were doing nothing about it.[12] Greater state involvement in the suppression of illegal gambling did not, therefore, necessarily mean improvements in the level of law enforcement; rather, the example above suggests there may have been a decline.

Perhaps the principal problem in enforcing Siam's gambling laws from the 1890s onwards was a lack of incentive: the gambling tax farmers had much more to lose from illegal gambling than the low-level state officials also charged with its suppression. Illicit gaming operations posed a serious threat to the gambling farmers' profits: underground *thua po* dens drew potential customers away from the gambling houses, while unauthorized individuals receiving stakes on the *huai* were essentially stealing directly from the lottery farmer. A further incentive for the tax farmers were the fines they stood to collect from those found guilty of gambling offences. In contrast, government officials had no such reason to pursue cases of illegal gambling. Given the inherent difficulties and dangers in detecting and busting gaming rings, their negligence is perhaps understandable. Bandit gangs and Chinese secret societies were often involved in running underground dens; just infiltrating these groups in order to gain information was highly risky.[13] Carrying out raids on illicit gaming operations could be even more so. In January 1919, for instance, four policemen were attacked when carrying out a bust in Nonthaburi province. One was knocked unconscious and another pushed down a well; the situation was brought under control only after the police shot dead one of their assailants.[14]

A lack of motivation was compounded by an array of institutional problems within the police force, not least of which was the poor salaries policemen received. In his first annual report, that for 1898/9, insufficient pay topped the list of factors that Jardine believed were retarding the Bangkok force's efficiency.[15] The low rate of remuneration remained an issue throughout the period in question: it not only meant police constables had little incentive to carry out their duties fully and encouraged corruption but, initially, it also made recruitment difficult. Consequently, around the turn of the twentieth century, the Bangkok force did not reach its sanctioned strength.[16] Moreover, those who did sign up were apparently of a low calibre: slaves, ex-convicts, the old, and the infirm.[17] Some improvements were made to the conditions of service during the 1900s and the manpower shortage was partially ameliorated by the introduction of conscription. But, while this latter measure ensured there were more young recruits, conscription had, according to Lawson, a malign effect on discipline and morale.[18] In 1920, conscripts were required to serve two years on a salary of just four baht a month and, understandably, their one concern was serving out their term.[19] Within the force as a whole, salaries did not keep pace with inflation, leading Lawson to observe that while 20 baht a month for a first-grade (non-conscripted) gendarme had been adequate in the 1890s, 'It is not a living wage now and it is not possible to obtain good men for such remuneration'.[20] Moreover, the force remained undermanned in spite of conscription. In 1915, E. W. Trotter, another British officer appointed to the Bangkok police, estimated there were 12,000 policemen – of whom only 7,000 were on active duty – in total in Siam, policing a population of about nine million. He recommended the force be increased by at least 6,000 in order to deal with crime adequately.[21] Manpower was still an issue in the mid-1930s; each district had only eight policemen and as one MP in the Assembly put it: 'how could they [the Assembly members] expect such a small force to successfully tackle gambling suppression work?'[22] Lastly, the Bangkok police force suffered from a lack of adequate equipment, firearms in particular, and general support from other state institutions. Lawson often claimed that the criminals were better armed than the police and complained about how difficult it was to get a case of assaulting police officers in the course of their duty tried in court.[23] No doubt this was partly due to the distrustful attitude of the Thai elite towards the British-dominated force, represented by Chulalongkorn's claim that 'the police are not ours, they are the police of the British'.[24] In short, the police force remained ill equipped, underpaid and undermanned throughout the period covered by this study. When these factors are combined with the large number of more serious offences that demanded police attention, it can be seen how suppressing illegal gambling was afforded a relatively low priority. Much the same considerations applied to other state officials responsible for detecting and investigating crime, who also suffered from a lack of experience and training. Commenting on the role of the district officer, Lawson noted in his 1901/2 report that:

> He is not a Policeman and has not the faintest idea how to set about making an enquiry, a duty in which he has never been trained, and for which he, probably, has neither aptitude, nor the necessary knowledge. Moreover, he has innumerable other duties to perform and has not the leisure to spend days, and weeks, if necessary, over a single case as ought to be done.[25]

This situation persisted into the 1920s, leading Lawson to lament that: 'The investigation of crime by Amphurs is a failure'.[26] Similarly, a newspaper article in 1928 asserted that if the government wanted to improve suppression efforts, it should increase the salaries of *kamnans* and village headmen so that they might take more pride in their work.[27]

Taking all these factors into consideration, it is not surprising that state officials might choose to turn a blind eye to illegal gambling in return for bribes or even conspire with illicit gaming rings in return for a cut of the profits. Corruption seems to have become especially acute in the post-1917 period. In his 1920 report, Lawson observed that: 'The abolition of gambling houses has not reduced gambling and has greatly increased bribery and corruption amongst the lower ranks of the Government services, not only in the Gendarmerie'.[28] If anything, the police became even more complicit in illegal gambling operations. By the mid-1920s, for instance, it was rumoured that police in *monthon* Ratchaburi were receiving 300 baht a month from each underground den in the area.[29] Police Commissioner Phraya Athikon Prakat and his Special Force were deeply implicated in such activities. Phraya Athikon had risen through the ranks of the police due to royal patronage and his reputation for being able to control the Chinese secret societies and organizations. Andrew Freeman, American editor of the *Bangkok Daily Mail* in the late 1920s, described the commissioner as:

> probably the most powerful nobleman in the city. His authority extended into every phase of life. The only persons he could not touch were members of the royal family [. ...] When he wanted evidence he did not have to use a search warrant. Despite the law which grants the subject the right to be arraigned within twenty-four hours after arrest, the commissioner would keep prisoners as long as he pleased. He could set bail or deny it according to his whim.[30]

In regard to the Special Force's involvement in illicit gambling, a former police officer testified after the 1932 coup that:

> high-ranking police officers of the Special Force are receiving monthly payments from Chinese casino operators; a given establishment is required to pay each officer 150 baht per month. If the money isn't paid by the first of the month, the casino owner is arrested the following day and required to double the payment in order to escape prosecution. Moreover, at Chinese New Year, the officers' men expect presents of gold and other things of value. Many casinos are operating by these arrangements, which I can personally attest have been in effect since at least 1923.[31]

So for every underground den busted by the police, there was another that flourished under their protection.

Under such circumstances it was vital that the state offer some incentive for officials to suppress illegal gambling. This was recognized by the Minister of Finance in 1890 but, while cash rewards for informing were offered from April that year, it was not until June 1903 that they were given to police officers for making arrests.[32] Even then, though, the police received rewards only for pursuing offences against the 1902 law. This led Lawson to reiterate the importance of such bonuses:

> Now it may not be a very high moral standpoint but as a matter of fact Constables will take far more interest in arresting cases of gambling if they receive rewards than they will if they do not. Also I would point out it is quite impossible to have illicit gambling on any scale without the fact being known to the Police. The gamblers will naturally try and bribe the Police but it is not possible to bribe them all. If therefore the fines or a considerable proportion of them were paid to the arresting Police it is certain that illicit gambling will be very hard indeed.[33]

In spite of these suggestions, little seems to have changed over a decade later. As Lawson noted in 1920:

> The law is not enforced because either rewards are paid not at all, or else after such a long delay that they might as well not be paid. But though Government will neither pay the Gendarmerie a living wage, nor give rewards the proprietors of the illicit gambling houses will and do.[34]

In short, the Thai case provides a good example of the futility of trying to suppress gambling with an undermanned, underpaid and overburdened police force. Indeed, it was the government's restrictionist policy that gave state officials the opportunity to profit from gambling's illegality by entering into alliance with criminal gaming rings. While the police may have been successful in busting some underground operations, the protection certain elements of the force afforded to other illicit enterprises ultimately rendered the law largely irrelevant. Since it was impossible to eliminate illegal gambling, the police had little option but to regulate it informally, and, in the process, they acquired a vested interest in the continued illegality of gambling. This then became not only an impediment to the enforcement of Siam's gambling laws but also a barrier to the liberalization of those laws.

Spies, informers and rewards

Having detailed some of the internal, institutional problems that hampered the enforcement of the gambling laws, it is time to consider external factors. By its very nature, illegal gambling is difficult to detect. It is often described as a 'victimless' crime, an epithet that, whilst crude, does emphasize the fact that when illegal gambling does take place there are no direct victims that might report the crime. Moreover, illicit gambling is usually conducted behind closed doors or in secretive, out-of-the-way places. Detecting gambling within private homes was complicated by police procedure. When the police wished to search a residence, they were required to produce a search warrant and to knock on the door. This gave those inside time to hide any evidence of wrongdoing or to flee the premises.[35] In the countryside, Siam's topography and sparse population made it ideal for conducting illegal activities. Dense jungle provided protection from prying eyes and rural people commonly gambled within its shadowy depths.[36] Farmer's shelters or isolated groves in the middle of paddy fields also made makeshift dens; players could see any officials approaching from afar and dispose of the evidence, throwing it in the flooded paddies or – in the case of games such as *bia bok* that were played with only a small number of cowries – swallowing it.[37] If gambling was being conducted within a village, scouts were posted to warn of police raids.[38] Under these circumstances, the detection of gambling offences was heavily dependent on surveillance operations by undercover police or spies, and tip-offs from informers.

Underground gambling rings naturally took precautions to protect their livelihoods, employing a wide range of security measures and stratagems to avoid detection and arrest. The *Nangsuphim thai* likened the underground gambling dens in the Sampheng district of Bangkok, which was a hotbed of illicit goings-on, to the hideouts of criminals in the movies, with their secret passages and elaborate escape routes.[39] The main entrances were usually stout wooden or metal doors; sometimes there was a series of them. Passwords were required to gain entry. Breaking these doors down took a long time, allowing the illegal gamblers to escape.[40] Watchmen, usually protégés of the treaty powers and thus protected by extraterritorial rights, were employed to give warning of a raid and obstruct the police.[41] One infamous den in the residence of a high-ranking government official had a sophisticated electric lighting warning system: when the white bulb was on, it was safe to play; the red one was switched on when there was a raid.[42] Organizers of banned games such as *po pan* might also take the precaution of having a card licence for their den, using it to delay officials and so gain time to hide any prohibited equipment.[43] Lastly, illicit gambling rings would change the location of their operations frequently.[44]

The underground *huai* lottery, which was based on the results of the official *huai* and was run in those provinces with rail links to Bangkok, was particularly difficult to suppress due to strong organizational support. Most of the unauthorized clerks were Chinese and, given the large amounts of cash involved, it can be surmised that these operations had the backing of Chinese secret societies. A conspiracy of silence seems to have existed between the organizers and the players, and everything was done to ensure there was no evidence of wrongdoing whatsoever.[45] If arrests were made, they were only of low-level employees who would be supported financially while serving out any prison sentence.[46] Elaborate codes were used to disguise transactions and communications between the various parts of the operation. Illegal lottery clerks in Nakhon Pathom, for instance, would send the daily register of stakes received in the form of a shopping list to their agents in Bangkok: an order for five bahts-worth of cardamom and ten of cloves meant five and ten baht had been placed on the letters *ko kai* and *kho khai* respectively. The governor of *monthon* Nakhon Chaisi managed to break this particular ring by using three women to place stakes on all 34 letters of the lottery – 12 letters for two of them and ten for the other – with four illegal clerks. By doing this, one of the girls was guaranteed to win with each of the clerks. When they went to collect their winnings, the local police were able to arrest the clerks, though one escaped.[47]

Given all the inherent difficulties in detecting illegal gambling, cash rewards were vital for not only ensuring the commitment of the police but also for securing the services of spies and informants. The issue was complicated, however, by the question of who should pay such rewards. Following the initial closures of the Bangkok gambling houses and the consequent increase in illegal gambling in the 1890s, rewards for information that led to convictions began to be offered for most gambling offences. Informants stood to receive half of the fine levied on the guilty party; if the latter could not pay their fine, the state would offer 80 baht.[48] Under the 1902 gambling law, however, the convicted party was expected to pay a reward in addition to any fine imposed; if unable to pay, they were liable to imprisonment. Crucially, this law did not commit the state to cover the reward if the guilty party defaulted.[49] This raised the problem of how rewards were to be paid, if at all, in such circumstances. The 1930 law, meanwhile, made no provision for their payment. The Minister of Justice Phraya Chinda Phirom (Chit na Songkhla) objected to the convicted party paying rewards in addition to a fine because it amounted to them paying for their own arrest. The government thus reverted to the original system whereby rewards were deducted from any fine imposed on the offender. The state would pay if the offender could not and a sum of money was budgeted for this purpose.[50] Finally, the 1936 law once more made the convicted party responsible for paying a reward in addition to a fine.[51] Nevertheless, the Ministry of the Interior still applied for an annual budget for the payment of rewards in those cases where the defendants could not pay, despite fierce opposition from the Ministry of Finance.[52] These constant changes to the payment system indicate that the government clearly recognized the necessity of offering rewards but was highly reluctant to cover the costs itself.

This thriftiness on the part of the state severely handicapped efforts at suppressing gambling. During the first half of the 1930s, there was a clear difference in the number of arrests made for gambling offences when rewards were paid and when the budget for them ran out.[53] Similarly, when the courts stopped ordering the payment of rewards in the mid-1910s, arrest rates fell.[54] Moreover, the complicated regulations and payment procedure led to frequent delays.[55] There were often cases where an informant thought they were entitled to a reward but did not receive one due to a technicality.[56] Such problems clearly had a demoralizing effect upon these spies and informers, and were hardly going to encourage others to offer their assistance. In 1936 one Nai Phrom summed up this situation in a petition to the Ministry of the Interior. Despite his frequent requests, he had yet to receive a reward for his part in helping bust a large, long-established den. He had taken a great risk in infiltrating the operation in order to gain the necessary information for a successful raid and he fully expected the defendants would seek their revenge. If the reward was not forthcoming, he, and others like him, would not be so willing to help the government in the future.[57]

The problems of privilege and extraterritoriality

Enforcement of the gambling laws suffered from a range of other problems. When the government first began to implement its restrictionist policy in the late 1880s and early 1890s, it laboured under two major constraints. Firstly, some aspects of the new legislation conflicted with established custom. As mentioned earlier, the Thai and Chinese new years and the Songkran festival were traditionally times when there was a free licence to gamble, on whatever and wherever one chose. However, the 1891 gambling house regulations and the 1893 law made it illegal to play *thua po* outside the gambling houses.[58] Nevertheless, the government felt that clamping down too heavily and too hastily on such gambling might antagonize segments of the population, especially the Chinese. It was thus initially willing to turn a blind eye to infringements during these festivities.[59] Secondly, the state lacked the administrative capabilities to fully enforce its will; the criminal justice system had neither the manpower nor the infrastructure to cope with an influx of illegal gambling cases. Events surrounding the Thai and Chinese new years in 1896 provide a good illustration of these points. They also mark the start of a more hard-line policy. Since the law had not previously been strictly enforced, it had given rise to the mistaken belief that these festivities were exempt from the law.[60] It had also encouraged royalty and government officials to indulge in gambling, behaviour that was considered inappropriate for their status and rank. Convinced by Prince Devawongse that the Chinese would not cause trouble, Chulalongkorn ordered that the law was now to be upheld and playing *thua po* outside the dens suppressed.[61]

Once both sets of festivities were over, Prince Phichit Prichakon, then Minister of Justice, wrote to the king concerning a report from the Criminal Court. One Nai Am had brought charges of illegal gambling, specifically playing *thua po* outside the gambling houses, against 49 Thai and Chinese, men and women. Since he suggested that the defendants be fined 500 baht each and that he, as plaintiff, should receive no less than half the total fines, it can be surmised that Nai Am was motivated by greed. Based on the argument that the accused were gambling during a time when it was traditionally allowed, the court sought advice on whether to try the case or not.[62] In Phichit's opinion it was unwise. If the court were to fine the defendants, he reasoned, it would set a precedent and lead to a flood of similar accusations because those who successfully prosecuted a case stood to make large sums of money. He feared troublemakers would be quick to take advantage at the expense of the general population. Moreover, the courts and judiciary would be overwhelmed with such cases. The poor, meanwhile, would be unable to pay their fines and would thus end up in prison, leading to overcrowding.[63] Despite these objections, Chulalongkorn insisted no exceptions could be made: the Gambling Act had been issued long ago and advance warning of a clampdown had also been given. If exceptions to the law were made on the basis of tradition, the people would not heed future legislation.[64] In short, Chulalongkorn considered enforcing the gambling laws to be essential for maintaining the state's authority.

One persistent obstacle to the enforcement of the gambling laws was the involvement of royals, nobles and government officials in illegal gambling. From the late 1910s on, this became particularly acute and, as Chapter 7 and Chapter 8 will detail, it was a major issue for the kingdom's popular press and some sections of the public. Due to their status and privileges, high-ranking members of society and those close to them seemed to enjoy near immunity from arrest and prosecution.[65] Although the police may have known full well that illegal gambling was going on in the residence of some prince or senior official, carrying out a raid on such a place was risky. As the *Bangkok Post* explained: 'it is essential that the raid should yield evidence that would prove the case to the hilt in Court',[66] the implication being that otherwise those hapless police officers involved in the arrests would face the wrath of the house owner. Similarly, the *Sara rat* noted that it was this fear of status and privilege that ensured only commoners were arrested for gambling offences.[67] It is revealing that when the long-running gambling den on the estate of Phraya Phuban Banthoeng – an important official within the Ministry of the Palace – was busted in May 1923, a number of senior police officers were in attendance as a mark of respect.[68] Moreover, the official apparently boasted that the police would be unable to touch him.[69] Similarly, one Phraya Mahathep, a senior officer in the Royal Bodyguard who was with Phraya Phuban Banthoeng at the time of the raid, dared one of the policemen to arrest him.[70] Clearly, both officials believed their rank guaranteed them protection from the law. However, although neither were at the actual scene of the crime, the fact that illegal gambling had been going on right under their noses was sufficient for charges to be brought against them. Significantly, this seems to have been the first time the police had successfully busted an illicit den in the home of such high-ranking officials.[71] The way in which Vajiravudh's government dealt with this case will be examined in Chapter 6.

A further obstacle was that the police had to obtain the king's permission to arrest and prosecute any member of the royal family, as well as to search any royal residences.[72] This latter process was time-consuming and meant these places were effectively off-limits to the police. Unsurprisingly, some royals and those close to them – relatives, servants, friends – took advantage of this protection. During January 1909, investigations into illegal gambling in Thanyaburi, a farming district on the outskirts of Bangkok, revealed that an illicit gambling ring was operating in the residence of a prince's wife (*mom*). This was a major operation: the residence was guarded by Sikhs and every evening towards the end of the harvest season (December–January) around 100 people, mostly migrant farmhands from the Northeast, would go there to gamble away their wages. The organizers included a government official, the younger brother of the prince's wife – Nai Chi – and one of her servants; each night it was estimated they were making between 600 and 1,200 baht in commission. For the local authorities, it was imperative something be done to stop this: they had had considerable success in arresting and prosecuting minor cases of illegal gambling but their failure to do anything about large-scale cases had led people to criticize them for being unjust.[73] Chaophraya Yomarat urged the governor of Thanyaburi to bring charges against those involved if he believed there was enough evidence but warned him to be careful not to fail.[74] Summons were issued for Nai Chi, identified as head of the ring, and his cohorts but they went into hiding in the residence, meaning royal permission was required before a raid could be conducted. A year later the gambling was still going on. Indeed, during Chinese New Year, the residence was apparently as crowded as one of the capital's gambling houses. As the governor observed, even if

Nai Chi and his followers were successfully prosecuted, the gambling would continue because the proceeds would be more than enough to cover any fine. Furthermore, since the residence was protected, the police would have to receive further permission before entering again, blocking the opportunity for a lightning raid to disrupt the operation.[75]

Even when it was more a case of bending the law rather than breaking it, such activities served as a vivid illustration of the uneven application of the law. Lawson summed up this state of affairs when he drew attention to how a prince had exceeded the time limit for licensed gambling to be conducted in his palace: 'It does not seem right to me that it should go on in this way, the festivities being over. More-over [sic] I hear that he proposes to have gambling every month and if the Police are to allow his Royal Highness to do it I really do not see how they can prevent any one else doing the same.'[76] As Chapter 7 will illustrate, Lawson's concern that such behaviour by members of the Thai elite was undermining efforts to reduce gambling was echoed by the popular Thai-language press of the 1910s. Indeed, the injustices resulting from the special status of the princes were one of the reasons cited by Luang Wichit Wathakan, chief ideologue of the Phibun regime, for the 1932 coup.[77]

Extraterritoriality and the participation of foreigners in illegal gambling presented a similar problem. Under the provisions of the numerous unequal treaties Siam signed with the various Western powers in the mid-nineteenth century and with Japan in 1898, both indigenous and colonial subjects of those countries enjoyed the right to be tried by their own consul rather than the Thai courts. The decision as to whether or not Thai law might be applied to foreigners and, by extension, whether they should be punished for any violations of it, was thus down to the consuls.[78] Following the decision to clamp down on the playing of *thua po* outside the gambling houses in 1896, for instance, the Bangkok police had to ask the British, French and Portuguese consuls to make this law applicable to their respective subjects.[79] Similarly, in May 1904, the US consul had to be asked to bring a halt to the roulette table being run by two Americans in Raffles Hotel.[80] Additionally, the Thai police had to apply to the relevant consul for warrants to search the property of their protected subjects and to arrest them: the arrested person was then turned over to the consul. Rather than give general warrants allowing for the arrest of all subjects committing a particular offence, certain consuls would require the name of the suspect and sometimes even evidence of their wrongdoing before issuing a warrant.[81] All of this created a time-consuming process that prevented the police from taking immediate action against foreign lawbreakers. Extraterritoriality thus afforded subjects of the treaty powers a great deal of protection from the Siamese authorities. The potential for abuse was compounded by the fact that other Asians, primarily Chinese immigrants, could also gain this protection by applying to one of the treaty powers for protégé status; these protection papers were commonly sold by consular officials or obtained through deception.[82]

According to Hong, the ease with which French papers could be secured made it the nationality 'of choice' for those involved in criminal activities.[83]

For the Siamese government, extraterritoriality meant it was dependent on the assistance and goodwill of the treaty powers for the successful suppression of illegal gambling. But this help was not always forthcoming. In 1917, for instance, the *Chino sayam warasap* newspaper criticized some unnamed consuls for protecting those of their subjects making a living through illegal gambling, instead of aiding Thai officials in its suppression.[84] The French were especially uncooperative at times. Indeed, during Chulalongkorn's reign, both Thai and British officials believed the French exploited extraterritoriality to stir up disorder within Bangkok and thereby further their imperial ambitions.[85] Moreover, following the Paknam crisis and the subsequent Franco-Siamese treaty in 1893, France was particularly aggressive in enrolling protégés amongst the kingdom's ethnic Khmer and Lao inhabitants, as well as the Chinese, in an attempt to increase its influence. Unsurprisingly, the French consul was disinclined to aid the Siamese authorities in suppressing illegal gambling. For instance, when the Bangkok police applied for warrants in January 1898 to search four properties in Sampheng where illegal gambling was suspected and which were supposedly owned by Chinese under French protection, the consul initially refused on the grounds that such gambling was traditionally permitted during Chinese New Year, which was fast approaching. Warrants were eventually granted but only with the condition that the police be accompanied by a French official when searching these properties. More seriously, it was even suggested that the French consul had been warning those under his jurisdiction of impending raids.[86]

Although France and Britain gave up extraterritorial rights for their Asian protégés in the border treaties concluded with Siam in 1907 and 1909 respectively, extraterritoriality remained an impediment to law enforcement. In the immediate aftermath of the abolition of the gambling houses, underground gambling rings commonly employed foreigners with extraterritorial rights, particularly Japanese citizens, to act as fronts for their illicit operations. These Japanese would become residents in houses doubling as gambling dens and thereby prevent the police from carrying out spontaneous raids. As with the French, the Japanese consul granted search and arrest warrants only on condition that a consular official was always in attendance.[87] The first raid on such a den was carried out on the night of 11 August 1917. Fifteen police officers, accompanied by the obligatory Japanese representative, raided a house in Bangkok's Hualamphong district, which, according to a sign in Thai, was the residence of a Japanese person called Ono. Despite Ono's attempts to delay the police while the gamblers disposed of the evidence and tried to escape, the raid was a success. Twenty-three people, mostly Chinese and Thai including one government official, were arrested. Cash and equipment for playing *po kam* were seized. Ono, meanwhile, was instructed to report to the Japanese embassy the following day. However, he was arrested later that night for assaulting a rickshaw coolie and a policeman. The police had planned a number of similar raids for the same night but, once they had returned to the station with the suspects and evidence, they received news that various dens had already shut up shop. While the evidence at the first raid was being collected, two other Japanese had briefly turned up there and it was assumed they had tipped off the other dens. Indeed, there were rumours that Ono and other Japanese 'doormen' like him were part of a citywide organization offering protection for illegal gambling dens.[88] Recognizing the seriousness of this situation, Chaophraya Yomarat urged that all involved should be heavily punished so as to deter others from using foreigners to protect themselves from the authorities: the Chinese were to be deported and the official dismissed. Furthermore, Vajiravudh felt it was imperative that they prosecute Ono in the Japanese consular court in order to set an example. However, the Japanese consul gave him the choice of either being prosecuted in Siam or voluntarily leaving the country. Ono chose the latter.[89] In this manner, extraterritoriality not only provided protection for the subjects and protégés of the treaty powers but also, indirectly, for Thai nationals.

In certain important aspects, the situation in Bangkok is reminiscent of that in Shanghai during the same period.[90] Both were port cities with large transient populations of migrants where gambling, drugs, and prostitution, and the associated lawlessness, flourished due to extraterritoriality and, in the case of Shanghai, the existence of the foreign concessions. The French Concession was especially notorious as a centre of vice but illicit activities were tolerated to a degree by the police in the International Settlement as well. Additionally, casinos tended to be registered with Latin American consulates in order to take advantage of extraterritoriality. Despite being banned, the concessions were also home to the headquarters of the local equivalent of the *huai*, the *huahui*, along with a number of legally operated horse and greyhound racing tracks. With the exception of the *huahui*, all these gambling facilities were patronized by a cosmopolitan mix of Europeans, Chinese and other Asians. As in Siam, gambling was blamed for much of the crime and destitution that plagued the city.[91] Furthermore, like the Thai government, the Chinese Nationalist administration, which assumed control of the Chinese sectors of the city in 1927, sought the removal of extraterritoriality through a demonstration of capable governance and, in particular, its ability to maintain law and order effectively.[92] Predictably, part of this strategy involved a clampdown on all forms of gambling. Unlike in the Thai case, however, the most significant legal gambling operations, namely the horse and greyhound racing tracks, were located in areas outside the jurisdiction of the Chinese municipality, and were largely foreign-owned and run. Consequently, Chinese community organizations were highly critical of the concessions' foreign authorities for allowing these forms of commercialized gambling that led their countrymen to ruin and demanded that if nothing was done to stop them, then extraterritoriality should be abolished. Under considerable pressure from the Chinese government, the Shanghai Municipal Council, which was responsible for administering the International Settlement, launched a crackdown on the concession's casinos in 1929 and then closed the greyhound tracks in 1931. Some of these operations merely moved to the French Concession, where the authorities continued to resist Chinese demands. After an exposé of police corruption by Chinese journalists, however, a reformist administration was appointed and tasked with stamping out organized crime and suppressing gambling. The campaign against gambling in Shanghai thus became part of the anti-imperialist struggle in a way that it did not, and indeed could not, in Siam, where legal facilities for gambling were mostly operated by the Thai government itself or influential members of Thai society. Nevertheless, the similarities between the cases of Shanghai and Bangkok underline Siam's semi-colonial status, something not lost on Chulalongkorn when he compared the problems engendered by extraterritoriality to those in Egypt at the end of the nineteenth century.[93] It is also worth noting that while the Chinese government was successful in getting the foreign concessions to close down Shanghai's casinos and racetracks, illicit gambling continued to prosper in Chinese-controlled parts of the city because of the corruption the profits from such operations fostered among the Chinese police.[94] In this respect, the susceptibility of the Shanghai police force to bribery was little different from that of the Bangkok force or, for that matter, any other in cities all over the world.

From an anti-gambling perspective, it was unfortunate that the creation of the Thai police force in its modern incarnation should coincide with the government's attempts to restrict gambling. The police were too ill equipped and unmotivated to successfully curb illegal gambling. They may have recorded the odd triumph here and there but the illicit gaming operators always remained one step ahead, continuously finding new tricks for evading the law. Indeed, there was a limit to the extent illegal gambling could be restricted, a limit that was dictated by the police, who were happy to tolerate certain underground operations in return for bribes. This informal regulation of illegal gambling by the police merely reflected the inherent contradiction within the government's broader policy, specifically, that, despite efforts to reduce gambling, certain forms of gambling in certain conditions with certain players were acceptable. In practice, however, it was the police, rather than the government, that was responsible for maintaining the regime of images, dragging illegal gambling offenders from the protected realm of the private into the public arena when it suited their interests or, as will be shown in Chapter 7, when facing pressure from the Bangkok press. The end result was that the force acquired a vested interest in gambling remaining illegal, making it the largest obstacle to the liberalization of the gambling laws.

6 The judiciary, punishment and the prison

Having examined the role of the police and the problems they faced in enforcing Siam's gambling laws, this chapter will consider the influence of the kingdom's legal and penal administrations upon the government's anti-gambling policy. Particular attention will be given to how convicted gambling offenders were punished. The Thai legal system that existed before the reforms of the late nineteenth and early twentieth centuries was based on the Indic concept of *dharma*, which denotes a universal moral law. Since wrongdoing was not so much a violation of man-made laws but of the cosmic order itself, punishment was pedagogic and corporal, with a strong element of spectacle designed to act as a deterrent to future wrongdoers.[1] Offenders were commonly paraded around town and forced to proclaim their crime and urge others not to follow their example. Similarly, executions and floggings were carried out in public. Torture was often used to obtain confessions while suspects were awaiting trial.[2] Unsurprisingly, such practices were cited by Westerners as evidence of the barbarity of the Siamese legal system and used to justify the need for extraterritoriality. Judicial and penal reform thus became a priority for the Thai elite as they perceived it to be a precondition for the revocation of the unequal treaties. Between the 1890s and 1930s, Western-educated Thai officials worked alongside American, European, Japanese and South Asian legal advisers in drafting the kingdom's modern law codes. The first of these to be promulgated was the Penal Code in 1908, under which imprisonment and fines became the principal penalties. Corporal punishment in the form of whipping was abandoned on the grounds that it was inhumane.[3] The code also established a system of conditional sentences and recidivism in an effort to control repeat offenders. Other provisions included special treatment for juvenile offenders and a system of maximum and minimum punishments. On the surface at least, the new criminal justice system seemed to be founded on principles of prevention and rehabilitation rather than suppression and retribution.[4] As this chapter will illustrate, however, certain pre-reform beliefs and practices persisted.

In the dock

Prior to the reforms of the 1890s, there were some 30-odd courts under the jurisdiction of the various traditional ministries. The Ministry of Justice was established in 1892 in order to rationalize this system along Western lines and to bring all the kingdom's courts under its centralized administration.[5] Three basic levels of court were established: courts of first instance, appellate courts, and the Supreme Court (*san dika*). Within Bangkok, the first tier included a civil court, a criminal court, and several misdemeanour or magistrate courts (*san porisapha*). Following the promulgation of the Law on the Provincial Courts in 1896, a three-tiered system of courts of first instance based on *monthon*, provinces (*muang*) and districts (*khwaeng*) was gradually implemented throughout Siam. Court procedure was a mixture of British and continental practices, utilizing both common and civil law.[6] According to Loos, the reform process coincided with a year-on-year increase in court cases due to 'better accounting systems; the penetration of the centralized state, its police force, and its laws into areas outside the capital; and the promulgation of standardized procedural law'.[7] During the 1890s, the newly reformed court system was faced with a backlog of cases, a situation exacerbated by a shortage of trained judges. Indeed, the courts remained overburdened and the judges overworked into the 1930s.

The following discussion of the judiciary's attitude towards illegal gambling is based largely on cases that were submitted to the Supreme Court. Although such cases came from all over the kingdom, they are by no means representative of gambling cases dealt with by the lower courts. There were strict limits on the circumstances in which a case could be appealed, usually on the basis of misapplied law, as opposed to the prosecutor's or defendant's dissatisfaction with the outcome.[8] Thus, those cases dealt with by the Supreme Court tended to be unusual or unique. Nevertheless, this does have some advantages for the historian. When the Supreme Court resolved complicated legal issues, its decisions often became the standard (*banthatthan*) to be applied to similar cases in the future.[9] For instance, it played a critical role in determining whether a particular game that was not mentioned specifically in the gambling laws was sufficiently similar to games that were mentioned as to bring it within the scope of the law. Moreover, the Supreme Court also set precedents on the appropriate sentence for particular offences. In other words, an examination of Supreme Court cases indicates how the judiciary wished the law to be applied. To this end, key rulings were published in *Thesaphiban*, the Ministry of the Interior periodical that contained guidelines for the kingdom's administrators, and the legal journal *Thammasan*. These cases have been supplemented by records of lower court decisions to build up a more detailed picture of how the law was actually applied.

The first aspect of the judiciary's work for consideration is how gambling offenders were punished and the circumstances under which custodial sentences were imposed. Many of the pre-1890 gambling laws prescribed strokes of the rattan as a penalty, in addition to a fine, but this was rarely applied following the judicial reforms of the mid-1890s.[10] Subsequently, a fine was the usual penalty for the majority of gambling convictions. Indeed, as mentioned in Chapter 4, the 1893 law prescribed terms of imprisonment only in lieu of payment of a fine. Moreover, given the Minister of Justice Prince Phichit's concerns about the ability of the criminal justice system to handle an influx of gambling cases, it can be surmised that during the 1890s the courts kept the amount people were fined for minor gambling offences to a minimum so as to prevent the prisons from being flooded with convicted gamblers who were unable to pay.[11] Indeed, fines seem to have remained the standard penalty for most minor cases throughout the period covered by this study, even though the 1902 law and its successors in the 1930s prescribed imprisonment as a penalty for playing both forbidden games and permitted ones without a licence. Up until the late 1910s, fines in these minor cases tended to be around 60 to 100 baht, with about 20 baht being the lowest and rising to 200 baht at most.[12] Along with the organizer or banker, the owner of the property in which the gambling took place usually received a heavier fine. Guilty pleas entailed a reduction in the offender's penalty: under Section 59 of the 1908 Penal Code this was set at a maximum of half the original sentence.[13] Nevertheless, despite the apparent leniency of the courts, there were times when the defendants were unable to pay these fines and thus found themselves imprisoned. In 1907, for instance, a Chinese man found guilty of being the banker for a forbidden game and two players were imprisoned for four months and two months respectively in lieu of paying their fines.[14] When it came to *huai* lottery offences, moreover, the courts did not hesitate to impose prison sentences. In 1915, for example, a Chinese man was sentenced to six months' imprisonment and fined 500 baht for illegally receiving stakes on the *huai*.[15] A year later the Bangkok Criminal Court gave two other Chinese terms of imprisonment for running underground lottery operations; both were sentenced to two years, with one receiving an additional eight months because he was a repeat offender.[16] These heavy sentences reflected the threat the underground *huai* posed to the lottery farm and its importance for state finances.

From the 1910s onwards, the public prosecutors and the courts began to take an increasingly hard line towards repeat offenders and those playing particular banned games. A Supreme Court judgment in 1912 seems to mark a watershed. That year the public prosecutor for Phetchaburi filed a petition against the light punishment of 11 Thais convicted of playing *thua* outside the gambling houses. The provincial court had passed sentence as follows: the banker, Nai Khian, had previously been convicted of playing a prohibited game; once this and his guilty plea had been taken into consideration he was fined 150 baht. The remaining defendants pleaded not guilty; two women and one man were fined 80 baht each, while the rest were acquitted. All the convicted managed to pay their fines. The prosecutor then appealed on the grounds that a mere fine was not going to deter them from offending again. Although the appellate court duly amended Nai Khian's fine, it was not enough for the prosecutor, whose petition to the Supreme Court was approved by Prince Damrong. The Supreme Court took the view that:

> The people of the outer and inner *monthons* are hopelessly addicted to gambling and repeatedly break the law. Nai Khian has already been fined once for illegal gambling but has not learned his lesson and persists in gambling. It is not fitting to show any mercy. He should be punished with imprisonment to set an example to the people.[17]

Nai Khian's fine was increased to 200 baht and he was sentenced to two months' imprisonment. The other three received one month. This desire on the part of the Supreme Court to make an example of these offenders shows the persistence of pedagogic principles within the Thai criminal justice system.

The need for harsher penalties was echoed by some sections of the press. Commenting on the prevalence of illegal gambling in Sampheng, the *Nangsuphim thai* noted that fines were ineffective because they were insignificant when compared with the proceeds from running an underground den. Only prison was a sufficient deterrent.[18] During the 1920s, heavier fines began to be levied for playing banned games. In June 1924, for instance, the Bangkok Criminal Court fined the female owner of a house in which *po kam* was being conducted 600 baht; others present were fined 400 baht.[19] The government also considered a range of other deterrents such as banishment from Bangkok to the provinces for all recalcitrant gamblers who had been convicted three times, 'as it is thought a good many people will think again before running that risk'.[20] Similarly, in contrast to most other offences, King Vajiravudh did not grant clemency to those convicted of illegal gambling.[21] By the mid-1920s, a significant fine and imprisonment seems to have become standard for those complicit in large-scale illegal gambling rings. In 1924, the Lopburi provincial court found 11 guilty of running a den where cockfighting and the prohibited games of *thua po* and *bia bok* were conducted: all received prison sentences ranging between six months for the ringleader and one month, and fines from 1,000 to 400 baht. When the defendants appealed, however, the appellate court found the lower court's judgment to be too severe and thus lifted the prison sentences. After the prosecutor petitioned against this decision, the Supreme Court, sending out a strong message as to the appropriate punishment for major gambling offences, upheld the judgment of the provincial court, though it did reduce the ringleader's term of imprisonment to three months.[22] In terms of heavy penalties for serious gambling offences, legislation lagged behind the general attitude of the judiciary: recall that it was not until the 1936 gambling law was enacted that imprisonment became the standard tariff for organizing most prohibited games, at least a decade after it had become the unwritten standard in court. In other words, the law was merely formalizing an established pattern. This suggests that it was the judiciary, rather than the legislature, that was driving the Siamese state's increasingly punitive stance towards illegal gambling.

Around the same time, the Supreme Court tried to make imprisonment the standard for playing some banned games, particularly those formerly conducted in the gambling houses. In 1926, the Bangkok Appeals Court overturned the criminal court's decision to acquit 11 people accused of playing *po kam* and fined each of them 400 baht. One defendant petitioned against this judgment. Unfortunately for him, however, the Supreme Court found there was incontrovertible proof of illegal gambling and, citing an earlier ruling as a precedent for imprisoning those convicted of playing *po*, sentenced the defendant to one month.[23] This Supreme Court ruling was in turn cited as justification for imprisoning some defendants in a similar case a couple of years later.[24] That the courts made a distinction between playing prohibited games and playing permitted ones without licence was not lost on the population; those charged with the former might insist they had actually been playing one of the latter, no doubt in the hope of avoiding a prison sentence. In January 1934, for instance, six people up before Samut Songkhram provincial court denied playing *po kam* but admitted to playing a dice game without a licence, despite all the evidence to the contrary. With the exception of a minor, all were fined and imprisoned.[25]

While a custodial sentence had become common for playing banned games by 1930, small fines remained the principal penalty for gambling without a licence or in contravention of one.[26] Nevertheless, even the smallest infraction might be punished, though the fine was usually light. In 1929, for example, a man was fined five baht for gambling without a permit. His only crime, though, was to have changed the location of the card game for which he had obtained a permit; one of his children had fallen ill and so the game had been moved to a friend's house.[27] Similarly, in 1935 seven were fined 16 baht each for exceeding the number of people, a maximum of six, that was specified on the card permit.[28] People were also penalized for playing games that, although permitted subject to licence, were not the game specified on the particular licence they had obtained.[29] These examples suggest both the public prosecutors and the judiciary could be ruthlessly pedantic in ensuring the letter of the law was upheld.

Having established that the majority of gambling offences were punished with fines, it is worth considering the impact they had upon the people of Siam. In the hierarchy of punishments, fines might have been preferable to imprisonment, which involved both a loss of liberty and the potential income that could have been earned while incarcerated, but their effects could still exceed a simple loss of money. Moreover, it is clear that not all could afford to pay and would consequently find themselves imprisoned anyway. A consideration of the typical income of the general population will put the punitive effects of these fines into perspective. At the beginning of the twentieth century, the fixed daily rate for a Bangkok coolie labourer was 0.5 baht and this had risen to 0.75 baht by the end of the Fifth Reign. In the mid-1920s, the average daily wage for such a labourer was 1 baht, falling to 0.8 baht during the 1930s.[30] In rural areas, meanwhile, agricultural wage labourers were usually paid at least 80 baht for a season's work (nine months), with free housing and food provided by their employer, though this fell to between 30 and 60 baht a season in the depression years.[31] From this it can be surmised that, for the majority of the population, even a small fine would have had a punitive impact disproportionate to the seriousness of most gambling offences.[32] Educated professionals in Bangkok were paid more, of course. In 1922, clerks in a foreign-run store had salaries of between 60 and 90 baht per month, for instance.[33] It is probably these people, and those better-off, to whom the *Bangkok Times* referred when it claimed: 'Many people do not mind a small fine, which is all that is inflicted in these card playing cases'.[34] This might partly explain why a number of Thai-language newspapers called incessantly for heavier penalties to be imposed.

Besides sentencing, the judiciary was also crucial in determining whether certain activities qualified as illegal gambling. Firstly, people did not always gamble for cash, instead using edibles or other items such as cigarettes as stakes. When such cases were brought to court, it was up to the judiciary to decide whether these items counted as property (*sap-sin*) and thus whether an offence had been committed. In 1922, for instance, a woman and two men were accused of playing cards for cash without a licence. The defendants admitted to playing cards but insisted they had been doing so for cakes not for money; the game had been taking place in the woman's food shop and none of them had any cash on their person. Both the *porisapha* and Bangkok Appeals Court dismissed the case on the grounds that the defendants had not been gambling for cash. Nevertheless, the prosecution petitioned the Supreme Court, claiming that cakes were a form of property and an offence had thus been committed. The Supreme Court ruled that it was impossible to determine whether the accused had been playing for cakes to eat, which was not an offence against the 1902 law, or had been playing for cakes as an item from which they might make a profit, which might be an offence. The prosecution's appeal was thus dismissed.[35] This ruling was subsequently used as a precedent to decide other cases in favour of the defendants.[36] However, the principle that gambling had to involve some form of profit-making, meaning that gambling for cigarettes or cakes amongst friends was not a wrong, was called into question by the 1930 law. Indeed, the lack of a precise definition of gambling and some ambiguous wording in this Act led the Chiang Rai provincial court to find nine guilty of playing *phai pok*, a prohibited card game, despite their insistence they had been playing without stakes and there being no evidence to the contrary. The Supreme Court eventually decided that no offence had been committed, reasoning that, since the 1930 law did not clearly state that playing a forbidden game without stakes was an offence, the accused should be given the benefit of the doubt. The Supreme Court also cited the ruling discussed above to further justify its stance.[37] The judiciary thereby established that gambling had to involve some transfer of value between the different parties.

The courts also played a role in determining the legality of games not specified in the legislation but which the prosecution deemed sufficiently similar to games that were listed for an offence to have been committed.[38] On the whole, the courts seem to have erred on the side of caution, dismissing most such cases on the grounds that any similarity had not been proven.[39] Nevertheless, by highlighting that a particular game was not covered by the existing legislation, the judiciary might then prompt the government to include it in a future law. This was the case with *yon chim*, a game of skill in which the players would pitch coins onto a checkerboard or other similar surface. In 1927, the Supreme Court judged that the method of playing *yon chim* was not similar to the dice games *si ngao lak* or *khluk khlik*, listed in the 1902 law, and, accordingly, could be played without a licence.[40] Under the 1930 law, however, *yon chim* was placed on the banned list.[41] In other cases, the courts' ruling on the legal status of an unlisted game preceded appropriate legislation. In 1916, for instance, the first *porisapha* court found four Chinese who had been gambling on mah-jong to be guilty of gambling without a licence, despite the fact that mah-jong was not specified in the current law.[42] Mah-jong was subsequently placed on the licensed list of the 1930 law.[43] In these instances, the judiciary had a semi-legislative function. Overall, it played a critical role in defining what exactly constituted gambling.

Disciplining government officials

Penalties under the pre-reform legal system were based on the principle of differential punishments determined by an individual's position within the Thai social hierarchy. This meant that a person of high rank convicted of wrongdoing would be given a harsher sentence than someone of a lower status who had committed the same offence because they had failed to behave in a manner that befitted their position.[44] Although this was abandoned under Chulalongkorn's reforms, the behaviour of government officials in the conduct of their duties was subjected to a much greater degree of regulation that it had been before. Furthermore, as this section will show, traces of the old system persisted in the attitude the government took towards gambling by its representatives.

Laws prohibiting government officials from partaking in certain forms of gambling date back to the Ayutthaya period and were later reiterated by Rama I in the early Bangkok era.[45] As should be apparent from previous chapters, however, gambling by Thai royals, nobles and government officials was commonplace. This state of affairs was a matter of considerable concern for Chulalongkorn and his successors. Firstly, they were well aware that gambling by these high-ranking members of society undermined efforts to discourage others from giving up the vice and could lead to accusations of hypocrisy.[46] At worst, this might involve those officials charged with upholding the law actually breaking it themselves. Such was the case in 1918, when the Minister of Justice informed the king about a judge and a public prosecutor in Samut Songkhram province who had confessed to gambling illegally.[47] Besides making a mockery of the government's restrictionist policy, the close association between the king and his officials meant that such behaviour on the latter's part reflected badly on the monarchy.[48] Their gambling habits might also lead them into debt, fraud and corruption. A 1926 government report, for example, attributed the increase in the number of officials driven into financial ruin over the previous ten years to gambling.[49] In turn, this undermined the functioning of the state and tarnished its legitimacy. In 1903, for instance, a treasury official in the town of Lang Suan, *monthon* Chumphon, was found to have embezzled over 1,500 baht from the local education budget and then gambled it away. Consequently, local teachers did not receive their monthly salary.[50] Gambling had a particularly detrimental effect upon the fledgling police force of the 1890s and 1900s. In his 1901/2 report, Commissioner Lawson observed, with regard to Thai as opposed to Lao policemen, that:

> gambling is generally the cause, not only of the desertions, but most of the serious crime in the force. What happens is this. A man gets his pay and goes straight to the gambling house. He loses all his previous month's pay, cannot pay his debts, and, consequently, cannot get any one to give him any more credit. Seeing no way of getting out of the difficulty, he runs away. Sometimes instead of running away he steals.[51]

Lastly, as Chapter 7 will illustrate, the hypocrisy and corruption that gambling fostered among the upper echelons of Siamese society gave the popular press of the 1910s and 1920s ammunition for its critiques of the absolutist social order. Indeed, if the Thai-language press is to be believed, state officials were some of the most inveterate gamblers in the country. Given all these reasons, it was imperative that the absolute monarchy be seen to take a hard line against gambling by officials.

Some measures to prevent officials from becoming too involved in gambling had been implemented long before this wave of press criticism, however. For instance, the decision to enforce the law against playing *thua po* outside the gambling houses during the various new year festivities in 1896 was partly motivated by a desire to discourage officials from taking part.[52] Moreover, the gambling house and lottery hall regulations issued in the 1890s prohibited any off-duty policemen or soldiers from entering these establishments while in uniform.[53] Until the 1920s, though, there were no such restrictions on civilian officials. Underlying the government's growing concern over the recreational activities of its officials was the change in the composition of the civilian bureaucracy and military. The expansion of state apparatus effected by Chulalongkorn's reforms created a need for young officials that the ranks of the royal family and nobility were unable to meet. Consequently, the lower echelons of the bureaucracy came to be filled by educated commoners, some of whom had studied in Europe and become infused with meritocratic and egalitarian ideals. Among these commoner officials, dissatisfaction with the glass ceiling of status and privilege that blocked their career advancement grew in tandem with their frustration over the economic mismanagement and profligacy of the Sixth Reign court. In her discussion of the Thai state's attempts to regulate the sexual comportment and relations of officials during this period, Loos highlights how Vajiravudh sought to neutralize the threat these commoners posed by discrediting them through charges of sexual promiscuity and hypocrisy.[54] Although a link between constitutional ideals and gambling is not made in any of the cases of illegal gambling by officials, it can be speculated that similar considerations might have been at work. Reprimanding and punishing certain officials for their gambling habits could have been used to discipline those with subversive ideas.

This suggestion is reinforced by the fact that the Sixth Reign government dealt with officials' involvement in illicit gambling on a case-by-case basis, rather than by instituting formal disciplinary procedures. Available sources indicate that those convicted for gambling offences were, upon approval from the king, stripped of their rank and dismissed from government service. In early 1918, for instance, a police captain was found guilty of conspiring to set up an underground *thua po* den. The Bangkok Criminal Court sentenced him to two months' imprisonment and fined him 800 baht. The police captain was subsequently dismissed.[55] Additionally, it seems that officials received heavier penalties than ordinary citizens. For example, in 1924 a *kamnan* was sentenced to six months' imprisonment for playing a banned game, in addition to a fine, while his fellow gamblers were merely fined.[56] Sometimes just a hint of wrongdoing was sufficient for action to be taken. In the case of the judge and public prosecutor who confessed to illegal gambling mentioned above, another official was implicated simply because he had been present and the Minister of Justice urged that he also be dismissed.[57] The dictum of there being no smoke without fire was also applied to the case of the two Phrayas in 1923, referred to in Chapter 5. Both Phraya Phuban Banthoeng and Phraya Mahathep held important positions within the royal household and the Wild Tigers, and, as will be shown in Chapter 7, the case provoked great excitement within some sections of the popular press. Both were charged with being an accessory to the underground dens that had operated on their estates, indeed it was implied that they were the effective heads of the gambling ring.

While Phraya Phuban was found guilty, and sentenced to two months' imprisonment and a 2,000 baht fine, Phraya Mahathep was acquitted due to doubts about the witnesses' testimony.[58] Nevertheless, the latter's reputation had been tarnished and, because he had also previously displeased the king, the feeling within the royal court was that an example needed to be set. Vajiravudh thus ordered that both officials be dismissed from office and stripped of all their ranks, although Phraya Mahathep was allowed to retain his title.[59] Yet, despite this warning, gambling by government officials remained a problem.

Upon coming to the throne, Prajadhipok took a number of steps to reverse this trend, instituting formal procedures for dealing with state officials implicated in illegal gambling. First, in April 1926, the king ruled that although officials may have been only an accessory to gambling offences – by letting others gamble in their residence, for instance – they should be severely reprimanded and even stripped of their rank or dismissed.[60] Later that year, Prajadhipok went further. Concerned about the increasing number of officials that were gambling, getting into debt and then being accused of embezzling government funds, the king believed that anyone who was a hardcore gambler was unfit to be an official. He ruled that if there was any hint of gambling on their part, they were to be censured. More significantly, any official charged with illegal gambling was to be expelled from office, regardless of whether the court found them guilty.[61] Records show both these rulings were applied. In October 1929, an air-force officer was acquitted of playing cards illegally only for Prajadhipok to order that he be dismissed.[62] Officials so accused had to undergo intense scrutiny. For example, even though a case of illegal gambling against one of its officials had been dismissed, the Ministry of Finance still examined every aspect of the verdicts in order to establish whether there had been any factual basis for the prosecution. Only then was that official reinstated.[63] This hard-line stance does not seem to have been effective, though. There was a steady stream of government officials prosecuted for illegal gambling throughout the Seventh Reign.[64]

Gambling by officials remained a concern in the post-1932 era. Since the constitutional regime's legitimacy rested partly on its claims that it represented a clean break from the hypocrisy of the absolutist order, it was vital that the fledgling government try to eradicate the iniquities of its predecessor. The cabinet issued a series of regulations, first in 1934 and again in 1938, that instructed all heads of departments to monitor the gambling of their subordinates. In any cases where it was deemed that the government's work was being adversely affected by an official's habit, even if it was legal gambling, that person was to be disciplined, with the threat of salary deductions or dismissal.[65] Moreover, certain officials, such as teachers and police officers, were prohibited from all forms of gambling, or indirectly having a stake in some gaming activity. Again, violations were liable to be punished with dismissal.[66]

To sum up, these increasingly strict regulations on gambling by officials reflected a number of government concerns, such as the fear that gambling, legally or illegally, might lead to corruption. Underlining these concerns, though, was the traditional idea that those in government service should adhere to a higher standard of behaviour than those of lesser status and be above vices such as gambling. Here it is important to note that government service was considered a Thai preserve. These attempts to discipline members of the bureaucracy and the military can, therefore, be seen as part of the state's broader aim of forging the modern Thai male. As the cases discussed above show, however, government officials were as resistant to these efforts, and as human, as the next person.

Behind bars

This final section will follow the convicted gambling offender into the kingdom's prisons to examine the role of the penal administration within the government's gambling policy. As with the police and judiciary, Chulalongkorn initiated a series of penal reforms to curb the abuses that plagued the traditional system in the 1890s; warders were now given salaries, for instance, rather than having to rely on prisoners' labour and bribes for remuneration. The first modern prison, the Bangkok Central Prison, which was modelled on the one in Singapore, was opened in the same period. Similar prisons were later established in all the major provincial centres and the notorious Bang Kwang Prison for long-term convicts was opened in 1930.

Gambling, along with other vices such as smoking opium and marijuana, was rife within the Siamese penal system. In 1902, Lawson commented on the jails in Bangkok's suburbs as follows:

> In these jails a good many luxuries are provided[...] at a certain gaol I have myself seen the excellent cockfighting ground provided for the use of the prisoners, on which the prisoners nightly pit their fighting cocks against each other. Houses for their wives are also provided, and they all have as much tobacco and opium as they like.[67]

Little appears to have changed almost 30 years later when a couple of newspapers carried exposés of prison conditions. After conducting interviews with prisoners and warders from various provincial prisons, a journalist for the *Ratsadon* newspaper wrote an article in 1928 entitled 'The State of Provincial Prisons'.[68] Amongst a list of other abuses, he observed that:

> prisons are excellent gambling dens. You [the convict] can gamble whenever you wish without having to ask for permission from anybody.

You are better off than people on the outside who always have to ask for permission from officials before gambling.[69]

In a similar article the same year, *Si krung* likened the kingdom's prisons to training schools for criminals. For the writer, the purpose of prison was to act as a deterrent to wrongdoers and discourage those incarcerated from re-offending once they were released. However, using the example of Samut Prakan provincial prison, the writer identified three factors that undermined any efforts at reform. First was the prevalence of gambling; Samut Prakan prison had a large, permanent den with all the equipment for games of *thua po*, dice, cards, and such like. Second was the widespread use of opium and marijuana, which were sold openly and were constantly available. Lastly, the intimidation and bullying of new prisoners by long-term convicts ensured that the former would feel pressurized into taking up gambling or drugs.[70] If a convict was not a compulsive gambler before entering prison, the chances were they would be by the time they left.

Such widespread violation of prison regulations and the law could not have escaped the notice of the penal authorities. Indeed, on occasion they were complicit in these illicit activities. On 21 October 1930, for instance, the police conducted a raid on Singburi provincial prison and found 40 to 50 convicts gambling. Among those arrested was Nai Am, a prison warder implicated as the organizer and banker.[71] The subsequent investigation concluded that the gambling was encouraged by a shortage of manpower and the negligence of the prison staff, especially the jailer. Nai Am, the warder, and the prisoners had often gambled in the past but previous attempts to catch them in the act had failed. A spy had therefore been placed inside to monitor them. Moreover, the superintendent had little faith in the abilities of the jailer to deal with the gamblers and their arrest was thus entrusted to the local police. Charges were subsequently brought against Nai Am and eight convicts. All pleaded guilty; the warder and one convict received two months' imprisonment for their part as organizers, while the others received one month.[72]

Besides the prison staff's negligence, the other problem was a lack of manpower. Although the Singburi prison had the full complement of nine warders, only five, including Nai Am, were present when the raid occurred. The other four were supervising extramural convict labour. Normally, only one warder would be on guard detail like this but, during October, the provincial authorities had been preparing for a visit by Prince Lopburi. Extra convict labourers, with warders to manage them, had been requisitioned to ensure all the outside preparatory work was completed in time. The prison was thus critically short-staffed at the time of the raid and it was decided, therefore, that the gambling could not be solely blamed on the negligence or incompetence of the jailer.[73] Nevertheless, the investigation failed to consider any underlying reasons why gambling was rife within Singburi prison and other penal institutions. For the prisoners, gambling was a break from the monotony of life inside. This can also be said for the warders who spent long hours in their company. Furthermore, providing convicts with opportunities to indulge in opium and gambling was a way of supplementing their salary. It can also be seen as an informal method of control. Convicts who were addicted to opium were less likely to cause trouble so long as they received their fix. While gambling certainly had the potential to cause arguments, if it was run correctly large numbers of prisoners could be engaged in an activity that required little warder supervision.

Following the 1932 coup, the new constitutional government launched a programme of prison reform with the aim of improving the moral standards and industrial training of convicts.[74] Greater efforts were made to ensure prisoners received a basic level of education. Recognizing that most had had no previous opportunity to study, the government sought to give them the necessary skills to make an honest living once freed, rather than having to resort to crime.[75] A special curriculum was drawn up that was designed to provide a primary-level education in two years. Besides reading, writing, and arithmetic, subjects included science, knowledge of the country, and ethics. This latter subject ranged from instruction in manners and etiquette to the work ethic and thriftiness. The aims of this last class were to encourage care for the home, tools and clothes, to dissuade spendthrift behaviour, and to encourage saving. Gambling was to be avoided.[76] There is no indication of how successful this education programme was, however. Given the prevalence of gambling within prisons, it can be assumed it had little effect in stopping people from gambling. Rather than being a solution to the gambling problem, imprisonment was part of the very problem.

Both the judiciary and the penal administration laboured under some of the same constraints as the police force, most noticeably a shortage of trained personnel. This clearly undermined the supposed reformatory role of the prison system and, in turn, government attempts to wean the population off their gambling habit. It is perhaps unsurprising, therefore, that the judiciary tried to avoid sentencing people convicted for minor gambling offences to terms of imprisonment. Nonetheless, the punitive effects of the fines imposed on such offenders should not be underestimated. Moreover, although the Thai criminal justice system that emerged from the reforms of the late nineteenth and early twentieth centuries was clearly modelled on Western lines, traditional practices and principles still persisted to some extent. For instance, the judiciary continued to make examples of gambling offenders in order to act as warnings to others. This pedagogic element to punishment was most pronounced in regard to the disciplining of government officials implicated in gambling. As the next chapter will show, the idea that people of high status and in positions of responsibility should be above gambling was also held by the middle class.

7 The press and the Bangkok middle class

During the first decades of the twentieth century, an embryonic middle class composed of low-level civil servants, teachers, lawyers, company clerks and such like emerged in Bangkok and other large urban centres as a result of the development of the nation-state and the commercial economy. These educated commoners began to exert an increasing influence over Thai social and cultural life, expressing their views and opinions on a diverse range of issues in the expanding print media. In their studies of the emergence of this public sphere, both Matthew Copeland and Scot Barmé have illustrated how the middle class used the media to challenge the discursive authority of the Thai ruling elite.[1] In the newspapers, novels, magazines and films of the 1920s and early 1930s, politically aware commoners mounted a sustained critique of the absolute monarchy and the social order it fostered, casting the former as 'an archaic, repressive institution which impeded Siam's progress' and the latter as 'moribund and profoundly corrupt'.[2] Moreover, the Thai-language press nurtured the development and articulation of a popular Thai nationalism that sharply opposed the official nationalism espoused by the absolute monarchy. Indeed, the press was a forum for a wide variety of hotly debated issues – social equality, gender relations, economic progress and such like – that were felt to reflect the socio-political malaise of the times and provided critics of absolutism with ammunition for their attacks. As this chapter will show, gambling was one of those issues.

The development of the Thai press

Before examining the debate on gambling it is worth considering the general development of the Thai press, its relationship with the government, and the characteristics – editorial stance, circulation figures, the readership, for example – of the particular newspapers used in this study.

Printing presses were introduced into Siam in the mid-1830s by the American missionary Dr Dan Beach Bradley, who also published the country's first periodical, the short-lived *Bangkok Recorder*, in 1844 and, later, the *Bangkok Calendar*. Another missionary, Dr Samuel Smith, was responsible for the English-language *Siam Weekly Advertiser* (1869–86) and the Thai-language *Sayam samai* (1882–86). Until the 1880s, publishing remained the preserve of these men and the royal court, which published a range of official and semi-official periodicals and journals such as *Ratchakitchanubeksa* (The Government Gazette) and *Darunowat*. During the last decades of the nineteenth century, American and European entrepreneurs set up the country's three principal, and long-running, English-language newspapers: the *Bangkok Times* (weekly, 1887–96, daily 1896–1942), the *Bangkok Daily Mail*, and the *Siam Observer*.[3] The latter two also had Thai-language editions. By 1910, all three were receiving annual subsidies from the Thai state and were regularly provided with news of government activities. Amongst the English-speaking inhabitants of the capital, the *Bangkok Times* was apparently the most influential and it claimed to have the largest circulation of any paper in the country. It was conservative in tone, a defender of the British Empire but sympathetic to Siam, and enjoyed a close working relationship with the Siamese government, to which it was not afraid to offer constructive criticism.[4] Under American editorship for much of its existence, the *Bangkok Daily Mail* was more outspoken and a constant thorn in the government's side. By 1912, it had a circulation of up to 1,500 copies per issue and there are indications this was considerably higher than those of its Thai- and English-language rivals.[5] After a series of critical commentaries of the king and the court, it was bought by Vajiravudh in 1917. But the *Bangkok Daily Mail* remained controversial, often carrying exposés of police corruption, and in 1927 Prajadhipok sold the paper to his father-in-law, Prince Svasti. It was closed by the constitutional regime in October 1933 because of its royalist connections. Like its contemporaries, the liberal *Siam Observer* had links with the government and seems to have occupied a middle-ground between the conservative, elitist *Bangkok Times* and the controversial, populist *Bangkok Daily Mail*. It ceased publication in early 1933 due to financial reasons.[6]

Of the numerous Thai-language newspapers that emerged in the early twentieth century, the *Nangsuphim thai* and the *Chino sayam warasap* deserve mention. The latter was founded in 1907 by Chinese nationalists and, as the name suggests, there was both a Thai-language edition and a Chinese one.[7] From around the start of the Sixth Reign, both the *Nangsuphim thai* and the *Chino sayam warasap* received government subsidies and, following an attempted coup in 1912, the former was purchased outright by Vajiravudh. This move was designed to counter the Thai inclination to 'believe everything they read in the papers' by 'seizing the press as a weapon' for promoting government policies.[8] Vajiravudh was responsible for its editorial policy and frequently used it as an outlet for his writings. It was widely recognized as the voice of the government.[9] Unsurprisingly, it was shut down following the 1932 coup.

According to Copeland, 1917 marked the advent of 'political journalism' in Siam, with one editor describing his paper as the kingdom's first political newspaper.[10] Driven by the growth of the Bangkok reading public, the early 1920s saw a proliferation of political journals such as the *Yamato* and the *Bangkok kanmuang*. These provided a forum in which the emergent middle class could discuss matters of national importance and air their grievances. It was the age of the popular press. Reflecting the growing antipathy for the absolutist order, these new publications had their sights firmly trained on the Sixth Reign court. As Barmé observes, 'Deference and respect for authority [...] were, for the most part conspicuously absent from the pages of the popular press' and 'irreverent, contemptuous attitudes towards authority figures in general, including the monarch himself, were commonplace'.[11] The first political daily, the Japanese-registered *Yamato*, was started in 1922. Until it was closed by the police in March 1924, its circulation exceeded that of the *Bangkok Daily Mail* and the government-run *Nangsuphim thai*.[12] The *Bangkok kanmuang*, meanwhile, enjoyed a longer existence; started in October 1922, it survived until 1932. Along with the *Krungthep Daily Mail*, it was considered 'the best of the news commentators'.[13] Under the two-year editorship of the noted political satirist and cartoonist Sem Sumanan, the *Bangkok kanmuang* frequently courted controversy, not least for its allegations of police corruption and involvement in illegal gambling. In October 1924, Sem left the paper for the new weekly *Kro lek*, an equally provocative and controversial publication.[14] Another luminary from this period was the sensationalist *Si krung*, which, along with the *Nangsuphim thai*, was the most influential of the Thai-language papers during the Seventh Reign.[15] Although many of these publications were short-lived, Benjamin Batson estimates that there were 10 to 15 Thai-language newspapers in Bangkok at any one time, along with the various English and Chinese ones.[16] The most popular had print runs of 2,000 to 3,000 copies per issue, though Barmé suggests they may actually have been read by up to 7,000 people or more, as the purchaser would invariably pass on their paper to friends, family or workmates.[17] Copeland has divided these 'voices of the capital' into two broad camps: the government-subsidized or, as termed herein, the mainstream press, which was generally supportive of the government, and the popular press, which acted as a forum for the government's critics.[18] When it came to discussions on gambling, however, this distinction was blurred.

Who read these publications? For much of the period in question, the readership was concentrated almost exclusively in Bangkok. During the Fifth Reign, a conservative estimate of the readership of both the Thai- and English-language press would be that it did not extend much beyond the Thai elite and a limited number of male commoners who had been fortunate to receive a modern education. Due to the growth of both the bureaucracy and the commercial economy, Barmé suggests that by the 1920s the reading public had broadened to include 'low- and middle-level government officials, salaried workers in the private sector, and literate members of the Thai working class, as well as educated middle-class women'.[19] Along with an 'incipient literati' of professional journalists, it was these groups that used the popular press of the 1920s to express their dissatisfaction with the absolutist order.[20] Even with the expansion of literacy in the constitutional era, the provincial reading public remained small.[21] The opinions expressed in the newspapers detailed above cannot, therefore, be said to be representative of the wider population; they were the viewpoints of just a small but highly vocal and significant minority.

As already noted, the absolute monarchy had an increasingly fractious relationship with the press. However, the government's ability to regulate and control it was limited by the unequal treaties, which guaranteed the rights of foreign nationals to conduct commercial activities within the kingdom. Additionally, some local publishers took advantage of extraterritoriality, by registering their publications to foreign frontmen, in order to avoid prosecution.[22] Others enjoyed the protection of powerful patrons.[23] Subsidies were one strategy the government employed to try to influence editorial policy, though, as the *Bangkok Daily Mail* and *Chino sayam warasap* frequently demonstrated, they were no guarantee of compliance. Moreover, the commercial boom in publishing during the 1920s further undermined their effectiveness.[24] Tighter regulation was the other option. According to Vella, however, Vajiravudh was an admirer of the free press in England and averse to state censorship.[25] Despite the recommendations of his ministers, a press law was not enacted until 1923. In its wake, scores of Bangkok publishers were prosecuted, printing presses confiscated and many papers, including the *Yamato* and *Chino sayam warasap*, closed.[26] A more comprehensive and stringent press law was passed in 1927, leading to further closures. This also had the effect of diluting the more libellous attacks upon individual members of the Thai elite, with criticisms now being framed in a more general and less personal manner.[27] Yet, in spite of this creeping tendency towards censorship and control, the last years of absolutist rule were a time of relative press freedom compared with the post-1932 period. Although formal censorship was briefly abolished in July 1932, increasing regulation and repression were the order of the day. Insecure and acutely sensitive towards criticism, the new regime closed a number of papers and enacted a new press law before the end of 1932. Over the next decade, further measures were initiated to curb public debate. Rather than attack the government, the press tended to be more supportive.[28]

To what extent did the press influence government policy in general? During the Fifth Reign, it can be argued that it was negligible for it was essentially just a debating forum for the elite. With the growth of the popular press from the 1910s onwards, however, the media began to wield a degree of influence. Both Vajiravudh and Prajadhipok apparently read all the principal Bangkok papers and were sensitive to writings that criticized their administrations. But the two differed in their understanding of press power. Vajiravudh saw it as the creator of public opinion, while Prajadhipok considered it to be a manifestation of general feeling. Tellingly, the latter and his ministers often discussed newspaper articles in order to decide which demanded some response or action.[29] Both governments collected extensive newspaper clippings on gambling; these not only form the documentary basis of much of this chapter but also provide physical evidence that the press was at least being heard, if not listened to.[30]

Portrayals of gambling in the press

Throughout the period covered by this study, the Thai- and English-language press articulated a more or less unanimous and consistent view on gambling that, in terms of both language and opinion, broadly mirrored that of the ruling elite. Gambling was a terrible vice (*abaiyamuk*); an evil, wicked thing; and a sure path to disaster and ruin.[31] Sometimes, more evocative terms were used: commentators often described gambling as a malign spirit (*phi kanphanan*) that had possessed the Thai people, for instance.[32] Similarly, the press echoed the government's assertions that gambling was a primary cause of poverty and crime: it not only threatened the moral and economic well-being of those people drawn into its web but also endangered the future of the nation.[33] Cautionary examples of the harmful effects of gambling were a regular feature within the kingdom's periodicals. Take, for instance, the woman whose fixation with cards resulted in her pawning away all her family's possessions and who was then divorced by her husband;[34] the young boy found begging for money so he could redeem the loincloth he had lost through gambling;[35] the son of a minor noble who resorted to theft to fund his gambling habit;[36] the pawnshop clerk who committed fraud in order to play billiards and was subsequently arrested;[37] and the numerous suicides attributed to gambling debts.[38] Commenting on the horror stories that surrounded the Winter Fairs of the Sixth Reign, the *Bangkok Times* suggested that Thai reporters tended to exaggerate and were getting some of their 'facts' from their imaginations.[39] It had good grounds to be suspicious. In 1923, a writer for the *Bangkok kanmuang* who used the pseudonym 'Knockout Punch' (*mat-det*) gave an eyewitness account of his trip to the Ratchaburi fair. Amongst other encounters, he described how he had seen a country lad lurking behind a food stall, scrabbling in the dirt for some discarded food that had already been half-eaten by a dog. When the journalist asked the boy if he was mad, he replied that he had gambled away all his cash and was desperately hungry.[40] However, one reader who had also attended the fair later questioned the veracity of this account by pointing out various discrepancies that suggested the reporter had not actually been there.[41] This incident suggests that Thai commentators felt justified in employing a little artistic licence to reinforce the damaging effects of gambling. It also raises questions, to be addressed in the Conclusion, about the exact nature and extent of the perceived gambling problem and implies that certain people might have exaggerated it so as to advance their own interests.

At the same time, and also like the Thai elite, the mainstream newspapers believed that gambling was an intrinsic part of human nature and were thus realistic about the extent to which it could be limited and controlled.[42] Stemming from this, commentators often gave suggestions as to how gambling might best be exploited for the greater good of the country. In 1914, for instance, one proposed that a system of government bonds might be instituted in place of the *huai* lottery; he believed such an initiative would be both less harmful and more beneficial than the *huai*.[43] Similarly, in 1928, another commentator made a strong case for an annual national lottery, referring to the fact that in civilized countries, lotteries were not considered a straightforward form of gambling since they were not as harmful. In his opinion, the benefits of a national lottery far outweighed the disadvantages, with the profits being invested in areas of national importance such as education.[44] Another manifestation of this pragmatic approach was the recognition of gambling as a form of entertainment and therefore that if it was to be restricted, some other amusement, such as sport, had to be encouraged: 'Prohibit gambling by all means, but something should be found to take its place'.[45]

Perhaps the earliest published critique of gambling by a Thai was a letter in Dr Smith's *Sayam samai* journal in 1886 on 'The Evils of Gambling In All Its Varieties'. There is no clear indication of the writer's identity but it can be surmised that he was well educated because the letter was later reproduced in the *Siam Weekly Advertiser* to 'show our European readers that *Siamese know how to write*'.[46] He started by noting his pleasure upon learning that Chulalongkorn had announced his intentions to close the gambling houses in the mid-1870s before lamenting the fact that this had yet to be carried out. Instead the Fifth Reign had seen a great increase in gambling. His was a personal tragedy, for his three sons had been ruined by the gambling houses, reduced to stealing and pawning goods to feed their addiction. Their debasement was indicative of a wider malaise afflicting Siamese society and the writer harked back to the reign of Rama III, when 'There were fewer public offenders than at present [...] There were few gambling houses, and as a consequence few thieves.' In a clear display of anti-Chinese sentiment, he concluded by highlighting the extravagant lifestyles of the Chinese gambling tax farmers and their tendency to remit large sums of money back to China: 'The Chinaman brought no money into the country. All which he spends comes from the people who gamble'.[47] While this bears some of the hallmarks of the anti-gambling discourse of the Thai elite, especially in the vilification of the Chinese, it is interesting to note the implicit criticism of the government itself for allowing the gambling problem to develop to the extent it had.

Similar opinions were voiced by the commoner intellectual Thianwan (T. W. S. Wannapho). This social campaigner and outspoken critic of the absolutist order was a key figure in the development of the Thai-language press.[48] Following a lengthy spell of imprisonment in the late nineteenth century, Thianwan started a journal, *Tulawiphak photchanakit*, in the 1900s in which to express his reformist ideas. These included universal education, a more representative system of government, equality for women, the abolition of slavery and polygamy, and a prohibition on gambling.[49] Thianwan's criticisms of the state's patronage of gambling show a well-rounded understanding of the issues. Recognizing the government's revenue needs, he lamented the fact that 'true Thais' and 'patriots' (*phuak rakchat*) did not have the opportunity to bid successfully for all the Bangkok gambling farms. If they did, they could then close all the dens but still pay the government, thereby freeing the people from ruin. He also highlighted how the money the government received from the gambling farms was equal to that spent by the tax farmers in, first, acquiring their monopoly through bribes and then running their operations, all of which came from the blood and sweat of the common man. The social costs were far greater than any advantages the government gained; the state was effectively crippling itself. Here Thianwan employed the metaphor of disease. But rather than infecting the people, gambling had infected the government itself. Combating the symptoms of gambling, namely crime, sapped the strength of the state, because the cost of building up the police force was more than the revenue from the gambling farms. Worse, however much the government spent, it could never be enough, for if the disease remained untreated, it would not go away by itself.[50] In other words, dealing with the effects of gambling was pointless so long as the government continued to endorse it. Through the use of such vibrant imagery, Thianwan was able to convey to his readership the true cost of the gambling tax farms. Such articles thereby generated a wider public awareness of how the government's short-sighted policies were counterproductive and responsible for many of Siamese society's ills.

On the whole, though, the mainstream press and its readership were sympathetic to the problem of how to abolish the gambling tax farms without throwing the kingdom's finances into turmoil.[51] Furthermore, it was understood that terminating all the farms at once would be counterproductive because gambling was so deeply ingrained in the Thai psyche that closure would invariably lead to a sharp upswing in illegal gambling.[52] When the *huai* lottery and the gambling tax farms were abolished, the mainstream press was united in approval. The *Bangkok Times*, for instance, likened the end of the *huai* to the abolition of the state monopoly on the sale of spirits in Russia.[53] The Thai-language press, meanwhile, lavished extravagant praise upon Vajiravudh and his administration.[54] The Thai-language edition of the *Siam Observer* even employed the discourse of *siwilai* to claim that the king had lifted Siam to a higher level of civilization.[55] As the following section will show, however, this was the high point of press approval for the Sixth Reign government's approach to gambling.

Gambling and critiques of the Sixth Reign government

As already noted, the late 1910s and early 1920s saw a proliferation of news journals that acted as a forum in which critics of the absolutist regime and social order could voice their grievances. Two aspects of the gambling issue were particularly provocative: first, the involvement or complicity of the nobility and government officials, especially the police force, in both legal and illegal gambling activities; and, second, the Sixth Reign court's continued reliance on gambling as a revenue provider, despite having renounced it publicly with the abolition of the gambling tax farms. Vajiravudh's regime thereby made itself vulnerable to accusations that it was directly responsible for the persistent gambling problem and the consequent socio-economic damage. Crucially, these criticisms were not confined to the popular press but also sometimes appeared in government-subsidized, mainstream newspapers. In short, the press was able to exploit the gambling issue to portray the absolute monarchy as inimical to the welfare of the nation.

Judging from the reports and editorials in some sections of the press, government officials and members of the upper class were among the most inveterate gamblers and, by setting a poor example to the rest of the population, were culpable for the extent of the gambling problem.[56] Writing in the *Siam Observer*, the commentator Prarop (literally, 'Thinking Out Loud') questioned the effectiveness of preaching about the evils of gambling while government officials continued to gamble illegally. The priority was getting them to renounce gambling; only then might others follow suit.[57] As with the Sixth Reign government's efforts to police the behaviour of its officials, the basis for such criticisms was the assumption that the behaviour of officials and nobles should reflect their lofty position within Siamese society. Failure to adhere to these standards led commoners to believe that if the upper classes could not resist the urge to gamble, then why should they?[58] Following this line of reasoning, even the participation of officials and nobles in legal gambling became a source of criticism. Commenting on the widespread card playing in the homes of officials during the Thai New Year in 1917, the *Krungthep Daily Mail* observed how invitations to parties were shamelessly explicit about the gambling that would take place. After glumly noting that most officials' morals were no different from those of the general population, it concluded that gambling by officials was more serious because they received a salary, derived from the labour of the people, which they then gambled away.[59] This critique was extended to high-class women and the wives of officials, whose gambling habits were a particular bête noire of the press. What seems to have most infuriated commentators was that these women led lives of relative luxury and, unencumbered by the need to go to work, squandered their free time taking part in illicit card circles rather than engaging in more useful activities.[60] In addition to these moralistic concerns, the press feared that the gambling habits of government officials, or their wives, might lead them into embezzlement and corruption.[61] These criticisms of the gambling habits of the nobility and government officials formed part of a broader critique upon the perceived misbehaviour – the drinking, womanizing, idleness, and general hedonism – of these social groups, the underlying aim of which seems to have been to shame them into conforming to a certain standard of propriety.[62]

Another controversial issue ripe for exploitation by critics of the absolutist social order was the double standard in law enforcement. As noted in Chapter 5, members of the Thai elite enjoyed virtual immunity from arrest or prosecution because of their social status and privileges. The *Sara rat* summed up this situation by noting that, despite all the arrests for illegal gambling made by the police, it was only the small fry that seemed to get caught while the big fish got away.[63] Given this, it is hardly surprising that the popular press had a field day in 1923 when two high-ranking nobles were implicated as heads of a large underground gambling ring – the case of the two Phrayas discussed in Chapter 5 and Chapter 6. Recognizing the significance of such high-profile arrests, the *Yamato* observed that it was a warning to all members of the nobility that their status would no longer protect them.[64] According to the *Awanti*, however, public opinion held that the two suspects would escape punishment; 'Could it be that the country's laws do not apply to people of rank?' it asked rhetorically.[65] Nevertheless, both papers were convinced the two nobles were guilty and, on account of the disregard they had shown for the country's laws and the king's will, called for them to be punished severely in order to set an example to others in similar positions.[66] The *Awanti* even wrote an open letter to the editors of five other newspapers, proposing they collectively petitioned the king to dismiss the two nobles from government service and strip them of rank.[67]

The press also commonly made thinly veiled allusions to police complicity in illicit gambling. Puzzled as to why illegal gambling had increased since 1917, the *Sara rat*, for instance, wondered how the gambling house tax farmers had managed to catch many more offenders before abolition than the police force was able to do in the early 1920s, despite the fact that the latter had ten times more men at its disposal.[68] Similarly, the *Awanti* concluded its praise for Police Commissioner Phraya Athikon Prakat's role in arresting the two nobles mentioned above by mischievously asking him if he had come across any other large illicit dens recently.[69] The *Chino sayam warasap*, meanwhile, ran an article detailing how villagers in a district on the outskirts of Bangkok, where underground gambling was rife, were protected from arrest by a 'heavenly being' (*thewada*). Whenever a household wished to gamble, a flag was raised. The 'heavenly being', presumably a corrupt official, would then fly to that house to collect an offering – of money rather than 'heavenly sustenance' (*thip-yahan*) – and in return would warn of any approaching police officers, thereby giving the illegal gamblers time to hide evidence of their crime.[70]

Perhaps one of the most controversial articles of its time, an outstanding example of satirical writing, and a brilliant synthesis of all the criticisms outlined above, was a piece by Sem Sumanan that appeared in the *Bangkok kanmuang* on 12 March 1923. It has already been discussed by Copeland, though not in its entirety, and, given its significance, merits further examination.[71] Sem started by commenting on the prevalence of 'unusually fat' police officers in the capital's Chinese districts since the closure of the gambling houses. This was unusual because:

> the police stationed in these districts ought to be getting plenty of exercise catching gamblers. Moreover, one would expect them to be irritated by the extra work but instead they are surprisingly happy – as happy as if they'd won the 100,000 baht jackpot in the lottery. Not only are they delighted by the opportunity to get exercise catching gamblers, but it would appear that it is precisely this type of exercise which is helping them to look so hearty. Without the Chinese ... our policemen might waste away.[72]

As Copeland highlights, this 'exercise' was a metaphor for bribes.[73] The article then went on to discuss the 'people with eighteen or nineteen crowns' (*phuak sip-paet sip-kao mongkut*) who also made a living from illegal gambling. The phrase 'eighteen crowns' refers to the eighteen monkey warriors that served Rama in the Indian epic *Ramayana*.[74] In popular parlance, however, it is used to refer to people of a duplicitous – or perhaps, more literally, multiplicitous – nature and in present-day Thailand might be applied to such characters as door-to-door salesmen or used-car dealers.[75] 'Nineteen crowns', meanwhile, was a phrase specially coined by Sem to refer to high-ranking government officials who, on account of their status, deserved an extra crown. Of course, the implication was that they were even more duplicitous and untrustworthy than those commoners involved in illegal gambling. By night they did not remain at home but drove helter-skelter through the streets to frequent various dens in which they won and lost huge sums of money. When these officials then ran up gambling debts that their salaries could not cover, they frantically tried to find more cash. Sem concluded by calling them bandits and thieves who stole from the people, whether it be private money that they won from others or the state's money when they blew their salaries.[76] As might be expected, this article caused quite a stir and Phraya Athikon brought a libel suit against the *Bangkok kanmuang*, in what became known as 'the Case of the Fat Policemen'. This eventually led to Sem being imprisoned in August 1923.[77] This did not deter him, however, and while inside he continued his campaign to expose police complicity in illegal gambling. On 15 September 1923, the *Bangkok kanmuang* carried one of his cartoons depicting a demon that personified gambling ushering people into hell (see Figure 7.1). Copeland observes that the caption – which reads: 'Is m'lord just going to sit there

Figure 7.1 Cartoon from *Bangkok kanmuang*, 15 September 1923 (courtesy of Matthew Copeland)

while demon gambling pulls fellow human beings down to hell?' – was a direct address to the Police Commissioner.[78] A year later, Sem reiterated his allegations in another cartoon, this time portraying Phraya Athikon as a dog tracking down illegal gamblers (see Figure 7.2). Again, as Copeland notes, the word 'gambling' on the side of the dog implied that 'the hunt need go no further than the Police Commissioner himself'.[79]

Perhaps more damaging to the Sixth Reign government were the criticisms surrounding its use of gambling as a fundraising device, specifically through fetes such as the Winter Fair and that in Ratchaburi. The press commonly carried sensationalist stories describing the harmful effects of these opportunities to indulge in gambling, with reports of families driven into poverty and people to suicide. The following extract from the *Kammakon* newspaper, reproduced in English in the *Bangkok Times*, is typical:

> in many cases husbands and fathers of families have pawned and sold everything they could lay their hands on in order to gamble away the proceeds at the Saranrom Gardens [the location of the Winter Fair].

Figure 7.2 Cartoon from *Kro lek*, 30 November 1924 (courtesy of Matthew Copeland).

> In a number of such cases [...] the young children in these households have been crying for hunger because there has been no money to buy rice, the families have been turned out of their dwellings because the rent has not been paid, and husbands and wives have parted in anger.[80]

Although the government mouthpiece the *Nangsuphim thai* was quick to blame the people for foolishly bringing ruin upon themselves, other sections of the press held the organizers of these events directly accountable for the social damage.[81] Additionally, many papers reasoned that the provision of public facilities for gambling at these fairs induced people to gamble, legally and illegally, at other times, while also encouraging other local authorities to set up similar fundraising events.[82]

Besides the ascribed social damage and blatant inducement to gamble, the press had a number of other objections to these fairs. First, while most newspapers recognized that the money went to worthwhile causes such as the development of the air force, many objected to the way in which charity was used as a pretext for gambling, especially since the harmful effects far outweighed the benefits. As a headline in the *Bangkok kanmuang* put it: 'Gambling in aid of the nation is like killing an elephant to acquire its tusks'.[83] The main culprits were the Wild Tigers, which was the principal beneficiary of the Winter Fair, and Phraya Nonthisen, Chief of Staff of the

Figure 7.3 Cartoon from *Kro lek*, 11 January 1925 (courtesy of Matthew Copeland).

corps and organizer of that event.[84] One newspaper compared the fundraising methods of the Wild Tigers with those employed by other organizations, such as the Siamese Red Cross, which relied on parades, exhibitions, and handicraft fairs in order to solicit donations from the public. Given these alternatives, it argued, the Wild Tigers had no excuse for promoting gambling to meet its financial requirements.[85] It is in this context that another cartoon by Sem Sumanan, published in the 11 January 1925 edition of *Kro lek*, should be viewed (see Figure 7.3). The cartoon's setting is most likely the clubhouse of the Royal Division of the Wild Tigers. In the upper left corner a figure that Copeland identifies as Vajiravudh is 'happily quaffing a beer' while locked in conversation with another person, perhaps Phraya Nonthisen himself.[86] Members of the Wild Tigers watch as two skeletons play a game of billiards. The caption reads: 'A competition between national development and the Wild Tigers'. Sem seems to have been implying that Vajiravudh and his court were enjoying the profits from the Wild Tigers' gambling enterprises at the expense of emaciated gamblers, represented by the skeletons. In other words, the development of the Wild Tigers was more important to the king than the welfare of the Thai people and the nation.

The press was also concerned as to the destination of the money raised from these events. For instance, when the committee responsible for the annual motor-racing meetings and air displays published its 1922/3 report on the donations it had made, the *Yamato* pointed out that the police force had received some money, despite the fact that the entrance-cum-lottery tickets for the event had not listed it as a recipient. Meanwhile, out of all the kingdom's hospitals, which were one of the indicated beneficiaries, only the Central Hospital had received any money. The paper observed bitterly that this was fair because the word 'hospital' (*rong phayaban*) on the ticket had no letter 'S' at the end and it was thus presumptuous to assume that it meant many hospitals.[87] Of course, the tickets were in the Thai language, which has no plural form for nouns, and the *Yamato* was being ironic in using an English language grammatical construction to explain why hospitals had not received their due. The implication was that the committee had distributed the funds dishonestly. Similarly, the *Chino sayam warasap* was alarmed at the way in which government officials sought to profit personally from the Winter Fairs by investing in running some of the gambling stalls. Noting how some shamelessly paraded their involvement, the paper commented that the only charity these officials were interested in was themselves. It then observed caustically that they believed they were entitled to make money in this manner, as it was entirely appropriate for their status.[88]

Another major objection was that the games at the fairs tended to be straightforward gambling games, such as *hi-lo* and *si ngao lak* which were played for cash, rather than more traditional fairground games, such as target shooting and fishing for prizes. The legality of gambling for cash at these events was highly ambiguous: for some papers it was merely bending the law, for others it was breaking it outright. The *Bangkok kanmuang* took a particularly hard line on this. Before the 1923 Winter Fair it apparently asked Phraya Nonthisen not to allow playing for money. Its plea fell on deaf ears, however, for after the event the *Wayamo* newspaper playfully noted that 'Chao Khun Nonthisen doesn't care who says what and because of this we could gamble for money and have fun'.[89] The *Wayamo* then teased the *Bangkok kanmuang* by inquiring what it might do now that its threats had had no effect, and praised the organizer of the Winter Fair for being steadfast. Nevertheless, the paper's flippant tone makes it clear who the real villain was. The *Bangkok kanmuang* also used satire to make a point, and one reporter's description of his visit to the 1924 Winter Fair is a fine example. Stopping at one stall, he takes great pleasure in watching some high-society ladies who, it is implied, were gambling there. But this did not last long:

> My delight turned to horror when I saw Chao Khun Nonthisen, the organizer of the Winter Fair, along with a few other officials and a beautiful lady come to sit at the stall. 'Hey! Why have you come? Ah, I see! Oh, yes! You've come to stop them gambling for money, for sure.' Immediately my shock turned to delight once more for I had actually seen a government official of Siam doing his duty! 'Hurrah for

Chao Khun Nonthisen.' But just as soon as I opened my mouth to thank Khun Nonthisen for coming to stop the gambling, he took a 20 baht note from his pocket and placed a 5 baht stake on *hi-lo*. He won as well. As the stallholder gave him his winnings, I was amazed. 'Chao Khun Nonthisen, organizer of the fair; Chao Khun Nonthisen, favourite of His Majesty; Chao Khun Nonthisen, you who know only too well that gambling for money does not conform with the wishes of the King. But alas! Instead of stopping this as you should have done, you do the opposite and start playing *hi-lo*. It's appropriate for a noble like yourself and in accordance with the wishes of His Majesty, right?' Tired of seeing Phraya Nonthisen's face, I decided it was better to go home. Just as I turned to leave, I heard Chao Khun say: 'This is good fun, playing like the truly civilized. Hey! I've won 10 baht!' The stallholder gave him 10 baht. 'Fine. It's fun just like you say. But the people will be ruined on account of this fun.'[90]

Through his feigned surprise and mock delight, the writer launches a withering assault on Phraya Nonthisen that leaves no doubt in the reader's mind as to who was to blame for the country's gambling problem. By describing Phraya Nonthisen's excitement in winning such a petty sum, the writer also suggests his greed and preoccupation with money. Lastly, the writer subverts the discourse of *siwilai* to show that the civilized state to which Phraya Nonthisen and, by extension, the Sixth Reign court aspired was immoral, materialistic and would ultimately destroy the country.

In sum, for the press, the extent of the gambling problem during the early 1920s represented all that was wrong with the absolutist social order: the corruption, hypocrisy, inequality, injustice and moral turpitude related to gambling was a manifestation of a wider social malaise afflicting Siamese society. Moreover, through critiques such as those outlined above, the press laid the blame for the gambling problem on the court, identifying certain government figures as the principal promoters and casting them as enemies of the nation. That these attacks had some influence on government policy can be deduced from the fact that, following Vajiravudh's death, the Winter Fairs were discontinued and the Seventh Reign government abandoned the use of gambling as a fundraiser. Additionally, as detailed in the previous chapter, Prajadhipok took a more serious view of government officials taking part in any form of gambling, instituting a number of regulations for disciplining those that did. However, there were also instances when the press exerted a much more direct influence.

The power of the press and horse racing

Perhaps the best example of Thai newspapers pressurizing the government into taking action against popular forms of gambling was the campaign against the one-baht sweepstakes at Bangkok's two horse racing clubs. In the early 1920s, horse racing experienced an enormous surge in popularity and every race day, of which there were three or four a month, the courses were packed with spectators. Every section of Bangkok society was present: men and women, nobles and commoners, government officials and military officers, coolies and clerks, wealthy businessmen and destitute beggars, even monks. Banks and government offices would close early so their employees could make haste to the races. Employers would be approached for loans by staff claiming that their parents or children were sick but who would then be found at the racecourse. Pawnshops would enjoy increased business. In 1923, at the height of racing's popularity, over 12,000 people attended one meeting at the Turf Club.[91] It was widely recognized that this had little to do with a sudden interest in the sport itself but, rather, was due to the opportunity for legal gambling that the race meetings provided.[92] According to the *Bangkok Times*, 'Nine-tenths of the outside public have no interest at all in the racing, and this they show by leaving the course the moment they have lost all their money'.[93] Of all the ways of betting, the most popular was the one-baht sweepstakes, introduced in 1920, which were held on each of the six to eight races run every race day. They were affordable to most, offered considerable prizes, and required no skill or knowledge of horse racing to play. When the sweepstakes were first launched, the prizes ranged from 200 baht to 1,800 but in 1923 the first prize was raised to the princely sum of 4,000 baht, further enhancing the appeal of the sweeps.[94] At one Turf Club meeting in July 1923, it was estimated that 35,000 baht changed hands on the sweeps alone.[95] For the press and some sections of the reading public, these sweeps were nurturing the population's gambling obsession, impoverishing Bangkok's lower classes, and accentuating social problems. In short, the race courses had become little more than open-air gambling dens.[96]

A number of specific criticisms were directed at the races. For instance, one paper highlighted how monks placing bets on the races was damaging to the Buddhist religion and might be criticized by foreigners.[97] Some papers questioned the legality of betting on the horses, the *Siam Observer* reasoning that the main reason it was tolerated in Siam was because it was done in Britain and France.[98] The *Sayam sakkhi* staged an especially vigorous campaign against the sweeps, vehemently insisting that they were in direct contravention of the law. It based this assessment on the argument that, apart from the ministerial regulations which listed specific games and activities, any form of betting that did not depend on either skill or knowledge could be considered gambling.[99] The paper then implied that the reason the relevant officials, Chaophraya Yomarat in particular, had failed to take action against the sweeps was because other nobles and high-ranking officials were the owners of the two race clubs. Here it repeated the claim that the country's laws had to be respected by all classes, nobles and commoners alike.[100] The paper then attempted to force the government's hand by expressing its confidence that Chaophraya Yomarat was not afraid of the important individuals with shares in the clubs and that Police Commissioner Phraya Athikon was just awaiting his orders.[101] The Thai elite were thus cast as the villains, exploiting the gambling habits of the masses for their private gain or just standing by and letting others do so.

Shortly after these articles appeared, the government took action. On 17 July 1923, Phraya Athikon informed the two clubs that the one-baht sweeps were henceforth prohibited.[102] The impact was immediate: the race meeting at the Royal Bangkok Sports Club on 21 July was practically deserted. Despite efforts by both the clubs to find new ways of appealing to the public, attendances never recovered.[103] The Thai-language press seems to have been almost unanimous in its approval of the prohibition, as was the general public apparently.[104] Noting that the governments of neighbouring countries such as Singapore had already forbidden them, the *Chino sayam warasap* thought it entirely appropriate that the Siamese administration should follow suit.[105] The *Sayam sakkhi*, meanwhile, attributed the prohibition to the success of its own editorials and issued the following warning:

> Since the words in our paper have resulted in officials cutting off a means of sucking the flesh and blood of the people, groups that have a vested interest in issuing the sweeps have been furious with us. But we aren't afraid of these wicked people, and let any that still try to suck the flesh and blood of the people know that we'll continue to call for officials to take action just as in this case.[106]

Clearly, the Thai-language press believed that, with sustained pressure, it could sway the government on certain matters and be a force for change. Furthermore, in some of the articles cited above there was an implicit criticism of the blind aping of Western practices, particularly as done by the Thai elite.[107] Indeed, underlying the campaign there were deep-rooted concerns about the extent of Western influence upon Thai society and these became more pronounced in the subsequent debate initiated by complaints about the ban on the sweeps in some of the English-language newspapers.

The main argument against the prohibition was based on the idea that the sweepstakes were a relatively harmless bit of fun. As the *Bangkok Times'* racing correspondent argued:

> The Sweeps were a very mild form of a game of chance and with their closure it is but natural to expect that new and more desperate means of gambling will be resorted to. For a hundred years the spirit of gambling has been encouraged in this country, and in the opinion of not a few experienced men it is an error of judgment to seek suddenly to prohibit any indulgence of this weakness of nature without providing a more gradual means to the end.[108]

Questions were also raised as to why no action had been taken against the sweeps earlier and about the motives of those behind the ban, Phraya Athikon and the Lord Mayor of Bangkok Phraya Phetchapani in particular.[109] The *Chino sayam warasap* and *Sayam sakkhi* responded by claiming that the prohibition was supported by most respectable Thai people and foreigners who had the best interests of the country at heart; the only people complaining were hardcore gamblers and foreigners who had forgotten their place and sought to impose their views upon others. These papers also contested the idea that the sweeps were comparatively harmless, insisting that gambling was gambling whatever form it took.[110]

Here it is worth returning to the case of Shanghai to note the similarities with the debate over greyhound racing in the foreign concessions.[111] Local Chinese community organizations were particularly concerned with these races because they were attended by all classes of Shanghai society, the majority of whom could ill afford to gamble. Chinese newspapers also carried lurid stories of suicides that were blamed on gambling debts. However, the Shanghai Municipal Council was reluctant to act; perhaps, because some of its councillors were directors of one of the courses. Notwithstanding this, defenders of greyhound racing also maintained that it was first and foremost a sport and the method of betting, namely the pari-mutuel or tote, was a 'safe' form of gambling as it decreased the risks of losing and allowed many to win a modest sum.[112] Greyhound racing was thus 'a legitimate form of pleasure' and 'a pleasant and innocent form of entertainment'. Drawing on the work of Anthony Giddens on modernity and risk management, Ning Jennifer Chang highlights how the pari-mutuel was 'an institutional device that managed risk' and, as such, 'reflected distinctive features of rising modernity' in the West.[113] However, the Chinese elites of Shanghai did not subscribe to the harmlessness of this new form of gambling. As Chang concludes, 'Taking a strong moral stand, they considered dog racing to be pure gambling and an incentive to crime. To pursue a cleaner sort of modernity, they linked morality, social order, and nationalism to campaign against dog racing.'[114] In this light, the Thai press campaign against the horse racing sweepstakes and gambling in general can also be seen as an attempt by the Bangkok middle class to negotiate the transition to modernity. The major difference between the two cases was that, while the campaign in Shanghai was directed against the municipal governments of the foreign concessions, the one in Siam targeted the indigenous absolutist elite, as it was they, rather than Western colonialists, who were the main agents of modernity.

In his analysis of the Bangkok middle class as a socio-cultural force, Barmé refers to the work of George Mosse on the link between the emergence of nationalism and notions of respectability in late eighteenth and early nineteenth century Europe.[115] For Mosse, respectability encompasses a wide array of concepts such as table manners but especially appropriate sexual behaviour, and 'served to legitimize and define the middle classes as against the lower classes and the aristocracy'.[116] For its part, nationalism 'absorbed and sanctioned middle-class manners and morals and played a crucial part in spreading respectability to all classes of the population'.[117] Barmé argues that the Bangkok middle class deployed similar ideas about respectability in an effort to regulate relations between the sexes, seeking to 'establish order through the creation of a new contemporary morality that was seen as fundamental to the nation's progress and prosperity'.[118] From the foregoing discussion in this chapter, it should be apparent that the issue of gambling was employed in an analogous manner. Indeed, it seems that the Bangkok middle class took the government campaign against gambling to heart more than the government itself. By appropriating the anti-gambling discourse articulated by the elite and turning it upon them, this new class of actors was able to have both a short-term impact on the government's gambling policy, through lurid stories highlighting the 'evils' of a particular form of gambling that then led to that form's regulation or prohibition, and a long-term influence, through piercing critiques of the hypocrisy and moral turpitude engendered by gambling that then resulted in the government regulating the behaviour of its officials more strictly. These criticisms were but one symptom of a broader and more deep-seated disenchantment with absolutist society that formed the backdrop to the 1932 coup that brought the absolute monarchy to an end. Nevertheless, it would be misleading to say that the Bangkok media and middle class spoke for the majority rural population. The attitudes of this section of Thai society will be considered in Chapter 8.

8 Buddhism, the Sangha and the silent majority

So far little has been said about the influence of the Buddhist religion upon attitudes and policies towards gambling. Given the supposed centrality of Buddhism within Thai society, this is perhaps surprising. But condemnations of gambling on religious grounds were noticeably absent from the minutes of government meetings, the preambles of the numerous gambling laws and the pages of the Bangkok press. Instead, as the previous chapters have shown, critiques of gambling were framed largely in the materialist terms of economic development and social order, with only fleeting references to morality. At times, members of the Sangha (the Buddhist monkhood) also adopted such an approach, as was the case in a short treatise titled 'The Dangers of Gambling' published by a monk in 1940. This text concentrates on the socio-economic costs of gambling and casts it not only as an impediment to people's happiness but also to the material progress of the country.[1] This suggests a markedly secular outlook towards the gambling issue, though it does not mean the monkhood had no impact upon policy or opinion. Besides exploring the role of the Sangha, this chapter will also examine the attitudes of the ordinary Thai person, whose influence has so far been limited to vague mentions about public opinion.

Gambling, Buddhism and the Sangha

According to the Buddha's teachings, gambling is one of four harmful vices (*abaiyamuk*) that all good Buddhists should avoid.[2] There are six particular ways in which gambling leads to suffering: first, when one wins, one provokes resentment; second, and conversely, when one loses, one regrets the money lost; third, gambling consumes one's wealth; fourth, as a gambler, no one believes what you have to say; fifth, one's friends will look down upon you; and, lastly, nobody will wish to marry you.[3] Moreover, it is generally considered that gambling comes under the strictures against stealing, the second of the five precepts that underlie the Thai Buddhist system of morality and that should be observed by all meritorious individuals.[4] As should be apparent by now, though, these proscriptions fell largely on deaf ears within Thai society. Perhaps this is unsurprising, for as Terwiel has noted in his study of Buddhism and its influence upon Thai behaviour: 'The general attitude seems to be that full adherence to the five precepts is not compatible with ordinary daily life and that people should not be sanctimonious'.[5] This indicates a highly pragmatic attitude towards Buddhist teachings, which was not just limited to the layperson. Indeed, this section will argue that the prevalence of gambling in Thai society was partly due to the monkhood's implicit condoning of gambling, at both an individual and institutional level.

For monks, the position on gambling is much clearer: it is something that is strictly forbidden under the rules governing monastic behaviour.[6] In addition to this religious injunction, there were a number of secular laws prohibiting monks from various forms of gambling; offenders were disrobed and punished as laypeople.[7] The regulations for the gambling houses and the *huai* issued during the early 1890s forbade the tax farmers and their employees from allowing monks to enter the dens or the lottery hall.[8] But, despite these religious and legal sanctions, gambling by monks was commonplace. In his memoirs, Phraya Anuman recalls how monks often placed stakes on the *huai*, for instance.[9] Similarly, the American Hermann Norden, who visited Siam during the Sixth Reign, notes how he often came across monks 'just around the corner from a Wat [temple], engaged in a sport that looked to me uncommonly like shooting craps', and being sorely tempted to join in.[10] Moreover, as mentioned in the previous chapter, monks were also to be seen placing bets at the horse races. While this was hardly saintly behaviour, it is not surprising, for not all who became monks did so out of religious piety. As one Westerner claimed in 1906, 'many enter the monasteries from no other motive than laziness, and some belong to the lowest criminal class who hope thus to escape from justice. These are the men who bring the monasteries into ill repute.'[11] Being ordained was also a way of avoiding conscription or corvée. Some might also have used it in order to get rid of their debts: 'they apply to some one who wishes to make merit with Buddha and induce him to pay the debt on condition of "taking orders"'.[12]

Monks took part not only in public, legal gambling. Kanchana highlights how sprawling temple grounds were an excellent location for illicit gambling because they provided many secluded places far from prying eyes.[13] Nonetheless, this was no guarantee of avoiding arrest. In 1912, for instance, the Phetchabun town court found a monk and a novice guilty of playing *bia bok*, a banned game, along with six laypeople, in the main chapel of their temple during the night. The two miscreants had denied the charges, claiming they had seen light coming from the chapel and, fearing it was a fire, had gone to investigate. It was then they had been arrested. Despite their protestations, there was sufficient evidence to convict them; the court ordered both to pay a fine of 100 baht. In a futile attempt to escape punishment, the monk pointed out that religious precepts forbade monks from possessing money and thus neither of them could pay. Furthermore, it was not permitted to imprison them in lieu of payment. Final judgment in a case such as this was the duty of the king: Vajiravudh ordered that the two be expelled from the monkhood and then punished accordingly.[14]

Clearly, such misconduct had a deleterious effect upon the Buddhist religion and the standing of the monkhood. It also set a terrible example for the lay population. Consequently, it was of grave concern for both the religious and secular authorities, which took numerous measures to prevent monks from gambling. In 1896, for instance, the Ministry of Public Instruction and Religion issued orders reminding the police to arrest any monk committing a range of listed offences. These included betting on the *huai*, and either entering a gambling house or getting someone else to place a bet for him.[15] Similarly, just prior to the annual fair at Wat Benchamabophit in 1903, the Ministry ordered the police to be especially rigorous in preventing monks from gambling during the festivities.[16] These repeated instructions to the police stemmed from the fact that, due to the great respect accorded to the monkhood, officers were loath to arrest miscreant monks. Commenting on the failure of two constables to arrest a monk who was drunk and disorderly in the lottery hall, Commissioner Lawson explained that: 'I think the reverence they feel for the priestly office was the cause of their dereliction of duty'.[17]

However, the damage done to state policy by the gambling habits of some reprobate monks was not nearly as great as that done by the implicit condoning and even active encouragement of the activity by some within the monkhood. The lottery prediction business is a relatively innocuous example of this. As noted in Chapter 2, people would often consult monks for tips on the winning letter of the *huai*. While not all monks were willing to indulge their audiences in such a manner,[18] it would seem that some actively encouraged this in order to increase the number of visitors making donations at their temple. For instance, while visiting a temple in Sampheng around the turn of the twentieth century, the Belgian traveller Charles Buls saw a Buddha's footprint:

> covered with hollow characters. After they [the worshippers] have lighted up some incense sticks, they randomly select the imprint of a character by detaching a piece of paper and thus derive a prediction from this for the lottery with the 36 animals [the *huai*].[19]

Such blatant pandering to people's superstitions suggests a tacit condoning of the lottery and, by extension, of gambling itself.

Nevertheless, this pales in comparison to the presence of gambling activities at temple fairs. Buls described such an event at the temple mentioned above as follows:

> Around this place of pilgrimage are crowded the elements of a fancy fair, especially gambling tables with the most varied games: cards,

dice, lottery numbers, turnstiles, roulette – the complete collection of all imaginable tricks to pluck the idiot possessed by the demon of gambling.[20]

The purpose of these fairs was to raise money for the host temple, often so that repairs to buildings might be carried out.[21] Although gambling at such events had been going on since time immemorial, Kanchana suggests there was a marked increase after the 1902 gambling law came into force.[22] By formalizing the procedure for organizing gambling at religious and secular festivals, this law may have inadvertently encouraged applications for permits. As with the similar, secular events discussed in Chapter 3, only Class 2 gambling was allowed; this was mostly gambling for prizes but, occasionally, gambling for cash was permitted.[23] Perhaps more important, though, was that gambling was allowed at the Wat Benchamabophit fair, held annually from around the turn of the twentieth century. This temple was the most important of those built during the Fifth Reign and had strong associations with the royal family. Its annual fair, which was regularly attended by Chulalongkorn, thus set a benchmark for what was acceptable. Indeed, when gambling at the fair was discontinued in the late 1900s, this was cited as the reason for denying permission for gambling at other temple fairs within the Greater Bangkok area.[24] One of the most significant temple fairs of the 1920s and 1930s, if not before, was that held during November on the site of the great stupa, Phra Pathom Chedi, in the provincial town of Nakhon Pathom. Every year, people from neighbouring provinces and the capital would descend upon the town to indulge in gambling. In 1923, the *Sayam rat* reported how every train from Bangkok to the town was packed but people were quite happy to stand.[25] That year there were over 100 gaming stalls offering all the favourites, such as *hi-lo* and *huai chap yi-ki*. The total rent from these stalls amounted to 57,750 baht, part of which went to the temple and part to the development of public facilities.[26] Needless to say, the presence of gambling at these temple fairs amounted to the Sangha condoning the vice, in direct contravention of Buddhist principles. As the *Bangkok Times* observed in connection with the Nakhon Pathom fair: 'It appears strange that such things should be connected with a Festival of Preaching'.[27] According to a female American missionary who resided in Siam during the late nineteenth century, the monkhood recognized that this was a sin but justified it on the grounds that nobody would come if there were no gaming facilities or other forms of entertainment.[28]

It would be unfair to hold the monkhood solely responsible for this state of affairs. Indeed, in most cases, these events were organized by laypeople, usually government officials and local nobles, on behalf of the temples.[29] But gambling at temple fairs received little or no condemnation from the monkhood and would surely have required the abbot's consent for the temple grounds to be used for such purposes. While one monk at the 1922

Nakhon Pathom fair may have 'waxed indignant and condemned the placing of the tables on the Pagoda premises at all', he seems to have been a lone dissenting voice.[30] To make matters worse, in some cases it was the monks themselves who organized the gaming. This was the case at a temple fair in 1925 in the southern province of Phang Nga where gambling went on for a whole week, 'both in and under priest's houses [sic], there being as many as ten circles going at a time – as many as one would see at the Tapan Lek [gambling] house in Bangkok in the old days'.[31] This was not so much condoning the vice as actively endorsing it and made a mockery of Buddhist precepts and state efforts to restrict it.

The whisper of the silent majority

Attempting to pin down something as nebulous and ephemeral as public opinion in late nineteenth- and early twentieth-century Siam is nigh on impossible. When newspapers claimed that the public was behind a particular initiative or reported the general feelings on a particular topic, it is difficult to know who exactly made up this public or shared these feelings. A conservative assessment would be that the press was really speaking only about and for its readership, namely the Bangkok middle class. In an attempt to gauge the opinions of a broader range of the population, this section draws on a variety of sources, primarily a number of letters and petitions from members of the public to the authorities. Many of these were anonymous and consisted of complaints about, for instance, a local fish-fighting den and the unsavoury characters it attracted or a government official abusing the procedure for issuing gambling permits.[32] These present snapshots into the mind of the writer but in most cases it is unclear who they were and just how representative their views were of the wider population. Apart from these sources, however, the historical record provides scant insight into what the ordinary Siamese person thought. With these problems and limitations in mind, this section will attempt to capture some of the opinions of the predominantly rural Siamese population on gambling and related government policy, and determine what influence the common man had on that policy.

Gambling obviously provoked an array of different views and feelings among the various sections of Siamese society. At one extreme were the professional gamblers and promoters, denizens of the gambling houses before their termination and patrons of the underground dens that sprung up after. For them, gambling was their life and their livelihood. These people appear in the historical record primarily as statistics for gambling convictions. At the other extreme were those people who considered gambling to be an evil that was, at best, retarding Siam's development or, at worst, slowly destroying the country. Such people might have been members of the Anti-Gambling League, which, under the leadership of Prince Damrong, was established around the turn of the twentieth century to press for the abolition of the gambling tax farms. Beyond a few cursory references, there is little information on this organization or its membership, however.[33] But, given its royal connections, it can be surmised that it was an elite movement. Between these two extremes was the bulk of the population, many of whom may have gambled occasionally: playing cards during the Songkran festival, purchasing the odd lottery ticket, or frequenting the gaming stalls at the Winter Fair, for instance. Others might not have gambled but saw little harm in it as long as it was not done to excess. Contemporary Western commentators may have depicted the Siamese as oblivious to the potential harm gambling could cause but, as Hong has shown, this was partly to reinforce 'the essential unfathomable difference' between East and West and to illustrate how Asian subjects subscribed to a different moral code that was impenetrable to the Western mind.[34] This was a strategy for emphasizing Western superiority and says more about the colonial mindset than that of the Thai. For those that had to live with an inveterate gambler, the damaging effects of their pastime – debt, poverty, and theft – were all too apparent. For those with no firsthand experience, the evils of unchecked gambling were conveyed through proverbs and fables. Take the following saying for example:

> If bandits plunder your home, you will have no belongings to use (*Tuk chon phlon, mai mi khong cha chai*).
> If a fire should burn, you will have no house in which to live (*Tuk phai mai, mai mi ruan cha yu*).
> If you lose at *po*, you will have no land on which to live (*Tuk po kin, mai mi phaen-din cha yu*).[35]

In this hierarchy of disasters, gambling is the worst because, unlike the other two, it leaves its victims with nothing at all with which to rebuild their lives.[36] Similarly, in the classical Thai folktale *Khun Chang Khun Phaen*, which dates back perhaps as far as the early sixteenth century, when one of the male protagonists asks for a woman to marry him his associates are questioned by that woman's parents as follows: 'Is he a gambler, a drunkard, a smoker of marijuana or opium?'[37] As Anuman observes, this indicates a deep-seated disapproval for men who indulged in such activities.[38]

Attitudes and opinions on gambling varied depending on the form. As noted in Chapter 2, the *huai* lottery had a much broader appeal than the gambling houses. Indeed, there are some tantalizing hints of public antipathy and opposition towards the latter. While visiting a town near Chiang Mai in the late nineteenth century, Holt Samuel Hallett learnt that tax farmers had been prevented from setting up gambling houses and opium dens 'by common consent'.[39] After all the gambling houses were closed in the southern *monthons* of Nakhon Si Thammarat and Chumphon in 1898, a missionary observed that: 'Regular *nakleng* gamblers are feeling rather sore over it, but the better class of people express great satisfaction and approval of the improvement this has wrought in the life of the people and in their general prosperity'.[40] Similarly, when all the provincial gambling houses were finally closed in 1906, public celebrations, organized by local governors, were staged in several central provinces. These involved religious ceremonies, such as the honouring of Buddha images and the giving of alms to monks, sporting contests, and theatrical performances.[41] Although many people attended and it is tempting to see their attendance as approval for government policy, it should be noted that these celebrations were held during the Songkran festival, a time of year traditionally associated with fun and games, and people may have been lured by the attractions rather than the cause. Nevertheless, these examples suggest there was a background hum of disapproval for the gambling houses.

In contrast, card playing seems to have been universally popular during the first decades of the twentieth century. This popularity may have been due in part to hardcore gamblers taking up different games following the closures of the gambling houses but the widespread passion for cards in particular probably stemmed from its social function. There was even a poem (*nirat*) extolling the joys of playing cards, in which the writer compared different cards to women.[42] Indeed, it has been suggested that the concession under the 1930 law for unlicensed card playing between family and friends, or in private members clubs, was a result of this popularity.[43] So enthusiastically was this taken up that the phrase *pai yat mit*, meaning 'to go [and see] relatives and friends', became slang for 'to play cards'.[44] Attitudes change with time, however. By the mid-1930s, the lack of restraint led to disgust and a public backlash, perhaps best illustrated by a popular song in which a man admonishes his wife, a regular patron of card dens, for neglecting their family, that sold extremely well as a record.[45] Around the same time, the constitutional regime annulled the concession for unlicensed card playing. This indicates how government policy was occasionally in tune with public opinion.

For the most part, however, the stance of the government and the attitudes of the mass population were not in unison. The loudest manifestation of this discord was the cacophony produced by contraventions of, and convictions under, the gambling laws. Throughout the 1920s and 1930s, gambling offences were consistently one of the top three classes of offences in terms of the number of people convicted.[46] Of course, this was but a fraction of the number gambling illegally. Unfortunately, these statistics do not give any indication of the exact nature and circumstances of the offence, or the sentence imposed. Nevertheless, it is reasonable to assume most convictions were for minor infringements of the gambling law committed by ordinary people, some perhaps ignorant of the law, who had the misfortune to be caught gambling illegally in the wrong place and at the wrong time. In support of this assessment, one Western judicial adviser attributed the sharp rise in the number of revenue convictions between 1902/3 and 1903/4 – from 234 to 1,150 – to the implementation of the 1902 gambling law in Bangkok:

> The general license to indulge in gambling with dice and cards granted during the new-year holidays was this year regulated more precisely as to time, and hundreds found themselves in the lock-up for gambling either before the official time had begun or after it expired.[47]

Clearly, people continued to gamble even when it was in contravention of the law, though this was probably due not so much to ignorance or outright defiance as to indifference. Indeed, if the aim of the government's gambling policy was to change people's behaviour by getting them to forgo particular games, then it is fair to say that for the period covered by this study it failed. That certain games continued to be played long after they had been prohibited is one of the clearest indications of this failure. In February 1940, for example, 15 people were arrested for playing *po kam*, some 50 years after that game had been confined to the gambling houses and nearly 25 years after it had been banned.[48] And this was not an isolated incident: underground *huai* lotteries continued to be run into the 1940s, if not longer.[49] The criminalization of certain types of popular gambling created a profound disconnect between the government and the general population as it is clear from the foregoing discussion that many did not see those games as criminal. This was just part of a process in which numerous forms of previously innocent behaviour were subjected to government regulation and proscription. As David Engel has noted:

> The rationality of the 'rationalized' legal system that brings such prohibitions to village society may escape local people. They do not see the total logic of the Thai legal system but only the specific rules that affect them and often contradict their own customary practices.[50]

The prevalence of illegal gambling was, and remains, a prominent example of the contradictions stemming from differences in the normative systems of the Thai government and large sections of the Thai population.

Some of the ruses illegal gamblers used to evade the law have already been discussed in Chapter 5. Perhaps none were more effective than those that sought to exploit these contradictions by targeting those officials charged with detecting and suppressing illegal gambling. As a woman from Bang Chan, a village once on the outskirts of Bangkok, explained in 1953:

> We have always played cards in this part of Bang Chan. [...] If the police came to arrest people, we would pay them or give them food or drink. ... Some police wanted to play cards and made good money gambling. When such a policeman came along, he took off his hat and

held it high on a pole to warn us he was coming, then we could see over the tall grass. People would stop and invite him to come in.[51]

With those state officials who were not so susceptible to bribery, meanwhile, people used other tactics to prevent them from doing their jobs. One commentator who had travelled widely throughout the country asserted that *kamnans* and village headmen were reluctant to arrest illegal gamblers in their localities because those gamblers came from within their own social circle. These grassroots officials feared that if they were to carry out their duties fully, then they might be ostracized from their own communities. Moreover, the commentator highlighted how villagers used malicious gossip and slander to undermine the authority of local officials who put their duty to the state before their perceived responsibility to their communities. He gave the example of a particularly strict *kamnan* in Loei province in the Northeast who arrested people without bias and had consequently been dubbed a jobsworth and ridiculed by local people.[52] This name-calling is a classic example of what James C. Scott has termed 'weapons of the weak', meaning techniques employed by the poor and downtrodden to ensure that those in their communities who are better off and more powerful conform to certain social norms.[53] The use of such tactics to subvert the enforcement of Siam's gambling laws reinforces the argument that those laws were not in accord with the worldview of many Thai people. For them, the gambling laws were an unwelcome and unrealistic imposition of the state.

But while some aspects of government attempts to restrict gambling may have been unpopular, the legitimacy of that policy was rarely openly questioned. One of the few exceptions was in relation to the 1939 prohibition on cockfighting imposed by the Phibun regime. This move provoked written protests from a group of northern farmers, who sent a petition bearing almost 100 signatures to the Ministry of the Interior, and from the MP for the southern province of Nakhon Si Thammarat.[54] Their principal objection to the ban was that cockfighting was a genuine, traditional Thai sport that had gone on since ancient times: its prohibition was thus cast as an attack upon Thai identity. Moreover, they directly challenged the government's arguments in support of the ban. For instance, both parties claimed that cockfighting encouraged agricultural development, rather than hindering it, because fighting cocks were an indigenous Thai breed. Indeed, since the prohibition, the chicken breeding industry had gone into decline. They also contested the claim that this type of gambling caused poverty and idleness, with the farmers stating that they only staged cockfights during the four months of the year following the harvest when there was little work for them to do and even then they had only four fights a month. The government was not swayed by these arguments, however, and the ban remained in place.[55] Presumably, this did not stop people from staging cockfights and, given the fact that they continue to this day, the prohibition eventually fell into abeyance.

Bringing officials to account

As noted in Chapter 6 and Chapter 7, gambling by government officials was a major concern among some sections of the public. From the mid-1910s, there was a steady stream of anonymous letters to the administration accusing certain officials of having gambling problems, running illicit gambling rings, covering up for others involved in such enterprises or neglecting their suppression duties.[56] Sometimes these claims were just part of a longer list of charges of official corruption and abuse.[57] It is not clear in all cases whether the authorities investigated these allegations, though it seems that the constitutional regime took them more seriously than its absolutist predecessor. When there was an investigation, the authorities usually found there was no factual basis for the allegations or, if there were hints of malpractice, not enough evidence for any action to be taken against the accused.[58] Questions could naturally be raised about the rigour and impartiality of the investigators. For instance, in January 1940 the governor of Pathum Thani province was accused of being a hardcore gambler who would compel other officials to play cards illegally. The only step the Ministry of the Interior apparently took was to ask the governor to explain himself. In response he produced a number of letters from various senior provincial officials and the police rebutting the allegations.[59] In some cases, the allegations arose from a misunderstanding on the part of the accuser. In 1940, for example, the deputy governor of Phrae province was accused of quashing a case against five officials who had been arrested for illegal gambling in a social club. The governor's subsequent investigation concluded that there had been no perversion of justice. The officials had merely been playing cards for cigarettes and alcohol; according to the public prosecutor and a judge this was not against the law and thus there was no basis for a criminal case.[60]

On a superficial level, these letters might be seen as indications of public antipathy to gambling or, at the very least, towards gambling by officials, and as indirect expressions of support for the government's restrictionist policy. For some, this certainly seems to have been the case. During the Seventh Reign clampdown on officials engaging in any form of gambling, the wife of a government clerk wrote to the *Lak muang* newspaper listing officials she had seen gambling on billiards. As she explained, she was not doing this for malicious reasons. Rather, her husband had become involved with this betting and had blown his salary; the couple now did not have enough money for food and were in debt.[61] Similarly, some wrote out of apparent concern for the negative effects that the gambling habits of government officials might have on their work and the government's reputation.[62] Others might have had more malign motives, though. By the late 1920s, the public had become aware that the government took a dim view of its officials gambling and that those so accused faced disciplinary action. Some people might thus have made false allegations against particular officials in order to discredit them and undermine the local administration; indeed, this was just the conclusion reached by an investigation into the conduct of the district chief of Damnoen Saduak and his wife, who had allegedly won on an underground *huai* lottery.[63] Similarly, the governor of Pathum Thani referred to above concluded that claims of him being an inveterate gambler had been cooked up by illegal gamblers in retaliation for the hard-line stance he had taken in suppressing their activities.[64] In this milieu of accusations and counterclaims it is difficult to determine who was telling the truth. What is clear, however, is that common people realized that they could use the government's anti-gambling policy and legislation for their own ends, to sully the reputations of local officials and possibly cause them to be removed from office or transferred.[65] The gambling laws and government policy enabled people to turn the tables on officials and bring them to account for their behaviour. Their willingness to do so raises questions about Thai attitudes towards authority that deserve more detailed examination.

One of the old axioms of Thai studies is that Thai people have traditionally shown respect and deference to government officials because they are representatives of the king and, as such, benevolent sources of protection.[66] However, the fact that so many tried to discredit officials through anonymous accusations suggests that this deference stemmed more from fear of their arbitrary power than actual respect for them. This observation tallies with some made by Engel in his study of lawsuits brought against government officials by villagers in the 1970s. Engel highlights how the courts provided a legal mechanism for ordinary Thai people to make officials accountable for abuses of power or other misdeeds, with 'the latent potential to act as social equalizers' and 'to place officials and villagers on an approximately equal footing'.[67] What the cases discussed above indicate, however, is that this search for such mechanisms of accountability goes back at least to the late 1930s, and that people saw the government's anti-gambling policy to be effective in this regard.

What should be clear from this chapter is that there was a deep-set ambivalence to gambling within both the day-to-day practice of Thai Buddhism and, more generally, Thai society as a whole. In spite of religious and secular injunctions against indulging in the vice, the Buddhist monkhood and the general public took a more practical approach to gambling, treating it as an indissoluble part of human nature that might be used to advance institutional or individual goals. Indeed, like successive Thai governments, the mass population may have considered gambling to be a crime only when it suited their interests: a little light gambling on cards between family and friends was perfectly acceptable but for government officials against whom they might hold a grudge it was not. Overall, the practicality of the monkhood towards gambling, represented most blatantly through the gaming stalls at temple fairs, contradicted and undermined the government's anti-gambling policy. More significantly, the general public exerted a subtle, indirect influence over government policy: people's ingenuity in avoiding legal restrictions on gambling and subverting those officials charged with upholding the law ensured that the government was constantly having to adapt its policies to suit the changing tastes and techniques of Thai society.

9 The criminalization of vice
Gambling policy in comparative perspective

Besides gambling, there were several other social problems that plagued Siam in the period under study, the two most prominent being opium use and prostitution.[1] Just as with gambling, the socio-economic changes the kingdom underwent in the nineteenth and early twentieth centuries led to a significant increase in opium consumption and commercial prostitution in Bangkok and, to a lesser extent, in the provinces. The Thai government subsequently took measures to control and limit the growth of these two phenomena, embarking upon a criminalization process similar to that of gambling: from taxation and limited control under the respective tax farms to increasing regulation and administration by the state itself, eventually concluding in prohibition. This chapter will tease out these comparisons in greater depth in an attempt to weigh the importance of the various political, economic and socio-cultural factors that determined government policies. These include the extent to which the Thai state depended on the taxation of each vice for revenue and the degree to which they were perceived to be Chinese problems. Perhaps the most obvious difference is that of timing: while gambling was more or less criminalized by 1945, opium and prostitution were not prohibited until 1959 and 1960 respectively. Moreover, prostitution was effectively re-legalized in 1966 through a semantic sleight-of-hand. This raises interesting questions about the priorities of the Thai elite in regard to these three social problems. The core argument of this chapter is that the government was more concerned about gambling than either opium use or prostitution, and that this prioritization was dictated in large measure by who was adversely affected by each of these vices.

Opium and prostitution in nineteenth-century Siam

Both opium and prostitution were features of Thai society long before the Bangkok era. Opium was probably introduced by the Chinese in the thirteenth century and its use in Ayutthaya was prohibited as far back as the fourteenth century for a variety of reasons, not least of all because it diminished the labouring and fighting capacity of Thai commoners.[2]

In contrast, prostitution was tolerated and taxed by the Thai state from the seventeenth century onwards. Most prostitutes were slaves who were confined to state-licensed brothels under the control of a bond master (*nai ngoen*). Some of these brothels were located near the port in Ayutthaya and catered to foreigners, particularly Chinese traders.[3] There were also special brothels reserved for elite men, in which they were served by noblewomen, including former consorts of the king, who had been forced into prostitution as punishment for sexual transgressions.[4] These differing approaches to managing opium and prostitution persisted into the nineteenth century. The prohibition on opium was reiterated in a series of laws, starting with the Three Seals Law Code of 1805. Rama III even managed to get Britain and the US to recognize the ban on imports in their respective treaties of 1826 and 1832. Following the promulgation of the last law in 1839, he launched a sustained military campaign against the Chinese secret societies involved in the illicit trade, burning a large quantity of seized opium in front of the royal palace. The same year a British envoy to Siam noted the almost prison-like structure of a Bangkok brothel:

> A few paces off the main street was a cage for some public women, with a row of twelve or fourteen small rooms, perhaps 6 feet by 4, opening in to a common verandah of about 4 feet wide and perhaps 6 feet high, closed in front with bars like the cage of some wild beast.[5]

That running a brothel was an accepted way of making money is underlined by the following comment by the wife of a brothel owner from the mid-nineteenth century:

> My husband has run a brothel for twenty-five years. Presently we have sixteen female slaves working for us. ... Both of us agree that there is no better form of business than obtaining beautiful young [slave] girls and having them work as prostitutes. They can earn you a living in the most comfortable way.[6]

Scholars have pointed to numerous socio-cultural factors in order to explain the prevalence and tolerance of prostitution in Thai society but the root causes were clearly the sexual double standard and the inferior status of women.[7] On the one hand, respectable women were expected to be pure and chaste, while on the other, notions of political power and masculinity being linked to sexual prowess ensured that men were allowed free sexual licence. As in many countries, the solution to this contradiction was prostitution. In the Thai context, Barmé highlights the contrasting terms for the loss of female and male virginity: whereas a woman's initial experience of sexual intercourse was referred to by the expression *sia tua*, which translates literally as 'spoiled body', a man was said to *khun khru*, which might be translated as 'getting on the teacher'. As Barmé notes, this implies that a man's first such sexual encounter was likely to be with an experienced practitioner, namely, a prostitute.[8] Moreover, Phraya Anuman used the term 'service institution' to describe the bathhouse-cum-brothel to which he was taken at a young age for a bath in order to emphasize how the sex industry was 'an essential and indispensable part of life' in Thai society.[9] Turning to the second factor, much attention has been paid to delineating the status of women in traditional Thai society and explaining the reasons for their inferior position to men.[10] What is clear is that women were subjugated to men in law: under the Three Seals Law Code a woman was literally 'owned' by her parents or, after marriage, her husband, the most graphic illustration of which was their right to sell her into slavery without her consent as if she were 'a water buffalo'.[11] The sexual double standard was also manifested in the law since it enabled men to have more than one wife, while restricting women to just the one husband. Moreover, the penalties for sexual offences such as adultery were greater for women than for men, and even included the death penalty in certain instances. Lastly, the Three Seals Law Code equated an adulterous woman with a prostitute, the specification of which as a distinct legal category effectively formalized prostitution.[12] Besides the potential to be sold as a slave or coerced into prostitution, the legal position of women also made them vulnerable to abandonment by their husbands, a situation in which they might then have resorted to prostitution to make ends meet.

During the nineteenth century there was a steady increase in both opium consumption and prostitution resulting from the growing imperial presence of the West in South-East Asia and the attendant socio-economic changes detailed in Chapter 1. As Carl Trocki has shown, the opium trade was instrumental in, firstly, funding the expansion of the British and other European empires in the region, and, secondly, in laying the foundations of the global capitalist structure through the creation of indigenous capitalist groups, particularly Chinese ones, and consumers.[13] In open defiance of the ban on importing opium, Western and Chinese merchants smuggled the drug into Siam, often in connivance with state officials. If they were caught, the governor of Singapore might voice his disapproval, resulting in the release of the merchants and their goods as the Thai elite sought to avoid a confrontation with the British.[14] Some of this opium was consumed by Thais, particularly members of the nobility.[15] But by far the largest market for the drug was the growing number of Chinese immigrants who came to work as coolies in the capital, on the plantations of the Central Plains or in the mines of the South. Some had acquired their habit back home in China, while others took it up after their arrival.[16] This sudden influx of large numbers of single, young Chinese men also created a demand for prostitution. It is no coincidence that in mid-nineteenth century Bangkok most of the brothels were concentrated in the Chinese district of Sampheng; the connection between the two is underscored by the fact that prostitutes were commonly called 'Sampheng women'.[17] This concentration persisted into the twentieth century: in May 1909, three-quarters of all the registered prostitutes in Bangkok were located in Sampheng.[18] As for the prostitutes themselves, the majority in the nineteenth century were local Thai women, who might nevertheless have changed their names to something Chinese in order to make themselves more appealing to their clientele.[19] Furthermore, the disruption caused by the emergence of a monetized market economy and the concomitant breakdown of the traditional labour system created a growing supply of potential prostitutes. People's need for cash to pay taxes and buy essentials they had previously made themselves might have induced them to sell their children and wives as slaves, who might later have ended up in a brothel. The gradual phasing out of slavery in the late nineteenth and early twentieth centuries did little to arrest this, however, since it merely removed a traditional safety net against destitution. Employment opportunities for women were severely limited in the new market economy and many may have had no better option than resorting to prostitution to feed themselves and their families. Others might have been tricked or coerced into indentured prostitution by brothel owners looking for replacements for their former slaves which they had had to release.[20]

By the mid-nineteenth century it had become clear to a new generation of the Thai elite that the government's attempts to suppress the smuggling of opium had failed. Moreover, the profits from trafficking had strengthened the Chinese secret societies and nurtured corruption among government officials.[21] Seeking an accommodation with the British and well aware that their insistence on free trade really meant the opium trade, Mongkut lifted the prohibition and established a tax farm on opium shortly after coming to the throne in 1851. While recognizing the harmful effects of the drug, he justified its legalization as follows:

> Although the former great kings have proclaimed the law forbidding opium for many reigns, it appears that the number of those who buy, sell, and smoke opium has not decreased. Thai and Chinese subjects who smoke and consume opium have greatly increased with every reign until opium spreads throughout the country. Thai and Chinese who buy and sell opium have smuggled money out of the country to buy opium to such an extent that money in the country has decreased every year.[22]

To prevent this currency flight, the government introduced a number of restrictions on how and from whom the opium farmers could purchase their supplies. Although these regulations were subsequently rendered void by the terms of the Bowring Treaty and the others concluded in its wake, British and other Western merchants could still only sell their opium to the tax farmer.[23] What is particularly interesting, though, is how opium, like gambling, was perceived to be first and foremost a Chinese problem. As Mongkut's explanation of his policy makes clear: 'those who clandestinely buy, sell and smoke opium are among the Chinese more than any other language group'.[24] Consequently, the government tried to confine opium use to the Chinese by prohibiting Thais and other local ethnic groups such as the Mon and the Khmer from purchasing or consuming it. Existing addicts were required to become 'Chinese', meaning they had to wear their hair in a Chinese-style pigtail and pay the triennial poll tax, though at a much higher rate than ethnic Chinese.[25] Failure to comply entailed the death penalty. Nevertheless, increasing numbers of Thai people began to smoke opium and even monks took up the habit, with the prohibition eventually falling into abeyance.[26] Revenue from the opium farms grew from 160,000 baht a year at the start of Mongkut's reign to 573,200 baht by its end.[27] This suggests a sharp rise in consumption but it is not clear to what extent it was due to the creation of new addicts or existing addicts smoking more.

The Fourth Reign also witnessed a subtle shift in attitudes towards women. Shortly before his death in 1868, Mongkut received a petition from a woman who had been sold into slavery by her husband against her will, leading him to decide that the current law was unjust. He thus decreed that henceforth a wife's consent was required for her sale to be valid. Moreover, Mongkut was particularly sensitive to the criticisms of polygamy by Western envoys and missionaries, taking a number of measures to deflect such attacks that included allowing the women of the Inner Palace to resign from royal service if they were unhappy with their lot.[28] But the criticisms of Westerners also provoked a defensive reaction from the Thai elite, with a member of the Bunnag family writing a defence of polygamy from the standpoint of Buddhism in which he claimed that having many wives ensured that a man need not force any to have sex with him against their will, thereby losing merit.[29] As Leslie Ann Jeffrey highlights, these debates over polygamy set the stage for the later struggles between the West and Siam over prostitution policy, with the male sexual prerogative as enshrined in polygamy becoming an issue of national identity.[30] Mongkut also undertook some reforms of the brothel system that prohibited people from forcing women into prostitution and limited some of the abuses perpetrated by brothel keepers to prevent their slaves from escaping servitude. Furthermore, the tax levied on brothels in the capital was remodelled as the Road Maintenance Tax and farmed out. This tax derived its name from the fact that any brothel keepers that violated these new regulations were required to provide the state with a specified amount of sand that would then be used to fill in roads.[31] Despite the slight improvements in the conditions of prostitutes, Dararat views the Road Maintenance Tax as primarily a revenue raising measure.[32] However, this tax on prostitution was never a significant item of state revenue: between 1890/1 and 1907/8, the last year in which it was collected, income from this source fluctuated between roughly 10,000 and 25,000 baht a year, a fraction of that from gambling and opium.[33]

154 *The criminalization of vice*

The growth in opium consumption and commercial prostitution continued into the late nineteenth century. In 1883, the postal directory for Bangkok listed over 250 opium dens and 27 brothels in the capital and its surrounds, though these figures probably do not record the more numerous smaller, temporary establishments.[34] Some of these brothels were little more than wooden huts catering to labourers, while others were well-furnished bordellos servicing high-class Thais and wealthy Chinese. There were also clubs and dancehalls where male members of the growing Western and Japanese communities might find a partner for the evening.[35] From the 1890s onwards, the growing ranks of the salaried bureaucracy and the gradual extension of the rail network throughout the country gave further impetus to the development of prostitution: increasing demand in the case of the former and providing new sources of recruits, willing or otherwise, in regard to the latter.[36] An increase in the number of brothels upcountry, meanwhile, is indicated by the levying of the Road Maintenance Tax in the provinces of the eastern seaboard and Phuket, where the large number of Chinese miners and the booming local economy fed the development of the sex industry.[37] These same factors also ensured that the Phuket opium farm accounted for around ten per cent of the total opium revenues for the kingdom in the early 1890s, the second highest contribution after Bangkok.[38] Opium was not just confined to areas of Chinese concentration, however; Aymonier reports its consumption throughout the Northeast in the 1880s, for example.[39] By the end of the nineteenth century, the receipts from the opium farms were the second most important item of state income after the various gambling farms, providing around 15 per cent of total revenue.[40] However, while this expansion in revenues was crucial in funding Chulalongkorn's reforms of the Thai state, the explosion in vice that it reflected was a matter of some concern for the government.

Regulating vice

As in the case of gambling, the Thai elite identified opium and prostitution as social evils that ruined people and imperilled the country. At a ministerial meeting on opium policy in 1908, for instance, Damrong warned that: 'If we let people smoke freely, it will affect the foundations and strength of the country until we will no longer be able to maintain our independence'.[41] Again like gambling, opium and prostitution were also cited as prime causes of crime, especially robbery, theft, assault and even murder. At the meeting of *monthon* commissioners for the year 1912/13, for instance, the commissioner of Ratchaburi reported that increasing numbers of young people in the town of Kanchanaburi were taking to opium, including some as young as seven years old. Many of these youths were implicated in cases of cattle rustling and burglary.[42] Besides theft, cravings for opium often made users violent: in 1896, for example, the owner of an opium den in Ayutthaya killed an addict who had gone into a frenzy and attacked him when he was refused credit.[43] Violence was also endemic in the sex industry, not all of it directed against prostitutes. Customers might fight among themselves over a particular woman, while others might be beaten and robbed by prostitutes and their pimps.[44] Here it should be noted that it was the women involved in prostitution, rather than the men, who bore the malice and the blame for the problems arising from it, as signified by the fact that one common term for prostitute was *phu-ying khon chua*, which literally means 'bad woman'.[45]

Besides concerns about crime, prostitution was also a public health issue. In the early twentieth century, if not before, venereal disease was rampant in Bangkok and other large urban centres. Barmé provides statistics showing that between 60 and 80 per cent of the male population had VD in the 1914 to 1920 period, while at least 90 per cent of prostitutes were claimed to be infected in 1927.[46] This was predominantly an urban phenomenon, however. Indeed, the government-sponsored rural economic survey of 1930–31 found that there was hardly any venereal disease outside the market centres.[47] Nevertheless, the threat of infection and the attached social stigma loomed large in the public mind. Anuman recalls a number of acquaintances contracting VD and dying at a young age, one committing suicide because he could not bear the shame of telling his parents.[48] Concerns about prostitution thus tended to focus on the prostitute as a carrier and cause of venereal disease; as Barmé observes, prostitutes were also called *tua kamarok*, meaning VD bodies: 'a derogatory expression which implied that women alone were responsible for making men ill'.[49] Significantly, this was made explicit in the preamble of the Venereal Disease Prevention Act of 1908:

> Some girls [prostitutes] have venereal disease that they might then pass on to the men that associate with them. If no doctors check or treat venereal disease then it will spread until it imperils the health and life of people greatly. Since there are no laws to guard against this at present, His Majesty has graciously decided to enact this legislation.[50]

The promulgation of this law was the end result of a lengthy discussion within the Thai government about how to bring the brothel industry under a greater degree of control. The Road Maintenance Tax was abolished and the government assumed direct responsibility for the licensing, taxing and regulating of prostitution in Bangkok.[51] All brothels and prostitutes were required to register with the Department of Public Health and pay a quarterly registration fee. Additionally, brothel keepers had to hang green lanterns bearing the registration number outside their premises and were prohibited from employing girls under the age of 15 as prostitutes. In order to limit the spread of venereal disease, brothel workers were required to have regular medical check-ups. If there was any indication of

VD, then the prostitute's licence was revoked until she could prove she was cured. This provision was not rigorously enforced, however, and many prostitutes refused to submit to examinations. Overall, despite instituting some additional protections against exploitation and abuse, scholars agree that there is a noticeable lack of concern for the prostitutes themselves. Indeed, the Act had no provisions for helping women escape from prostitution and the registration fees, amounting to 48 baht a year and a considerably greater tax burden than that levied on the majority of the population, 'represented a marked form of exploitation of women by the state'.[52] As Dararat and Jeffrey both claim, the underlying purpose of the law was to protect men from infection by prostitutes.[53] Given the above figures for the incidence of VD in the 1910s and 1920s, it would seem that the Act failed in this respect.

The Thai government also brought the sale of opium under its control in the first decade of the twentieth century. During the 1890s and early 1900s, the government had implemented a number of reforms in the opium farming system, most importantly experimenting with different configurations of the territory covered by the various farms in an attempt to discourage smuggling from one area to another.[54] These arrangements worked to the advantage of both the government, which enjoyed greater revenues, and the opium farmers, who benefitted from improved control and efficiency. As the profits from opium farming grew, however, so did the competition for the consolidated regional monopolies. In 1907, the farming syndicate that held the combined monopoly for the central region and the North collapsed due to the machinations of a rival group. The government had been considering taking over the administration of the opium monopoly itself but had been waiting to train its officials. Its hand was now forced.[55] Chulalongkorn justified the establishment of the government monopoly by claiming it was the first step toward the complete elimination of opium in Siam:

> Prohibiting the smoking of opium is difficult for a number of reasons. Firstly, the proceeds of the kingdom will fall considerably. Secondly, there is the question of how to get those who are already addicted to quit: should they be forced to stop immediately or when it suits them? Regardless, they'll still be actively looking to smoke illicit opium. If the government is unable to prevent the sale of illicit opium effectively, trying to prohibit people from smoking opium will be a waste of the kingdom's money[...] Prohibiting the smoking of opium has not been entirely successful in any country in the world. Nevertheless, it is not appropriate that our subjects should fall into the evils of opium use. After careful consideration, it was decided to reform the opium monopoly so that the number of smokers, and the state's revenue from the monopoly, might be gradually reduced until opium use is eventually eliminated.[56]

As this statement makes clear, financial considerations were one of the key determinants of government opium policy. Indeed, the closure of the provincial gambling houses in the mid-1900s had made the government even more dependent upon opium receipts. Under government administration, revenue from the monopoly grew dramatically, from just under 10 million baht in 1907/8 to an all-time high of just over 23 million baht in 1919/20. This accounted for between 20 and 25 per cent of the government's total income.[57] Suphaphon identifies two factors behind this increase. First, by eliminating one level of middlemen, namely the tax farmers, the government ensured it received a greater percentage of the profits from opium sales. Second, the government was better equipped for combating smuggling. An important innovation in the 1910s was the packaging of opium for retail in collapsible lead tubes bearing a government stamp and sealed by a machine. This made it easier to identify contraband opium as smugglers did not have access to the same machinery and the tubes were destroyed once used. It also prevented retailers from adulterating government opium.[58] As opium revenues grew, however, so too did government expenditure and it became increasingly difficult for the government to find alternative sources. This dependence was magnified by the abolition of the gambling houses and the *huai* lottery in the early twentieth century. Additionally, the financial problems that beset the government following the First World War made opium revenues even more critical.[59] There was nothing unusual in this 'addiction' to opium revenue, however. Indeed, the government monopoly was modelled on those in French Indochina and the Netherlands East Indies. Despite international commitments to reducing opium consumption, opium revenue remained a financial mainstay of the South-East Asian colonial states, with the exception of the Philippines under the US where opium was prohibited, until the Second World War.[60] Naturally, this lent further legitimacy to the Thai state's monopoly.

In contrast to those on gambling and opium, the government's prostitution policy was not dictated by financial necessity. In 1908/9, the first year of registration, the government collected about 40,000 baht in fees from registered brothels and prostitutes.[61] Over a decade later, this amount remained the same and was but a trifle compared to the millions brought in by opium.[62] A common factor in determining policy to all three vices, however, was the evasion of regulations or, to put it another way, the impossibility of prohibition. The most noticeable effect of the Venereal Disease Prevention Act was to drive prostitutes out of the registered brothels and into establishments such as opium dens and teahouses, which were little more than fronts for prostitution, or onto the streets, as they sought to avoid the embarrassment of submitting to VD checks and paying the registration fee. Moreover, before the law was implemented in the provinces in 1913, many prostitutes from Bangkok chose to relocate upcountry. While the number of registered prostitutes declined in the 1920s, the illicit sex trade boomed.[63] Similarly, stricter government controls on opium combined with an increase in its price and a decrease in the number of licensed dens meant many addicts turned to alternatives such as morphine or started smoking the dross from opium pipes instead.[64] Consequently, the government issued a number of laws forbidding the unlicensed importation, sale and possession of opium-based medicines and derivatives, along with other drugs such as cocaine, in the first three decades of the twentieth century.[65] By far the greatest threat to government control efforts, however, was the thriving trade in illicit opium. Some of this contraband came from the mountains of the North where ethnic minority hill tribes cultivated poppies and produced opium mainly for their own consumption, though most of it was smuggled across the country's land and sea borders. The main sources of this opium were the southern Chinese province of Yunnan, where production boomed in the chaos unleashed by the 1911 Republican Revolution, and the Shan States, where the British exerted little control over the Shan *sawbwas* (local chiefs) who received a large proportion of the hill-tribes' harvest as tribute.[66] In the mid-1920s, the Thai government tried to check this smuggling of contraband by reopening a number of opium dens in rural areas in order to encourage licit consumption.[67] Nevertheless, the transnational nature of the illicit opium trade meant that such measures would have little impact unless other countries adopted similar control policies.

During the early twentieth century there was also a significant change in the Bangkok sex trade as a growing number of women trafficked from China appeared in the city's brothels. Although there was a greater number of registered Thai brothels compared to Chinese ones in 1908/9, there were more registered Chinese prostitutes than Thai, with highs of 389 registered in the case of the former and 260 for the latter.[68] By the mid-1920s, this Chinese dimension to prostitution had become more pronounced. In 1925/6, there were as many as 155 registered Chinese brothels with over 700 Chinese prostitutes compared to a maximum of 18 Thai brothels and less than 100 Thai prostitutes.[69] This shift was observed by Anuman, who noted how Chinese women were more popular than those of other ethnic groups.[70] Indeed, this was just part of a region-wide phenomenon that saw increasing numbers of Chinese women and girls trafficked by ship from Hong Kong or Canton to meet the demand of Chinese male labourers in Siam and its colonized South-East Asian neighbours. Some of these women and girls were kidnapped and physically coerced into prostitution, while others were duped by promises of work or marriage. During this period, Bangkok emerged as a transit point for this trafficking, with Chinese women and also some Thais then being sent on to Singapore and British Malaya by train. This development drew much criticism from the local Thai press, which was concerned about how it was affecting the country's reputation, and the Singaporean government.[71] It also placed Siam firmly in the sights of the League of Nations and its attempts to control the international trafficking of women and children.

The international dimension and Thai prestige

The key difference between the Thai government's policies on opium and prostitution compared to those on gambling was that the former were shaped to a much larger degree by the need to conform to international norms. Although the Thai state's reliance on gambling for revenue may have drawn some criticism from Western missionaries and envoys, this never translated into concrete efforts on their part to force the government to abolish the gambling tax farms. In contrast, the transnational natures of the opium trade and – through its close links to human trafficking – prostitution meant that the success of control measures in any one country was dependent upon the cooperation of others. This necessitated, first, the building of some degree of international consensus on these issues and then commitments on the part of individual countries to implement common measures to deal with them. It also made the creation of an international body that might act as a forum for discussion and as a means of encouraging compliance an imperative.

From the mid-nineteenth century on, there was growing concern in Europe and the US about the use of opium and its effects as the practice of smoking opium, rather than ingesting it in some form as it had been commonly used, spread beyond Chinese immigrant communities. Missionaries also began to raise awareness about the impact of the opium trade upon China, leading to calls for it to be curbed. By the start of the twentieth century, these fears had been translated into domestic legislation that restricted and in some cases prohibited opium use.[72] Over the same period, prostitution in Asia became an issue as panic was whipped up about Western women being forced into sexual servitude by 'wicked Oriental' traffickers in what was called the 'white slave trade'. European governments held a number of conferences on human trafficking around the turn of the twentieth century, which led, first, to the establishment of an International Bureau for the Suppression of Traffic in Women and Children in 1899 and then the International Agreement for the Suppression of the White Slave Traffic in 1904. This treaty was followed in 1910 by a convention bearing the same name whereby the participating European states made the procurement of women for prostitution a criminal offence, regardless of whether those women gave their consent. As Jeffrey highlights, these initiatives reflected the prevailing Western assumptions about correct gender roles and cast the prostitute as a victim. Thus, when the West sought to ensure the adherence of non-Western countries to these and subsequent agreements, it was 'seeking not to impose a more equitable gender arrangement but, rather, a gender code that reflected Western understandings of civilized gender roles'.[73] Accordingly, prostitution, and the related issue of polygamy, became a source of friction between the West and the Thai elite, who might challenge these notions in the name of preserving Thai identity.

The growing spirit of international cooperation on human trafficking encouraged similar initiatives for controlling the drugs trade, with the main impetus coming from the US. Its decision to ban opium in the Philippines in 1908 meant the United States was dependent on the cooperation of other countries and gave it a powerful incentive to establish a regional control regime.[74] The US and Britain were also concerned about the destabilizing effect the drug was having upon China.[75] Consequently, the British concluded a treaty with the Chinese in 1906 whereby they agreed to progressively reduce exports of Indian opium. The significance of this cannot be understated for as Trocki notes: 'So long as the British government profited from and perpetuated the opium industry, there could be no stopping it'.[76] For its part, the Chinese government committed itself to the elimination of domestic opium production within ten years. Following American suggestions, the first international conference on opium control was held in Shanghai in 1909 with several European countries and Persia, China, Japan and Siam participating alongside the US. Nothing concrete emerged from this meeting but it did serve to raise international awareness. Subsequent US pressure for a binding international agreement on opium then led to the Hague Opium Conference, again attended by Siam, in 1911 and the resulting convention of 1912. This agreement reflected the mixed agendas of the participants: committing its signatories to the eventual eradication of opium through programmes of gradual suppression but also acknowledging state opium monopolies as an effective control mechanism. Moreover, it required near universal ratification, a process that was delayed by the outbreak of the First World War. Nevertheless, Siam ratified the convention in 1914.[77]

The turmoil and destruction of the First World War served to reaffirm the desire for international cooperation and led to the formal establishment of the League of Nations in 1920, with Siam as one of the founding members.[78] By joining the war on the side of the Allies, Siam had also earned the right to sit at the negotiating table in Versailles and gained the US's commitment to helping it regain its full fiscal and judicial sovereignty. Under the terms of the Versailles Peace Treaty, ratification of the 1912 Hague Opium Convention was mandatory for all parties and the task of supervising compliance with this and future control efforts was entrusted to the League. The Thai elite had been especially anxious about securing a place in the new international organization, seeing it as a means of affirming Siam's position as a sovereign state, and they remained committed to the organization and its goals throughout the 1920s and the first half of the 1930s.[79] Indeed, Stefan Hell argues that membership of the League was at the core of Siam's foreign policy during this period, summarizing its importance as follows:

> League membership was a means for Siam to regain its full sovereignty and fiscal autonomy during the early 1920s, a means to maintain and strengthen this autonomy during the later 1920s and the subsequent decade, an important tool to modernise the country in different areas of society, and a key element in enabling the Thai elite

to demonstrate and reinforce its modernity or progressiveness domestically and internationally.[80]

Membership of the League thus served to legitimize the rule of the absolute monarchy and, post-1932, the constitutional regime both symbolically, as it demonstrated that Siam was now recognized as a bona fide member of the international community, and materially, as involvement in such League programmes as public health improved the lot of the population.[81] But membership had a price: Siam had to adhere to certain international norms and ensure it fulfilled its international obligations. Consequently, the League had a direct impact on the country's opium and prostitution policies. In the early 1920s, the Sixth Reign government turned this to its advantage, however, as it was able to press for the revision of the unequal treaties by claiming that they prevented it from meeting its international commitments.[82] For instance, the Opium Act B. E. 2464, promulgated in 1921 to meet Siam's obligations under the 1912 Hague Convention, had a provision for the registration of all opium smokers, which was to be implemented at a later date.[83] This was expected to lead to a decrease in opium consumption because casual smokers would not wish to register and, consequently, it would impact heavily upon opium revenue. As the Financial Adviser noted:

> It is not likely, however, that this step [registration] will be taken until Siam attains complete fiscal autonomy, and is free to revise her tariffs with a view to obtaining additional revenue from other sources. In the meantime, she has the satisfaction of knowing that she is complying strictly with the terms of her international obligations, and that the new Opium Law provides for machinery for the efficient control of the opium régie within her borders.[84]

Similarly, when the League sent out questionnaires enquiring about the legislation its member states had in place for combating human trafficking, the Thai government replied that:

> With regard to the rest of the questionnaire, H. M.'s Government is contemplating new legislation on the subject; but, owing to the fact that at the present moment the treaties with foreign powers, with the exception of the United States of America, have not yet been revised, the putting into force of such legislation will be acquired with much difficulty.[85]

As may be recalled from Chapter 3, the Thai government had tried to use its scheme for abolishing the gambling houses in the mid-1900s in a similar manner but had failed. Now, with the weight of international commitments behind it, the government was much more successful, with revisions to the fiscal provisions of the various agreements with all the treaty powers being completed by the mid-1920s.

Beside the aforementioned opium law, the Thai government issued a series of other laws on human trafficking, immigration and narcotics that were all the direct result of the international treaties it had signed on these issues.[86] In 1921, for example, Siam attended the League's Conference on the Suppression of the Traffic in Women and Children in Geneva and signed the resulting convention, which aimed at improving immigration procedures in order to limit trafficking. As a result of this agreement, the government issued, first, the Immigration Act B. E. 2470 in 1927 and then the Trafficking of Women and Children Act B. E. 2471 the following year. Both these laws were designed primarily to stem the influx of Chinese women, which had increased significantly in the 1920s.[87] However, while the Thai elite seem to have shared the League's commitment to opium control, and the belief that gradual suppression rather than immediate prohibition was the best means, doubts must be cast on their commitment to restricting human trafficking. Indeed, according to Hell, Siam only attended the 1921 trafficking conference because China and Japan did so and signed the convention for international recognition rather than for domestic purposes.[88] Moreover, he goes on to highlight how the Thai elite showed little interest in the issue in the early 1920s, with the Thai delegate in Geneva, Prince Charoon, informing Prince Devawongse ahead of the conference that: 'I know there are the cases in Siam of Chinese girls brought in from China but I am not aware of circumstances'.[89] Although Hell claims that the League's efforts succeeded in creating awareness about the extent of the trafficking problem, the subsequent course of government policy on the matter displays a singular lack of genuine concern.[90] For instance, the Seventh Reign government refused to cover the expenses of the visit of the League's Commission of Enquiry on Trafficking in Women and Children to Siam in 1930, in sharp contrast to the financial support it gave to the League's other commissions and the red carpet treatment it afforded that on opium in 1929, in particular.[91] Even here in the realm of opium policy, however, there are suggestions that the government enacted legislation because it felt it had to rather than because it wanted to. As Hell highlights once more, the Opium Act B. E. 2472, which provided for a system of licensing and registering dross addicts, was enacted in 1929 just ahead of the commission's visit so that the government might show it had complied with the agreements it signed at the opium conferences in Geneva in the winter of 1924–25.[92] To be fair to the Thai government it was the forerunner in East Asia in adopting certain opium control measures such as confining the smoking of opium to state-run or licensed establishments and its system for returning all dross to the government, drawing praise for these pioneering initiatives in the commission's report.[93] Overall, though, it is hard to shake the impression that the Thai government was more committed to membership of the League, and the material and symbolic benefits it brought, than to the actual causes of restricting opium and human trafficking. It is in this light that the Seventh Reign government's invitation to the League to hold its 1931 opium conference in Bangkok should be read. Indeed, as Prince Traidos Prabandh Devakul, son of Prince Devawongse and his successor as Minister of Foreign Affairs, explained to the king, this was a 'unique chance to glorify Siam'.[94] Similarly, the League's acceptance was hailed by Prajadhipok as 'a signal honour conferred on Siam'.[95] This was a real coup for the Thai elite as it was the first time the country hosted an international meeting of this kind, with all the East Asian major powers, except China, attending and the US sending an observer. In practical terms, the conference achieved few far-reaching commitments, with the prevailing opinion being that individual governments could not enforce domestic opium regulations effectively until smuggling was curbed. From the point of view of the Thai elite, however, the conference was a success in raising the profile and changing Western perceptions of Siam for the better.

Nevertheless, the foregoing discussion should not be taken to mean that the Thai government unquestioningly implemented all the requirements of the League and attendant treaties. For example, the scheme for the registration of opium smokers outlined in the 1921 law was never implemented in the League's lifetime; initially, because the Sixth Reign government could not afford the anticipated drop in revenue and, from the late 1920s on, because smuggling reached such heights that the scheme would have proven ineffective. As the Financial Adviser James Baxter concluded in the 1934/5 budget report:

> Until the contraband trade can be effectively dealt with, the Government is not disposed to introduce a system of licensing and registration since this would result in an extension of the illicit traffic to the advantage of the smuggler and to the detriment of the fisc, without there being any reason to believe that the consumption of opium was thereby diminished. The suppression of the contraband trade which goes on mainly over the north and north-eastern frontiers, will become progressively more difficult as Siam's internal communications develop.[96]

Whereas the amount of contraband opium, about 1.5 metric tons, seized by the Thai authorities in 1925/6 represented only 2.6 per cent of total government sales, the seizure of approximately 4.5 tons in 1936/7 accounted for 16 per cent. This was thought to be just a small proportion of the total illicit traffic, with the actual quantity of contraband in the country perhaps equalling the amount sold by the government.[97] Concomitantly, revenue from the opium monopoly dropped to under 10 million baht by the mid-1930s, representing less then 10 per cent of total revenues compared to the 20 per cent and more it had in the early 1920s.[98] Ironically, it was the very control measures advocated by the League and adopted in Siam and elsewhere in Asia that fed the growth of the illicit opium trade.[99] Consequently, in the mid-1930s, the constitutional government decided to reduce the price of monopoly opium and reopen opium dens in order to weaken the attraction of contraband.[100] A global decline in opium production during the 1930s, meanwhile, meant the constitutional government had to find new sources of opium, initially relying heavily on its seizures of contraband.[101] In 1938, the government moved further away from control when it initiated an experimental scheme for purchasing raw opium from the hill tribes in the north of the country. This was intended to relieve the government's dependence on opium imports, decrease monopoly expenses and reduce smuggling. Two years later, the Phibun government declared the experiment a success and that it now planned to expand official opium production.[102] This was to prove essential in the war years as Thailand was cut off from other sources of opium. As Hell explains, this abandonment of international control measures must be understood in the context of the League's declining global influence as a result of its failure in the area of collective security.[103] Moreover, under Phibun, Thailand was re-orientating itself away from Europe towards Japan; there was even talk that the country might follow Japan's lead and withdraw from the League in the late 1930s.[104]

This resistance to international control efforts was also apparent in the government's prostitution policy in the 1930s. In 1932, the League's commission on human trafficking published its report, in which it concluded that the licensing of brothels by the state encouraged the trafficking in women and children.[105] Consequently, League efforts focused on getting the Thai government to abolish its registration and licensing system. While the constitutional regime placed a greater emphasis on women's rights and gender equality, with some members of the new elite being proponents of abolition, entrenched interests resisted such reforms. Jeffrey sums up the situation as follows: 'In post-absolutist Thailand the "woman question" reflected a tension between the desire to present Thai women to the world as modern wives and mothers within an equitable gender system and a continued defence of male sexual prerogative'.[106] Perhaps the best example of this tension was the practice of polygamy, which, despite being outlawed when Siam adopted monogamy as the marital standard in 1935, continued to be practised indirectly through the taking of minor wives (*mia noi*) and mistresses (*mia lap*). The government, meanwhile, defended the system of licensed brothels as vital for keeping venereal disease under control. During the 1930s, there was a decline in the trafficking of Chinese women to Siam and a resulting decrease in the number working as prostitutes. While the number of registered Thai brothels remained the same and the number of registered Thai prostitutes only declined slightly between 1930 and 1936, the number of Chinese brothels and prostitutes halved, from 137 brothels to 63 and from 646 prostitutes to 326.[107] This trend was due to the economic depression and the tighter immigration controls aimed specifically at reducing Chinese immigration instituted by the constitutional regime.[108] Nevertheless, the illicit sex trade flourished as increasing numbers of Thai women were forced into prostitution in order to avoid destitution.[109] In 1936, a Committee Considering the Abolition of Licensed Brothels was established in order to determine the government's stance ahead of the Bandung Conference on Trafficking in Women and Children to be held the following year. The committee decided that Siam could commit itself to the abolition of licensed brothels only as a long-term goal. At the actual conference, Hell notes how the Thai delegation was able to skilfully avert any binding concrete measures being adopted in the convention by submitting a draft resolution stating that the conference committed itself to the long-term abolition of licensed brothels, which was subsequently agreed on by all participants.[110] In short, the Thai government was able to drag its feet on implementing internationally endorsed control measures on both opium and prostitution, thereby maintaining its dependence on opium revenue and defending the male sexual prerogative, by pointing to the prevalence of illicit contraband and the incidence of venereal disease respectively.

The politics of criminalization

The pattern of international pressure and Thai resistance outlined above continued in the post-World War Two period, with the United Nations taking on the mantle of the disbanded League and renewing pressure on the Thai government to reform its system of licensed prostitution and abolish its opium monopoly. Despite this international pressure to conform, however, the actual timing of the prohibitions on opium and prostitution was dictated by domestic politics. During the Second World War, the Thai government had intensified opium production in the North to avert shortages and opium revenues became a financial mainstay once more. Meanwhile, in 1943, the US succeeded in getting the British and the Dutch to commit themselves to the abolition of their opium monopolies once they had regained their South-East Asian colonies. By the end of the war, state opium monopolies had become an anachronism. Moreover, from 1949, the communists in China were successful in eradicating poppy cultivation and during the 1950s the major opium producing countries of Europe, the Middle East and South Asia abandoned the export of the drug for non-medicinal purposes. The stage was thus set for an area encompassing northern Thailand, Burma and Laos, known infamously as 'the Golden Triangle', to become the centre of world opium production. By the end of the 1950s, this area was producing about half of the world's contraband opium and Bangkok had become the distribution centre, the 'opium capital of Asia'.[111] As for prostitution, there had been a dramatic increase in the number of registered brothels and prostitutes during the war as a result of the Japanese occupation and the mass mobilization of Thai men. While these numbers returned to pre-war levels by the end of the war, illicit prostitution flourished due to the subsequent economic downturn.[112] Although this wartime boom in prostitution led to greater concerns about the spread of venereal disease and new legislation was discussed, there was no significant change in government policy and the system of licensed brothels remained in place.[113]

In the immediate post-war period, there was fierce jockeying for power among the various factions of the Thai elite, from which Phibun, who had been deposed in 1944 for his involvement with the Japanese, emerged as premier once more in 1948. However, his control was not as complete as it had been in the pre-war period. In the 1950s, the real power lay with the army head Sarit Thanarat and the police chief Phao Siyanon, who both vied for control over the illicit opium trade to build up their rival powerbases. In order to strengthen his position, meanwhile, Phibun sought US support and military aid by espousing anti-communist sentiments. Moreover, he wished to cement Thailand's position as a respected member of the international community and, consequently, advocated strong involvement with the UN. Indeed, Bangkok became the South-East Asian hub for UN activities. In 1949, the UN issued its Convention for the Suppression of Traffic in Persons and of the Exploitation of the Prostitution of Others, which collected together all similar previous agreements and called for the immediate abolition of licensed brothels. Underlying the convention was the idea that prostitutes were social deviants with an abnormal sexual appetite. As such they required psychological treatment and rehabilitation so that their sexual behaviour might be 'normalized'.[114] Although Thailand did not sign the convention immediately, the government suspended the registration of new brothels and new prostitutes in 1949 and 1955 respectively. However, as the only Asian member of the UN to have legalized brothels, Thailand was still under pressure to abolish the system once and for all. In 1956, the government tried to draw up legislation for this purpose, but no agreement could be reached due to elite male resistance and public indifference.[115] As a 1957 UN report noted: 'Among men, prostitution is often viewed as an accepted part of life. On the part of women it is apparently looked upon either as "a necessary evil" or with outward indifference.'[116] When prostitution was eventually prohibited in 1960 it was as a result of a change in the balance of power within the Thai government.

Domestic politics were also critical in leading to the prohibition of opium. In 1955, the power struggle between Sarit and Phao neared its conclusion after Phao was implicated in a scandal over the payment of rewards for the seizure of a large quantity of illicit opium. In an attempt to counter Sarit's growing influence, Phibun then held elections in 1957, which he won in an alliance with Phao. Shortly after, however, Sarit staged a coup, following which Phibun and Phao went into exile. To cement his grip on power, Sarit then staged another coup, his self-styled 'revolution', in 1958. After using the proceeds he had accumulated through the opium trade to pay off rival elements in the military, Sarit subsequently declared the prohibition of opium in 1959:

Now, the designated time has arrived. The first minute after midnight on 1 July 1959 marks the termination of opium smoking in Thailand. Therefore, 1 July 1959 is a historic day for it is the first day of a new chapter and a new society in Thai history. We will be able to claim fully that we are a civilized nation (*chat araya*), and national prestige will be free from international criticism. No longer will foreign newspapers publish pictures of opium addicts [in Thailand].

I thus announce that from the first minute after midnight on 1 July 1959 the use and sale of opium is illegal, and I believe it is a major crime. Any who violate the law will be severely punished. If they are an alien, they will be deported. If they are Thai, they will be considered a traitor who refuses to make sacrifices for the honour of the nation.[117]

All the remaining government opium dens were closed and existing addicts were required to enter hospital and undergo a rehabilitation programme. This was part of a broader social order campaign through which Sarit sought to legitimize his rule. Besides opium addicts, he also targeted 'hooligans' (*anthaphan*), rickshaw drivers and prostitutes as anti-social elements within Thai society whose behaviour needed to be reformed.[118] Given this, it is hardly surprising that the Prostitution Prohibition Act issued in 1960 targeted the prostitute as the cause of the problem, with the definition of prostitution focusing on the 'promiscuity of the act' rather than the monetary aspect.[119] As with opium addicts, prostitutes were to be rehabilitated and it is here that the influence of the prevailing international discourse on prostitution can be discerned. A number of reform homes were established in order to transform former sex workers into domesticated women. Under the provisions of the new law, meanwhile, the offences of pimping and procuring carried lighter sentences than they had in the Penal Code. Moreover, there were numerous loopholes that still allowed for some forms of legal prostitution. Rather than criminalizing prostitution, the law just criminalized the prostitute. In its wake, the sex trade diversified and went underground, with a predictable rise in the number of women arrested for prostitution.[120] Moreover, in 1966, Sarit's heirs, Thanom Kittikhachon and Praphat Charusathian, issued the Entertainment Places Act, which effectively re-legalized the prostitution industry. These two laws remain in place today, allowing prostitution to flourish in this legal grey area. Similarly, Sarit's prohibition on opium did little to curb the illicit drugs trade, as it was more a crackdown on the addict rather than the supplier.[121] Indeed, perhaps one of the most striking aspects of the Thai government's policies on opium and prostitution throughout the period covered in this chapter is the general lack of concern for those most exploited by the opium trade and prostitution industry: the addict and the prostitute.

When compared with the government's policy on gambling, a few curious aspects stand out. The first and most obvious is the timing of criminalization: gambling was essentially criminalized by the end of the Second World

War but opium use and prostitution were not criminalized until over a decade later in spite of the fact that Thailand was under international pressure to prohibit the latter two for a period of at least 40 years. Related to this is the fact that there were no comparable international efforts aimed at the control of gambling: no League or UN convention on the restriction of lotteries, for instance, that might go alongside the international agreements on opium and prostitution discussed above.[122] In other words, the criminalization of gambling was primarily a result of internal, domestic forces whereas the criminalization of opium and prostitution were heavily influenced by international norms and the pressure to conform. Second, the Thai government issued a much greater level of legislation related to the control of gambling than it did on prostitution and, to a lesser extent, opium. Indeed, throughout the entire period covered in this chapter, there were only two laws that dealt with prostitution explicitly. Of these, the Venereal Disease Prevention Act was not amended once in over 50 years despite being recognized as deficient for at least 20 years.[123] When compared to the myriad of laws and amendments on gambling issued over the same period, not to mention the amount of time spent drafting and discussing those laws, it seems clear that regulating gambling was a bigger priority for the Thai elite than controlling prostitution. Third, at the start of the twentieth century, gambling and opium were the two largest sources of government revenue, between them accounting for over a third of total revenue.[124] It is highly unlikely that the government could have afforded to forgo both at the same time and so it had to choose. Moreover, in abolishing one source the government was aware that its dependence upon the other would be magnified, forestalling the possibility that it might be abolished in the near future. Finally, it did not choose the one providing the least revenue at that time but the one providing the most: gambling. Given all this, it seems fair to say that the Thai elite thought restricting gambling was more important than limiting opium consumption. In a hierarchy of social problems, gambling seems to have occupied the top spot. This begs the question: why? What was the big deal about gambling that made it such a concern of the Thai government?

Numerous answers spring to mind, not least of all that, for the Thai elite, gambling must have seemed to be more manageable than either opium or prostitution. Unlike the latter two, gambling was a domestic problem rather than an international one. Putting aside the issue of extraterritoriality, which was nonetheless a barrier to dealing with all three vices in equal measure, the Thai government was not reliant on international cooperation for its policy of restricting gambling to be successful. Perhaps more important, though, was the fact that gambling was much more visible than opium use and, to a lesser extent, prostitution. This is mainly down to the private nature of these latter two activities: whereas large numbers of people might have gathered to play a particular gambling game together, opium smoking and the sexual act of prostitution were commonly done away from prying eyes in the privacy of a den or a room in some brothel or hotel. Indeed, opium smoking was primarily a solitary activity: the smoker might have someone present to prepare their pipes or a drink but this was not a necessity. This private aspect was reflected in the way the Thai government tried to confine opium consumption and prostitution to licensed dens and brothels throughout the period of this study. In this respect, it is revealing that government and public concerns about prostitution increased only after streetwalkers became a regular sight in Bangkok. In contrast, gambling was engaged in much more publicly, pervading everyday life in a way that opium and prostitution did not. For instance, as described in Chapter 2, clerks selling lottery tickets could be found on every street in the capital throughout the life of the *huai* and young men might be seen pitching coins along the side of the road. Moreover, gambling was an essential ingredient of most festive occasions: no temple fair was complete without a wheel of fortune or a game of *hi-lo*, and, for much of the nineteenth century, the Thai and Chinese new years seem to have been little more than excuses for unfettered indulgence in games of chance.

Related to this issue of visibility was the number of people that engaged in the three activities. Although there are no statistics that might indicate how many people might have gambled in the past, it is estimated that in present-day Thailand some 70 per cent of the population regularly gamble in some form or another.[125] Given that the opportunities for legal gambling at present are much less than those in the nineteenth and early twentieth centuries, it can be surmised that at least as many people gambled then as they do now. Opium addicts, meanwhile, made up only a fraction of the population. A survey conducted by the League of Nation's commission of enquiry in 1930 found that nearly 90,000 people entered licensed dens in a 24-hour period. Based on this and other figures, the subsequent report concluded that there were some 110,000 people who regularly smoked in a licensed den and about 20,000 illicit smokers, out of a total population of about 11 million, in 1930.[126] By 1939, the number of licit smokers had declined to roughly 60,000, though it is not clear whether this reflected a decline in the actual number of smokers or an increase in illegal ones.[127] Estimates as to the number of prostitutes are hazier but, again, they suggest that the number of women working in the sex trade was only a small proportion of the population. Newspaper reports from 1927 estimated that there were at least 30,000 prostitutes in the country, of which two-thirds were working in Bangkok.[128] A UN report from 1957, meanwhile, placed the number of sex workers at 20,000 out of a population of 22 million, with half in the Bangkok area.[129] Of course, the number of men buying sex from these women must have been a substantial part of the male population but, as should be apparent by now, the client was all but missing in discussions and legislation on prostitution. It can thus be argued that part of the reason the Thai government focused its resources on restricting gambling was because this vice affected a far greater number of people, in what it perceived to be a negative manner, than either opium or prostitution. Just as important, however, was the issue of *who* was affected by these vices.

Among the Thai elite and Westerners alike, the general consensus was that opium smoking was primarily a Chinese vice and that only a small number of Thais were addicted to the drug.[130] Indeed, it was believed that the Chinese had a peculiar inclination for opium. As a 1921 Ministry of Finance memo noted: 'The Chinaman's usual method of enjoying himself, when in funds, is to meet his friends and smoke opium, even though he may not be addicted to the drug – much in the same way as Europeans meet and partake of alcohol'.[131] Additionally, it was claimed that opium was less harmful for Chinese consumers than for other ethnic groups. The League commission explained the reasons for this as follows:

> they [the Chinese] have better control over themselves, avoiding excessive use and keeping the daily consumption within the limits which the individual by experience has found to be the quantity which will not endanger his earning capacity or bring other undesirable results.[132]

In contrast, 'The indigenous smoker is likely to lose control of himself in a short time and to keep on increasing the dose until he becomes physically, mentally, and morally wrecked and financially ruined'.[133] The idea that it was okay for Chinese people to smoke opium, and that they needed it to some extent, provided a convenient justification for the Thai and colonial states of South-East Asia for their exploitation of the opium-smoking habit for financial gain. As the preamble to the 1890 opium law makes clear, it was only Thai people that needed protecting:

> Opium has extreme downsides but if prohibited it might upset some groups of people, such as the Chinese, who are already addicted to it. But if they are allowed to acquire opium to their heart's content without any restrictions, it will encourage the Siamese people to indulge in bad habits in the form of taking drugs. Thus we need to consider ways of preventing people from taking up opium while also finding a way to improve revenue collection to meet state expenditures.[134]

Moreover, given the professed anti-Chinese sentiments of both the Sixth Reign and constitutional governments, it is not surprising that they should show a relative disinterest in opium regulation compared to restricting gambling. This lack of concern was mirrored among some of the Bangkok middle class. In the mid-1910s, for instance, one newspaper commentator argued that Thais should be prohibited from smoking as they must become soldiers to defend the nation but the Chinese should be allowed to continue.[135] In a perfect illustration of the callous indifference of both the Thai and Western attitudes to Chinese opium consumption, Virginia Thompson claimed that:

Opium smoking is not a Siamese vice; and when its own people are suffering from diseases like malaria and only a third of the nation's children are able to go to school, the Government is not going to spend its money on alien coolies who have voluntarily contracted an ignoble habit.[136]

In short, opium consumption was a problem for the Chinese community, not for the Thai government.

Similarly, the comparative lack of interest in regulating prostitution and improving the lot of prostitutes during the nineteenth century might have come down simply to the fact that it was women who were adversely affected rather than men. The inferior status of women within Thai society has already been referred to and it seems that this had some influence on policy making. One obvious example of this was in regard to the education of women during the Fifth Reign. Despite the efforts of Queen Saowapha, the most important and influential of Chulalongkorn's many wives, to promote female education, her enthusiasm was not shared by the king. In a clear display of his priorities, Chulalongkorn told the Minister of Education in 1901 that: 'The government's revenue had better be used for boy's education [sic]. Do not promote girls' education too much'.[137] Turning to prostitution policy it is revealing that, when the draft of the Venereal Disease Prevention Act came up for discussion in February 1908, Chulalongkorn gave the final say to his ministers because he claimed he did not know enough about the issue to make an informed decision.[138] It is no surprise that, as clearly manifest in this law, prostitution was only an issue for the elite in the sense that it might threaten the male population with infection by venereal disease. Furthermore, although there was a growing focus on women's rights and gender equality in the 1910s and 1920s, the fact that the majority of prostitutes in Bangkok at the time were women that had been trafficked from China might account for the Sixth Reign government's lack of interest in the issue.[139] Here it is interesting to note that the greater levels of concern shown in the late 1920s and 1930s coincided with an increase in the number of Thai women entering prostitution and the growing sense of popular Thai nationalism. A number of scholars have noted the connection between nationalism and the need to police women's sexual behaviour; as Jeffrey observes:

> Because of women's reproductive role, the regulation of women's bodies is an integral part of inscribing national/ethnic identities. As both the literal and figurative reproducers of the race (through biological reproduction and cultural reproduction, respectively), women and the control of their sexuality are key to the national(ist) project.[140]

With this in mind, it is no coincidence that the increase in public concern about prostitution in the 1950s occurred at a time when the number of Thai prostitutes was increasing to meet the demands of US servicemen and government advisers stationed in the country, a foreign presence that was not entirely welcome among all sections of the Thai population. The Prostitution Prevention Act of 1960 can thus be seen as an attempt to defend the Thai nation's virtue against a foreign threat.[141] It is also worth noting that the government prohibited opium use only after mass Chinese immigration came to a halt in the early 1950s. Coupled with the government's insistence that the Chinese now integrate into Thai society by adopting the Thai language and other signifiers, this meant that any new addicts would be Thai addicts.

Although the boom in gambling described in Chapter 1 can be attributed in part to the rapid increase in Chinese immigration during the nineteenth century and despite the fact the Thai elite did hold gambling to be a Chinese vice just like opium, the large numbers of people that took part in gambling meant that, unlike opium and prostitution, it also came to be perceived as a Siamese vice. This then was the reason for the elite's seeming obsession with regulating gambling: it was a vice that had a negative impact upon large numbers of ethnic Thais, especially men, and thus threatened the emerging Thai nation of the early twentieth century to a greater extent than either of the 'Chinese' problems of opium and prostitution. For the Thai elite, gambling was a Siamese vice that belonged in the past; they did not want it to be a 'Thai' one.

Conclusion

> Gambling is the heritage of mankind. Lucidness or wit may help some escape from ruin, but most of us human beings must keep on gambling. Wherever gambling is illegal, it must be carried out secretly. If the authorities in Siam were serious about arresting gamblers, the kingdom's jails would overflow.
>
> Arkartdamkeung Rapheephat, *The Circus of Life*[1]

The setting is Monte Carlo, probably sometime in the 1920s, and Wisoot, the protagonist of Arkartdamkeung Rapheephat's ground-breaking 1929 novel *The Circus of Life* (*Lakhon haeng chiwit*), is moved to make the above observation while morbidly contemplating the ruin caused by unchecked gambling in the resort's casinos. It is one of many occasions in the novel where the distinction between fiction and fact becomes blurred and where Wisoot's voice seems to become that of the author. Indeed, the story of Wisoot's life closely shadows that of Arkart, and, as Marcel Barang notes, even at the time of its release, the novel was considered to be 'a thinly disguised autobiography'.[2] A love of gambling is not the least of the similarities between creator and creation, though in the author's case it had tragic consequences. Arkart was born in November 1905; his father was Prince Rabi (Ratburi Direkrit), one of Chulalongkorn's many sons and the Minister of Justice from 1896 to 1910. According to Arkart, the two were never close and his sense of estrangement from his father was compounded when his parents divorced in 1918. Arkart then went to live with his mother, who had been accused by her husband of being an inveterate gambler. It is from her that Arkart is said to have acquired his passion for gambling. In 1924, he went to study in England, before moving on to Georgetown University in the United States. Returning to Bangkok via Japan in 1928, Arkart then entered government service and proceeded to write his masterpiece *The Circus of Life*, in which he draws heavily on his experiences of life overseas to depict Wisoot's own journey around the world. However, after incurring substantial debts, and having been implicated in a string of financial scandals, he fled to Hong Kong in 1931, from where he often visited the casinos in Macao. Arkart committed suicide in May 1932. As Rachel Harrison observes, Wisoot's description of gamblers that had lost everything in Monte Carlo's casinos and then taken their own lives thus seems chillingly prescient.[3] What makes the novel most remarkable, though, is its international scope: by venturing overseas, Wisoot gains the perspective to offer constructive criticisms of Siamese society, with the practice of polygamy coming in for particular condemnation.[4] *The Circus of Life* thus suggests Arkart's desire for social change and it is in this light that Wisoot's comments on gambling should be considered.

The quote is insightful on a number of levels. Firstly, Arkart displays a profound recognition of gambling's fundamental human appeal and, stemming from this, the futility of attempts to restrict it. Secondly, in questioning the authorities' resolve in arresting illicit gamblers, he alludes to the corruption arising from gambling's illegality in a very matter-of-fact, non-condemnatory manner. On a deeper level, however, this statement challenges the Thai government's very commitment to the suppression of gambling: was it truly serious about restricting the vice? In turn, this raises questions about the real purpose of government policy, and whether or not the government was successful in achieving those aims. Moreover, by asserting that 'the kingdom's jails would overflow' if all illicit gamblers were imprisoned, Arkart is making an assumption about the amount of illegal gambling in Siam. But was it really as great as he implies and members of the political elite and literati claimed? More importantly, was the Siamese population's gambling habit actually as problematic and harmful as was depicted? These are some of the questions to be addressed in the following section.

Gambling in Siam in perspective

In order to evaluate the success of the Thai government's gambling policy, it is first necessary to clarify what the ruling elite actually wished to achieve. As should be familiar by now, they considered gambling to be a social evil that was a potent source of crime, poverty and, before its formal abolition in 1905, debt slavery. Moreover, gambling encouraged moral laxity and indolence amongst the population and, through a combination of all these factors, retarded economic development. At times, it is almost as if gambling was held to be the cause of all Siam's ills, a view the ruling elite shared with missionaries, foreign advisers and the emerging indigenous middle class. Indeed, such a view of gambling was repeated mantra-like in government reports, travelogues and newspapers until it became a self-evident truth that required no explanation.[5] It thereby followed that if gambling could be restricted or even eliminated, then poverty and crime would be reduced and Siam's prosperity assured.[6] The reality was a little different, however.

A lack of comprehensive statistical information on the volume of gambling in Siam, the amount of crime, levels of poverty, and the incidence of debt slavery makes it extremely difficult to evaluate the success of the government's restrictionist policy towards gambling or to judge the extent to which it was based on accurate perceptions. Indeed, as noted in Chapter 4, government policy was based predominantly on general impressions rather than hard facts. Naturally, this had profound implications, allowing different groups of people to make largely unsubstantiated claims about gambling and its effects in order to advance personal or institutional interests. It has already been noted in Chapter 7, for instance, that some newspaper commentators exaggerated the damage caused by gambling and, on occasion, even resorted to outright fabrication in order to drive home their point. It would be unfair and naive to assume they were the only ones to do so. The reasons for this and its effects will be considered later but first it is necessary to try to determine the actual impact of government policy.

Turning first to the issue of gambling as a cause of debt slavery, it can be surmised that the gradual closure of the gambling houses in the late nineteenth and early twentieth centuries did little to reduce this form of human bondage, for the simple reason that it was implemented too late to have much effect. The main impetus for the abolition of slavery came from a decree issued by Chulalongkorn in 1874. This ruled that anyone born a hereditary slave from 1868 onwards would gain their liberty at the age of 21 and, more pertinently with regards to gambling, any free person born after 1868 could not sell themselves or be sold into slavery upon reaching 21. While the 1874 decree did not affect existing debt slaves and still allowed parents to sell their children into slavery, it seems that it did have a significant indirect impact on this latter practice. Many people mistakenly believed that the decree had actually forbidden the buying and selling of children born after 1868, leading some to complain about the difficulties of finding a buyer in order to service or discharge a debt.[7] By the time the final abolition decree was issued in 1905, the number of slaves and potential slaves had been greatly diminished.[8] Given that the initial closures of the Bangkok gambling houses during the late 1880s and early 1890s probably did little to reduce gambling in the capital and that the first provincial dens were closed only in 1898, it is difficult to see how these moves had more than a negligible impact upon debt slavery.

Similarly, there are few firm indications that the government's attempts to restrict gambling had much effect upon crime rates or levels of poverty in Siam. Indeed, both of these social problems, and fluctuations in their prevalence, arise from a wide range of socio-economic factors, of which gambling can reasonably be considered only a minor one at best. Throughout the period covered by this study, the incidence of crime appears to have grown inexorably almost year-on-year. The most comprehensive and complete statistics on criminal behaviour for early twentieth-century Siam are those showing the number of people convicted for criminal offences: this figure increased almost tenfold during the first four decades of the twentieth century, from 11,353 convictions in 1903/4 to well over 100,000 a year in the second half of the 1930s.[9] To a certain extent, this was a reflection of Siam's growing population, which increased from about 8.1 million in 1910 to around 14.5 in 1937.[10] However, the number of convictions grew at a far greater rate than the population: from 36.82 convictions per 10,000 people in 1911/12 to 77.04 in 1937/8.[11] In other words, a higher proportion of people were being convicted for criminal offences in the late 1930s than in the early 1910s. Of course, these statistics for convictions may better reflect the activities and attitudes of the police and the judiciary than the incidence of crime. Besides reflecting institutional biases, crime statistics in general are subject to a number of other variables, such as changes in the methods of recording crime and administrative reforms within police forces and judiciaries. As was recognized at the time, the rise in the number of reported crimes and the number of criminal cases brought before the Thai courts in the 1900s were largely due to increasing public confidence in the police, improvements in detection and prosecution, and the expanding territorial jurisdiction of the Ministry of Justice.[12] Despite these factors, however, both Thai and Western government officials believed the rate of crime in the country was rising and maintained that gambling was a primary cause.[13] In his report on the police for the year 1919/20, Lawson presented statistics indicating a notable increase in serious crime over the previous ten years (see Table 1). He attributed the sharp jump in 1910/11 to the deleterious effects of conscription, introduced for the police force in 1908/9. As noted in Chapter 5, conscripts tended to be ill disciplined and, due to the poor rates of pay, their morale was low, thereby limiting the effectiveness of the police force as a deterrent to crime. The marked rise in 1919/20, meanwhile, was due to habitual criminals interned in the penal settlement on Koh Pai being removed from the island and distributed throughout the country.[14] Interestingly, the cancellation of the concession

Table 1 Number of cases of homicide, gang robbery and robbery between 1909/10 and 1919/20

Year	Homicide	Gang robbery	Robbery
1909/10	429	281	310
1910/11	658	598	347
1911/12	661	709	303
1912/13	859	707	346
1913/14	1052	610	296
1914/15	1218	701	345
1915/16	1201	691	448
1916/17	1222	612	665
1917/18	1139	668	404
1918/19	1299	653	405
1919/20	1493	963	559

Source: NA R 6 N 4.1/165, 'A Report on work of Police and Gendarmerie and on the Criminal Statistics of Siam for the year B. E. 2462', p. 62.

for unlicensed gambling during the Thai and Chinese new years and Songkran in 1913, the abolition of the *huai* lottery in 1916, and the closure of the last Bangkok gambling houses in 1917 do not seem to have made any significant impression on the number of these offences. Indeed, as Lawson and other members of the administration suggested, abolition may actually have encouraged crime, since it fuelled an increase in underground gambling dens.[15] Although there may have been some short-term victories in curbing crime, in the long term government policy had little discernible impact.

In spite of what the ruling elite, government officials, foreign advisers and newspaper commentators may have thought, the link between gambling and crime was not so clear-cut. As noted in Chapter 4, crimes of acquisition, and theft in particular, were closely associated with gambling. Remarkably, however, the number of people per 10,000 of population convicted for offences against property – theft, snatching and robbery, gang robbery, extortion, cheating and fraud, criminal misappropriation, receiving stolen property, and mischief – remained surprisingly stable between the early 1910s and late 1930s, despite all the changes and initiatives in the government's restriction or promotion of gambling. In 1910/11, the ratio of convictions per 10,000 people for these crimes was 12.91 and the following year it was 14.38.[16] From 1919/20 to 1938/9, this figure then fluctuated between 11.74 (1933/4) and 14.95 (1929/30), the only exception being the year 1920/21 when, perhaps due to the impact of the post-war economic crisis, it soared to 17.89.[17] This consistency of convictions for property offences per 10,000 of Siam's population suggests the rate of crimes of acquisition was largely unaffected by the government's attempts to suppress gambling. Additionally, in 1936, the Ministry of the Interior conducted a survey of convicts in 53 prisons to find out what had driven them to crime: factors included revenge, drunkenness, love, anger, and unemployment. Out of 7,399 cases, the most common answer was poverty, with 1,819 respondents or nearly a quarter of the total. Only 42 prisoners gave gambling as the reason for their criminal behaviour, the least of all the categories.[18] It could be argued that many might have been forced into crime by gambling-induced poverty but this would suggest a surprising lack of self-awareness among those interviewed for this survey. It is more reasonable to conclude that gambling was actually not the major cause of crime that many in Siam thought it to be.

Similar doubts can be raised about gambling as a prime cause of poverty. Over the course of the previous chapters, numerous examples of its insidious effects – children stealing from parents, starving families, huge gambling debts leading to suicide and so on – have been cited; the overall impression created by government reports and newspaper commentaries is that such happenings occurred with depressing regularity. But this seems unlikely, if only for the simple reason that these examples derived their efficacy as cautionary tales of the dangers of unchecked gambling from their extreme nature. Undoubtedly, some people succumbed to addiction and were ruined by their gambling habit – the case of Arkart discussed in the opening section is testament to that – but it is reasonable to assume that the majority gambled within their means and for the sake of entertainment. Indeed, as alluded to in Chapter 4, the idea that gambling was the root of all Siamese society's ills seems to have been based on a misguided and patronizing view of the mass population as indolent and morally lax. Perhaps the best example of this was the condemnatory and derisive attitude that Chaophraya Wongsanupraphat had towards the Thai farmer, which was discussed in that chapter. In his study of the recession that hit the rice trade in the late 1900s, and the Minister of Agriculture's suggestions for dealing with it, Brown concludes that Wongsanupraphat's unsympathetic view of the Thai cultivator blinded him to the necessity of developing an adequate irrigation system and prevented him from formulating an impartial and precise assessment of the causes of the recession, which might act as a basis for action.[19] This hints at one reason why the gambling problem received such prominence in debates on the state of the nation: it was easier for the ruling elite to blame Siam's social and economic troubles on the population's gambling habit than it was to recognize the state's failure to provide and maintain the necessary economic infrastructure. Consequently, their solution was to discipline people into being more efficient producers and loyal citizens of the Thai nation-state.

The Thai elite's rigid conviction that gambling was the cause of all the country's woes stemmed in large part from their educational background and experience of the West. From around the 1830s, the elite of King Mongkut's generation acquired a fascination for Western ideas and technology, cultivating contacts with missionaries, such as Dr Bradley, and other Westerners. The future King Chulalongkorn and his brother princes – most prominently, Damrong and Devawongse – accordingly received an education that combined traditional Siamese elements with modern Western ones. Starting in the last decades of the nineteenth century, young members of the royal family, including nearly all of Chulalongkorn's sons, and the nobility were sent to study in England and other imperial metropoles, with many spending their formative years overseas. For instance, Arkart's father, Prince Rabi, lived in England from the age of 11 to 22, studying law at Oxford before returning to Siam to take up government service in 1896. Significantly, while abroad, he required tuition in the Thai language to ensure he did not forget his mother tongue.[20] With the expansion of the military and civilian bureaucracy in the 1890s and 1900s, increasing numbers of commoners were also given the opportunity for an overseas education. It was in Paris in the mid-1920s where Pridi and Phibun, among others, first discussed their plans to overthrow the absolute monarchy. To a greater or lesser extent, these elite and non-elite Thais not only acquired Western knowledge and skills but also Western tastes and prejudices. As noted in Chapter 4, for example, it was during his time in England that Vajiravudh became enamoured with participation in sport as a means of promoting camaraderie and restoring the virility, dissipated in part by gambling, of the common Thai man. This bears all the hallmarks of the anti-gambling discourse prevalent in England at the time, in which gambling on professional sport had allegedly superseded taking part in 'manly' outdoor activities and was thus seen as a threat to masculinity.[21] Similarly, it was probably while living in Europe that Chaophraya Wongsanupraphat acquired his disdainful opinion of the Thai farmer.[22] Here it is interesting to note that the memorandum he prepared on ideas for alleviating the economic hardship caused by the above-mentioned recession was written in English.[23] While it is not clear why, it can be speculated that perhaps he felt more comfortable writing in English than Thai. Upon returning to Siam, it is fair to say that these Westernized Thai elites, especially those of high status, had more in common with the foreign advisers who aided them in the process of administrative, legal, and financial reform, than they did with Siam's rural population, to whom – in terms of dress, conduct, and, most significantly, mindset – they were only marginally less alien.[24] This cultural distance between rulers and ruled left ample ground for misunderstandings; what the Thai elite saw as problem gambling may have been nothing of the sort to the Thai commoner.

More crucially, in late nineteenth and early twentieth century Britain, if not elsewhere in Europe, conventional wisdom held that gambling, crime and poverty were closely connected. Just as in Siam, this link was based on general impressions and statements of opinion rather than on statistical evidence.[25] As Dixon puts it while commenting on the Home Office's fierce articulation of this view, 'It was not necessary to *prove* that betting caused crime and other social problems: acceptance of the causal connection was a matter of common sense'.[26] Since it was established orthodoxy in the seat of empire that gambling was a virulent cause of crime and poverty, it should not be surprising that the Thai elite adhered to this opinion. Moreover, within Siam the causal connection was reinforced and exaggerated by a range of actors. As already suggested, for the ruling elite, the gambling problem disguised some of the inadequacies and failures of the state: for instance, it could be claimed that crime was rife because gambling was so prevalent, not because the police force was too small and ill equipped to cope with it. Conversely, gambling's undesirability gave the constitutional regime of the 1930s the pretext for monopolizing the provision of lotteries and other gaming facilities: gambling was an evil but, since it could not be eliminated entirely, it was better that the state, and only the state, provide some tightly regulated outlet for it. For the missionaries and colonialists of the early nineteenth century, meanwhile, the Thai state's reliance on the gambling tax farms was evidence of the backward and exploitative nature of the indigenous regime: the prevalence of gambling justified their presence and possible intervention in the country, while also underlining their supposed superiority. Similarly, for the emerging middle-class intelligentsia of the 1910s and 1920s, the gambling problem gave them grounds to criticize the ruling regime: the absolute monarchy was inimical to the good of the nation partly because it exploited people's love of gambling for revenue purposes. For the undermanned and underpaid police force, the illegality of gambling was both a burden and a blessing: by entering into alliance with illicit gambling promoters, the police were able to regulate gambling to some extent, reduce their workload, and supplement their meagre income. For the ordinary Siamese farmer or Chinese labourer, gambling's illegality enabled them to bring government officials to account: as detailed in Chapter 7 and Chapter 8, even mere allegations of gambling were sometimes enough for an official to be dismissed from service. From these differing perspectives, the ultimate success or failure of government attempts to restrict gambling becomes immaterial: the gambling issue derived its utility from the mere occurrence of gambling. What is more, the varied nature of gambling meant its numerous forms and games could be placed in a hierarchy based on their overall impact upon society. This made the anti-gambling discourse more flexible than that on, say, opium, and allowed different actors to employ it to advance a range of different interests. Whereas the discourses on opium and prostitution were, due to the hegemony of Western norms articulated through international treaties and organization, portrayed as black-and-white issues, the debates on gambling allowed for a shade of grey.[27] While many of the actors mentioned above relied on depicting gambling as a social evil that brought nothing but disaster in its wake in order to further their agendas, others sometimes exploited the ambiguities in the anti-gambling discourse to promote certain forms of gambling for their own advantage. The most effective in this regard was the Thai state which used the discourse to control and direct the gambling passions of the Thai population away from types of gambling from which it did not stand to gain, such as card playing in the 1910s and again in the 1930s, towards forms on which it did profit, lotteries in particular. On the whole, though, gambling was a problem in late nineteenth and early twentieth-century Siam largely because it suited people's interests for it to be perceived as a problem.

Nevertheless, as this study should have made clear, the prevalence of gambling in this period was not the cause of the kingdom's problems but rather a symptom of, and even a driving force behind, its transition to modernity and transformation from Siam to Thailand. In Chapter 1 it was argued that the increase in gambling during the nineteenth century was a result of the expanding monetized, market economy, indeed that gambling aided this process. The gambling boom was a sign of growing prosperity. People gambled more because they had both the money and time to do so: rice farmers could buy lottery tickets with their cash surplus, while clerks in Bangkok could visit the horse races on their day off and stake a portion on their favourite. More importantly, as detailed in Chapter 3, the boom in gambling provided the Thai government with the revenue from which it was able to transform the semi-feudal Siamese kingdom into the modern nation-state of Thailand. This connection between the increase in gambling and economic development was often acknowledged implicitly but rarely celebrated. For instance, while the Financial Adviser W. J. F. Williamson noted in his 1904/5 budget report that the increases in revenue from the gambling house, *huai* lottery and alcohol tax farms 'may be regarded with satisfaction, as showing an expected improvement in the condition of that section of the population which derives its income from the land', he qualified this statement by observing that 'The Gambling Farms are, however, open to obvious objections'.[28] More interestingly, Vajiravudh, writing under his penname Asavabahu in the *Siam Observer*, pointed to the widespread gambling in his kingdom to argue that poverty was not a problem:

> Are the Siamese as a whole really poor? I have elsewhere expressed it as my own individual opinion that they are not, and nothing has occurred since to make me alter my opinion. It appears to me very easy to prove this contention, as several things tend to prove it. Let me bring only two of them to your notice:
>
> (1) In our county, no one has ever been known to die of starvation.
>
> (2) The trains from the provinces still bring in loads of passengers, who come to Bangkok to put their money into the pockets of the Huay and Gambling Farmers. It is obvious that if people are starving, they would scarcely be able to continue doing so.[29]

Continuing in this somewhat bizarre manner, Vajiravudh went on to claim that people had no need for money as they could obtain all they needed to survive from nature or through barter, concluding that: 'What money the people earn they only use for two purposes, namely, for paying taxes and for gambling!'[30] Such comments show the deep-seated ambivalence of the Thai elite towards gambling and betray the underlying reason for their seeming obsession with regulating it. The increase in gambling was a manifestation of wrenching socio-economic changes over which they had little or no control. Nevertheless, unlike the problems of opium and prostitution, which transcended the borders and the abilities of individual states to successfully manage, gambling was one aspect of Siam's transition to modernity that the Thai elite thought it could negotiate on its own terms. Rather than fearing an increase in gambling, however, perhaps they should have been more concerned about a decrease. As an elderly woman in Bang Chan village observed in the early 1950s: 'Gambling disappeared two years ago. People in the same hamlet used to hear about a game of cards and gather together. Now the money is all gone. There are more poor people.'[31] A rise in the cost of living and the incidence of poverty had done what government policy could not: bring a halt to gambling.

Gambling in Thailand today: the past in the present

Fast-forward to present day Thailand and the government's attitude and policies towards gambling seem to have changed little, in spite of the further socio-economic transformations the country has undergone over the last 60 plus years. Indeed, the legal and regulatory framework established during the 1930s and 1940s has created an environment in which gambling has become ever more deeply entrenched in the illegal economy. Apart from the twice-monthly state lotteries and the totes on horse racing, most forms of gambling either remain illegal or are subject to such a complex and restrictive licensing system as to render them virtually so.[32] Nevertheless, gambling remains as prevalent as it did in the past: 70 per cent of the Thai population are said to take part in the gaming economy.[33] Illegal gambling takes three principal forms: gaming in casinos, the underground lottery (*huai tai din*), and betting on football matches. Underground casinos and gambling dens of all sizes, styles and clientele can be found throughout the country. In 1996, it was estimated that there were between 187 and 300 such establishments in Bangkok alone and at least 89 in the provinces.[34] These are frequented by people from all walks of life: businessmen, politicians, artists, housewives, office workers, teenage students, and the unemployed. However, the largest illicit gambling enterprise in the country, both in economic and organizational terms, is the underground lottery: in their late 1990s study of the gaming economy, Pasuk et al. claimed about four million people were then involved in its sales and administration network, with an estimated annual turnover equivalent to eight per cent of GDP.[35] The underground lottery is run in tandem with the state lottery, upon which the winning numbers are based. There are various ways of placing a stake: most commonly, punters bet on the last two or three digits of the first prize number in the official draw. These variants, and the slightly better odds some offer, make the underground lottery a serious rival to the government one. Furthermore, while state lottery tickets cost 40 baht each, punters can stake just a few baht on its illegal twin, which also pays out more in prize money: 70 to 75 per cent of the total money staked as opposed to 60 per cent.[36] A more recent gambling craze is betting on the results of football matches, with games in international tournaments and the English Premier League being the most popular. The development of football gambling is a graphic example of globalization and has been facilitated by advances in technology: people watch the games on satellite TV, place bets by mobile phone or the Internet, and transfer money electronically.[37] During the 2010 World Cup in South Africa, over 1,700 people were arrested for gambling offences, the majority of whom were punters. Significantly, the amount of cash seized by the police and the amount of money found in circulation was but a fraction of that during the 2006 World Cup because bookmakers had moved online, making detection more difficult.[38] Additionally, Thais regularly go abroad to gamble, visiting Macao, Hong Kong, and Las Vegas among other locations.[39] Closer to home, there are numerous casinos just across the border in Burma, Cambodia, and Laos, many of which are Thai-owned.[40] According to the National Economic and Social Development Board (NESDB), nearly three million Thais visited these cross-border establishments in 2001.[41] Similarly, offshore liners replete with gaming tables ply the Gulf of Thailand.

Huge sums of money are involved in the illegal gambling economy. In 2001, the underground lottery is reckoned to have made 542 billion baht, while the turnover of Bangkok casinos was estimated to be 673 billion baht and that of provincial ones 142 billion.[42] Moreover, Thais are said to bet over 100 billion baht on football a year.[43] Lastly, so great is the amount being gambled in foreign casinos that it is claimed to affect the baht exchange rate.[44] The social cost to the country is also high, with the proceeds from illicit gambling enterprises going to organized crime. Indeed, the government's restrictive policy may inadvertently have nurtured crime syndicates. In the late 1930s, the American academic Kenneth P. Landon claimed that organized crime had yet to gain a foothold in the country.[45] This assessment appears to be supported by the government reports and other sources used in this study; apart from the Chinese secret societies, large-scale criminal organizations are hardly ever referred to in connection with gambling. It was only in the 1940s and 1950s that organized crime took off in Bangkok, running some casinos and collecting protection money from others.[46] The organizations behind present-day cross-border casinos are also involved in the drug trade, smuggling and money laundering.[47] Furthermore, policing illegal gambling is a strain on the police force and diverts precious resources away from the suppression of more serious crimes. This is to say nothing of the corrupting influence it has upon the police and, since the development of party politics, politicians.

Given the potential revenue from gambling the Thai state currently forgoes, along with the economic and social costs of illegal gambling, it is not surprising that governments frequently contemplate adopting a more liberal stance and legalizing casinos in particular. A 1996 survey conducted by a group of academics at Chulalongkorn University among the Bangkok middle class and opinion makers found a majority in favour of legalizing casinos, though people were divided over lifting restrictions on other forms of gambling.[48] However, although the case for government-run casinos is persuasive, such proposals have generally attracted fierce criticism and have consequently been shelved. Whereas gambling has been progressively decriminalized in many developed and developing countries over the last half-century – for instance, Singapore opened its first casinos in 2010 – Thailand has stood still. Moreover, with the advent of the Internet and online gambling, controlling gambling becomes ever more difficult and unrealistic. As Pasuk et al. recognize, the end result is that the Thai government's stance on gambling looks increasingly out-of-date and out-of-step with economic sense, technological developments, and people's behaviour.[49]

Unsurprisingly, the primary impediment to the decriminalization of gambling in Thailand remains the police force. In 2002, a senior police officer revealed that 'up to 10 gambling dens in Bangkok each pay up to 10 million baht a month for the police force to turn a blind eye'.[50] Lawson's observation, quoted in Chapter 5, that it was impossible to conduct illicit gambling on any scale without the police knowing about it, remains as true today as it was 100 years ago. One justification the police use for their 'informal taxes' on casinos is that they do not receive enough money in their budget for crime suppression work, particularly because much of it requires paying informers.[51] So long as police salaries and budgets remain inadequate, it is not in their interest to see a liberalization of the kingdom's gambling laws. Similarly, some politicians have close connections with illicit gambling promoters or are themselves involved. The proceeds of the underground lottery are used to buy votes at election time and to finance the campaigns of some candidates. Additionally, the extensive administrative and client network of this enterprise is used as an electioneering machine and vote bank.[52] In short, too many influential actors still have a vested interest in the illegality of gambling.

Of course, many people still object to gambling on moral and social grounds. More intriguing though is the way in which the anti-gambling discourse continues to be used to demonize proponents of decriminalization. The most significant public figure to fall victim to such attacks was Thaksin Shinawatra, Thailand's most successful politician at the ballot box and easily its most controversial. Following its electoral success in 2001, his Thai Rak Thai (literally, Thai love Thai) party absorbed two other parties to become the first to wield an outright parliamentary majority. Combined with new constitutional provisions designed to strengthen the prime minister and to encourage more stable governments, this meant Thaksin acquired an unprecedented degree of political power for an elected Thai premier.[53] The manner in which he chose to wield it ensured he had many enemies. Among businessmen involved in the entertainment industry and international investors, it was generally acknowledged that Thaksin represented the best opportunity for legalizing casinos.[54] Such a move was certainly in keeping with the former prime minister's economic policy, branded Thaksinomics, in which he sought to bring illicit business enterprises above ground in order to contribute to growth and government revenue.[55] As part of this strategy, in 2003 the Government Lottery Office (GLO) instituted a large number of draws of two- and three-digit numbers for fixed prizes in order to undermine the underground lottery, a tactic that met with some success.[56] A year later, the NESDB proposed the establishment of state-run casinos as a means of combating corruption and the underground economy, while also creating jobs and investment.[57] While controversial, this was totally overshadowed by the uproar caused by the Liverpool Football Club lottery scheme.[58] In May 2004, Thaksin, as part of a consortium of Thai Rak Thai billionaires, tried to buy a 30 per cent stake in the English Premier League club. After this was denounced as unconstitutional, he announced he was going to purchase the shares on behalf of 'Thailand as a country', using public money. Predictably, this too was denounced, on the grounds that it was inappropriate. Thaksin then proposed raising the funds through a lottery. Tickets would cost 1,000 baht, with a first prize of one billion baht, a second of 100 million, and others going down to 100,000 baht for the last place.[59] In addition, all purchasers would receive a 200 baht share in the football club. The lottery scheme generated a storm of protest from academics, press commentators, social activists, and students. For instance, the *Khao sot* newspaper pointed out that ticket-holders' shares might become worthless due to fluctuations in the London stock exchange and that the proposal totally contradicted the government's campaign to rid the nation of vice, including the underground lottery.[60] Following criticisms from his one-time mentor, Chamlong Srimuang, that the scheme would spur greed and incite a lending rush, Thaksin kicked the Liverpool lottery proposal into touch.[61]

Gambling has remained a divisive issue throughout the political turmoil since Thaksin was deposed from power by a palace-backed military coup in September 2006. In December 2009, the GLO gave the go ahead for the Thai-foreign consortium Loxley-GTech Technology to roll out its online lottery booths.[62] This had been another of Thaksin's initiatives, which was designed to stem the rampant corruption within the distribution system for government lottery tickets but had been placed on hold following the 2006 coup. Despite the GLO's approval for the scheme to be finally implemented, then PM Abhisit Vejjajiva, leader of the military-backed anti-Thaksin coalition government, announced his intention to cancel it entirely in January 2010, citing fears about the effects the online lottery might have on the young.[63] This sudden u-turn raised some protest from lottery vendors who had already installed some 7,000 vending machines and Loxley-GTech executives threatened to sue the government for at least three billion baht in compensation.[64] Jatuporn Prompan, an opposition party MP and a leader of the pro-Thaksin United Front for Democracy against Dictatorship, accused the PM of using the story to divert attention away from the corruption scandals and inter-party conflicts plaguing his coalition government.[65] One newspaper commentator described the move as 'a morally correct decision that defies reality', while others speculated that Abhisit was merely protecting the influential groups that had a vested interest in the existing distribution system.[66]

The anti-gambling discourse deployed in the recent debates over decriminalization is little changed from that which was articulated during the period covered by this study. One critic of the Liverpool lottery scheme, for instance, claimed it would 'increase crime, lead to gambling addiction and ruin families'.[67] As in the past, concerns were raised about gambling's effects on children: it was claimed that if casinos were legalized it would encourage them to believe that gambling was a legitimate activity, with disastrous consequences for society.[68] Even the new two- and three-digit lottery draws, the revenue from which goes to providing scholarships for the education of children from low-income families, were condemned on similar grounds.

At a seminar at Thammasat University, a Bangkok senator argued that: 'doing this is like using money from committing a sin to make merit. It is a way to justify the lottery run. More importantly, it has confused children and caused them to feel grateful to the lottery.'[69] One slight difference, however, is that a greater emphasis now seems to be placed on the immorality of gambling and how it contravenes Buddhism. For instance, a poll conducted in January 2010 found that 58 per cent thought the online lottery project should be cancelled because a Buddhist-dominated society such as Thailand should not be promoting vice.[70] Thaksin, meanwhile, has all but been accused of being a 'bad' Buddhist, with the senator quoted above claiming that the proposals for legalizing casinos showed that he lacked true understanding of Buddhist principles. Similarly, at the same seminar a Thai academic claimed that the Thaksin government's 'moral standard was lower than its ability to perform economic work' and that it 'had failed to follow Buddhist precepts'.[71] Proposals for decriminalizing gambling were thus evidence of how Thaksin focused only on economic development without considering the social costs of his schemes. Just as the popular press in the 1920s used the anti-gambling discourse to undermine the legitimacy of the absolute monarchy, Thaksin's opponents deployed it to illustrate why his premiership was detrimental to the Thai nation and how he personally was morally unfit to govern.

There is one new element in the present-day anti-gambling discourse, though it draws its potency from the past. In February 2003, *Matichon*, a weekly aimed at the urban middle class, ran an article discussing the legalization of casinos.[72] Revealingly, the article included a photograph of King Chulalongkorn and opened with a quotation in which he expressed his fears about the spread of gambling within Bangkok in the nineteenth century. After reporting how the legalization of casinos was on the political agenda once more, the writer claimed that their proponents were being wilfully ignorant about Chulalongkorn's attitude towards gambling, his policy of closing the dens and his reasons for doing so. The writer went on to quote a lengthy passage from Chulalongkorn's study of the Songkran festival in which the king attributed the longevity of the Chakri dynasty to its determination to rid the country of vice. Chulalongkorn then stated that any member of the royal family or government official that respected the magnanimity of the monarchy should refrain from gambling or seeking to profit from it. The article's writer concluded by observing how the great threat posed by gambling that Chulalongkorn had foreseen and tried to forestall was now in danger of coming to pass.[73] What is striking is that the writer makes no attempt to explain why legalization might be disadvantageous for present-day Thailand; it is enough to present some examples of Chulalongkorn's thoughts on gambling. In short, the writer's argument amounts to little more than gambling is bad because Chulalongkorn said so. Although never spelt out, and ignoring the historical myopia of the writer, the implications are clear. To be a proponent of decriminalization is to be not only a 'bad' Buddhist but, even more seriously in a country where the monarchy is highly revered and loyalty to it is considered the very essence of Thai identity, to be anti-monarchist and un-Thai. By contemplating the legalization of casinos, it was insinuated that Thaksin was challenging the wisdom of Chulalongkorn and, by association, that of the current monarch, King Bhumibol Adulyadej.[74] It is an unfortunate irony that a study that has sought to decentralize the monarchy in the historical narrative of Thailand should end by giving the last word to one of those monarchs. Nevertheless, this is only meant to underline the continuing discursive authority of the Thai monarchy. In the Thai deck of cards, the king is always trump; playing this card invariably guarantees a winning hand.

The world has turned and turned since the legal and conceptual framework of the Thai government's restrictionist policy on gambling was formulated but, as a consequence of the entrenched interests of the police and politicians and, perhaps just as crucially, the long shadow cast by one of the country's most revered monarchs, the pendulum has yet to swing back.

Notes

Introduction

1 Kukrit Pramoj, *Four Reigns (Si phaen-din)*, trans. Tulachandra, Chiang Mai: Silkworm Books, 1998 [1953], p. 629.
2 Marcel Barang (comp.), *The 20 Best Novels of Thailand*, Bangkok: Thai Modern Classics, 1994, p. 285.
3 Jan McMillen, 'Understanding Gambling: History, Concepts and Theories' in Jan McMillen (ed.), *Gambling Cultures: Studies in History and Interpretation*, London and New York: Routledge, 1996, p. 7.
4 Ibid., p. 6.
5 Ibid.
6 Roger Munting, *An Economic and Social History of Gambling in Britain and the USA*, Manchester: Manchester University Press, 1996, p. 3.
7 Mannot Sutthiwatthanaphrut, *Kham athibai pramuan kotmai phaeng lae phanit wa duai yumfaksap kepkhong nai khlangsinkha prani-pranom yomkhwam kanphanan lae khanto* [Explanation of the Civil and Commercial Code Concerning Borrowing and Depositing Property, Reconciliation and Compromise, Consent, Gambling and Betting], 2nd ed., Bangkok: Ramkhamhaeng University Press, 1975, pp. 262–63; Thanongsak Thinsinuan, 'Kotmai kieokap kanphanan' [Laws about Gambling], MA thesis, Faculty of Law, Thammasat University, 1986, p. 85; Institute of Linguistics (comp.), *Pathanukrom chabap luang* [Government Dictionary], np, nd, p. 402; *Saranukromthai chabap ratchabanditthayasathan* [Thai Encyclopaedia: National Bar Association Edition], vol. 20, Bangkok: Thai-mit Press, 1975–76, pp. 12653–54.
8 NA R7 Kh 2/2, 'Extract from the Council of Ministers Meeting, 18 August 1928'.
9 Equating the game or activity on which gambling takes place with gambling itself is common. In British English, for instance, to say that someone 'likes the horses' is to imply that they like gambling on the horses rather than horses per se.
10 *PKPS*, 18, p. 276.
11 *PKPS*, 10, pp. 129–30; *PKPS*, 18, p. 254.
12 For a contemporary overview of the problems of defining crime, see Stephen Jones, *Criminology*, 3rd ed., Oxford: Oxford University Press, 2006, pp. 31–41.
13 For a critique of this argument see ibid., pp. 31–34.
14 Pasuk Phongpaichit, Sungsidh Piriyarangsan and Nualnoi Treerat, *Guns, Girls, Gambling, Ganja: Thailand's Illegal Economy and Public Policy*, Chiang Mai: Silkworm Books, 1998, p. 215.

15 Jones, *Criminology*, pp. 34–41.
16 Ted Robert Gurr, Peter N. Grabosky and Richard C. Hula, *The Politics of Crime and Conflict: A Comparative History of Four Cities*, Beverley Hills, California: Sage Publications, 1977, pp. 683, 697–98.
17 Ibid., pp. 14, 681–82; Pasuk et al., *Guns, Girls, Gambling, Ganja*, p. 216.
18 Gurr et al., *Politics of Crime and Conflict*, p. 678.
19 David Dixon, *From Prohibition to Regulation: Bookmaking, Anti-Gambling, and the Law*, Oxford: Clarendon Press, 1991, p. 28.
20 Ibid., p. 29.
21 These axioms were first elucidated by Benedict Anderson in his seminal work on Thai studies. See Benedict R. O'G. Anderson, 'Studies of the Thai State: The State of Thai Studies' in Eliezer B. Ayal (ed.), *The Study of Thailand: Analyses of Knowledge, Approaches, and Prospects in Anthropology, Art History, Economics, History and Political Science*, Papers in International Studies, Southeast Asia Series 54, Athens, Ohio: Ohio University, 1978, pp. 193–98.
22 David K. Wyatt, *The Politics of Reform in Thailand: Education in the Reign of King Chulalongkorn*, New Haven and London: Yale University Press, 1969; Walter F. Vella, *Chaiyo! King Vajiravudh and the Development of Thai Nationalism*, Honolulu: University of Hawaii Press, 1978.
23 Anderson, 'Studies of the Thai State', p. 196.
24 In addition to Wyatt, *Politics of Reform*, and Vella, *Chaiyo!*, see also Benjamin A. Batson, *The End of the Absolute Monarchy in Siam*, Singapore: Oxford University Press, 1984; and Stephen L. W. Greene, *Absolute Dreams: Thai Government Under Rama VI, 1910–1925*, Bangkok: White Lotus, 1999.
25 For a discussion of these critical discourses, see Craig J. Reynolds and Hong Lysa, 'Marxism in Thai Historical Studies', *Journal of Asian Studies*, 43, 1 (November 1983), pp. 77–104; and Thongchai Winichakul, 'The Changing Landscape of the Past: New Histories in Thailand since 1973', *Journal of Southeast Asian Studies*, 26, 1 (March 1995), pp. 104–7.
26 Matthew Copeland, 'Contested Nationalism and the 1932 Overthrow of the Absolute Monarchy in Siam', PhD dissertation, Australian National University, 1993; Nakkharin Mektrairat, *Kanpathiwat sayam pho so 2475* [The Siamese Revolution of 1932], Bangkok: The Foundation for the Social Sciences and Humanities, 1992.
27 Scot Barmé, *Woman, Man, Bangkok: Love, Sex and Popular Culture in Thailand*, Lanham: Rowman and Littlefield, 2002.
28 Tamara Loos, *Subject Siam: Family, Law and Colonial Modernity in Thailand*, Ithaca, New York, and London: Cornell University Press, 2006, Ch. 2.
29 Ibid., p. 184.
30 Once again, Anderson was the first to articulate the dual nature of the Thai state. Anderson, 'Studies of the Thai State', pp. 199, 209–10.
31 Chatthip Nartsupha and Suthy Prasertset (eds), *The Political Economy of Siam, 1851–1910*, Bangkok: The Social Science Association of Thailand, 1981; Hong Lysa, 'Extraterritoriality in Bangkok in the Reign of King Chulalongkorn: The Cacophonies of Semi-Colonial Cosmopolitanism', *Itinerario: European Journal of Overseas History*, 27, 2 (July 2003), pp. 125–46; Hong Lysa '"Strangers within the Gates": Knowing Semi-Colonial Siam as Extraterritorials', *Modern Asian Studies*, 38, 2 (May 2004), pp. 327–54.
32 Thongchai Winichakul, *Siam Mapped: A History of the Geo-Body of a Nation*, Honolulu: University of Hawaii Press, 1994; Chaiyan Rajchagool, *The Rise and Fall of the Thai Absolute Monarchy: Foundations of the Modern Thai State from Feudalism to Peripheral Capitalism*, Bangkok: White Lotus, 1994.
33 Loos, *Subject Siam*, p. 6.
34 Ibid., p. 182.

35 See, for instance, the National Assembly Committee for Financial Affairs, Banking and Financial Institutions, *Rai-ngan phon-kanphicharana suksa ruang kanpoet kasino nai prathet hai thuktong tam kotmai* [Report on Study Considering the Opening of Casinos in Accordance with the Law], Bangkok: Secretariat of the National Assembly, 2003; and *Bangkok Post*, 28 March and 11 June 2004.
36 Prince Damrong Rachanuphap, *Prachum phongsawadan phak thi 17: Ruang tamnan kanloek bonbia lae huai* [Collected Chronicles, Part 17: The Abolition of the Gambling Dens and the *huai* Lottery], Bangkok: Cremation Volume, 1960. For a detailed discussion of Damrong's work and influence upon Thai historiography, see Kennon Breazeale, 'A Transition in Historical Writing: The Works of Prince Damrong Rachanuphap', *Journal of the Siam Society*, 59, 2 (July 1971), pp. 25–49.
37 *BTWM*, 15 June 1904.
38 Damrong [Abolition], pp. 89–92.
39 Ibid., pp. 52, 88.
40 See, respectively, Kanchana Chintakanon, 'Naiyobai khong ratthaban kieokap phasi-akon kanphanan pho so 2367–2460' [Government Policy Towards Gambling Taxes, 1824–1917], MA thesis, Sinlapakon University, 1987; and Nuttaya Ussavaponganat, 'Bonbia nai sangkhom thai pho so 2367–2460: Kansuksa choeng sangkhom watthanatham' ['Bonbia' – Chinese Gambling in Thai Society, 1824–1917: A Socio-Cultural Study], MA thesis, Thammasat University, 2005.
41 Ian Brown, *The Creation of the Modern Ministry of Finance in Siam, 1885–1910*, London: MacMillan, 1992, pp. 23–24, 88–92.
42 See, for instance, David K. Wyatt, *Thailand: A Short History*, 2nd ed., New Haven and London: Yale University Press, 2003, pp. 169, 171, 177, 190; and Chris Baker and Pasuk Phongpaichit, *A History of Thailand*, New York: Cambridge University Press, 2005, pp. 34, 40, 48, 52, 75, 91, 131, 171.
43 Throughout the text this is abbreviated to *PKPS* followed by the volume number.
44 *Rai-ngan kanprachum sapha phu-thaen ratsadon* [Records of the National Assembly], Bangkok: Office of the Parliamentary Secretary, 1933+.
45 Sthirakoses (Phraya Anuman Rajdhon), *Looking Back: Book One*, Bangkok: Chulalongkorn University Press, 1992, and *Looking Back: Book Three*, Bangkok: Chulalongkorn University Press, 2001. Travelogues and memoirs by Westerners include Carl Bock, *Temples and Elephants: Travels in Siam in 1881–82*, Singapore: Oxford University Press, 1986 [1884]; and H. Warrington Smyth, *Five Years in Siam: From 1891–1896*, Bangkok: White Lotus, 1994 [1898], 2 vols.

1 Gambling and socio-economic change in nineteenth-century Siam

1 Simon de la Loubère, *The Kingdom of Siam,* Kuala Lumpur: Oxford University Press, 1969 [1693], pp. 46, 50.
2 Prince Damrong Rachanuphap, *Prachum phongsawadan phak thi 17: Ruang tamnan kan-loek bonbia lae huai* [Collected Chronicles, Part 17: The Abolition of the Gambling Dens and the *huai* Lottery], Bangkok: Cremation Volume, 1960, p. 6.
3 See, for example, La Loubère, *Kingdom of Siam*, p. 50; and Sir John Bowring, *The Kingdom and People of Siam*, vol. 1, London: Oxford University Press, 1969 [1857], p. 154.
4 *Bangkok Calendar*, 1871, p. 119.

5 See, for instance, the comments of David Abeel in Anthony Farrington (ed.), *Early Missionaries in Bangkok: The Journals of Tomlin, Gutzlaff and Abeel, 1828–1832*, Bangkok: White Lotus, 2001, pp. 122–23.
6 Quoted in B. J. Terwiel, *Through Travellers' Eyes: An Approach to Early Nineteenth Century Thai History*, Bangkok: Editions Duang Kamol, 1989, p. 216.
7 These figures are taken from Constance Wilson's detailed examination of archival records on tax farming. See Constance M. Wilson, 'Revenue Farming, Economic Development and Government Policy during the Early Bangkok Period, 1830–92' in John Butcher and Howard Dick (eds), *The Rise and Fall of Revenue Farming: Business Elites and the Emergence of the Modern State in Southeast Asia*, London: MacMillan, 1993, p. 152; and 'State and Society in the Reign of Mongkut, 1851–68: Thailand on the Eve of Modernization', PhD dissertation, Cornell University, 1970, p. 995, respectively.
8 Kanchana Chintakanon, 'Naiyobai khong ratthaban kieokap phasi-akon kanphanan pho so 2367–2460' [Government Policy Towards Gambling Taxes, 1824–1917], MA thesis, Sinlapakon University, 1987, pp. 9–10; Damrong [Abolition], pp. 8–9.
9 Damrong, [Abolition], p. 7.
10 Ibid., p. 17; Terwiel, *Travellers' Eyes*, p. 214.
11 On the growth of trade and attendant socio-economic changes in the late eighteenth and early nineteenth centuries, see Hong Lysa, *Thailand in the Nineteenth Century: Evolution of the Economy and Society*, Singapore: Institute of Southeast Asian Studies, 1984, Ch. 3, esp. pp. 42–55; and Nidhi Eoseewong, *Pen and Sail: Literature and History in Early Bangkok (including the History of Bangkok in the Chronicles of Ayutthaya)*, edited by Chris Baker and Ben Anderson, with Craig J. Reynolds, Hong Lysa, Pasuk Phongpaichit, Patrick Jory and Ruth T. McVey, Chiang Mai: Silkworm Books, 2005 [1982], pp. 57–114.
12 Kanchana, [Government Policy], p. 30.
13 Hong, *Thailand*, pp. 51, 84.
14 Damrong, [Abolition], p. 17.
15 On the decline of forced labour, see Pasuk Phongpaichit and Chris Baker, *Thailand: Economy and Politics*, 2nd ed., New York: Oxford University Press, 2002, pp. 24–26; James C. Ingram, *Economic Change in Thailand, 1850–1970*, Stanford, California: Stanford University Press, 1971, pp. 58–61.
16 Pasuk and Baker, *Thailand*, p. 24.
17 Hong, *Thailand*, p. 55.
18 Nidhi, *Pen and Sail*, pp. 76–77.
19 Ibid., pp. 121–24.
20 On the prevalence of gambling among the Thai elite see Frederick Arthur Neale, *Narrative of a Residence in Siam*, Bangkok: White Lotus, 1996 [1852], pp. 143–44; and *The Burney Papers*, vol. 1, pt. 2, Bangkok: Vajiranana National Library, 1910, p. 202.
21 *Bangkok Calendar*, 1871, p. 119.
22 Gerda Reith, *The Age of Chance: Gambling in Western Culture*, London and New York: Routledge, 1999, p. 59.
23 Ibid., p. 59.
24 Nidhi, *Pen and Sail*, p. 102.
25 Terwiel, *Travellers' Eyes*, p. 252.
26 In 1868, the total revenue from the numerous gambling tax farms was 599,400 baht. The total tax farming revenue was 2,874,236 baht. Wilson, 'State and Society', pp. 995–1000.

27 The most comprehensive study of Chinese immigration and its impact upon nineteenth-century Siam remains G. William Skinner, *Chinese Society in Thailand: An Analytical History*, Ithaca, New York: Cornell University Press, 1957, Chs 2–4.
28 Ibid., p. 58.
29 Pasuk and Baker, *Thailand*, p. 188.
30 Skinner, *Chinese Society*, pp. 73–74, 79.
31 On the *angyi* in nineteenth-century Siam see ibid., pp. 139–45; Pasuk and Baker, *Thailand*, pp. 189–91, 233–35.
32 Kanchana, [Government Policy], p. 30.
33 Wilson, 'Revenue Farming', pp. 151–52; B. J. Terwiel, *Thailand's Political History: From the 13th Century to Recent Times*, rev. ed., Bangkok: River Books, 2011, p. 128.
34 Kanchana, [Government Policy], p. 25.
35 Damrong, [Abolition], p. 17 fn. 2.
36 For examples, see Kanchana, [Government Policy], pp. 31, 48–49, 74–75.
37 Terwiel, *Travellers' Eyes*, pp. 190–91.
38 NA K Kh 0301.1.30/15, 'H. E. Chao Phya Yomaraj's letter of 1 March 2458 (1916) to H. M. the King on the Chinese Question'.
39 Perhaps the best treatment of the toils and temptations of male Chinese immigrants to South-East Asia is James Francis Warren, *Rickshaw Coolie: A People's History of Singapore*, Singapore: Singapore University Press, 2003 [1986], esp. Ch. 14.
40 Skinner, *Chinese Society*, p. 123.
41 Ibid., p. 120.
42 Ibid., p. 125.
43 Hong, *Thailand*, pp. 92–93.
44 Kanchana, [Government Policy], pp. 75–76.
45 Skinner, *Chinese Society*, p. 110.
46 Suehiro Akira, *Capital Accumulation in Thailand, 1855–1985*, Tokyo: The Centre for East Asian Cultural Studies, 1989, p. 69.
47 H. Warrington Smyth, *Five Years in Siam: From 1891–1896*, Bangkok: White Lotus, 1994 [1898], vol. 1, p. 328.
48 John G. Butcher, 'The Demise of the Revenue Farm System in the Federated Malay States', *Modern Asian Studies*, 17, 3 (July 1983), pp. 395–97.
49 In his overview of the Thai economy in 1850, James Ingram states bluntly that: 'We have no information on the amount of money in circulation'. Ingram, *Economic Change*, p. 32.
50 Nidhi, *Pen and Sail*, pp. 93–94.
51 In Thai, these coins are called *phot duang*, literally meaning 'curled worm', again, in reference to their shape. Reginald Le May, *The Coinage of Siam*, Bangkok: The Siam Society, 1932, p. 1.
52 John Crawfurd, *Journal of an Embassy to the Courts of Siam and Cochin China*, Kuala Lumpur: Oxford University Press, 1967 [1828], p. 331.
53 Bowring, *Kingdom of Siam*, 1, p. 257.
54 Wilson, 'State and Society', p. 619.
55 While in Ayutthaya in 1862, Adolf Bastian observed that cowries were 'measured out in painted baskets or in not so accurate coconut shells because the counting of large amounts would be too time-consuming'. Adolf Bastian, *A Journey in Siam (1863)*, trans. Walter E. J. Tips and ed. Christian Goodden, Bangkok: White Lotus, 2005 [1867], p. 35.
56 Le May, *Coinage*, pp. 63–65.
57 Rujaya Abhakorn, for instance, notes that in the 1870s 'the barter system prevailed in the remoter areas' of Ratchaburi province and that 'it was by no

means out of fashion in the market centers' either. Similarly, small purchases continued to be made by barter in Chiang Rai in the 1880s. M. R. Rujaya Abhakorn, 'Ratburi, An Inner Province: Local Government and Central Politics in Siam, 1868–92', PhD dissertation, Cornell University, 1984, p. 31; Holt Samuel Hallett, *A Thousand Miles on an Elephant in the Shan States*, Edinburgh and London: William Blackwood and Sons, 1890, p. 163.
58 For examples see Hong, *Thailand*, p. 52.
59 B. O. Cartwright, 'The Huey Lottery', *Journal of the Siam Society*, 18, 3 (1924), p. 221. There is some dispute over the year the *huai* was established as the records of the court astrologers date its introduction to 1829. See Terwiel, *Travellers' Eyes*, pp. 215–16.
60 Hong, *Thailand*, p. 90.
61 Cartwright, 'Huey Lottery', p. 222.
62 This remained an important argument for the *huai* throughout its existence. *Bangkok Daily Mail*, 14 February 1916.
63 Bullet coins were not demonetized until 1904. Le May, *Siamese Coinage*, p. 85; Terwiel, *Political History*, pp. 159–60.
64 Wilson, 'State and Society', p. 620.
65 The most comprehensive account and catalogue of these gambling counters is H. A. Ramsden, *Siamese Porcelain and Other Tokens*, Yokohama, Japan: Jun Kobayagawa, 1911, esp. pp. 4–7.
66 Cited in Le May, *Siamese Coinage*, p. 99.
67 For Bangkok, see Bowring, *Kingdom of Siam*, 1, p. 257.
68 Bastian, *Journey in Siam*, p. 15.
69 Ibid., p. 19. Bastian attributes this to the fact that there were no Chinese living there; underlining once more the crucial role they played in the Thai economy and also their association with gambling.
70 Terwiel, *Political History*, pp. 180–81.
71 Sthirakoses (Phraya Anuman Rajdhon), *Looking Back: Book One*, Bangkok: Chulalongkorn University Press, 1992, p. 141.
72 Damrong, [Abolition], p. 22.
73 Le May, *Coinage*, pp. 99–100.
74 *PKPS*, 9, pp. 128–30
75 Ramsden, *Siamese Porcelain*, pp. 4–5.
76 Étienne Aymonier, *Isan Travels: Northeast Thailand's Economy in 1883–1884*, trans. Walter E. J. Tips, Bangkok: White Lotus, 2000 [1895, 1897], pp. 240, 257–58; Hallett, *Thousand Miles*, p. 234.
77 Rujaya, 'Ratburi', p. 167.
78 Sthirakoses, *Looking Back*, 1, pp. 135–36.
79 See Mr and Mrs Émile Jottrand, *In Siam: The Diary of A Legal Adviser of King Chulalongkorn's Government*, trans. Walter E. J. Tips, Bangkok: White Lotus, 1996 [1905], p. 186; W. A. R. Wood, *Consul in Paradise: Sixty-Nine Years in Siam*, London: Souvenir Press, 1965, pp. 22–23.
80 NA R5 KS 4.5/6, 'Graham to Chaophraya Thewet Wongwanit, November 1902'.
81 Ingram, *Economic Change*, pp. 15, 65; Nidhi, *Pen and Sail*, p. 107.
82 Foreign banks opened branches in Siam in the 1880s and 1890s, while the first Thai bank, the Siam Commercial Bank, was founded in 1907. These were concentrated in Bangkok, however, and the average Thai villager still had no access to banking facilities or savings institutions in the early 1930s. See Ian Brown, *The Élite and the Economy in Siam, c.1890–1920*, Singapore: Oxford University Press, 1988, pp. 125–35; and Carle C. Zimmerman, *Siam: Rural Economic Survey, 1930–31*, Bangkok: Bangkok Times Press, 1931, p. 46.

2 Games, dens and players

1 Originally, the whole of Bangkok constituted a single farm. This was divided into 20 different farms in the early 1870s. *PKPS*, 8, pp. 266–67.
2 Prince Damrong Rachanuphap, *Prachum phongsawadan phak thi 17: Ruang tamnan kanloek bonbia lae loek huai* [Collected Chronicles Part 17: The Abolition of Gambling Dens and the *huai* Lottery], Bangkok: Cremation Volume, 1960, pp. 19–21.
3 Recognizing this, J. Antonio called the gambling houses 'one of the greatest sights in the country' in his travel guide. J. Antonio, *The 1904 Travellers' Guide to Bangkok and Siam*, Bangkok: White Lotus, 1997 [1904], p. 3.
4 See Sthirakoses (Phraya Anuman Rajdhon), *Looking Back: Book One*, Bangkok: Chulalongkorn University Press, 1992, pp. 134–48; and Phraya Anuphap Traiphop, *Phramaha-nakhon-krungthep nai khwamsongcham khun ayu chetsip* [Bangkok as Remembered by a Seventy-Year Old], Bangkok: Cremation Volume, 1961, pp. 147–50.
5 For a comprehensive account of the shifting locations of the dens see Nuttaya Ussavaponganat, 'Bonbia nai sangkhom thai pho so 2367–2460: Kansuksa choeng sangkhom watthanatham' ['Bonbia' – Chinese Gambling in Thai Society, 1824–1917: A Socio-Cultural Study], MA thesis, Thammasat University, 2005, Ch. 2.
6 Carl Bock, *Temples and Elephants: Travels in Siam in 1881–82*, Singapore: Oxford University Press, 1986 [1884], p. 43.
7 *Bangkok Calendar*, 1873, p. 65.
8 *PKPS*, 11, p. 127.
9 Sthirakoses, *Looking Back,* 1, p. 143.
10 *PKPS*, 13, p. 43.
11 *Siam Repository*, 1873, p. 89.
12 Kanchana Chintakanon, 'Naiyobai khong ratthaban kieokap phasi-akon kanphanan pho so 2367–2460' [Government Policy Towards Gambling Taxes, 1824–1917], MA thesis, Sinlapakon University, 1987, pp. 75, 145–46.
13 *PKPS*, 16, pp. 288–91.
14 The following descriptions of these games and the methods of betting are drawn from a variety of sources. The most authoritative are Damrong, [Abolition], pp. 27–29; Lisut Thonchai, *Khu-mu kanphanan* [Gambling Handbook], 2nd ed., Bangkok, nd, pp. 93–99; and Nuttaya, ['Bonbia'], pp. 121–24. The best English-language descriptions are in Sthirakoses, *Looking Back*, 1, pp. 134–39; and *Siam Repository*, 1873, pp. 88–89, which refers to *thua* as the 'mat game' and *po pan* as the 'brass-cup game'.
15 The minimum stake was increased from one *salung* (quarter of a baht) to one baht in the early twentieth century. Nuttaya, ['Bonbia'], p. 147.
16 Ibid., pp. 63–64.
17 Sthirakoses, *Looking Back*, 1, pp. 134–35.
18 W. A. R. Wood, *Consul in Paradise: Sixty-Nine Years in Siam*, London: Souvenir Press, 1965, p. 21.
19 Nuttaya, ['Bonbia'], p. 128; Sthirakoses, *Looking Back*, 1, pp. 136–37.
20 Lucien Fournereau, *Bangkok in 1892*, trans. Walter E. J. Tips, Bangkok: White Lotus, 1998 [1894], p. 52.
21 Nuttaya, ['Bonbia'], pp. 117–18.
22 NA R5 N 8.1/142, 'A. J. A. Jardine to Prince Naret Worarit, 13 December 1897: Statements A, A1 & B'.
23 Otto E. Ehlers, *On Horseback through Indochina: Volume 3. Vietnam, Singapore, and Central Thailand*, trans. Walter E. J. Tips, Bangkok: White Lotus, 2002 [1894], pp. 166–67.

24 Sthirakoses, *Looking Back*, 1, p. 147.
25 For examples of criminal activities in the dens see *Siam Repository*, 1870, pp. 114, 172–73, 358; Fournereau, *Bangkok in 1892*, p. 52; and Walter E. J. Tips, *Crime and Punishment in King Chulalongkorn's Kingdom: The Special Commission for the Reorganisation of the Provincial Courts in Ayuthia (1896–1897)*, Bangkok: White Lotus, 1998, pp. 113–15, 166–67.
26 Prince Damrong Rachanuphap, *Ruang sonthana kap phuraiplon* [Interview with a Bandit], Bangkok: Cremation Volume, 1925, pp. 5–6, 41–42; Tips, *Crime and Punishment*, pp. 85–89, 103–6, 132–36, 276.
27 For the Bangkok dens, see Sthirakoses, *Looking Back*, 1, pp. 148–50; and Fournereau, *Bangkok in 1892*, pp. 51–52; and for the provincial ones, Adolf Bastian, *A Journey in Siam (1863)*, trans. Walter E. J. Tips and ed. Christian Goodden, Bangkok: White Lotus, 2005 [1867], p. 27; and Étienne Aymonier, *Isan Travels: Northeast Thailand's Economy in 1883–1884*, translated by Walter E. Tips, Bangkok: White Lotus, 2000 [1895, 1897], p. 259.
28 Sthirakoses, *Looking Back*, 1, p. 161.
29 Nuttaya, ['Bonbia'], pp. 51, 72, 99.
30 As a British official in the Royal Survey Department observed: 'The railways [...] are not without their bad side, for they enable the country people so easily to come into Bangkok and gamble away the price of their rice crop. That they actually have such an effect is shown by the great increase in value of the Bangkok gambling farm since the railways were started.' See P. A. Thompson, *Siam: An Account of the Country and the People*, Bangkok: White Lotus, 1987 [1910], p. 73.
31 Anuphap, [Bangkok], pp. 149–50; Ernest Young, *The Kingdom of the Yellow Robe*, London: Archibald Constable and Co., 1900, p. 18.
32 *RFAB (1901–02)*, p. 3.
33 Arnold Wright and Oliver Breakspear (eds), *Twentieth Century Impressions of Siam: Its History, People, Commerce, Industries, and Resources*, Bangkok: White Lotus, 1994 [1908], p. 108.
34 NA R5 Kh 14.1.Kh/22, 'Prince Mahit Ratchaharithai to Chulalongkorn, 13 August 1901'.
35 *RPAB Year 120* [1901/2], p. 22.
36 Ibid.
37 See Tips, *Crime and Punishment*, pp. 109–10; and Kanchana, [Government Policy], pp. 86–87.
38 *RPAB Year 123* [1904/5], p. 18.
39 NA R6 N 4.1/51, 'Phraya Phirentharathibodi to E. W. Trotter, 29 June 1915'; NA R6 N 4.1/73, 'Trotter to Chaophraya Yomarat, 23 December 1915'.
40 See, for instance, NA R5 N 42.11/15, 'Chin Hoi to Finance Office, 4 June 1897'; NA R5 N 42.11/16, 'Prince Alangkan to Phraya Phetchaphani, 15 November 1897'; NA R5 N 3.3.K/28, 'Chin Chieo to Finance Office, 27 January 1898'.
41 NA R5 N 42.11/23, 'Chin Hu to Finance Office, 26 August 1899'.
42 NA R5 N 42.11/27, 'Chin Cheng to Finance Office, 22 October 1900'.
43 Kanchana, [Government Policy], p. 107; Nuttaya, ['Bonbia'], p. 144.
44 *PKPS*, 13, p. 56.
45 NA R5 N 8.1/142, 'Jardine to Naret, 13 December 1897 and 8 July 1898'; *RPAB 1898–99*, pp. 9–10.
46 NA R5 N 42.11/16, 'Alangkan to Phetchaphani, 15 November 1897'; NA R5 N 42.11/23, 'Chin Hu to Finance Office, 26 August 1899'.
47 NA R5 N 42.11/15, 'Chin Hoi to Finance Office, 4 June 1897'.
48 NA R5 N 42.11/27, 'Chin Cheng to Finance Office, 22 October 1900'.
49 See, for instance, *RPAB 120* [1901/02], p. 14; and Tips, *Crime and Punishment*, pp. 94–101.

50 NA R5 N 6.2/929, 'Naret to Prince Sommot, 17 May 1902', 'Lawson to Naret, 18 June 1902'.
51 *RPAB Year 123* [1904/05], p. 17.
52 *Siam Observer* (Thai edition), 5 April 1917.
53 NA R5 M 2.11/11, 'Report on Meeting of Provincial Governors, 8 September 1906'; NA R6 Kh 2/12, 'Prince Chanthaburi to Vajiravudh, July 1917'.
54 *Chino sayam warasap*, 17 April 1917.
55 Scot Barmé, *Woman, Man, Bangkok: Love, Sex and Popular Culture in Thailand*, Lanham: Rowman and Littlefield, 2002, p. 45.
56 Nuttaya, ['Bonbia'], pp. 151–52.
57 The most detailed accounts of the *huai* are Sthirakoses, *Looking Back*, 1, Ch. 15; and B. O. Cartwright, 'The Huey Lottery', *Journal of the Siam Society*, 18, 3 (1924), pp. 221–39.
58 Cartwright, 'Huey Lottery', p. 228.
59 The area covered by the *huai* lottery farm mirrored the growth of greater Bangkok. In the early 1850s, Mongkut extended it to include the provinces of Nonthaburi and Pathum Thani. With the creation of *monthon* Krungthep (Greater Bangkok administrative area) around the turn of the twentieth century, the farm came to encompass Samut Prakan, Nakhon Khuan Khan (Phra Pradaeng), Minburi and Thanyaburi. Kanchana [Government Policy], pp. 46–47, 168.
60 Kullada Kesboonchoo Mead, *The Rise and Decline of Thai Absolutism*, London and New York: RoutledgeCurzon, 2004, p. 52.
61 Cartwright, 'Huey Lottery', pp. 234–35.
62 *Bangkok Calendar*, 1873, p. 63.
63 Cartwright, 'Huey Lottery', p. 238. One att was 1/64 of a baht.
64 Damrong, [Abolition], p. 61.
65 Cartwright, 'Huey Lottery', pp. 228–29.
66 Damrong, [Abolition], p. 62.
67 For details of these rituals and monks, see Cartwright, 'Huey Lottery', pp. 230–31; Sthirakoses, *Looking Back*, 1, pp. 161–64; and *Siam Repository*, 1873, p. 24.
68 *BTWM*, 29 March 1916.
69 Ibid.; Sthirakoses, *Looking Back*, 1, p. 157.
70 Damrong, [Abolition], p. 90.
71 *Bangkok Calendar*, 1873, p. 64.
72 Cartwright, 'Huey Lottery', p. 239.
73 *RFAB 1902–03*, p. 4.
74 *BTWM*, 26 October 1904.
75 Ibid.; Cartwright, 'Huey Lottery', p. 239.
76 Kanchana, [Government Policy], pp. 23–24.
77 In 1851, revenue from the gambling den and lottery farm was 213,200 baht compared to just 16,000 baht from the other gambling farm. Constance M. Wilson, 'State and Society in the Reign of Mongkut, 1851–68: Thailand on the Eve of Modernization', PhD dissertation, Cornell University, 1970, pp. 995–96.
78 Ibid., pp. 635, 1045–46.
79 *PKPS*, 13, p. 53.
80 Monsignor Jean-Baptiste Pallegoix, *Description of the Thai Kingdom or Siam: Thailand under King Mongkut*, trans. Walter E. J. Tips, Bangkok: White Lotus, 2000 [1854], p. 123.
81 Aymonier, *Isan Travels*, p. 173.
82 Ibid.
83 Anthony Reid, *Southeast Asia in the Age of Commerce, 1450–1680. Volume One: The Lands Below the Winds*, New Haven and London: Yale University Press, 1988, p. 193.

84 Ibid., p. 194. See also Clifford Geertz, 'Deep Play: Notes on the Balinese Cockfight' in his *The Interpretation of Cultures: Selected Essays*, New York: Basic Books, 1973, pp. 412–53.
85 For descriptions of these games see Wood, *Consul in Paradise*, pp. 76–79; and Ehlers, *On Horseback*, pp. 189–90.
86 Bock, *Temples and Elephants*, pp. 233–36.
87 For descriptions of these kite-flying contests see Young, *Kingdom of the Yellow Robe*, pp. 150–53; and Wright and Breakspear (eds), *Twentieth Century Impressions*, pp. 236–37.
88 Sombat Plainoi, *Sorties into Thai Cultural History*, Bangkok: Ministry of Education, 1982, pp. 36–37.
89 *BTWM*, 25 October 1913.
90 Anek Bunyaphakdi, *Phai phong thai* [Thai Card Games], Bangkok: Cremation Volume, 1967, pp. 12–13.
91 *BTWM*, 25 October 1913.
92 Anek, [Card Games], pp. 11–12.
93 See Thompson, *Siam*, pp. 135–36; and Young, *Kingdom of the Yellow Robe*, pp. 160, 304–5.
94 Damrong, [Abolition], p. 18.
95 See, for instance, Ehlers, *On Horseback*, p. 166; *Siam Repository*, 1874, p. 413; Thompson, *Siam*, p. 69.
96 In addition to Figure 2.2, see the temple murals of people playing three-stick trick and *hi-lo* in Preecha Kanchanakom, Sinchai Krabuansaeng, Marut Amranondha and Kamol Chayawatana, *Dhonburi Mural Painting*, Bangkok: The Society for the Conservation of National Art Treasures and the Environment, 1980, pp. 68–69.
97 Damrong, [Abolition], p. 13.
98 *PKPS*, 5, pp. 65–71.
99 King Chulalongkorn, *Phithi songkran* [Songkran Ceremonies], Bangkok: Cremation Volume, 1978, p. 96.
100 The large number of women kept within the Inner City of the Grand Palace, for instance, 'spent countless hours in gambling', while princes were known to sell regalia such as their swords in order to pay off gambling debts. Government officials and princes might also be seen in the capital's gambling dens. See Mary Lovina Cort, *Siam: Or, the Heart of Farther India*, New York: Anson D. F. Randolph and Co., 1886, p. 51; Thompson, *Siam*, p. 165; and Wilson, 'State and Society', p. 503.
101 *BTWM*, 25 October 1913.
102 NA R5 N 11.3 K/6, 'Chaiyan to Chulalongkorn, 25 October 1893'.
103 See, for instance, *Siam Repository*, 1873, p. 90; and *BTWM*, 9 July 1904.
104 Thompson, *Siam*, p. 217; Sthirakoses, *Looking Back*, 1, p. 140.
105 Bock, *Temples and Elephants*, p. 131.
106 Nuttaya, ['Bonbia'], pp. 141–42.
107 *PKPS*, 9, pp. 204–5; Tips, *Crime and Punishment*, p. 165.
108 As Munting notes, 'behaviourists have explained gambling as being stimulated or reinforced by experience, so that some learn to gamble'. Soft forms of gambling such as coin tossing might then lead to harder forms such as *thua po*. Roger Munting, *An Economic and Social History of Gambling in Britain and the USA*, Manchester: Manchester University Press, 1996, p. 191.
109 *PKPS*, 8, pp. 207–11, 224–25; *PKPS*, 9, pp. 204–6.
110 NA R5 M 2.11/12, 'Report on the Meeting of Provincial Governors, 16 September 1905'.
111 Maxwell Sommerville, *Siam on the Meinam: From the Gulf to Ayuthia*, Bangkok: White Lotus, 1985 [1897], pp. 87–88. See also Thompson, *Siam*, p. 69.

112 Gerda Reith, *The Age of Chance: Gambling in Western Culture*, London and New York: Routledge, 1999, pp. 145–46.
113 Kanchana, [Government Policy], pp. 31–32.
114 Young, *Kingdom of the Yellow Robe*, p. 162; Henry Norman, *The People and Politics of the Far East: Travels and Studies in the British, French, Spanish and Portuguese Colonies, Siberia, China, Japan, Korea, Siam and Malaya*, London: T. F. Unwin, 1895, p. 421.
115 This is the conventional explanation for gambling in many different social and cultural settings. See Munting, *History of Gambling*, pp. 189–90; and Reith, *Age of Chance*, pp. 130–36.
116 Reith, *Age of Chance*, pp. 128–29.
117 Damrong, [Abolition], p. 21.
118 Thompson, *Siam*, pp. 143–44.
119 Alan Klima, *The Funeral Casino: Meditation, Massacre, and Exchange with the Dead in Thailand*, Princeton and Oxford: Princeton University Press, 2002, pp. 250–51.
120 Cort, *Siam*, p. 116.
121 Until 1940, the Thai year started on 1 April and during the nineteenth century this was celebrated separately from the Songkran festival, which now marks the Thai New Year. See Antonio, *Guide to Bangkok*, pp. 38–39; and Bastian, *Journey in Siam*, pp. 167–68.
122 Damrong dates this dispensation back to the reign of King Taksin, attributing it as a morale raising measure during those years of sustained conflict. Damrong, [Abolition], pp. 12–13.
123 For descriptions of these festivals and the gambling see Bastian, *Journey in Siam*, pp. 167–68; Cort, *Siam*, pp. 178–80; Sthirakoses, *Looking Back*, 1, pp. 171–72.
124 Two of the most influential studies in this regard are Erving Goffman, 'Where the Action Is' in his *Interaction Ritual: Essays on Face-to-Face Behavior*, New York: Pantheon Books, 1967, pp. 149–270; and Geertz, 'Deep Play'.
125 Goffman, 'Where the Action Is', p. 240.
126 Reith, *Age of Chance*, p. 94.
127 Klima makes a similar observation in his description of gambling among army cadets from differing socio-economic backgrounds at the Chulachomkhlao Military Academy. Klima, *Funeral Casino*, p. 256.
128 See Reith, *Age of Chance*, pp. 81–87, 150–51; and Munting, *History of Gambling*, pp. 190–91.
129 Ruth Benedict, *Thai Culture and Behavior: An Unpublished War Time Study dated September, 1943*, Ithaca, New York: Data Paper Number 4, Southeast Asia Program, Cornell University, 1952, pp. 23–24.
130 Ibid., p. 24. Emphasis in original.
131 Anuman observes how village people around the turn of the twentieth century usually had only four or five baht in cash at home. Any excess would be kept hidden in containers around the house or, if a very large sum, buried somewhere secret. Sthirakoses (Phraya Anuman Rajdhon), *Looking Back: Book Three*, Bangkok: Chulalongkorn University Press, 2001, p. 35.
132 R. McKibbin, 'Working-Class Gambling in Britain, 1880–1939', *Past and Present*, 82, 1 (February 1979), p. 161.
133 Ibid., pp. 161–63.

3 Gambling revenue and the creation of the modern Thai nation-state

1 *The Economist*, 24 February 2011.

2 The role of tax farming in the creation of modern, rationalized bureaucratic states in South-East Asia is examined at length in John Butcher and Howard Dick (eds), *The Rise and Fall of Revenue Farming: Business Elites and the Emergence of the Modern State in Southeast Asia*, London: MacMillan, 1993.
3 Hong Lysa, *Thailand in the Nineteenth Century: Evolution of the Economy and Society*, Singapore: Institute of Southeast Asian Studies, 1984, p. 93.
4 This point is made most forcibly in Constance M. Wilson, 'Revenue Farming, Economic Development and Government Policy during the Early Bangkok Period, 1830–92' in Butcher and Dick (eds), *Revenue Farming*, p. 161.
5 Prince Damrong Rachanuphap, *Prachum phongsawadan phak thi 17: Ruang tamnan kanloek bonbia lae huai* [Collected Chronicles, Part 17: The Abolition of the Gambling Dens and the *huai* Lottery], Bangkok: Cremation Volume, 1960, p. 90.
6 By the late 1900s, competition for the principal opium farm had become so intense that it led to the collapse of the entire system. See Ian Brown, 'The End of the Opium Farm in Siam, 1905–7' in Butcher and Dick (eds), *Revenue Farming*, pp. 233–45.
7 The most comprehensive overviews of tax farming in Siam are Hong, *Thailand*, Ch. 4; and Wilson, 'Revenue Farming'.
8 Bangkok's outlying provinces and tributaries had their own tax farms. Following the extension of Bangkok's control in the 1870s and 1880s, local rulers were stripped of their power to appoint tax farmers and some local gambling farms were abolished. See the map and related comments in Wilson, 'Revenue Farming', pp. 150–51; and Kanchana Chintakanon, 'Naiyobai khong ratthaban kieokap phasi-akon kanphanan pho so 2367–2460' [Government Policy Towards Gambling Taxes, 1824–1917], MA thesis, Sinlapakon University, 1987, pp. 76–77, 120.
9 Wilson, 'Revenue Farming', p. 148; Kanchana, [Government Policy], p. 101.
10 This was a feature of tax farming throughout South-East Asia, see John Butcher, 'Revenue Farming and the Changing State in Southeast Asia' in Butcher and Dick (eds), *Revenue Farming*, p. 24.
11 Hong, *Thailand*, p. 103.
12 Kanchana, [Government Policy], p. 66. *Sakdina* literally means 'power over the fields' and the number of marks indicated one's position in the official hierarchy.
13 Damrong, [Abolition], p. 21.
14 Holt Samuel Hallett, *A Thousand Miles on an Elephant in the Shan States*, Edinburgh and London: William Blackwood and Sons, 1890, p. 243.
15 Nuttaya Ussavaponganat, 'Bonbia nai sangkhom thai pho so 2367–2460: Kansuksa choeng sangkhom watthanatham' ['Bonbia' – Chinese Gambling in Thai Society, 1824–1917: A Socio-Cultural Study], MA thesis, Thammasat University, 2005, p. 87.
16 Howard Dick, 'A Fresh Approach to Southeast Asian History' in Butcher and Dick (eds), *Revenue Farming*, pp. 5–6.
17 John G. Butcher, 'The Demise of the Revenue Farm System in the Federated Malay States', *Modern Asian Studies*, 17, 3 (July 1983), p. 393.
18 Ibid.; Kanchana, [Government Policy], p. 83.
19 *PKPS*, 8, p. 135.
20 Butcher, 'Revenue Farming', pp. 19, 37.
21 Kanchana, [Government Policy], pp. 81, 94–95.
22 Hong, *Thailand*, p. 103.
23 Ibid., pp. 93, 103.
24 Constance M. Wilson, 'State and Society in the Reign of Mongkut, 1851–68: Thailand on the Eve of Modernization', PhD dissertation, Cornell University, 1970, p. 635.

25 Pasuk Phongpaichit and Chris Baker, *Thailand: Economy and Politics*, 2nd ed., New York: Oxford University Press, 2002, p. 231.
26 *PKPS*, 8, pp. 266–67.
27 Nuttaya, ['Bonbia'], p. 66.
28 Hallett, *Thousand Miles*, p. 238.
29 On the Finance Office and the attendant fiscal reforms see Ian Brown, *The Creation of the Modern Ministry of Finance in Siam, 1885–1910*, London: MacMillan, 1992, pp. 14–18; and Hong, *Thailand*, pp. 116–19.
30 Kullada Kesboonchoo Mead, *The Rise and Decline of Thai Absolutism*, London and New York: RoutledgeCurzon, 2004, pp. 53, 65.
31 *PKPS*, 13, pp. 40–44.
32 NA R5 Kh 14.1.Kh/1, 'Narathip to Chulalongkorn, 5 October 1890 and 15 October 1891'.
33 *PKPS*, 13, pp. 51–60, 275–84.
34 Nuttaya, ['Bonbia'], pp. 45, 133–40.
35 Ibid., pp. 102–3.
36 Ibid., pp. 100–102.
37 NA R5 N 42.11/31, 'Mahit to Prince Naret Worarit, 23 May 1902', 'Lawson to Naret, 31 May 1902'.
38 *PKPS*, 18, p. 441.
39 NA R5 Kh 14.1.Kh/1, 'Narathip to Chulalongkorn, 15 October 1891'.
40 Kanchana, [Government Policy], p. 150.
41 Hong, *Thailand*, p. 128.
42 See Brown, *Ministry of Finance*, pp. 64–65.
43 Dick, 'Fresh Approach', p. 9.
44 For the Thai government's annual revenue and expenditures from 1892 to 1950, see James C. Ingram, *Economic Change in Thailand, 1850–1970*, Stanford, California: Stanford University Press, 1971, pp. 328–29.
45 For details of these closures see *PKPS*, 16, pp. 288–91, 475–79; NA R5 Kh 14.1.Kh/12, 'Mahit to Chulalongkorn, 21 December 1899'; NA R5 Kh 14.1.Kh/15, 'Mahit to Chulalongkorn, 13 December 1900'; NA R5 Kh 14.1.Kh/18, 'Mahit to Chulalongkorn, 9 December 1901 and 12 December 1902'.
46 NA R5 Kh 14.1.Kh/8, 'Mahit to Chulalongkorn, 11 May 1898'; NA R5 Kh 14.1.Kh/10, 'Mahit to Chulalongkorn, 27 November 1898'.
47 Kanchana, [Government Policy], p. 150.
48 Brown, *Ministry of Finance*, p. 89.
49 For the complete Act, see *PKPS*, 18, pp. 275–79.
50 NA R5 M 1.3/20, 'Damrong to Chulalongkorn, 19 March 1902'. For the inner *monthons*, *monthon* Phayap and Bangkok regulations, see *PKPS*, 18, pp. 264–69, 269–74, 548–53, respectively.
51 *SY 1931–33*, p. 294.
52 NA R5 M 2.11/11, 'Report of Meeting of Provincial Governors, 8 September 1906'. The licence fees for cards, for instance, were raised from 1 baht a circle per day to 4 baht per day and 8 baht a night in the provinces, and to 6 baht a day and 12 baht a night in Bangkok. Licence fees revenue, meanwhile, only rose 100,000 baht between 1905/6 and 1906/7. See *PKPS*, 20, p. 512; *PKPS*, 21, p. 59; *SY 1931–33*, p. 294.
53 *PKPS*, 21, pp. 120–21, 166–67; NA R5 Kh 14.1.Kh/20, 'Damrong to Chulalongkorn, 5 June 1906'.
54 Thongchai Winichakul, *Siam Mapped: A History of the Geo-Body of a Nation*, Honolulu: University of Hawaii Press, 1994.
55 NA R5 Kh 14.1.Kh/18, 'Report of Meeting of the Council of Ministers, 15 December 1904'.

56 NA R5 Kh 14.1.Kh/18, 'Report of Meeting on Closing the Gambling Houses and Raising Taxes, 14 January 1905'.
57 NA R5 Kh 14.1.Kh/18, 'Notification by the Minister of Finance on the Abolition of Gambling, 124'.
58 NA R5 Kh 14.1.Kh/18, 'Report of Meeting on Closing the Gambling Houses and Raising Taxes, 14 January 1905'.
59 Brown, *Ministry of Finance*, pp. 91–92.
60 *SY 1931–33*, pp. 292, 294.
61 Ingram, *Economic Change*, p. 178.
62 Kanchana, [Government Policy], p. 163.
63 *Bangkok Daily Mail*, 14 February 1916.
64 Nuttaya, ['Bonbia'], pp. 105–7; *SY 1931–33*, p. 295.
65 NA R5 Kh 14.1.Kh/22, 'Chanthaburi to Chulalongkorn, 3 March 1910'; Nuttaya, ['Bonbia'], pp. 109–10.
66 NA R6 Kh 18/5, 'Chanthaburi to Vajiravudh, 27 March 1915'.
67 NA R6 Kh 18/5, 'Chanthaburi to Vajiravudh, 25 February 1916'; *RFAB 1916–17*, p. 5.
68 NA K Kh 0301.1.3/5, 'Vajiravudh to Chanthaburi, 10 November 1916'.
69 See, for instance, NA R6 Kh 2/12, 'Chanthaburi to Vajiravudh, July 1917'.
70 *PKPS*, 28, pp. 472–73; *PKPS*, 29, p. 327.
71 NA R6 B 11/2, 'Chanthaburi to Prince Prachin, 5 December 1919'.
72 NA K Kh 0301.1.3/7, 'Translation of Finance letter to H. M. No. 37/2785 dated 21 May B. E. 2461 (1918)'.
73 Ibid.
74 NA R6 B 11/2, 'Chanthaburi to Prachin, 5 December 1919'.
75 The Royal Division alone, which was under the direct control of the king, received 600,000 baht annually from the Privy Purse. Stephen L. W. Greene, *Absolute Dreams: Thai Government Under Rama VI, 1910–1925*, Bangkok: White Lotus, 1999, p. 164.
76 Ibid., p. 140; NA R6 B 11/7, 'Phraya Nonthisen to Vajiravudh, 17 August 1923 and 11 April 1924'.
77 Ingram, *Economic Change*, p. 190; Greene, *Absolute Dreams*, pp. 141–42, 158–59, 166.
78 On the security fears of the absolute monarchy and the establishment of the army aviation corps, see Walter F. Vella, *Chaiyo! King Vajiravudh and the Development of Thai Nationalism*, Honolulu: University of Hawaii Press, 1978, pp. 79–87.
79 NA R6 B 11/2, 'Yomarat to Prachin, 4 December 1919', 'Chanthaburi to Prachin, 5 December 1919'; NA R6 B 11/5, 'Prince Nen to Devawongse, 4 December 1920'.
80 NA R6 B 11/2, 'Yomarat to Phraya Chakraphan Sisinwisut, 23 February 1922', 'Prince Khamrop to Chaophraya Ram Rakkhop, 26 January 1923'.
81 NA R6 B 11/5, 'Prince Supphayokha to Chakraphan, 29 July 1922'; NA R6 B 11/7, 'Chaophraya Mahithon to Nonthisen, 20 August 1923'.
82 NA R6 B 11/2, 'Yomarat to Chakraphan, 23 February 1922'.
83 *Bangkok Times*, 22 August 1923.
84 NA R6 B 11/4, 'Nai Hong Heng to Vajiravudh, 17 December 1919', 'Chanthaburi to Vajiravudh, 22 December 1919'.
85 On some of the problems associated with lotteries in the early 1920s, see *BTWM*, 21 March 1925.
86 On the scandal and subsequent court cases, see *BTWM*, 3 September 1925; Greene, *Absolute Dreams*, pp. 164, 167; NA R7 Y 4/1, 'Phraya Anuphap to Ram Rakkhop, 24 July 1925', 'Mahithon to Phraya Thepwithura, 25 July 1925', 'Prince Phanurangsi to Phraya Chinda, 6 October 1927'.

87 On the construction of the park, and planning of the exhibition and lottery, see *BTWM*, 29 January 1925; Vella, *Chaiyo!*, pp. 174–75, 258; Greene, *Absolute Dreams*, pp. 164–65, 168–69.
88 Vella, *Chaiyo!*, p. 259.
89 Greene, *Absolute Dreams*, p. 165.
90 Erik Seidenfaden, *Guide to Bangkok with Notes on Siam*, Singapore: Oxford University Press, 1984 [1928], p. 61.
91 *San phranakhon*, 24 November 1924.
92 *Chino sayam warasap*, 13 February 1923.
93 *BTWM*, 17 July 1923 and 25 November 1924.
94 *Samphan thai*, 19 January 1924; *BTWM*, 21 January 1924.
95 David K. Wyatt, *Thailand: A Short History*, 2nd ed., New Haven and London: Yale University Press, 2003, p. 227.
96 NA R7 M 15/4, 'Prince Boriphat to Mahithon, 17 June 1932', 'Wibun to Damrong, 24 June 1932'; NA (2) SR 0201.101/1, 'Cover Sheet – Royal Opinion, 20 June 1932'.
97 Virginia Thompson, *Thailand: The New Siam*, New York: MacMillan, 1941, p. 696.
98 NA (2) SR 0201.101/1, 'President of People's Committee to Minister of the Interior, 11 August 1932'.
99 Pridi Banomyong, *Pridi by Pridi: Selected Writings on Life, Politics, and Economy*, trans. Chris Baker and Pasuk Phongpaichit, Chiang Mai: Silkworm Books, 2000, pp. 100, 120, 123 n. 10.
100 The first lottery had 383 prizes amounting to 500,000 baht in total, ranging from a first prize of 80,000 baht to 250 prizes of 400 baht. The second introduced 100 baht prizes for all tickets that shared the same three final numbers as the winning ticket, meaning there were over 1,000 prizes in total. NA (2) SR 0201.101/5, 'Chaophraya Mukhamontri to Phraya Manopakon, 12 June 1933', 'Report of State Lottery Committee Meeting, 12 June 1933'; NA K Kh 0301.1.3/10, 'D. G. of Revenue's Memo on State Lottery Scheme B. E. 2477 to S. C. Finance dated 2 January B. E. 2476'.
101 NA (2) SR 0201.101/6, 'Report on Issuing Million baht State Lottery (1st Occasion), B. E. 2477'.
102 NA (2) SR 0201.101/5, 'Cabinet Secretary to Minister of the Interior, 18 April 1933'; NA (2) SR 0201.101/6, 'Minister of Finance to PM, 25 January 1934'.
103 NA (2) SR 0201.101/6, 'Cabinet Secretary to Minister of Finance, 15 February 1934'.
104 NA (2) SR 0201.101/12, 'Chairman of the Siamese Red Cross to Phraya Phahon, 12 March 1934'.
105 The second lottery sold out within four months and yielded profits of 440,000 baht. NA (2) SR 0201.101/6, 'Report on Issuing Million baht State Lottery (1st Occasion), B. E. 2477'. On the problems related to the lotteries, see NA (2) SR 0201.101/5, 'Mukhamontri to PM, 18 September 1933', 'Mukhamontri to Cabinet Secretary, 1 November 1933'.
106 NA (2) SR 0201.101/8, 'President of the Constitution Celebration Lottery Committee to Cabinet Secretary, 18 November 1933'.
107 As Pridi explained in a radio broadcast on the fourth anniversary of the coup: 'The constitution is the highest dhamma to enable the Siamese people to survive as an independent nation'. Similarly, the chief ideologue of the new regime, Luang Wichit Wathakan, proclaimed: 'Let everybody be confident that this constitution will bring progress and happiness to our country. We must make our constitution secure as it is the basis of our nation.' See, respectively, Pridi, *Pridi*, p. 196; Scot Barmé, *Luang Wichit Wathakan and the Creation of a Thai Identity*, Singapore: Institute of Southeast Asian Studies, 1993, p. 109.

108 Wyatt, *Thailand*, p. 239.
109 Barmé, *Luang Wichit Wathakan*, pp. 111–13.
110 See Anake Nawigamune (comp.), *A Century of Thai Graphic Design*, London: Thames and Hudson, 2000, p. 65.
111 NA (2) SR 0201.101/13, 'Report of Meeting Establishing the Framework for 1st Municipal Lotteries, B. E. 2477'.
112 NA (2) SR 0201.101/13, 'Minister of Interior to PM, 8 November 1935'.
113 *BTWM*, 19 May 1934.
114 NA (2) SR 0201.31/6, 'Minister of Economic Affairs to PM, 22 May 1934'.
115 *PKPS*, 52, pp. 88–91.
116 Quoted in *BTWM*, 4 May 1939.
117 *BTWM*, 2 and 6 May 1939.
118 *BTWM*, 4 May 1939. A photo taken at the casino showed only two Westerners among all the guests. Kenneth P. Landon, *The Chinese in Thailand*, New York: Russell and Russell, 1941, p. 90.
119 *BTWM*, 28 September 1939.
120 *BTWM*, 28 January and 22 February 1940.
121 *BTWM*, 20 March 1940.
122 Pridi, *Pridi*, p. 181; Ingram, *Economic Change*, p. 184.
123 *BTWM*, 22 February 1940.
124 *BTWM*, 20 March 1940.
125 *BTWM*, 28 May 1940.
126 Thanongsak Thinsinuan, 'Kotmai kieokap kanphanan' [Laws about Gambling], MA thesis, Faculty of Law, Thammasat University, 1986, pp. 80–81; *Thai mai*, 1 and 5 June 1945.

4 The Thai elite, anti-gambling and lawmaking

1 On the influence of Western ideas, see Thongchai Winichakul, 'The Quest for "*Siwilai*": A Geographical Discourse of Civilizational Thinking in the Late Nineteenth and Early Twentieth-Century Siam', *Journal of Asian Studies*, 59, 3 (August 2000), pp. 528–49; Scot Barmé, *Luang Wichit Wathakan and the Creation of a Thai Identity*, Singapore: Institute of Southeast Asian Studies, 1993, pp. 17–21; and Kullada Kesboonchoo Mead, *The Rise and Decline of Thai Absolutism*, London and New York: RoutledgeCurzon, 2004, pp. 36–37.
2 Thongchai, 'Quest for "*Siwilai*"', p. 529.
3 Phra Ratcha-woramuni (Prayut Payutto), *Photchanukrom phutthasat: Chabap pramuan tham* [Dictionary of Buddhism], Bangkok: Chulalongkorn University Fund for Publishing a Dictionary of Buddhism, 1985, pp. 175–76; George Bradley McFarland (ed.), *Thai-English Dictionary*, Stanford, California: Stanford University Press, 1944, p. 964.
4 Kanchana Chintakanon, 'Naiyobai khong ratthaban kieokap phasi-akon kanphanan pho so 2367–2460' [Government Policy Towards Gambling Taxes, 1824–1917], MA thesis, Sinlapakon University, 1987, pp. 27–28.
5 Monsignor Jean-Baptiste Pallegoix, *Description of the Thai Kingdom or Siam: Thailand under King Mongkut*, trans. Walter E. J. Tips, Bangkok: White Lotus, 2000 [1854], p. 123.
6 Kanchana, [Government Policy], pp. 49–50.
7 *Siam Repository*, 1869, p. 113.
8 NA R5 N 2/95, 'Nai Ki and Chin Kai Ho to Prince Mahit, 20 April 1903'; *PKPS*, 19, pp. 11–12.
9 See, for instance, NA R5 N 2/95, 'Prince Naret Worarit to Chulalongkorn, 7 February 1903'; NA R6 N 11.5.Ch/17, 'Ministry of Interior Consultation on

Class 2 Gambling'; NA R7 Kh 2/2, 'Prince Boriphat to Prajadhipok, 8 August 1928'.
10 NA R6 KS 1/4, 'Memorandum on our Domestic Economy'.
11 Prince Damrong Rachanuphap, *Prachum phongsawadan phak thi 17: Ruang tamnan kanloek bonbia lae huai* [Collected Chronicles, Part 17: The Abolition of the Gambling Dens and the *huai* Lottery], Bangkok: Cremation Volume, 1960, pp. 90–91.
12 Ibid., p. 90; NA R7 Kh 2/2, 'Boriphat to Prajadhipok, 8 August 1928'.
13 See, for instance, NA R7 Kh 2/2, 'Boriphat to Prajadhipok, 8 August 1928'; and P. A. Thompson, *Siam: An Account of the Country and the People*, Bangkok: White Lotus, 1987 [1910], p. 69.
14 *RPAB Year 122* [1903/4], pp. 1, 3.
15 Ibid., p. 25.
16 NA R6 N 4.1/73, 'E. W. Trotter to Yomarat, 23 December 1915'.
17 NA R5 N 6.2/963, 'Damrong to Chulalongkorn, 5 March 1907'.
18 NA R5 M 1.3/20, 'Damrong to Chulalongkorn, 27 June 1902'; *PKPS*, 18, pp. 431–32.
19 NA R5 Kh 14.1.Kh/18, 'Damrong to Prince Sommot, 13 February 1904'.
20 There were two categories of debt slaves: redeemable ones, whose labour had essentially been mortgaged by the seller and who had some limited civil rights, and non-redeemable ones, who had been sold outright and had little legal protection. During the nineteenth century, the majority of debt slaves were redeemable and the relative number of such slaves was apparently increasing.
21 H. Warrington Smyth, *Five Years in Siam: From 1891–1896*, Bangkok: White Lotus, 1994 [1898], vol. 2, p. 255.
22 Prince Dilok Nabarath, *Siam's Rural Economy under King Chulalongkorn*, trans. Walter E. J. Tips, Bangkok: White Lotus, 2000 [1908], p. 36.
23 Nuttaya presents the tragic life story of one Amdeng Chan, whose parents sold themselves into slavery to pay off their gambling debts and, later in her life, whose gambler husband sold her to a brothel keeper to work as a prostitute. Nuttaya Ussavaponganat, 'Bonbia nai sangkhom thai pho so 2367–2460: Kansuksa choeng sangkhom watthanatham' ['Bonbia' – Chinese Gambling in Thai Society, 1824–1917: A Socio-Cultural Study], MA thesis, Thammasat University, 2005, pp. 130–31.
24 Chatchai Panananon, 'Siamese "Slavery": The Institution and its Abolition', PhD dissertation, University of Michigan, 1982, p. 236.
25 Thanet Aphornsuvan, 'Slavery and Modernity: Freedom in the Making of Modern Siam' in David Kelly and Anthony Reid (eds), *Asian Freedoms: The Idea of Freedom in East and Southeast Asia*, Cambridge: Cambridge University Press, 1998, p. 176.
26 Andrew Turton, 'Thai Institutions of Slavery' in James L. Watson (ed.), *Asian and African Systems of Slavery*, Oxford: Basil Blackwell, 1980, p. 285.
27 On the issues of polygamy and slavery see, respectively, Craig J. Reynolds, *Seditious Histories: Contesting Thai and Southeast Asian Pasts*, Seattle and London: University of Washington Press, 2006, Ch. 9; and Thanet, 'Slavery and Modernity', pp. 161–86.
28 NA K Kh 0301.1.3/5, 'The Abolition of Gambling (Communiqué by Ministry of Finance)'.
29 NA R5 Kh 14.1.Kh/18, 'Hamilton King to Prince Devawongse, 20 April 1905'.
30 *BTWM*, 20 November 1939.
31 Peter A. Jackson, 'The Thai Regime of Images' and 'The Performative State: Semi-coloniality and the Tyranny of Images in Modern Thailand', *Sojourn*, 19, 2 (October 2004), pp. 181–218, 219–53.
32 Jackson, 'Regime of Images', p. 181.

33 Jackson, 'Performative State', p. 235.
34 Kullada, *Thai Absolutism*, pp. 36, 87.
35 Barmé, *Luang Wichit Wathakan*, pp. 20–21.
36 Kullada, *Thai Absolutism*, pp. 46–47.
37 NA R6 Kh 18/5, 'Chanthaburi to Vajiravudh, 25 February 1916'.
38 Kullada, *Thai Absolutism*, p. 51.
39 Chris Baker and Pasuk Phongpaichit, *A History of Thailand*, New York: Cambridge University Press, pp. 77–78.
40 NA R5 Kh 14.1.Kh/18, 'Notification by the Minister of Finance on the Abolition of Gambling, 124'.
41 NA K Kh 0301.1.30/15, 'H. E. Chao Phya Yomaraj's letter of 1 March 2458 (1916) to H. M. the King on the Chinese Question'.
42 NA R5 Kh 14.1.Kh/18, 'Memorandum containing proposals at to the manner in which revenue can be raised to supply the deficiency which will be caused by the abolition of gambling in the provinces'.
43 NA R6 KS 1/4, 'Memorandum on our Domestic Economy'.
44 Ian Brown, *The Élite and the Economy in Siam, c.1890–1920*, Singapore: Oxford University Press, p. 93 n. 113.
45 J. G. D. Campbell, *Siam in the Twentieth Century: Being the Experiences and Impressions of a British Official*, London: Edward Arnold, 1902, p. 102.
46 Walter F. Vella, *Chaiyo! King Vajiravudh and the Development of Thai Nationalism*, Honolulu: University of Hawaii Press, 1978, pp. 144–46.
47 *PKPS*, 26, pp. 285–86.
48 *BTWM*, 21 October 1913.
49 Vella, *Chaiyo!*, p. 144.
50 *Thesaphiban*, 39, p. 1574.
51 On these reforms see Barmé, *Luang Wichit Wathakan*, pp. 144–60; Thamsook Numnonda, 'Pibulsongkram's Thai Nation-Building Programme during the Japanese Military Presence, 1941–45', *Journal of Southeast Asian Studies*, 9, 2 (September 1978), pp. 234–47; and Kobkua Suwannathat-Pian, *Thailand's Durable Premier: Phibun Through Three Decades, 1932–1957*, Kuala Lumpur: Oxford University Press, 1995, pp. 103–35.
52 NA (2) SR 0201.31/8, 'Explanation Concerning the Prohibition of Fish Fighting and Cockfighting'.
53 Scot Barmé, *Woman, Man, Bangkok: Love, Sex and Popular Culture in Thailand*, Lanham: Rowman and Littlefield, 2002, pp. 232–33.
54 Dilok, *Siam's Rural Economy*, p. 36. See also Campbell, *Siam in the Twentieth Century*, p. 148.
55 Kanchana, [Government Policy], pp. 113–14, 207.
56 Ibid., pp. 151–53.
57 Ian Brown, 'The End of the Opium Farm in Siam, 1905–7' in John Butcher and Howard Dick (eds), *The Rise and Fall of Revenue Farming: Business Elites and the Emergence of the Modern State in Southeast Asia*, London: MacMillan, 1993, pp. 243–44.
58 *PKPS*, 11, pp. 126–27.
59 Ibid., pp. 127–28.
60 NA R6 N 4.1/9, 'Vajiravudh to Yomarat, 13 June 1916'.
61 As in Siam, the Chinese gambling habit was used to justify the existence of the gambling tax farms in the Federated Malay States. John G. Butcher, 'The Demise of the Revenue Farm System in the Federated Malay States', *Modern Asian Studies*, 17, 3 (July 1983), pp. 392–93.
62 Such attitudes were common among the Western advisers to the Thai government in the early twentieth century. See Campbell, *Siam in the Twentieth Century*, pp. 108, 278–79, 283–84; and W. A. Graham, 'Siam, and Her Relations

206   Notes

with Other Powers', *Journal of the Royal Institute of International Affairs*, 7, 5 (September 1928), p. 316.
63 As Carl Trocki notes, this was the Thai state's justification for the opium farm. Carl A. Trocki, *Opium, Empire and the Global Political Economy: A Study of the Asian Opium Trade*, London and New York: Routledge, 1999, pp. 150–51.
64 *PKPS*, 18, pp. 348–49; NA R5 Kh 14.1.Kh/22, 'Mahit to Chulalongkorn, 5 April 1902'; Damrong, [Abolition], pp. 48–49.
65 NA R5 M 1.3/20, 'Damrong to Chulalongkorn, 10 March 1906'.
66 NA R5 M 2.11/11, 'Report of Meeting of Provincial Governors, 8 September 1906'.
67 NA R6 Kh 2/12, 'Chanthaburi to Vajiravudh, July 1917'.
68 *SY 1931–33*, p. 294.
69 NA R6 Kh 2/12, 'Chanthaburi to Vajiravudh, 30 March 1918'.
70 NA K Kh 0301.1.3/11, 'Subject: Issue of Lotteries by Public Authorities, 30 June 1934'.
71 NA R7 M 15/4, 'Boriphat to Chaophraya Mahithon, 17 June 1932'.
72 Pridi Banomyong, *Pridi by Pridi: Selected Writings on Life, Politics, and Economy*, trans. Chris Baker and Pasuk Phongpaichit, Chiang Mai: Silkworm Books, 2000, p. 123 n. 10.
73 See the numerous newspaper clippings on billiards competitions in NA R6 N 20.17/3, 'Billiards Gambling'.
74 On the development of horse racing in Siam see Arnold Wright and Oliver Breakspear (eds), *Twentieth Century Impressions of Siam: Its History, People, Commerce, Industries, and Resources*, Bangkok: White Lotus, 1994 [1908], p. 236.
75 NA R5 N 20/10, 'Translation of Draft of Royal Charter'.
76 NA R5 N 20/10, 'Naret to Chulalongkorn, 28 June 1901', 'Contract for the Leasing of Land to the RBSC'.
77 NA R5 N 20/10, 'Olarovsky to Chulalongkorn, August 1901'.
78 NA R5 N 20/10, 'Olarovsky to Sommot, 17 and 18 August 1901'.
79 NA R5 M 1.3/20, 'Damrong to Chulalongkorn, 19 March 1902'.
80 *Sayam sakkhi*, 7 July 1923.
81 *BTWM*, 19 May 1934 and 4 May 1939; NA (2) SR 0201.31/4, 'Phraya Khathathonbodi to Phraya Phahon, 20 March 1934'.
82 Arkartdamkeung Rapheephat, *The Circus of Life*, trans. Phongdeit Jiang-phattanarket and ed. Marcel Barang, Bangkok: Modern Thai Classics, 1995, pp. 194–96. See also Thongchai, 'Quest for "Siwilai"', pp. 537–40.
83 Arkartdamkeung, *Circus of Life*, pp. 194–96.
84 Prince Narathip Phongpraphan (ed.), *Chumnum phranipphon khong than wan* [Collected Writings of Prince Wan], Bangkok: Padung Suksa, 1965, pp. 145–50.
85 NA R6 N 26/6, 'Letter from B. Boon Long, 1 February 1921'.
86 NA R6 N 26/6, 'Yomarat to Phraya Chakraphan, 26 February 1921'.
87 *Rai-ngan kanprachum sapha phu-thaen ratsadon samai ti 2 saman p. s. 2482*, vol. 2 [Records of the National Assembly, 1939/40], p. 687.
88 For the complete Acts, see *PKPS*, 13, pp. 250–58; and *PKPS*, 18, pp. 275–79, respectively.
89 NA R7 Kh 2/2, 'Boriphat to Prajadhipok, 8 August 1928'.
90 For the complete Act and Regulations, see *PKPS*, 43, pp. 143–55.
91 For the complete Act and the first edition of the Ministerial Regulations, see *PKPS*, 48, pp. 1772–81, 1804–8.
92 See the seventeenth and eighteenth editions of the law's Ministerial Regulations in Lisut Thonchai, *Khu-mu kanphanan* [Gambling Handbook], 2nd ed., Bangkok, nd, pp. 11–29.

93 For the inner *monthons*, *monthon* Phayap and Bangkok Regulations, see *PKPS*, 18, pp. 264–65, 270, 548–49, respectively.
94 For a contemporary explanation for some of these differences see NA R5 N 2/95, 'Naret to Chulalongkorn, 7 February 1903'.
95 Emphasis added. NA K Kh 0301.1.3/7, 'Memorandum of a discussion, on 5 March 1917, between H. R. H. the Minister of Finance, the Financial Adviser, and the Legal Adviser to the Ministry, on Phya Indra Montri's proposed new Gaming Law'.
96 NA R6 Kh 2/12, 'Chanthaburi to Vajiravudh, 30 March 1918'.
97 *PKPS*, 31, pp. 3–6.
98 *PKPS*, 43, p. 153.
99 *Thammasan*, 16, pp. 96–97, 391–92.
100 NA R5 M 1.3/20, 'Damrong to Chulalongkorn, 19 March 1902'.
101 *Krungthep Daily Mail*, 25 May 1928.
102 See NA K Kh 0301.1.3/7, 'Note on the draft Gaming Law prepared by the Director General of the Revenue Department'; NA R7 Kh 2/2, 'Boriphat to Prajadhipok, 8 August 1928'; and *Rai-ngan kanprachum sapha phu-thaen ratsadon samai ti 2 saman p. s. 2478* [Assembly Records, 1935/6], pp. 2031–53.
103 NA K Kh 0301.1.3/7, 'Memorandum of a discussion, on 5 March 1917, between H. R. H. the Minister of Finance, the Financial Adviser, and the Legal Adviser to the Ministry, on Phya Indra Montri's proposed new Gaming Law'; NA R7 Kh 2/2, 'Extract from the report of the Council of Ministers, 18 August 1928'; *Rai-ngan kanprachum sapha phu-thaen ratsadon samai ti 2 saman p. s. 2478* [Assembly Records, 1935/6], pp. 2045–53.
104 *PKPS*, 13, p. 55.
105 Ibid., pp. 254–55.
106 *PKPS*, 18, p. 278.
107 *PKPS*, 20, pp. 505–6; NA R5 M 1.3/20, 'Damrong to Chulalongkorn, 10 March 1906'.
108 *PKPS*, 43, pp. 145–46.
109 *PKPS*, 48, pp. 1776–77.
110 Lisut, [Gambling Handbook], p. 6.
111 *PKPS*, 43, pp. 144–45.
112 *Thesaphiban*, 30, pp. 739–41.
113 *BTWM*, 15 March 1933.
114 *Thesaphiban*, 34, p. 1011.
115 *BTWM*, 24 November 1934.
116 *Thesaphiban*, 34, pp. 1012–15.
117 *BTWM*, 11 November 1935.
118 See, for instance, R7 Kh 2/2, 'Ideas about Suppressing Gambling'; and *Rai-ngan kanprachum sapha phu-thaen ratsadon samai ti 2 wisaman p. s. 2478*, vol. 2 [Assembly Records, 1935/6], pp. 1103–10.
119 For the complete act and Regulations, see *PKPS*, 51, pp. 901–4, 938–39.
120 Anek Bunyaphakdi, *Phai phong thai* [Thai Card Games], Bangkok: Cremation Volume, 1967, pp. 16–17.
121 Ibid., p. 19.
122 For instance, managers of card dens stockpiled large quantities of unstamped cards. When licensing officials tried to enforce the law, these managers took advantage of an omission in the act to claim they were merely keeping the cards for the purpose of play, rather than for sale, and thus the cards did not require a stamp. *Rai-ngan kanprachum sapha phu-thaen ratsadon samai ti 2 saman p. s. 2482*, vol. 2 [Assembly Records, 1939/40], pp. 727–29.
123 For the complete Act and Regulations, see Lisut, [Handbook], pp. 373–77, 380–82.

5 The police and enforcement

1. On the creation and development of the modern Thai police, see Purachai Piusombun, *The Evolution of Thai Law Enforcement*, School of Public Administration, The National Institute of Development Administration, 1982, pp. 10–20.
2. *RPAB 1898–99*, p. 2. The lack of respect for the police stemmed in part from the 'ridiculous' uniform they wore, which made them look like 'scarecrows' and 'clowns'. See ibid. and H. Warrington Smyth, *Five Years in Siam: From 1891–1896*, Bangkok: White Lotus, 1994 [1898], vol. 1, pp. 36–37.
3. *RPAB 1898–99*, p. 3; *RPAB 1899–1900*, p. 6; *RPAB Year 120* [1901/2], p. 6.
4. Cecil A. Carter, *The Kingdom of Siam*, New York and London: G. P. Putnam's Sons, 1904, p. 121.
5. *RPAB Year 122* [1903/4], pp. 1, 25; *RPAB Year 123* [1904/5], p. 9.
6. David B. Johnston, 'Rural Society and the Rice Economy in Thailand, 1880–1930,' PhD dissertation, Yale University, 1975, pp. 181–84.
7. For a detailed description of the Provincial Gendarmerie see Arnold Wright and Oliver Breakspear (eds), *Twentieth Century Impressions of Siam: Its History, People, Commerce, Industries, and Resources*, Bangkok: White Lotus, 1994 [1908], pp. 110–11.
8. *PKPS*, 13, pp. 57, 277, 282.
9. Ibid., p. 256.
10. *RPAB 1899–1900*, p. 52.
11. *PKPS*, 18, pp. 268, 273, 551.
12. NA R5 N 42.11/22, 'Chin Sieo Chu to Prince Mahit, 13 July 1899'.
13. See, for instance, the 1924 report on the operations and hangouts of three criminal gangs in *monthon* Prachinburi. NA R6 N 4.1/234, 'Chaophraya Yomarat to Phraya Phetchapani, 21 January 1924'.
14. NA R6 N 4.1/9, 'Phraya Si Woraphotthirat to Prince Prachin, 22 January 1919 and 8 March 1919'.
15. *RPAB 1898–99*, p. 2.
16. *RPAB 1898–99*, pp. 3–4; *RPAB 1899–1900*, pp. 4–6; *RPAB Year 120* [1901/2], pp. 6–7; *RPAB Year 122* [1903/4], pp. 5–7.
17. *RPAB 1898–99*, p. 2; *RPAB 1899–1900*, p. 6.
18. NA R6 N 4.1/165, 'A Report on work of Police and Gendarmerie and on the Criminal Statistics of Siam for the year B. E. 2462', pp. 62–64.
19. Andrew A. Freeman, *A Journalist in Siam* (originally published as *Brown Women and White*), Bangkok: White Lotus, 2007 [1932], p. 225.
20. NA R6 N 4.1/165, 'A Report on work of Police and Gendarmerie and on the Criminal Statistics of Siam for the year B. E. 2462', p. 3.
21. NA R6 N 4.1/73, 'Trotter to Yomarat, 23 December 1915'.
22. *BTWM*, 6 November 1935.
23. See, respectively, NA R5 N 8.1/216, 'Special Report on Crime in the two Divisions of the Suburbs with recommendations with a view to reduce Crime and improve the administration of Criminal Justice and Police'; and NA R5 Kh 14.1.Kh/25, 'Lawson to Naret, 27 July 1905'.
24. Quoted in Hong Lysa, 'Extraterritoriality in Bangkok in the Reign of Chulalongkorn, 1868–1910: The Cacophonies of Semi-Colonial Cosmopolitanism', *Itinerario: European Journal of Overseas History*, 27, 2 (July 2003), p. 132.
25. *RPAB 1901–02*, p. 66.
26. NA R6 N 4.1/165, 'A Report on work of Police and Gendarmerie and on the Criminal Statistics of Siam for the year B. E. 2462', p. 64.
27. *Si krung*, 12 May 1928.

28 NA R6 N 4.1/165, 'A Report on work of Police and Gendarmerie and on the Criminal Statistics of Siam for the year B. E. 2462', p. 66.
29 NA R7 Kh 2/2, 'Ideas about Suppressing Gambling'.
30 Freeman, *Journalist in Siam*, pp. 227–28.
31 Quoted in Matthew Copeland, 'Contested Nationalism and the 1932 Overthrow of the Absolute Monarchy in Siam', PhD dissertation, Australian National University, 1993, pp. 86–87.
32 NA R5 N 11.3.K/1, 'Prince Narathip to Chulalongkorn, 11 April 1890'; *PKPS*, 12, pp. 113–15; *PKPS*, 19, pp. 126–27.
33 NA R5 N 8.1/306, 'Lawson to Nares, 17 January 1904'.
34 NA R6 N 4.1/165, 'A Report on work of Police and Gendarmerie and on the Criminal Statistics of Siam for the year B. E. 2462', p. 66.
35 The *Nangsuphim thai* (12 December 1916) identified this as one of the main difficulties for the police in suppressing illegal gambling.
36 NA R5 Kh 14.1.Kh/18, 'Damrong to Prince Sommot, 13 February 1904'.
37 NA MT 4/153, 'Discussion on the Suppression of Illegal Gambling – Meeting of Provincial Governors B. E. 2478'.
38 *BTWM*, 20 March 1908.
39 *Nangsuphim thai*, 12 December 1916.
40 *Krungthep Daily Mail*, 14 February 1930.
41 NA R6 N 4.1/51, 'Phraya Phirentharathibodi to Director-General of the Police Department, 29 June 1915'; NA R6 N 4.1/9, 'Phraya Si Woraphotthirat to Prachin, 11 September 1917'.
42 *Yamato*, 25 May 1923.
43 *Krungthep Daily Mail*, 12 January 1917.
44 *BTWM*, 2 October 1923.
45 *Krungthep Daily Mail*, 19 September 1913.
46 NA R6 N 4.1/9, 'Phraya Maha Ammat to Vajiravudh, 19 March 1915'.
47 NA R5 N 6.2/982, 'Damrong to Sommot, 13 August 1910'.
48 *PKPS*, 12, pp. 113–15.
49 *PKPS*, 18, p. 278.
50 NA R7 Kh 2/2, 'Report of the Council of Ministers, 23 June 1930'; NA MT 4/153, 'Discussion on Gambling Rewards – Meeting of Provincial Governors, B. E. 2478'.
51 *PKPS*, 48, p. 1777.
52 NA (2) SR 0201.31/7, 'Minister of the Interior to PM, 22 March 1937'.
53 NA MT 4/153, 'Discussion on Gambling Rewards – Meeting of Provincial Governors, B. E. 2478'.
54 NA R6 N 11.5.Ch/4, 'Yomarat to Phetchapani, 5 June 1915'.
55 See, for instance, NA R5 N 42.11/2, 'Phra Siri-aisawan to Phra Antinarakon, 27 May 1892'.
56 See, for example, NA MT 0201.1.1/690, 'Nakhon Si Thammarat Provincial Committee to Undersecretary of the Interior, November 1937'.
57 NA MT 0201.1.1/19, 'Nai Phrom to Minister of the Interior, 21 March 1936'.
58 *PKPS*, 13, pp. 53, 252–53.
59 NA R5 N 11.3.K/3, 'Prince Devawongse to Sommot, 1 February 1896'; NA R5 N 11.3.K/4, 'Prince Phichit to Chulalongkorn, 29 April 1896'.
60 NA R5 N 11.3.K/4, 'Phichit to Chulalongkorn, 29 April 1896'.
61 NA R5 N 11.3.K/3, 'Naret to Sommot, 24 January 1896', 'Devawongse to Sommot, 1 February 1896', 'Chulalongkorn to Naret, 4 February 1896'.
62 NA R5 N 11.3.K/4, 'Report of Criminal Court, 7 April 1896', 'Phraya Thammasan to Phra Si Thammasan, 7 April 1896'.
63 NA R5 N 11.3.K/4, 'Phichit to Chulalongkorn, 29 April 1896'.
64 NA R5 N 11.3.K/4, 'Chulalongkorn to Phichit, 9 May 1896'.

65 In theory, Chulalongkorn's legal and judicial reforms established a principle of equality for all before the law, though in reality royals, nobles and government officials remained protected, to a certain extent, by various preconditions for bringing suits against them. See David Engel, *Law and Kingship in Thailand during the Reign of King Chulalongkorn*, Michigan Papers on South and Southeast Asia No. 9, Ann Arbor: University of Michigan, Center for South and Southeast Asian Studies, 1975, pp. 100–103.
66 *BTWM*, 19 July 1924.
67 *Sara rat*, 8 May 1923.
68 *Yamato*, 5 May 1923.
69 *Awanti*, 11 May 1923.
70 *Yamato*, 25 May 1923.
71 *Yamato*, 5 May 1923.
72 See, for instance, NA R7 M 99/3, 'Prince Lopburi to Chaophraya Mahithon, 12 June 1926'; and NA R7 Y 4/8, 'Chinda to Mahithon, 15 March 1930 and 7 June 1930'.
73 NA R5 N 3.2.K/111, 'Khun Naranukunkit to Phraya Nonthaburi, 28 January 1909'.
74 NA R5 N 3.2.K/111, 'Yomarat to Nonthaburi, 31 January 1909'.
75 NA R5 N 3.2.K/111, 'Nonthaburi to Yomarat, 15 February 1910'.
76 NA R5 N 8.1/236, 'Lawson to Nares, 19 December 1902'.
77 Engel, *Law and Kingship*, pp. 121, 125 n. 1.
78 For an overview of extraterritoriality in Siam, see Francis Bowes Sayre, 'The Passing of Extraterritoriality in Siam', *American Journal of International Law*, 22, 1 (January 1928), pp. 70–88.
79 NA R5 N 11.3.K/4, 'Naret to Chulalongkorn, 26 February 1896', 'Phra Anan Nararak to Naret, 13 February 1896'.
80 NA R5 N 7.7.Ng/14, 'Lawson to Naret, 24 May 1904'.
81 NA R5 N 11.3.K/5, 'Chulalongkorn to Naret, 3 February 1898'; *Chino sayam warasap*, 27 April 1917.
82 Sayre, 'Passing of Extraterritoriality', p. 73; W. A. R. Wood, *Consul in Paradise: Sixty-Nine Years in Siam*, London: Souvenir Press, 1965, p. 19.
83 Hong, 'Extraterritoriality in Bangkok', p. 134.
84 *Chino sayam warasap*, 17 April 1917.
85 Hong, 'Extraterritoriality in Bangkok', p. 129.
86 NA R5 N 11.3.K/5, 'Naret to Chulalongkorn, 21 January 1898', 'Chulalongkorn to Devawongse, 24 January 1898', 'Devawongse to Chulalongkorn, 28 January 1898'.
87 NA R6 N 4.1/9, 'Yomarat to Prachin, 15 August 1917'.
88 NA R6 N 4.1/9, 'Phirentharathibodi to Prince Khamrop, 13 August 1917'.
89 NA R6 N 4.1/9, 'Yomarat to Prachin, 15 August 1917', 'Vajiravudh to Yomarat, 17 August 1917', 'Si Woraphotthirat to Prachin, 25 September 1917'.
90 As Frederic Wakeman Jr. notes in his comprehensive study on the Shanghai police, 'police efforts to control the city's entertainment industries [i.e. gambling, narcotics and prostitution] illustrate better than practically any other law enforcement activity the limitations imposed upon the Chinese police by extraterritoriality'. Frederic Wakeman Jr., *Policing Shanghai, 1927–1937*, Berkeley: University of California Press, 1995, p. 97.
91 This discussion of gambling in Shanghai, and Chinese responses to it, is drawn from ibid., Ch. 7, esp. pp. 97–105; and Ning Jennifer Chang, 'Pure Sport or A Gambling Disgrace? Greyhound Racing and the Formation of Modern Shanghai' in Peter Zarrow (ed.), *Creating Chinese Modernity: Knowledge and Everyday Life, 1900–1940*, New York: Peter Lang, 2006, pp. 147–81.
92 Wakeman, *Policing Shanghai*, p. 14.

93 NA R5 N 11.3.K/5, 'Chulalongkorn to Devawongse, 24 January 1898'.
94 Wakeman, *Policing Shanghai*, pp. 104–5.

6 The judiciary, punishment and the prison

1. On the pre-reform legal system, see David Engel, *Law and Kingship in Thailand during the Reign of King Chulalongkorn*, Michigan Papers on South and Southeast Asia No. 9, Ann Arbor: University of Michigan Center for South and Southeast Asian Studies, 1975, pp. 1–8; and Sarasin Viraphol, 'Law in Traditional Siam and China: A Comparative Study', *Journal of the Siam Society*, 65, 1 (January 1977), pp. 81–136.
2. See Carl Bock, *Temples and Elephants: Travels in Siam in 1881–82*, Singapore: Oxford University Press, 1986 [1884], pp. 110–14, 161–62, 238–39, 314–15; Holt Samuel Hallett, *A Thousand Miles on an Elephant in the Shan States*, Edinburgh and London: William Blackwood and Sons, 1890, pp. 449–51; and Monsignor Jean-Baptiste Pallegoix, *Description of the Thai Kingdom or Siam: Thailand under King Mongkut*, trans. Walter E. J. Tips, Bangkok: White Lotus, 2000 [1854], pp. 193–94.
3. Tokichi Masao, 'The New Penal Code of Siam,' *Yale Law Journal*, 18, 2 (December 1908), pp. 88–89.
4. For an official statement of such, see the report of the Committee of Redaction of 1917, which was tasked with revising the 1908 code. 'Report on the Revision of the Penal Code of 1908 (28 July 1917)' reproduced in M. B. Hooker (ed.), *The Laws of Southeast Asia, Volume 2: European Laws in Southeast Asia*, Singapore: Butterworth and Co., 1988, p. 607.
5. The transformation of the judicial system is described in depth in Engel, *Law and Kingship*, pp. 59–90.
6. Frank C. Darling, 'The Evolution of Law in Thailand', *The Review of Politics*, 32, 2 (April 1970), pp. 215–16.
7. Tamara Loos, 'Gender Adjudicated: Translating Modern Legal Subjects in Siam', PhD dissertation, Cornell University, 1999, p. 60.
8. Ibid., p. 63.
9. As the compiler of a collection of Supreme Court rulings on gambling cases eloquently put it, these judgments were like a whetstone on which to sharpen a knife. See 'Foreword' in Phra Borirak Nitikaset (comp.), *Phraratchabanyat kanphanan kap khamphiphaksadika banthatthan* [The Gambling Act and Supreme Court Rulings], np, nd.
10. Under an 1896 regulation all sentences inflicting up to 50 lashes were to be replaced by imprisonment. Engel, *Law and Kingship*, p. 69.
11. NA R5 N 11.3.K/4, 'Phichit to Chulalongkorn, 29 April 1896'.
12. For examples of fines in this range see NA R5 N 3.5.K/5, 'List of Criminal Cases, August 1903'; NA R5 N 3.5.K/12, 'List of Criminal Cases, January 1905'; NA R5 N 3.5.K/67, 'List of Criminal Cases, May 1905', 'List of Criminal Cases, June 1905'; NA R5 N 3.3.Ch/16, 'Phra Thepphlu to Minister of Local Government, 8 June 1907, 11 March and 5 April 1908'; *Nangusphim thai*, 27 January, 16 February and 12 May 1917; *Thammasan*, 1, pp. 303–7; *Thammasan*, 2, pp. 31–34, 85–89; Borirak, [Gambling Act], pp. 31–32.
13. *The Penal Code for the Kingdom of Siam R. S. 127 (1908)*, Bangkok: American Presbyterian Mission Press, 1908, pp. 17–18.
14. NA R5 N 3.3.K/87, 'Thepphlu to Naret, 10 July 1907'.
15. *Krungthep Daily Mail*, 10 November 1915.
16. *Krungthep Daily Mail*, 12 August 1916.
17. *Thesaphiban*, 15, pp. 293–94.

18 *Nangsuphim thai*, 5 January 1917.
19 *BTWM*, 27 June 1924.
20 *BTWM*, 2 October 1923.
21 *BTWM*, 19 July 1924.
22 Borirak, [Gambling Act], pp. 51–53.
23 Ibid., pp. 56–58.
24 *Thammasan*, 12, pp. 225–28.
25 *Thammasan*, 17, pp. 980–82.
26 For example cases from the 1920s and 1930s see *Thammsan*, 7, pp. 5–7; *Thammasan*, 9, pp. 258–61; *Thammasan*, 12, pp. 215–17; *Thammasan*, 21, pp. 632–38; and *Thammasan*, 22, pp. 554–57.
27 *Thammasan*, 13, p. 15.
28 *Thammasan*, 19, pp. 171–75.
29 *Thammasan*, 19, pp. 70–73, 713–18; *Thammasan*, 20, p. 1974.
30 Mr and Mrs Émile Jottrand, *In Siam: The Diary of A Legal Adviser of King Chulalongkorn's Government*, trans. Walter E. J. Tips, Bangkok: White Lotus, 1996 [1905], p. 284; Benjamin A. Batson, *The End of the Absolute Monarchy in Siam*, Singapore: Oxford University Press, 1984, p. 90; Constance M. Wilson, *Thailand: A Handbook of Historical Statistics*, Boston: G. K. Hall and Co., 1983, p. 95.
31 Prince Dilok Nabarath *Siam's Rural Economy under King Chulalongkorn*, trans. Walter E. J. Tips, Bangkok: White Lotus, 2000 [1908], p. 91; Wilson, *Thailand*, p. 95.
32 This was the view taken in an article in the *Siam Observer* (Thai edition), 2 February 1916.
33 *BTWM*, 9 May 1922.
34 *BTWM*, 19 July 1924.
35 Borirak, [Gambling Act], pp. 41–42.
36 See, for instance, ibid., pp. 81–83.
37 *Thammasan*, 15, pp. 1204–6.
38 Under the 1902 law, any games similar to those specified as forbidden were also prohibited. Under the 1930 and 1936 laws, meanwhile, any games that were similar to those permitted subject to licence also required a licence. See *PKPS*, 18, pp. 264–65, 270, 548; *PKPS*, 20, pp. 508–9; *PKPS*, 43, pp. 143–44; *PKPS*, 48, pp. 1773–74.
39 See, for example, Borirak, [Gambling Act], pp. 54–55, 65–66; *Thammasan*, 16, pp. 478–80; *Thammasan*, 20, pp. 1515–17; *Thammasan*, 21, pp. 452–55; *Thammasan*, 24, p. 526.
40 Borirak, [Gambling Act], pp. 65–66.
41 *PKPS*, 43, p. 149.
42 *Nangsuphim thai*, 17 and 28 October 1916, 20 November 1916.
43 *PKPS*, 43, p. 150.
44 See Engel, *Law and Kingship*, p. 104; Sarasin, 'Law in Traditional Siam', pp. 117–20.
45 Prince Damrong Rachanuphap, *Prachum phongsawadan phak thi 17: Ruang tamnan kanloek bonbia lae huai* [Collected Chronicles, Part 17: The Abolition of the Gambling Dens and the *huai* Lottery], Bangkok: Cremation Volume, 1960, pp. 8, 13.
46 King Chulalongkorn, *Phithi songkran* [Songkran Ceremonies], Bangkok: Cremation Volume, 1978, p. 96; NA R7 Kh 2/2, 'Ideas about Suppressing Gambling'.
47 NA R6 N 4.1/9, 'Chaophraya Aphairacha to Vajiravudh, 8 July 1918'.
48 This reflexive association was particularly strong in the case of officials appointed directly by the king himself. Tamara Loos, *Subject Siam: Family, Law and*

Colonial Modernity in Thailand, Ithaca, New York, and London: Cornell University Press, 2006, pp. 160–61; Engel, *Law and Kingship*, p. 102.
49 NA R7 Kh 2/2, 'Ideas about Suppressing Gambling'.
50 Kanchana Chintakanon, 'Naiyobai khong ratthaban kieokap phasi-akon kanphanan pho so 2367–2460' [Government Policy Towards Gambling Taxes, 1824–1917], MA thesis, Sinlapakon University, 1987, pp. 112–13.
51 *RPAB Year 120* [1901/2], p. 11.
52 NA R5 N 11.3.K/2, 'Chulalongkorn to Prince Phitthayalap, 10 July 1895'.
53 *PKPS*, 13, pp. 56, 277, 281.
54 As Loos notes, the sexual activities of some commoner officials were little different from those of the royal family and nobility since the number of wives a man possessed was an indication of his status and masculinity. Vajiravudh differentiated the elite and non-elite practices of polygamy by claiming that the manner in which commoner officials furtively took mistresses or 'secret wives' (*mia lap*) undermined the institution of the family and, by association, the Thai nation, whereas members of the aristocracy publicly acknowledged and supported their wives. Loos, *Subject Siam*, pp. 160–72.
55 NA R6 N 4.1/9, 'Yomarat to Prachin, 1 February 1918', 'Vajiravudh to Yomarat, 6 March 1918'.
56 *BTWM*, 27 June 1924.
57 NA R6 N 4.1/9, 'Aphairacha to Vajiravudh, 8 July 1918'.
58 NA R6 N 4.1/9, 'Chaophraya Thammathikon to Vajiravudh, 12 September 1923'.
59 NA R6 N 4.1/9, 'Vajiravudh to Thammathikon, 13 September 1923'. The public prosecutor later successfully appealed against Phraya Mahathep's acquittal. The official received the same sentence as Phraya Phuban Banthoeng. *BTWM*, 12 November 1923.
60 NA MT 2.2/1, 'Chaophraya Mahithon to Prince Lopburi, 21 April 1926'.
61 *Thesaphiban*, 31, pp. 234–36.
62 NA R7 Y 4/7, 'Cover Sheet – Royal Order, 5 October 1929', 'Chinda to Mahithon, 4 October 1929'.
63 NA R7 Y 4/2, 'Summary of Criminal Cases, 10 January 1927'.
64 See, for instance, NA R7 Y 4/2, 'Summaries of Criminal Cases, 1 May 1926, 28 March 1927, 15 February 1928, 25 September 1928 and 2 March 1929'; NA R7 Y 4/7, 'Chinda to Mahithon, 7 March 1930 and 6 January 1931', 'Chaophraya Sithamma Thibet to Mahithon, 7 June 1932'.
65 *Thesaphiban*, 34, pp. 1162–64(k); *BTWM*, 25 October 1938.
66 NA MT 2.2/1, 'Report on Regulations for Gambling by Officials', 'Secretary of Civil Service Commission to Undersecretary of the Interior, 5 September 1938'.
67 NA R5 N 8.1/216, 'Special Report on Crime in the two Divisions of the Suburbs with recommendations with a view to reduce Crime and improve the administration of Criminal Justice and Police'.
68 *Ratsadon*, 14 and 17 December 1928.
69 *Ratsadon*, 17 December 1928.
70 *Si krung*, 16 August 1928.
71 NA MT 4.5/13, 'Extract from *Si krung*, 28 October 1930'.
72 NA MT 4.5/13, 'Superintendent of Singburi prison to Prince Upphatthaphong, 11 November and 1 December 1930'.
73 NA MT 4.5/13, 'Luang Phiphat to Phra Borihanthanthanit, 10 December 1930', 'Superintendent to Upphatthaphong, 16 December 1930'.
74 Virginia Thompson, *Thailand: The New Siam*, New York: MacMillan, 1941, p. 289; Kenneth P. Landon, *Siam in Transition: A Brief Survey of Cultural Trends in the Five Years since the Revolution of 1932*, London: Oxford University Press, 1939, p. 155.

214 *Notes*

75 NA MT 4/46, 'Penitentiary Department to Chao Khun Prichanusat, January 1934'.
76 NA MT 4/46, [Curriculum for Primary Level Education of Prisoners].

7 The press and the Bangkok middle class

1 Matthew Copeland, 'Contested Nationalism and the 1932 Overthrow of the Absolute Monarchy in Siam', PhD dissertation, Australian National University, 1993; Scot Barmé, *Woman, Man, Bangkok: Love, Sex and Popular Culture in Thailand*, Lanham: Rowman and Littlefield, 2002.
2 Barmé, *Woman, Man, Bangkok*, p. 2.
3 On the ownership and editors of these three newspapers see Arnold Wright and Oliver Breakspear (eds), *Twentieth Century Impressions of Siam: Its History, People, Commerce, Industries, and Resources*, Bangkok: White Lotus, 1994 [1908], pp. 293–95; and Virginia Thompson, *Thailand: The New Siam*, New York: MacMillan, 1941, pp. 789–90.
4 Benjamin A. Batson, *The End of the Absolute Monarchy in Siam*, Singapore: Oxford University Press, 1984, pp. 72–73; Walter F. Vella, *Chaiyo! King Vajiravudh and the Development of Thai Nationalism*, Honolulu: University of Hawaii Press, 1978, p. 255; Thompson, *Thailand*, p. 793.
5 Copeland, 'Contested Nationalism', p. 56 n. 16; Vella, *Chaiyo!*, p. 254.
6 Batson, *End of the Absolute Monarchy*, p. 73.
7 Copeland, 'Contested Nationalism', pp. 35–36 n. 17.
8 Ibid., p. 36.
9 Vella, *Chaiyo!*, p. 254.
10 Copeland, 'Contested Nationalism', p. 52.
11 Barmé, *Woman, Man, Bangkok*, p. 97.
12 Copeland, 'Contested Nationalism', p. 54.
13 Thompson, *Thailand*, p. 792.
14 Copeland, 'Contested Nationalism', p. 109.
15 Batson, *End of the Absolute Monarchy*, p. 73.
16 Ibid., p. 72.
17 Barmé, *Woman, Man, Bangkok*, p. 98.
18 Copeland, 'Contested Nationalism', p. 58.
19 Barmé, *Woman, Man, Bangkok*, p. 98.
20 Ibid., pp. 7–8.
21 Thompson, *Thailand*, p. 799.
22 Copeland, 'Contested Nationalism', pp. 16, 72–73.
23 Barmé, *Woman, Man, Bangkok*, p. 99.
24 Copeland, 'Contested Nationalism', pp. 56–57.
25 Vella, *Chaiyo!*, p. 253.
26 Copeland, 'Contested Nationalism', p. 72, 72 n. 97.
27 Barmé, *Woman, Man, Bangkok*, p. 99.
28 For details, see ibid., pp. 231–32; Thompson, *Thailand*, pp. 795–98.
29 Vella, *Chaiyo!*, pp. 251–52; Copeland, 'Contested Nationalism', pp. 129–30; Batson, *End of the Absolute Monarchy*, p. 16.
30 Most of the newspapers clippings used in this chapter come from the file series NA R6 N 20.17 Newspapers – Gambling.
31 For examples see *Nangsuphim thai*, 13 March 1916; *Siam Observer* (Thai edition), 16 November 1916; *Sayam sakkhi*, 7 July 1923; *Bangkok kanmuang*, 19 July 1923; *Lak muang*, 20 October 1928.
32 *Krungthep Daily Mail*, 14 April 1917; *Kro lek*, 7 February 1930.
33 In addition to the newspapers cited in the two footnotes above see *BTWM*, 15 June 1904; *Awanti*, 18 May 1923; *Yamato*, 5 May 1923.

34 *Bangkok Calendar*, 1873, pp. 66–67.
35 *Siam Repository*, 1869, p. 94.
36 *Chino sayam warasap*, 13 March 1917.
37 *Nangsuphim thai*, 5 July 1928.
38 *Samphan thai*, 19 January 1924; *BTWM*, 21 January 1924.
39 *BTWM*, 21 January 1924.
40 *Bangkok kanmuang*, 28 August 1923.
41 NA R6 N 20.17/27, 'Letter from *khon* Pet in reply to Knockout Punch, 31 August 1923'.
42 Perhaps the best expression of this was the *Siam Observer*'s editorial on 31 March 1917 about the abolition of the gambling houses.
43 *Krungthep Daily Mail*, 11 June 1914.
44 *Si krung*, 25 October 1928.
45 *BTWM*, 17 October 1913.
46 *Siam Weekly Advertiser*, 27 February 1886. Italics in the original.
47 Ibid.
48 For an overview of Thianwan's life see Walter F. Vella, 'Thianwan of Siam: A Man Who Fought Giants' in Ronald D. Renard (ed.), *Anuson Walter Vella*, Chiang Mai: W. F. Vella Fund, Payap University; and Honolulu: Center for Asian and Pacific Studies, University of Hawaii at Manoa, 1986, pp. 79–81.
49 Ibid., pp. 81–89.
50 This summary of Thianwan's views on gambling is drawn from one of his articles reproduced in Sangop Suriyin, *Thianwan*, 3rd ed., Bangkok: Ruamsan Press, 2000, pp. 118–23.
51 See, for instance, *Chino sayam warasap*, 8 and 16 December 1914; *Nangsuphim thai*, 13 March 1916; and *Siam Observer* (Thai edition), 16 November 1916.
52 See, for example, *Siam Observer* (Thai edition), 19 June 1915; *Krungthep Daily Mail*, 3 February 1917.
53 *BTWM*, 15 March 1916.
54 In addition to a glowing editorial on 13 November 1916, the *Nangsuphim thai* published various letters expressing gratitude for the king's grace and mercy in its 24 and 25 November 1916 issues.
55 *Siam Observer* (Thai edition), 16 November 1916.
56 See, for instance, *Krungthep Daily Mail*, 26 November 1916.
57 *Siam Observer* (Thai edition), 19 June 1915.
58 *Siam Observer* (Thai edition), 17 January 1917.
59 *Krungthep Daily Mail*, 14 April 1917.
60 *Krungthep Daily Mail*, 23 January 1917; *BTWM*, 12 July 1924.
61 See, for instance, *Siam Observer* (Thai edition), 17 January 1917; *Krungthep Daily Mail*, 23 January 1917; *Chino sayam warasap*, 10 February 1917.
62 For an analysis of the media's treatment of the misbehaviour of the elite see Barmé, *Woman, Man, Bangkok*, Ch. 4.
63 *Sara rat*, 2 May 1923.
64 *Yamato*, 5 May 1923.
65 *Awanti*, 11 May 1923.
66 *Yamato*, 17 May 1923.
67 *Awanti*, 9 May 1923.
68 *Sara rat*, 2 May 1923.
69 *Awanti*, 9 May 1923.
70 *Chino sayam warasap*, 16 December 1916.
71 See Copeland, 'Contested Nationalism', pp. 86–87.
72 Quoted in ibid., p. 86.
73 Ibid.

74 George Bradley McFarland, (ed.), *Thai–English Dictionary*, Stanford, California: Stanford University Press, 1944, p. 867.
75 My thanks to Chatnopdol Aksornsawad for explaining this usage.
76 This article is reproduced in the archival file NA R6 N 4.1/214, 'Extract from *Bangkok kanmuang*, 12 March 1923'.
77 Copeland, 'Contested Nationalism', p. 87.
78 Ibid.
79 Ibid., p. 111.
80 *BTWM*, 21 January 1924.
81 *Nangsuphim thai*, 22 November 1924; *Chino sayam warasap*, 14 February 1923.
82 See, for instance, *Yamato*, 26 July 1923; *Samphan thai*, 8 December 1923; *Sayam rat*, 28 November 1924.
83 *Bangkok kanmuang*, 8 February 1924.
84 See, for example, *Sayam rat*, 10 September 1923.
85 NA R6 N 20.17/29, 'The Fundraising Methods of the Wild Tigers Compared with those of Other Organizations'.
86 Copeland, 'Contested Nationalism', p. 112.
87 *Yamato*, 1 August 1923.
88 *Chino sayam warasap*, 15 February 1923.
89 *Wayamo*, 21 February 1923.
90 *Bangkok kanmuang*, 10 January 1924.
91 *BTWM*, 9 May 1922 and 18 July 1923; *Nangsuphim thai*, 18 April 1923; *Chino sayam warasap*, 25 June 1923; *Sayam Sakkhi*, 9 July 1923.
92 'Why is horse racing so popular with the general public?' asked one Thai newspaper rhetorically. 'The answer is easy: it's the lotteries.' *Sayam sakkhi*, 7 July 1923.
93 *BTWM*, 9 May 1922.
94 Ibid.; *BTWM*, 13 May 1922; *Chino sayam warasap*, 18 July 1923.
95 *BTWM*, 18 July 1923.
96 For examples of these sentiments, see *Sayam sakkhi*, 9 July 1923; *Chino sayam warasap*, 18 July 1923; *BTWM*, 28 and 31 January 1924.
97 *Sayam sakkhi*, 9 July 1923.
98 *Siam Observer* (Thai edition), 22 December 1922.
99 *Sayam sakkhi*, 9 July 1923.
100 *Sayam sakkhi*, 7 July 1923.
101 *Sayam sakkhi*, 9 July 1923.
102 *BTWM*, 18 July 1923.
103 *Yamato*, 26 July 1923.
104 Ibid.; *Chino sayam warasap*, 21 July 1923; *Krungthep Daily Mail*, 25 July 1923.
105 *Chino sayam warasap*, 18 July 1923.
106 *Sayam sakkhi*, 18 July 1923.
107 See, for instance, *Siam Observer* (Thai edition), 22 December 1922.
108 *BTWM*, 20 July 1923.
109 *Siam Observer*, 19 and 20 July 1923.
110 *Chino sayam warasap*, 21 July and 13 August 1923; *Sayam sakkhi*, 10 August 1923.
111 The following discussion is drawn from Ning Jennifer Chang, 'Pure Sport or A Gambling Disgrace? Greyhound Racing and the Formation of Modern Shanghai' in Peter Zarrow (ed.), *Creating Chinese Modernity: Knowledge and Everyday Life, 1900–1940*, New York: Peter Lang, 2006.
112 In the pari-mutuel or tote system the players bet against one another rather than against the racetrack or house. All the money bet, minus expenses, taxes and commissions, is then divided among the winners.
113 Chang, 'Pure Sport', pp. 166–67.
114 Ibid., p. 180.

115 Barmé, *Woman, Man, Bangkok*, pp. 10–11.
116 George L. Mosse, *Nationalism and Sexuality: Respectability and Abnormal Sexuality in Modern Europe*, New York: Howard Fertig, 1985, p. 9.
117 Ibid.
118 Barmé, *Woman, Man, Bangkok*, p. 11.

8 Buddhism, the Sangha and the silent majority

1 Phra Thepphawethi, *Thot khong kanphanan* [The Dangers of Gambling], Bangkok: Mahamakut Buddhist University Press, 1940, pp. 8–9.
2 The other three are womanizing, taking intoxicants and associating with bad characters.
3 Phra Ratcha-woramuni (Prayut Payutto), *Photchanukrom phutthasat: Chabap pramuan tham* [Dictionary of Buddhism], Bangkok: Chulalongkorn University Fund for Publishing a Dictionary of Buddhism, 1985, pp. 176–78.
4 B. J. Terwiel, *Monks and Magic: An Analysis of Religious Ceremonies in Central Thailand*, 3rd ed., Bangkok: White Lotus, 1994, p. 166.
5 Ibid., p. 169.
6 Ibid., pp. 95–97.
7 See, for instance, the prohibition on monks and novices participating in cock, bird and fish fighting. *PKPS*, 5, pp. 16–18.
8 *PKPS*, 13, pp. 56, 277, 281.
9 Sthirakoses (Phraya Anuman Rajdhon), *Looking Back: Book One*, Bangkok: Chulalongkorn University Press, 1992, p. 157.
10 Hermann Norden, *From Golden Gate to Golden Sun: A Record of Travel, Sport, and Observation in Siam and Malaya*, London: H. F. and G. Witherby, 1923, p. 111.
11 P. A. Thompson, *Siam: An Account of the Country and the People*, Bangkok: White Lotus, 1987 [1910], p. 125.
12 Carl Bock, *Temples and Elephants: Travels in Siam in 1881–82*, Singapore: Oxford University Press, 1986 [1884], p. 101.
13 Kanchana Chintakanon, 'Naiyobai khong ratthaban kieokap phasi-akon kanphanan pho so 2367–2460' [Government Policy Towards Gambling Taxes, 1824–1917], MA thesis, Sinlapakon University, 1987, p. 117.
14 NA R5–6 RL-KhPh/17, 'Prince Sawat to Vajiravudh, 3 June 1912', 'Vajiravudh to Sawat, 30 June 1912'.
15 NA R5 N 49.5/15, 'Prince Naret to Phra Anan, 10 August 1896'.
16 NA R5 N 49.5/50, 'Phraya Wisut Suriyasuk to Phraya Intharathipbodi, 1 December 1903'.
17 NA R5 N 8.1/370, 'Lawson to Nares, 30 May 1906'.
18 For an example of a revered, and beleaguered, monk who tried to escape the constant demands for tips on the *huai*, see B. O. Cartwright, 'The Huey Lottery', *Journal of the Siam Society*, 18, 3 (1924), p. 230.
19 Charles Buls, *Siamese Sketches*, trans. Walter E. J. Tips, Bangkok: White Lotus, 1994 [1901], p. 35.
20 Ibid.
21 See, for instance, NA R5 N 7.7.Ng/12, 'Phra Ratsadakonkoson to Naret, 13 February 1904'; NA R5 N 7.7.Ng/22, 'Luang Senaphonsitthi to Naret, 23 April 1905'.
22 Kanchana, [Government Policy], p. 111.
23 See NA R5 N 49.5/59, 'Lawson to Nares, 4 November 1904' in which Lawson raises concerns as to whether gambling for cash was to be permitted at the Wat Yuen fair: 'If so the same very disgraceful scenes as those witnessed last year at the Pu-Kow-Tong [the Golden Mount] festival will occur again'.

24 NA R5 N 7.7.Ng/28, 'Naret to Ratsadakonkoson, 19 January 1907'; NA R5 N 7.7.Ng/31, 'Naret to Ratsadakonkoson, 27 March 1907'; NA R5 N 49.5/84, 'Order No. 13/17958, 10 December 1908'.
25 *Sayam rat*, 23 November 1923.
26 *Krungthep Daily Mail*, 25 November 1923.
27 *BTWM*, 24 November 1923.
28 Mary Lovina Cort, *Siam: Or, the Heart of Farther India*, New York: Anson D. F. Randolph and Co., 1886, p. 116.
29 The Nakhon Pathom festival, for instance, was organized by a committee that included the Lord Lieutenant of *monthon* Nakhon Chaisi and the governor of the province.
30 *BTWM*, 24 November 1923.
31 *BTWM*, 4 September 1925.
32 NA R6 N 42/37, 'A "Gentleman" to Phetchapani, 28 April 1917'; NA R6 N 42/26, 'The Oppressed to Yomarat, 20 September 1915'.
33 *BTWM*, 15 June 1904; W. A. Graham, *Siam: A Handbook of Practical, Commercial and Political Information*, London: Alexander Moring, 1924, vol. 1, p. 340.
34 To illustrate this point, Hong presents an almost farcical scene from the British Consular Court in which the judge tries in vain to make a Siamese woman see the error of her ways in sending one of her young sons to place a stake on the *huai* lottery. Hong Lysa, '"Stranger within the Gates": Knowing Semi-Colonial Siam as Extraterritorials', *Modern Asian Studies*, 38, 2 (May 2004), pp. 340–41.
35 Phra Thepphawethi, [Dangers of Gambling], p. 5.
36 Ibid., p. 6.
37 Sthirakoses (Phraya Anuman Rajdhon), *Looking Back: Book Three*, Bangkok: Chulalongkorn University Press, 2001, p. 16.
38 Ibid.
39 Holt Samuel Hallett, *A Thousand Miles on an Elephant in the Shan States*, Edinburgh and London: William Blackwood and Sons, 1890, p. 366.
40 *BTWM*, 3 October 1898.
41 NA R5 Kh 14.1.Kh/18, 'Damrong to Prince Sommot, 27 April and 2 May 1906'.
42 Nai Charoen, *Nirat phai lae nirat pen tahan* [The Card Poem and the Poem about Being a Soldier], Bangkok: Ruang Sin, 1979 [1925/6], pp. 1–53.
43 Anek Bunyaphakdi, *Phai phong thai* [Thai Card Games], Bangkok: Cremation Volume, 1967, p. 14.
44 Khun Wichit Matra, *80 pi nai chiwit khapphachao* [80 Years in My Life], Bangkok: Cremation Volume, 1980, p. 95.
45 Anek, [Card Games], p. 15.
46 The other two classes were offences against property and offences in contravention of the opium and excise laws. See *SY 1924–25*, pp. 248–49; *SY 1929–30*, pp. 302–3; *SY 1931–33*, pp. 354–55; *SY 1933–35*, pp. 370–71; *SY 19373/8–1938/39*, pp. 358–59.
47 *Ministry of Justice Report for the Year 122 (1903–04)*, p. 8.
48 *BTWM*, 24 February 1940.
49 *BTWM*, 5 February 1940.
50 David Engel, *Code and Custom in a Provincial Thai Court: The Interaction of Formal and Informal Systems of Justice*, Tuscon, Arizona: University of Arizona Press, 1978, pp. 188–89.
51 Lauriston Sharp and Lucien Hanks, *Bang Chan: Social History of a Rural Community in Thailand*, Ithaca, New York, and London: Cornell University Press, 1978, pp. 127–28.
52 *Si krung*, 12 May 1928.

53 James C. Scott, *Weapons of the Weak: Everyday Forms of Peasant Resistance*, New Haven: Yale University Press, 1985, esp. pp. 22–25, 234–35, 282.
54 NA MT 0201.1.1/1577, 'Nai Khwai Kaenkaeo, Nai Tan Wongbaipet and Associates to Minister of the Interior, 24 September 1940'; NA MT 0201.1.1/1579, 'MP for Nakhon Si Thammarat to Minister of the Interior, 23 September 1940'.
55 NA MT 0201.1.1/1577, 'Secretary of Minister of Interior to Nai Khwai and associates, 3 October 1940'; NA MT 0201.1.1/1579, 'Secretary of Minister of Interior to MP for Nakhon Si Thammarat, 3 October 1940'.
56 See, for example, NA R6 N 42/32, 'An Honest Person to the Minister of Local Government, July 1916'; NA R6 N 42/95, 'Anonymous Letter from People of Pak Klong Phra Khanong, 22 March 1925'; NA MT 0201.1.1/185, 'Anonymous Letter, 9 October 1936'; NA MT 0201.1.1/1354, 'People of Sukhothai to Phibun, 1 December 1939'.
57 See, for instance, NA R6 N 42/85, 'Mr Watching the Government to the Minister of the Interior, 19 June 1923'; NA R6 N 42/92, 'The People, 25 June 1925'; NA R6 N 42/114, 'The People of Phra Pradaeng Province'; NA MT 0201.1.1/2, 'Villagers of Tambon Talat Mai to PM, 18 February 1934'; NA MT 0201.1.1/898, 'Nai Sawat to Chaikan, 3 August 1938'; NA MT 0201.1.1/1007, 'Nai Lek to Phibun, 1 March 1939'.
58 See, for example, NA MT 0201.1.1/2, 'Ang Thong Provincial Committee to Undersecretary of the Interior, 13 June 1934'; NA MT 0201.1.1/1007, 'Ang Thong Provincial Committee to Director-General of the Department of the Interior, 27 July 1939'.
59 NA MT 0201.1.1/1221, 'Undersecretary of the Interior to Governor of Pathum Thani, 27 January 1940', 'Governor of Pathum Thani to Undersecretary of the Interior, 8 February 1940'.
60 NA MT 0201.1.1/1581, 'Anonymous letter to PM, 15 May 1940', 'Governor of Phrae to Undersecretary of the Interior, 14 June 1940'.
61 NA R7 M 26.2/6, 'Extract from *Lak muang*, 22 January 1927'.
62 NA MT 0201.1.1/1354, 'People of Sukhothai to Phibun, 1 December 1939'; NA MT 0201.1.1/1221, 'Nai Prasoet to PM, January 1940'.
63 NA MT 0201.1.1/297, 'Ratchaburi Provincial Committee to Undersecretary of the Interior, 15 August 1936'.
64 NA MT 0201.1.1/1221, 'Governor of Pathum Thani to Undersecretary of the Interior, 8 February 1940'.
65 Of all the anonymous letters cited in this section, however, there was only one that resulted in an official being dismissed from office. See NA R6/1 N 42/103, 'Report No. 3360, 17 May 1926'.
66 For examples of this view, see Engel, *Code and Custom*, pp. 190–91.
67 Ibid., p. 191.

9 The criminalization of vice

1 Compared to gambling, opium and prostitution in Thailand have commanded far greater academic attention. Besides a number of English-language studies, this chapter draws on two Thai-language master's theses in particular, which focus on opium and prostitution respectively: Suphaphon Charanphattana, 'Phasifin kap naiyobai dankankhlang khong ratthaban thai pho so 2367–2468' [Opium Revenue and the Fiscal Policy of the Thai Government, 1824–1925], MA thesis, Chulalongkorn University, 1980; and Dararat Mettarikanon, 'Sopheni kap naiyobai ratthaban thai pho so 2411–2503' [Prostitution and Thai Government Policy, 1868–1960], MA thesis, Chulalongkorn University, 1983.

2 Wit Thiangburannatham, *Fin su heroin* [From Opium to Heroin], Bangkok: Phaenphitthaya, 1978, pp. 85–86; Kasian Tejapira, 'Pigtail: A Pre-History of Chineseness in Siam' in Tong Chee Kiong and Chan Kwok Bun (eds), *Alternate Identities: The Chinese of Contemporary Thailand*, Singapore: Brill, 2001, p. 55.
3 Dararat, [Prostitution and Government Policy], pp. 13–16.
4 Thanh-Dam Truong, *Sex, Money and Morality: Prostitution and Tourism in Southeast Asia*, London: Zed Books, 1990, p. 148.
5 Anthony Farrington (ed.), *Dr Richardson's Missions to Siam, 1829–1839*, Bangkok: White Lotus, 2004, p. 206.
6 Quoted in Scot Barmé, *Woman, Man, Bangkok: Love, Sex and Popular Culture in Thailand*, Lanham: Rowman and Littlefield, 2002, p. 76.
7 Barmé, for instance, has suggested that the long-standing practice of men providing monetary compensation for sexual transgressions with another's wife or unmarried daughter might have naturalized the idea of commercialized prostitution. Ibid., p. 20.
8 Ibid., p. 158.
9 Sthirakoses (Phraya Anuman Rajdhon), *Looking Back: Book Three*, Bangkok: Chulalongkorn University Press, 2001, p. 16.
10 A number of scholars have claimed that there is an inherent gender bias against women in Buddhism, though this argument has been heavily critiqued. See Craig J. Reynolds, *Seditious Histories: Contesting Thai and Southeast Asian Pasts*, Seattle: University of Washington Press, 2006, pp. 186–88; and Thanh-Dam, *Sex, Money and Morality*, pp. 131–49, on the one hand; and Leslie Ann Jeffrey, *Sex and Borders: Gender, National Identity, and Prostitution Policy in Thailand*, Honolulu: University of Hawaii Press, 2002, pp. xvii–xix, on the other.
11 This was the expression used in both the law and in Mongkut's later criticism of the practice. See Reynolds, *Seditious Histories*, pp. 191, 198.
12 Barmé, *Woman, Man, Bangkok*, pp. 20–21; Thanh-Dam, *Sex, Money and Morality*, pp. 146–49.
13 Carl A. Trocki, *Opium, Empire and the Global Political Economy: A Study of the Asian Opium Trade*, London and New York: Routledge, 1999, pp. 9–11, 58–59, 156.
14 Wichai Photsa-yachinda, *Botrian chak banhafin nai sattawat raek khong krungrattanakosin* [Lessons from the Opium Problem in the First Century of the Rattanakosin Era], Bangkok: Health Research Institute, Chulalongkorn University, 1983, pp. 4–5; Suphaphon, [Opium Revenue], pp. 26–27.
15 Frederick Arthur Neale, *Narrative of a Residence in Siam*, Bangkok: White Lotus, 1996 [1852], pp. 143–44.
16 The question as to whether Chinese opium smokers in South-East Asia brought their habit with them has long been debated. The British Malaya Opium Commission of 1924 found that most had started after leaving China and this was probably the case in nineteenth-century Siam as well. League of Nations, Commission of Enquiry into the Control of Opium-Smoking in the Far East, *Report to the Council, Volume 1: Report with Comparative Tables, Maps and Illustrations*, Geneva, 1930, p. 24.
17 Sthirakoses, *Looking Back*, 3, pp. 16–18.
18 Dararat, [Prostitution and Government Policy], pp. 19–21.
19 Sthirakoses, *Looking Back*, 3, pp. 18, 32–33.
20 Barmé, *Woman, Man, Bangkok*, pp. 77–78; Dararat, [Prostitution and Government Policy], pp. 37–42.
21 Suphaphon, [Opium Revenue], pp. 27–28; Wichai, [Lessons from the Opium Problem], p. 4.
22 Quoted in Kasian, 'Pigtail', p. 56.

23 Wichai, [Lessons from the Opium Problem], p. 6.
24 Quoted in Kasian, 'Pigtail', p. 56.
25 For a detailed discussion of these 'fake Chinese' (*chin plaeng*), see ibid., pp. 54–59.
26 Suphaphon, [Opium Revenue], p. 35; Wichai, [Lessons from the Opium Problem], p. 6.
27 Constance M. Wilson, 'State and Society in the Reign of Mongkut, 1851–68: Thailand on the Eve of Modernization', PhD dissertation, Cornell University, 1970, pp. 995–1000.
28 Reynolds, *Seditious Histories*, pp. 195–99.
29 See ibid., pp. 203–12.
30 Jeffrey, *Sex and Borders*, pp. 3, 8.
31 On the Road Maintenance Tax, see Dararat, [Prostitution and Government Policy], pp. 58–72.
32 Ibid., p. 63.
33 Ibid., pp. 68–69.
34 Constance M. Wilson, 'Bangkok in 1883: An Economic and Social Profile,' *Journal of the Siam Society*, 77, 2 (1989), p. 56.
35 Barmé, *Woman, Man, Bangkok,* pp. 79–80, 91 n. 38; Sthirakoses, *Looking Back*, 3, pp. 20, 39–41.
36 Barmé, *Woman, Man, Bangkok,* pp. 77, 93 n. 60.
37 Dararat, [Prostitution and Government Policy], pp. 66–70.
38 Suphaphon, [Opium Revenue], p. 107.
39 Étienne Aymonier, *Isan Travels: Northeast Thailand's Economy in 1883–1884*, trans. Walter E. J. Tips, Bangkok: White Lotus, 2000 [1895, 1897], pp. 46, 132.
40 Suphaphon, [Opium Revenue], pp. 170–71.
41 Quoted in Wichai, [Lessons from the Opium Problem], p. 13.
42 NA R6 N 19/3, 'Points from the *thesaphiban* Meeting, 1912/13'.
43 Walter E. J. Tips, *Crime and Punishment in King Chulalongkorn's Kingdom: The Special Commission for the Reorganisation of the Provincial Courts of Ayutthaya (1898–1897)*, Bangkok: White Lotus, 1998, pp. 126–29.
44 Barmé, *Woman, Man, Bangkok*, p. 78.
45 Dararat, [Prostitution and Government Policy], p. 4; Sthirakoses, *Looking Back*, 3, p. 17.
46 Barmé, *Woman, Man, Bangkok*, p. 173.
47 Carle C. Zimmerman, *Siam: Rural Economic Survey, 1930–31*, Bangkok: Bangkok Times Press, 1931, p. 230.
48 Sthirakoses, *Looking Back*, 3, pp. 21–26, 46–47.
49 Barmé, *Woman, Man, Bangkok*, pp. 177–78 n. 60.
50 *PKPS*, 22, pp. 345–46.
51 On the Venereal Disease Prevention Act see Barmé, *Woman, Man, Bangkok*, pp. 78–79; and Dararat, [Prostitution and Government Policy], pp. 73–79, 83–84.
52 Barmé, *Woman, Man, Bangkok*, p. 93 n. 53.
53 Dararat, [Prostitution and Government Policy], p. 78; Jeffrey, *Sex and Borders*, p. 12.
54 For the 1893/4 to 1895/6 lease, the government put the monopoly for the entire kingdom up for auction as a single farm, while for the 1896/7 to 1898/9 period it auctioned off farms by *monthon*. In the 1900s, these *monthon* farms were grouped together into larger regional blocs. Suphaphon, [Opium Revenue], pp. 79–92.
55 See Ian Brown, 'The End of the Opium Farm in Siam, 1905–7' in John Butcher and Howard Dick (eds), *The Rise and Fall of Revenue Farming: Business Elites and the Emergence of the Modern State in Southeast Asia*, London: MacMillan, 1993, pp. 233–41.

56 Quoted in Chali Iamkrasin, *Khwam songcham chak phraphuttha chaoluang* [Episodes from King Rama V's Reign], Bangkok: Samnakphim Tonmai, 2004, pp. 135–36.
57 Suphaphon, [Opium Revenue], pp. 170–71.
58 Ibid., pp. 168–69.
59 Ibid., pp. 175–78.
60 For the opium revenues of the South-East Asian colonies in 1920 and 1929, see League of Nations, *Report to Council*, pp. 47–52.
61 Barmé, *Woman, Man, Bangkok*, p. 79.
62 Ibid., p. 93 n. 53.
63 Ibid., pp. 80–81; Dararat, [Prostitution and Government Policy], pp. 48–49, 87, 90–91, 100–110.
64 Suphaphon, [Opium Revenue], pp. 187–91; Wichai, [Lessons from the Opium Problem], pp. 11–13.
65 See, for example, *PKPS*, 18, pp. 248–50; NA R6 N 2/22, 'The Morphine and Cocaine Act, B. S. 2456'; and *PKPS*, 35, pp. 383–99.
66 League of Nations, *Report to the Council*, pp. 82–83; Alfred W. McCoy with Cathleen B. Read and Leonard P. Adams II, *The Politics of Heroin in Southeast Asia*, Singapore: Harper and Row, 1972, pp. 71–72.
67 *RFAB 1923–24*, p. 14.
68 Dararat, [Prostitution and Government Policy], pp. 80–82.
69 Ibid., pp. 100–101.
70 Sthirakoses, *Looking Back*, 3, pp. 18, 20, 32–33.
71 Dararat, [Prostitution and Government Policy], pp. 111–13; Stefan Hell, *Siam and the League of Nations: Modernisation, Sovereignty and Multilateral Diplomacy, 1920–1940*, Bangkok: River Books, 2010, pp. 170, 175.
72 William B. McAllister, *Drug Diplomacy in the Twentieth Century: An International History*, London and New York: Routledge, 2000, pp. 16–24; Trocki, *Opium, Empire and the Global Political Economy*, pp. 164–65.
73 Jeffrey, *Sex and Borders*, pp. 10–11.
74 Anne L. Foster, 'Prohibition as Superiority: Policing Opium in South-East Asia, 1898–1925', *The International History Review*, 22, 2 (June 2000), p. 255.
75 McAllister, *Drug Diplomacy*, pp. 24–28.
76 Trocki, *Opium, Empire and the Global Political Economy*, p. 164.
77 Suphaphon, [Opium Revenue], pp. 184–85.
78 On Thai involvement in and attitudes towards the League, see Hell, *Siam and the League*, Chs 1 and 2.
79 See the comments of Vajiravudh in 1923 and the People's Party in 1932 in ibid., p. 41.
80 Ibid., p. 13.
81 Ibid., p. 244.
82 Ibid., pp. 35–37, 42–43.
83 For the complete Act and accompanying Regulations, see *PKPS*, 33, pp. 266–93.
84 *RFAB 1921–22*, p. 2.
85 Quoted in Hell, *Siam and the League*, p. 167.
86 This is directly acknowledged in the preamble to these Acts. See, for instance, that of the Narcotics Act B. E. 2465 (1922) in *PKPS*, 35, p. 383.
87 On the League convention and the resulting laws see Dararat, [Prostitution and Government Policy], pp. 117–18, 120–27; Hell, *Siam and the League*, pp. 167–74; and Jeffrey, *Sex and Borders*, pp. 12–14.
88 Hell, *Siam and the League*, pp. 167, 169.
89 Quoted in ibid., p. 168.
90 Ibid., pp. 188, 243.
91 Ibid., pp. 102–3, 176–77.

92 Ibid., p. 101.
93 League of Nations, *Report to the Council*, pp. 34, 40, 45–46, 79–82.
94 Quoted in Hell, *Siam and the League*, p. 105.
95 Quoted in ibid.
96 *RFAB 1934–35*, p. 22.
97 *RFAB 1937–38*, p. 21.
98 *SY 1931–33*, p. 293; Hell, *Siam and the League*, p. 115.
99 Hell, *Siam and the League*, p. 110; McAllister, *Drug Diplomacy*, pp. 120, 133.
100 *RFAB 1934–35*, p. 21; *RFAB 1936–37*, pp. 16–17; *SY 1937–38 & 1938–39*, p. 528.
101 In the early 1930s, the British-Indian government, then the world's largest opium producer, curtailed its exports.
102 On this scheme, see *RFAB 1939 & 1939–40*, pp. 30–31; and Kenneth P. Landon, *The Chinese in Thailand*, New York: Russell and Russell, 1941, pp. 94–95.
103 Hell, *Siam and the League*, p. 118.
104 Ibid., pp. 47–48.
105 Dararat, [Prostitution and Government Policy], pp. 129–30.
106 Jeffrey, *Sex and Borders*, p. 15.
107 Landon, *Chinese in Thailand*, pp. 95–96.
108 Dararat, [Prostitution and Government Policy], pp. 124–25; Hell, *Siam and the League*, p. 180.
109 Jeffrey, *Sex and Borders*, p. 15.
110 Hell, *Siam and the League*, pp. 183–84.
111 McCoy et al., *Politics of Heroin*, pp. 91–92.
112 Dararat, [Prostitution and Government Policy], pp. 98–99, 139–40, 144–45.
113 Jeffrey, *Sex and Borders*, p. 16.
114 Ibid., pp. 19–20.
115 Ibid., pp. 20–23; Dararat, [Prostitution and Government Policy], pp. 140–41, 155–56.
116 Morris G. Fox, 'Problem of Prostitution in Thailand' in Department of Public Welfare, Ministry of Interior, *Social Service in Thailand*, Bangkok: Ministry of Interior Press, 1960, p. 143.
117 Wit, [Opium to Heroin], p. 100; Thak Chaloemtiarana, *Thailand: The Politics of Despotic Paternalism*, rev. ed., Ithaca, New York: Cornell Southeast Asia Program, 2007, p. 126.
118 Thak, *Thailand*, pp. 121–24.
119 Jeffrey, *Sex and Borders*, p. 26.
120 Dararat, [Prostitution and Government Policy], pp. 159–66.
121 McCoy et al., *Politics of Heroin*, p. 144.
122 From the viewpoint of today, when lotteries and casinos are used by countries all over the world for revenue purposes, the idea of such an agreement on gambling seems laughable in a way that the UN conventions on the suppression of human trafficking and the narcotics trade do not.
123 This was explicitly stated in the draft Venereal Disease Control Act B. E. 2485 (1942) that was never enacted. See Fox, 'Problem of Prostitution', p. 151.
124 *SY 1931–33*, pp. 292–95; James C. Ingram, *Economic Change in Thailand, 1850–1970*, Stanford, California: Stanford University Press, 1971, pp. 328–29.
125 Philip Cornwel-Smith, *Very Thai: Everyday Popular Culture*, Bangkok: River Books, 2005, p. 197.
126 League of Nations, *Report to the Council*, pp. 20–21, 78.
127 Landon, *Chinese in Thailand*, p. 95.
128 Barmé, *Woman, Man, Bangkok*, p. 82.
129 Fox, 'Problem of Prostitution', p. 141.
130 See, for example, NA K Kh 0301.1.30/15, 'Chaophraya Yomarat to Vajiravudh, 1 March 1916'; League of Nations, *Report to the Council*, p. 78.

224 *Notes*

131 Quoted in Hell, *Siam and the League*, p. 87.
132 League of Nations, *Report to the Council*, p. 25.
133 Ibid., p. 26.
134 *PKPS*, 12, p. 84.
135 *Krungthep Daily Mail*, 24 May 1916.
136 Virginia Thompson, *Thailand: The New Siam*, New York: MacMillan, 1941, p. 740.
137 Quoted in Barmé, *Woman, Man, Bangkok*, p. 22.
138 Dararat, [Prostitution and Government Policy], p. 76.
139 This is how Hell accounts for the similar lack of interest in human trafficking. Hell, *Siam and the League*, p. 167.
140 Jeffrey, *Sex and Borders*, p. xx. See also Reynolds, *Seditious Histories*, pp. 123–25.
141 Jeffrey, *Sex and Borders*, pp. 22–23.

Conclusion

1 Arkartdamkeung Rapheephat, *The Circus of Life*, trans. Phongdeit Jiangphattanarket and ed. Marcel Barang, Bangkok: Modern Thai Classics, 1995, p. 195.
2 Ibid., p. 9.
3 Rachel Harrison, 'Thailande: Between East and West' in Monique Zaini-Lajoubert (ed.), *États et literature en Asie: L'emergence des états modernes*, Paris: Les Indes Savantes, 2003, p. 180.
4 Ibid., pp. 172–73.
5 See, for instance, NA R5 Kh 14.1.Kh/18, 'Memorandum containing proposals as to the manner in which revenue can be raised to supply the deficiency which will be caused by the abolition of the gambling houses in the provinces'; and NA R6 N 11.5.Ch/17, 'Ministry of the Interior Consultation on Class 2 Gambling'.
6 In 1910, for example, Chaophraya Wongsanupraphat claimed that within five years of closing the gambling house and *huai* lottery tax farms 'the country will enter into a healthy state of prosperity which it has never know before'. See NA R5 KS 1/4, 'Memorandum on our Domestic Economy'.
7 Chatchai Panananon, 'Siamese "Slavery": The Institution and its Abolition', PhD dissertation, University of Michigan, 1982, pp. 235–37.
8 Ibid., pp. 7, 269–78.
9 *Ministry of Justice Report for the Year 122 (1903–04)*, p. 13; *SY 1937–38 & 1938–39*, p. 358.
10 David K. Wyatt, *Thailand: A Short History*, 2nd ed., New Haven and London: Yale University Press, 2003, p. 301.
11 The 1911/12 figure is a result of calculations based on the population and conviction figures from *SY 1916*, pp. 16, 193, and the 1937/8 figure is taken straight from *SY 1937–38 & 1938–39*, p. 359.
12 *RPAB 1899–1900*, p. 21; *Ministry of Justice Report for the Year 122 (1903–04)*, p. 8; *Ministry of Justice Report for the Year 123 (1904–05)*, pp. 5, 11; *Ministry of Justice Report for the Year 126 (1907–08)*, pp. 7–8.
13 See, for instance, NA R5 Kh 14.1.Kh/18, 'Damrong to Chulalongkorn, 4 August 1903'; NA R6 N 4.1/73, 'E. W. Trotter to Chaophraya Yomarat, 23 December 1915'; NA R7 Kh 2/2, 'Ideas about Suppressing Gambling'.
14 NA R6 N 4.1/165, 'A Report on work of Police and Gendarmerie and on the Criminal Statistics of Siam for the year B. E. 2462', pp. 62–63.
15 Ibid., p. 66; NA R7 Kh 2/2, 'Ideas about Suppressing Gambling'.
16 These figures are the result of calculations using the population and crime statistics from *SY 1916*, pp. 16, 192–93; and Wyatt, *Thailand*, p. 301.

17 *SY 1924–25*, p. 249; *SY 1929–30*, p. 303; *SY 1931–33*, p. 355; *SY 1933–35*, p. 371; *SY 1937–38 & 1938–39*, p. 359.
18 Kenneth P. Landon, *Siam in Transition: A Brief Survey of Cultural Trends in the Five Years since the Revolution of 1932*, London: Oxford University Press, 1939, p. 154.
19 Ian Brown, *The Élite and the Economy in Siam, c.1890–1920*, Singapore: Oxford University Press, 1988, pp. 87–88.
20 Tamara Loos, *Subject Siam: Family, Law and Colonial Modernity in Thailand*, Ithaca, New York, and London: Cornell University Press, 2006, p. 49.
21 See David Dixon, *From Prohibition to Regulation: Bookmaking, Anti-Gambling, and the Law*, Oxford: Clarendon Press, 1991, p. 58.
22 Wongsanupraphat had received marine training in Denmark and then lived in Europe for some period of time.
23 NA R6 KS 1/4, 'Memorandum on our Domestic Economy'.
24 Batson makes a similar point in regards to the Bangkok-appointed Siamese officials who were sent to administer the outlying areas of the kingdom during the late nineteenth century, noting their similarity to the Western colonial officials in other parts of South-East Asia. Benjamin A. Batson, *The End of the Absolute Monarchy in Siam*, Singapore: Oxford University Press, 1984, p. 12.
25 Dixon, *From Prohibition to Regulation*, pp. 194–97.
26 Ibid., p. 197.
27 In this respect, the debate over gambling is more comparable to that on drugs in general.
28 *RFAB 123 (1904–05)*, p. 7.
29 Robert E. Speer, Dwight H. Day and Dr. David Bovaird, *Report of Deputation of the Presbyterian Board of Foreign Missions to Siam, the Philippines, Japan, Chosen and China, April–November 1915*, New York: Board of Foreign Missions of the Presbyterian Church in the U.S.A., 1916, p. 15.
30 Ibid., p. 16.
31 Lauriston Sharp and Lucien Hanks, *Bang Chan: Social History of a Rural Community in Thailand*, Ithaca, New York, and London: Cornell University Press, 1978, p. 194.
32 Pasuk Phongpaichit, Sungsidh Piriyarangsan and Nualnoi Treerat, *Guns, Girls, Gambling, Ganja: Thailand's Illegal Economy and Public Policy*, Chiang Mai: Silkworm Books, 1998, pp. 216–17.
33 Philip Cornwel-Smith, *Very Thai: Everyday Popular Culture*, Bangkok: River Books, 2005, p. 197.
34 Pasuk et al., *Guns, Girls, Gambling, Ganja*, pp. 33–34.
35 Ibid., p. 45.
36 Ibid., pp. 45–46.
37 Ibid., p. 73.
38 During the 2010 tournament, 166,200 baht in cash was confiscated and 3.6 million baht in circulated money found, compared to figures of 7.5 million in cash and 845 million baht in circulation in the previous one. *Pattaya Daily News*, 13 July 2010. Online, available HTTP: <http://www.pattayadailynews.com/en/2010/07/13/national-world-cup-gambling-crackdown-successful/> (accessed 10 November 2010).
39 Pasuk et al., *Guns, Girls, Gambling, Ganja*, pp. 19–20.
40 Pasuk Phongpaichit and Chris Baker, *Thaksin: The Business of Politics in Thailand*, Chiang Mai: Silkworm Books, 2004, p. 116.
41 *Bangkok Post*, 30 May 2004.
42 Cornwel-Smith, *Very Thai*, p. 198.
43 Ibid., p. 197.

44 Ibid., p. 198.
45 Landon, *Siam in Transition*, p. 154.
46 See Pasuk et al., *Guns, Girls, Gambling, Ganja*, pp. 25–33, 39–40.
47 Ibid., p. 14.
48 For the details of the survey see ibid., pp. 219–30.
49 Ibid., p. 218.
50 Quoted in Cornwel-Smith, *Very Thai*, p. 198.
51 Pasuk et al., *Guns, Girls, Gambling, Ganja*, p. 35.
52 Ibid., pp. 64–68.
53 Pasuk and Baker, *Thaksin*, pp. 94–95.
54 *Matichon*, 19 February 2003.
55 Pasuk and Baker, *Thaksin*, p. 116.
56 Ibid.; Cornwel-Smith, *Very Thai*, p. 198.
57 *Bangkok Post*, 30 May and 11 June 2004.
58 Unless indicated the information on the Liverpool lottery scheme is taken from Pasuk and Baker, *Thaksin*, pp. 243–46.
59 *Bangkok Post*, 30 May 2004.
60 *Khao sot*, 25 May 2004.
61 *Bangkok Post*, 4 and 6 June 2004.
62 *Bangkok Post*, 5 December 2009.
63 *Bangkok Post*, 4 January 2010.
64 *Bangkok Post*, 6 January 2010.
65 *Bangkok Post*, 5 January 2010.
66 Ibid.; *The Nation*, 11 January 2010.
67 *Bangkok Post*, 31 May 2004.
68 *Bangkok Post*, 28 March 2004.
69 Quoted in *Bangkok Post*, 13 June 2004.
70 *Bangkok Post*, 6 January 2010.
71 *Bangkok Post*, 13 June 2004.
72 *Matichon*, 19 February 2003.
73 Ibid.
74 On the symbolic linking of Chulalongkorn and King Bhumibol see Irene Stengs, *Worshipping the Great Moderniser: King Chulalongkorn, Patron Saint of the Thai Middle Class*, Singapore: NUS Press, 2009, Ch. 5.

Bibliography

Archival materials

The archival research for this study was carried out in the National Archives of Thailand, Bangkok. In the notes, all archival sources from this source are prefixed with NA and are referenced according to the catalogue system used by the National Archives. Most of the pre-1932 archival records are organized by reign and then by ministry. After 1932, they are grouped by ministry or office. Listed below are the reference numbers of the file series and their sub-series that were consulted, followed by their respective titles. When only one file has been referenced from a particular series then it is listed with its individual reference number and title.

Documents from the Fifth Reign **(R5)**

Ministry of Agriculture (KS)

4.5/6   'Report of Mr Giles on the Rate of Land Tax'

Ministry of Finance (Kh)

14.1.Kh   Taxes. Revenue Department. Gambling Houses

Ministry of the Interior (M)

1.3   General. Announcements and Legislation
2.11   Administrative Division. Administrative Meetings

Ministry of Local Government (N)

2   Announcements and Legislation
3.2.K   Provincial Administration in *monthon* Krungthep. Thanyaburi. General
3.3.K   Provincial Administration in *monthon* Krungthep. Nakhon Khuan. General
3.3.Ch   Provincial Administration in *monthon* Krungthep. Nakhon Khuan Khan. Prisoners

228 Bibliography

3.5.K Provincial Administration in *monthon* Krungthep. Pathum Thani. General
6.2 Prison Department (Serious Offences). Prisoners
7.7.Ng Bangkok Revenue Department. Revenue. Gambling and Entertainment
8.1 Police Department. General
11.3.K Provincial Gendarmerie and Metropolitan Police. Patrol Department. Gambling
20 Clubs and Associations
42.11 Correspondence with Ministry of Finance. Gambling Houses
49.5 Correspondence with Ministry of Public Instruction and Religion. Monks and Novices

Combined documents from the Fifth and Sixth Reigns (R5–6)

Ministry of the Royal Secretariat (RL)

RL-KhPh Court Verdicts

Documents from the Sixth Reign (R6)

Ministry of Agriculture (KS)

1 General

Ministry of Finance (Kh)

2 Announcements and Legislation
18 Taxes and Revenue

Ministry of Local Government (N)

2 Announcements and Legislation
4.1 Metropolitan Police Department. General
11.5.Ch Revenue Department. Taxes and Revenue. Gambling and Entertainment
19 *Thesaphiban* Meetings
20.6 Newspapers. Articles
20.17 Newspapers. Gambling
26 Clubs and Associations
42 Anonymous Letters

Miscellaneous (B)

11 Lotteries

Documents from the Seventh Reign (R7)

Ministry of Finance (Kh)

2 Announcements and Legislation

Ministry of the Interior (M)

15 Lotteries
26 Newspapers
99 Miscellaneous

Ministry of Justice (Y)

4 Court Cases

Office of the Financial Adviser **(K Kh 0301.1)**

3   Gaming and Lotteries
30/15 'The Chinese Question'

Documents from the Office of the Prime Minister's Secretariat **((2) SR 0201)**

31   Gambling
101 Lotteries

Documents from the Ministry of the Interior **(MT)**

2.2 Office of the Undersecretary. Central Division
4   Department of Corrections
4.5 Department of Corrections. Newspaper Reports

Documents from the Office of the Undersecretary of the Interior **(MT 0201)**

1.1 Office of the Ministerial Secretariat. Investigations and Ideas Division

Newspapers and periodicals

Awanti
Bangkok Calendar
Bangkok Daily Mail
Bangkok kanmuang
Bangkok Post
Bangkok Times
Bangkok Times Weekly Mail
Chino sayam warasap
Khao sot
Kro lek
Krungthep Daily Mail
Lak muang

230 Bibliography

Matichon
Nangsuphim thai
The Nation
Pattaya Daily News (online newspaper)
Ratsadon
Samphan thai
San phranakhon
Sara rat
Satri sap
Sayam rat
Sayam sakkhi
Siam Observer (Thai and English editions)
Siam Repository
Siam Weekly Advertiser
Si krung
Thai Mai
Thammasan
Thesaphiban
Wayamo
Yamato

Articles, books and theses

1. Thai-language sources

Anek Bunyaphakdi, *Phai phong thai* [Thai Card Games], Bangkok: Cremation Volume, 1967.
Anuphap Traiphop, Phraya, *Phramaha-nakhon-krungthep nai khwamsongcham khun ayu chetsip* [Bangkok as Remembered by a Seventy-Year-Old], Bangkok: Cremation Volume, 1961.
Borirak Nitikaset, Phra (comp.), *Phraratchabanyat kanphanan kap khamphiphaksadika banthatthan* [The Gambling Act and Supreme Court Rulings], np, nd.
Chali Iamkrasin, *Khwam songcham chak phraphuttha chaoluang* [Episodes from King Rama V's Reign], Bangkok: Samnakphim Tonmai, 2004.
Charoen, Nai, *Nirat phai lae nirat pen tahan* [The Card Poem and the Poem about Being a Soldier], Bangkok: Ruang Sin, 1979 [1925/6].
Chulalongkorn, King, *Phithi songkran* [Songkran Ceremonies], Bangkok: Cremation Volume, 1978.
Damrong Rachanuphap, Prince, *Prachum phongsawadan phak thi 17: Ruang tamnan kanloek bonbia lae huai* [Collected Chronicles, Part 17: The Abolition of the Gambling Dens and the *huai* Lottery], Bangkok: Cremation Volume, 1960.
——, *Ruang sonthana kap phuraiplon* [Interview with a Bandit], Bangkok: Cremation Volume, 1925.
Dararat Mettarikanon, 'Sopheni kap naiyobai ratthaban thai pho so 2411–2503' [Prostitution and Thai Government Policy, 1868–1960], MA thesis, Chulalongkorn University, 1983.

Institute of Linguistics (Thailand) (comp.), *Pathanukrom chabap luang* [Government Dictionary], np, nd.
Kanchana Chintakanon, 'Naiyobai khong ratthaban kieokap phasi-akon kanphanan pho so 2367–2460' [Government Policy Towards Gambling Taxes, 1824–1917], MA thesis, Sinlapakon University, 1987.
Lisut Thonchai, *Khu-mu kanphanan* [Gambling Handbook], 2nd ed., Bangkok, nd.
Mannot Sutthiwatthanaphrut, *Kham athibai pramuan kotmai phaeng lae phanit wa duai yumfaksap kepkhong nai khlangsinkha prani-pranom yomkhwam kanphanan lae khanto* [Explanation of the Civil and Commercial Code Concerning Borrowing and Depositing Property, Reconciliation and Compromise, Consent, Gambling and Betting], 2nd ed., Bangkok: Ramkhamhaeng University Press, 1975.
Nakkharin Mektrairat, *Kanpathiwat sayam pho so 2475* [The Siamese Revolution of 1932], Bangkok: The Foundation for the Social Sciences and Humanities, 1992.
Narathip Phongpraphan, Prince (ed.), *Chumnum phranipphon khong than wan* [Collected Writings of Prince Wan], Bangkok: Padung Suksa, 1965.
National Assembly Committee for Financial Affairs, Banking and Financial Institutions, *Rai-ngan phon-kanphicharana suksa ruang kanpoet kasino nai prathet hai thuktong tam kotmai* [Report on Study Considering the Opening of Casinos in Accordance with the Law], Bangkok: Secretariat of the National Assembly, 2003.
Nuttaya Ussavaponganat, 'Bonbia nai sangkhom thai pho so 2367–2460: Kansuksa choeng sangkhom watthanatham' ['Bonbia' – Chinese Gambling in Thai Society, 1824–1917: A Socio-Cultural Study], MA thesis, Thammasat University, 2005.
Rai-ngan kanprachum sapha phu-thaen ratsadon [Records of the National Assembly], Bangkok: Office of the Parliamentary Secretary, 1933+.
Ratchaworamuni (Prayut Payutto), Phra, *Photchanukrom phutthasat: Chabap pramuan tham* [Dictionary of Buddhism], Bangkok: Chulalongkorn University Fund for Publishing a Dictionary of Buddhism, 1985.
Sangop Suriyin, *Thianwan*, 3rd ed., Bangkok: Ruamsan Press, 2000.
Saranukromthai chabap ratchabanditthayasathan [Thai Encyclopaedia: National Bar Association Edition], vol. 20, Bangkok: Thai-mit Press, 1975–76.
Sathian Laiyalak et al. (comps), *Prachum kotmai pracham sok* [Collected Laws in Chronological Order], Bangkok: Daily Mail Press, Nitiwet, 1935+, 70 vols.
Suphaphon Charanphattana, 'Phasi fin kap naiyobai dan-kankhlang khong ratthaban thai pho so 2367–2468' [Opium Revenue and the Fiscal Policy of the Thai Government, 1824–1925], MA thesis, Chulalongkorn University, 1980.
Thanongsak Thinsinuan, 'Kotmai kieokap kanphanan' [Laws about Gambling], MA thesis, Faculty of Law, Thammasat University, 1986.
Thepphawethi, Phra, *Thot khong kanphanan* [The Dangers of Gambling], Bangkok: Mahamakut Buddhist University Press, 1940.
Wichai Photsa-yachinda, *Botrian chak banhafin nai sattawat raek khong krungrattanakosin* [Lessons from the Opium Problem in the First Century of the Rattanakosin Era], Bangkok: Health Research Institute, Chulalongkorn University, 1983.
Wichit Matra, Khun, *80 pi nai chiwit khapphachao* [80 Years in My Life], Bangkok: Cremation Volume, 1980.
Wit Thiangburannatham, *Fin su heroin* [From Opium to Heroin], Bangkok: Phaenphitthaya, 1978.

2. English-language sources

Akira, Suehiro, *Capital Accumulation in Thailand, 1855–1985*, Tokyo: The Centre for East Asian Cultural Studies, 1989.
Anake Nawigamune (comp.), *A Century of Thai Graphic Design*, London: Thames and Hudson, 2000.
Anderson, Benedict, 'Studies of the Thai State: The State of Thai Studies' in Eliezer B. Ayal (ed.), *The Study of Thailand: Analyses of Knowledge, Approaches, and Prospects in Anthropology, Art History, Economics, History and Political Science*, Papers in International Studies, Southeast Asia Series 54, Athens, Ohio: Ohio University, 1978, pp. 193–247.
Antonio, J., *The 1904 Traveller's Guide to Bangkok and Siam*, Bangkok: White Lotus, 1997 [1904].
Arkartdamkeung Rapheephat, *The Circus of Life*, trans. Phongdeit Jiangphattanarket and ed. Marcel Barang, Bangkok: Modern Thai Classics, 1995.
Aymonier, Étienne, *Isan Travels: Northeast Thailand's Economy in 1883–1884*, trans. Walter E. J. Tips, Bangkok: White Lotus, 2000 [1895, 1897].
Baker, Chris and Pasuk Phongpaichit, *A History of Thailand*, New York: Cambridge University Press, 2005.
Barang, Marcel (comp.), *The 20 Best Novels of Thailand*, Bangkok: Thai Modern Classics, 1994.
Barmé, Scot, *Woman, Man, Bangkok: Love, Sex and Popular Culture in Thailand*, Lanham: Rowman and Littlefield, 2002.
——, *Luang Wichit Wathakan and the Creation of a Thai Identity*, Singapore: Institute of Southeast Asian Studies, 1993.
Bastian, Adolf, *A Journey in Siam (1863)*, trans. Walter E. J. Tips and ed. Christian Goodden, Bangkok: White Lotus, 2005 [1867].
Batson, Benjamin A., *The End of the Absolute Monarchy in Siam*, Singapore: Oxford University Press, 1984.
Benedict, Ruth, *Thai Culture and Behavior: An Unpublished War Time Study dated September, 1943*, Ithaca, New York: Data Paper Number 4, Southeast Asia Program, Cornell University, 1952.
Bock, Carl, *Temples and Elephants: Travels in Siam in 1881–82*, Singapore: Oxford University Press, 1986 [1884].
Bowring, Sir John, *The Kingdom and People of Siam*, 2 vols, London: Oxford University Press, 1969 [1857].
Breazeale, Kennon, 'A Transition in Historical Writing: The Works of Prince Damrong Rachanuphap', *Journal of the Siam Society*, 59, 2 (July 1971), pp. 25–49.
Brown, Ian, 'The End of the Opium Farm in Siam, 1905–7' in John Butcher and Howard Dick (eds), *The Rise and Fall of Revenue Farming: Business Elites and the Emergence of the Modern State in Southeast Asia*, London: MacMillan, 1993, pp. 233–45.
——, *The Creation of the Modern Ministry of Finance in Siam, 1885–1910*, London: MacMillan, 1992.
——, *The Élite and the Economy in Siam, c.1890–1920*, Singapore: Oxford University Press, 1988.
Buls, Charles, *Siamese Sketches*, trans. Walter E. J. Tips, Bangkok: White Lotus, 1994 [1901].
Burney Papers, The, 5 vols, Bangkok: Vajiranana National Library, 1910–14.

Butcher, John G., 'Revenue Farming and the Changing State in Southeast Asia' in John Butcher and Howard Dick (eds), *The Rise and Fall of Revenue Farming: Business Elites and the Emergence of the Modern State in Southeast Asia*, London: MacMillan, 1993, pp. 19–44.

———, 'The Demise of the Revenue Farm System in the Federated Malay States', *Modern Asian Studies*, 17, 3 (July 1983), pp. 395–412.

Campbell, J. G. D., *Siam in the Twentieth Century: Being the Experiences and Impressions of a British Official*, London: Edward Arnold, 1902.

Carter, Cecil A., *The Kingdom of Siam*, New York and London: G. P. Putnam's Sons, 1904.

Cartwright, B. O., 'The Huey Lottery', *Journal of the Siam Society*, 18, 3 (1924), pp. 221–39.

Chaiyan Rajchagool, *The Rise and Fall of the Thai Absolute Monarchy: Foundations of the Modern Thai State from Feudalism to Peripheral Capitalism*, Bangkok: White Lotus, 1994.

Chang, Ning Jennifer, 'Pure Sport or A Gambling Disgrace? Greyhound Racing and the Formation of Modern Shanghai' in Peter Zarrow (ed.), *Creating Chinese Modernity: Knowledge and Everyday Life, 1900–1940*, New York: Peter Lang, 2006, pp. 147–81.

Chatchai Panananon, 'Siamese "Slavery": The Institution and its Abolition', PhD dissertation, University of Michigan, 1982.

Chatthip Nartsupha and Suthy Prasertset (eds), *The Political Economy of Siam, 1851–1910*, Bangkok: The Social Science Association of Thailand, 1981.

Copeland, Matthew, 'Contested Nationalism and the 1932 Overthrow of the Absolute Monarchy in Siam', PhD dissertation, Australian National University, 1993.

Cornwel-Smith, Philip, *Very Thai: Everyday Popular Culture*, Bangkok: River Books, 2005.

Cort, Mary Lovina, *Siam: Or, the Heart of Farther India*, New York: Anson D. F. Randolph and Co., 1886.

Crawfurd, John, *Journal of an Embassy to the Courts of Siam and Cochin China*, Kuala Lumpur: Oxford University Press, 1967 [1828].

Darling, Frank C., 'The Evolution of Law in Thailand', *The Review of Politics*, 32, 2 (April 1970), pp. 197–218.

Dick, Howard, 'A Fresh Approach to Southeast Asian History' in John Butcher and Howard Dick (eds), *The Rise and Fall of Revenue Farming: Business Elites and the Emergence of the Modern State in Southeast Asia*, London: MacMillan, 1993, pp. 3–18.

Dilok Nabarath, Prince, *Siam's Rural Economy under King Chulalongkorn*, trans. Walter E. J. Tips, Bangkok: White Lotus, 2000 [1908].

Dixon, David, *From Prohibition to Regulation: Bookmaking, Anti-Gambling, and the Law*, Oxford: Clarendon Press, 1991.

Ehlers, Otto E., *On Horseback through Indochina: Volume 3. Vietnam, Singapore, and Central Thailand*, trans. Walter E. J. Tips, Bangkok: White Lotus, 2002 [1894].

Engel, David M., *Code and Custom in a Provincial Thai Court: The Interaction of Formal and Informal Systems of Justice*, Tuscon, Arizona: University of Arizona Press, 1978.

———, *Law and Kingship in Thailand during the Reign of King Chulalongkorn*, Michigan Papers on South and Southeast Asia, No. 9, Ann Arbor: University of Michigan, Center for South and Southeast Asian Studies, 1975.

Farrington, Anthony (ed.), *Dr Richardson's Missions to Siam, 1829–1839*, Bangkok: White Lotus, 2004.
——, *Early Missionaries in Bangkok: The Journals of Tomlin, Gutzlaff and Abeel, 1828–1832*, Bangkok: White Lotus, 2001.
Foster, Anne L., 'Prohibition as Superiority: Policing Opium in South-East Asia, 1898–1925', *The International History Review*, 22, 2 (June 2000), pp. 253–73.
Fournereau, Lucien, *Bangkok in 1892*, trans. Walter E. J. Tips, Bangkok: White Lotus, 1998 [1894].
Fox, Morris G., 'Problem of Prostitution in Thailand' in Department of Public Welfare, Ministry of Interior, *Social Service in Thailand*, Bangkok: Ministry of Interior Press, 1960, pp. 139–65.
Freeman, Andrew A., *A Journalist in Siam* (originally published as *Brown Women and White*), Bangkok: White Lotus, 2007 [1932].
Geertz, Clifford, 'Deep Play: Notes on the Balinese Cockfight' in his *The Interpretation of Cultures: Selected Essays*, New York: Basic Books, 1973, pp. 412–53.
Goffman, Erving, 'Where the Action Is' in his *Interaction Ritual: Essays on Face-to-Face Behavior*, New York: Pantheon Books, 1967, pp. 149–270.
Graham, W. A., 'Siam, and Her Relations with Other Powers', *Journal of the Royal Institute of International Affairs*, 7, 5 (September 1928), pp. 297–318.
——, *Siam: A Handbook of Practical, Commercial and Political Information*, London: Alexander Moring, 1924, 2 vols.
Greene, Stephen L. W., *Absolute Dreams: Thai Government Under Rama VI, 1910–1925*, Bangkok: White Lotus, 1999.
Gurr, Ted Robert, Grabosky, Peter N., and Hula, Richard C., *The Politics of Crime and Conflict: A Comparative History of Four Cities*, Beverley Hills, California: Sage Publications, 1977.
Hallett, Holt Samuel, *A Thousand Miles on an Elephant in the Shan States*, Edinburgh and London: William Blackwood and Sons, 1890.
Harrison, Rachel, 'Thailande: Between East and West' in Monique Zaini-Lajoubert (ed.), *États et literature en Asie: L' emergence des états modernes*, Paris: Les Indes Savantes, 2003, pp. 154–84.
Hell, Stefans, *Siam and the League of Nations: Modernisation, Sovereignty and Multilateral Diplomacy, 1920–1940*, Bangkok: River Books, 2010.
Hong Lysa, '"Stranger within the Gates": Knowing Semi-Colonial Siam as Extraterritorials', *Modern Asian Studies*, 38, 2 (May 2004), pp. 327–54.
——, 'Extraterritoriality in Bangkok in the Reign of Chulalongkorn, 1868–1910: The Cacophonies of Semi-Colonial Cosmopolitanism', *Itinerario: European Journal of Overseas History*, 27, 2 (July 2003), pp. 125–46.
——, *Thailand in the Nineteenth Century: Evolution of the Economy and Society*, Singapore: Institute of Southeast Asian Studies, 1984.
Ingram, James C., *Economic Change in Thailand, 1850–1970*, Stanford, California: Stanford University Press, 1971.
Jackson, Peter A., 'The Thai Regime of Images', *Sojourn*, 19, 2 (October 2004), pp. 181–218.
——, 'The Performative State: Semi-coloniality and the Tyranny of Images in Modern Thailand', *Sojourn*, 19, 2 (October 2004), pp. 219–53.
Jaiser, Gerhard, *Thai Mural Painting, Volume 2: Society, Preservation and Subjects*, Bangkok: White Lotus, 2010.

Jeffrey, Leslie Ann, *Sex and Borders: Gender, National Identity, and Prostitution Policy in Thailand*, Honolulu: University of Hawaii Press, 2002.
Johnston, David B., 'Rural Society and the Rice Economy in Thailand, 1880–1930,' PhD dissertation, Yale University, 1975.
Jones, Stephen, *Criminology*, 3rd ed., Oxford: Oxford University Press, 2006.
Jottrand, Mr and Mrs Émile, *In Siam: The Diary of A Legal Adviser of King Chulalongkorn's Government*, trans. Walter E. J. Tips, Bangkok: White Lotus, 1996 [1905].
Kasian Tejapira, 'Pigtail: A Pre-History of Chineseness in Siam' in Tong Chee Kiong and Chan Kwok Bun (eds), *Alternate Identities: The Chinese of Contemporary Thailand*, Singapore: Brill, 2001, pp. 41–66.
Klima, Alan, *The Funeral Casino: Meditation, Massacre, and Exchange with the Dead in Thailand*, Princeton and Oxford: Princeton University Press, 2002.
Kobkua Suwannathat-Pian, *Thailand's Durable Premier: Phibun Through Three Decades, 1932–1957*, Kuala Lumpur: Oxford University Press, 1995.
Kukrit Pramoj, *Four Reigns (Si phaen-din)*, trans. Tulachandra, Chiang Mai: Silkworm Books, 1998 [1953].
Kullada Kesboonchoo Mead, *The Rise and Decline of Thai Absolutism*, London and New York: RoutledgeCurzon, 2004.
La Loubère, Simon de, *The Kingdom of Siam*, Kuala Lumpur: Oxford University Press, 1969 [1693].
Landon, Kenneth P., *The Chinese in Thailand*, New York: Russell and Russell, 1941.
——, *Siam in Transition: A Brief Survey of Cultural Trends in the Five Years since the Revolution of 1932*, London: Oxford University Press, 1939.
Le May, Reginald, *The Coinage of Siam*, Bangkok: The Siam Society, 1932.
League of Nations, Commission of Enquiry into the Control of Opium-Smoking in the Far East, *Report to the Council, Volume 1: Report with Comparative Tables, Maps and Illustrations*, Geneva, 1930.
Loos, Tamara, *Subject Siam: Family, Law and Colonial Modernity in Thailand*, Ithaca, New York, and London: Cornell University Press, 2006.
——, 'Gender Adjudicated: Translating Modern Legal Subjects in Siam', PhD dissertation, Cornell University, 1999.
Masao, Tokichi, 'The New Penal Code of Siam', *Yale Law Journal*, 18, 2 (December 1908), pp. 85–100.
McAllister, William B., *Drug Diplomacy in the Twentieth Century: An International History*, London and New York: Routledge, 2000.
McCoy, Alfred W. with Read, Cathleen B., and Adams II, Leonard P., *The Politics of Heroin in Southeast Asia*, Singapore: Harper and Row, 1972.
McFarland, George Bradley, (ed.), *Thai–English Dictionary*, Stanford, California: Stanford University Press, 1944.
McKibbin, R., 'Working-Class Gambling in Britain, 1880–1939', *Past and Present*, 82, 1 (February 1979), pp. 147–78.
McMillen, Jan, 'Understanding Gambling: History, Concepts and Theories' in Jan McMillen (ed.), *Gambling Cultures: Studies in History and Interpretation*, London and New York: Routledge, 1996, pp. 6–42.
Mosse, George L., *Nationalism and Sexuality: Respectability and Abnormal Sexuality in Modern Europe*, New York: Howard Fertig, 1985.
Munting, Roger, *An Economic and Social History of Gambling in Britain and the USA*, Manchester: Manchester University Press, 1996.

Neale, Frederick Arthur, *Narrative of a Residence in Siam*, Bangkok: White Lotus, 1996 [1852].
Nidhi Eoseewong, *Pen and Sail: Literature and History in Early Bangkok (including the History of Bangkok in the Chronicles of Ayutthaya)*, edited by Chris Baker and Ben Anderson, with Craig J. Reynolds, Hong Lysa, Pasuk Phongpaichit, Patrick Jory and Ruth T. McVey, Chiang Mai: Silkworm Books, 2005 [1982].
Norden, Hermann, *From Golden Gate to Golden Sun: A Record of Travel, Sport, and Observation in Siam and Malaya*, London: H. F. and G. Witherby, 1923.
Norman, Henry, *The People and Politics of the Far East: Travels and Studies in the British, French, Spanish and Portuguese Colonies, Siberia, China, Japan, Korea, Siam and Malaya*, London: T. F. Unwin, 1895.
Pallegoix, Monsignor Jean-Baptiste, *Description of the Thai Kingdom or Siam: Thailand under King Mongkut*, trans. Walter E. J. Tips, Bangkok: White Lotus, 2000 [1854].
Pasuk Phongpaichit and Baker, Chris, *Thaksin: The Business of Politics in Thailand*, Chiang Mai: Silkworm Books, 2004.
——, *Thailand: Economy and Politics*, 2nd ed., New York: Oxford University Press, 2002.
Pasuk Phongpaichit, Sungsidh Piriyarangsan and Nualnoi Treerat, *Guns, Girls, Gambling, Ganja: Thailand's Illegal Economy and Public Policy*, Chiang Mai: Silkworm Books, 1998.
Penal Code for the Kingdom of Siam R. S. 127 (1908), The, Bangkok: American Presbyterian Mission Press, 1908.
Preecha Kanchanakom, Sinchai Krabuansaeng, Marut Amranondha and Kamol Chayawatana, *Dhonburi Mural Painting*, Bangkok: The Society for the Conservation of National Art Treasures and the Environment, 1980.
Pridi Banomyong, *Pridi by Pridi: Selected Writings on Life, Politics, and Economy*, trans. Chris Baker and Pasuk Phongpaichit, Chiang Mai: Silkworm Books, 2000.
Purachai Piusombun, *The Evolution of Thai Law Enforcement*, School of Public Administration, The National Institute of Development Administration, 1982.
Ramsden, H. A., *Siamese Porcelain and Other Tokens*, Yokohama, Japan: Jun Kobayagawa, 1911.
Reid, Anthony, *Southeast Asia in the Age of Commerce, 1450–1680. Volume One: The Lands Below the Winds*, New Haven and London: Yale University Press, 1988.
Reith, Gerda, *The Age of Chance: Gambling in Western Culture*, London and New York: Routledge, 1999.
Report on the Police Administration of Bangkok Town, Suburbs, and Railway District (title varies), 1899+.
Reynolds, Craig J., *Seditious Histories: Contesting Thai and Southeast Asian Pasts*, Seattle: University of Washington Press, 2006.
Reynolds, Craig J., and Hong Lysa, 'Marxism in Thai Historical Studies', *Journal of Asian Studies*, 43, 1 (November 1983), pp. 77–104.
Rujaya Abhakorn, M. R., 'Ratburi, An Inner Province: Local Government and Central Politics in Siam, 1868–92', PhD dissertation, Cornell University, 1984.
Sarasin Viraphol, 'Law in Traditional Siam and China: A Comparative Study', *Journal of the Siam Society*, 65, 1 (January 1977), pp. 81–136.

Sayre, Francis Bowes, 'The Passing of Extraterritoriality in Siam', *American Journal of International Law*, 22, 1 (January 1928), pp. 70–88.
Scott, James C., *Weapons of the Weak: Everyday Forms of Peasant Resistance*, New Haven: Yale University Press, 1985.
Seidenfaden, Erik, *Guide to Bangkok with Notes on Siam*, Singapore: Oxford University Press, 1984 [1928].
Sharp, Lauriston, and Hanks, Lucien, *Bang Chan: Social History of a Rural Community in Thailand*, Ithaca, New York, and London: Cornell University Press, 1978.
Skinner, G. William, *Chinese Society in Thailand: An Analytical History*, Ithaca, New York: Cornell University Press, 1957.
Smyth, H. Warrington, *Five Years in Siam: From 1891–1896*, Bangkok: White Lotus, 1994 [1898], 2 vols.
Sombat Plainoi, *Sorties Into Thai Cultural History*, Bangkok: Ministry of Education, 1982.
Sommerville, Maxwell, *Siam on the Meinam: From the Gulf to Ayuthia*, Bangkok: White Lotus, 1985 [1897].
Speer, Robert E., Day, Dwight H. and Bovaird, Dr. David, *Report of Deputation of the Presbyterian Board of Foreign Missions to Siam, the Philippines, Japan, Chosen and China, April–November 1915*, New York: Board of Foreign Missions of the Presbyterian Church in the U.S.A., 1916.
Stengs, Irene, *Worshipping the Great Moderniser: King Chulalongkorn, Patron Saint of the Thai Middle Class*, Singapore: NUS Press, 2009.
Sthirakoses (Phraya Anuman Rajdhon), *Looking Back: Book One*, Bangkok: Chulalongkorn University Press, 1992.
——, *Looking Back: Book Three*, Bangkok: Chulalongkorn University Press, 2001.
Terwiel, B. J., *Thailand's Political History: From the 13th Century to Recent Times*, rev. ed., Bangkok: River Books, 2011.
——, *Monks and Magic: An Analysis of Religious Ceremonies in Central Thailand*, 3rd ed., Bangkok: White Lotus, 1994.
——, *Through Travellers' Eyes: An Approach to Early Nineteenth Century Thai History*, Bangkok: Editions Duang Kamol, 1989.
Thailand, Committee of Redaction of 1917, 'Report on the Revision of the Penal Code of 1908, 28 July 1917' in M. B. Hooker (ed.), *The Laws of Southeast Asia, Volume 2: European Laws in Southeast Asia*, Singapore: Butterworth and Co., 1988.
Thailand, Ministry of Finance, *Report of the Financial Adviser upon the Budget of the Kingdom of Siam*, 1902+.
Thailand, Ministry of Finance, Department of Commerce and Statistics (name varies), *Statistical Yearbook of the Kingdom of Siam* (title varies), 1916+.
Thailand, Ministry of Justice, *Ministry of Justice Annual Report*, various years, 1902+.
Thak Chaloemtiarana, *Thailand: The Politics of Despotic Paternalism*, rev. ed., Ithaca, New York: Cornell Southeast Asia Program, 2007.
Thamsook Numnonda, 'Pibulsongkram's Thai Nation-Building Programme during the Japanese Military Presence, 1941–45', *Journal of Southeast Asian Studies*, 9, 2 (September 1978), pp. 234–47.
Thanet Aphornsuvan, 'Slavery and Modernity: Freedom in the Making of Modern Siam' in David Kelly and Anthony Reid (eds), *Asian Freedoms: The Idea*

of Freedom in East and Southeast Asia, Cambridge: Cambridge University Press, 1998, pp. 161–86.

Thanh-Dam Truong, *Sex, Money and Morality: Prostitution and Tourism in Southeast Asia*, London: Zed Books, 1990.

Thompson, P. A., *Siam: An Account of the Country and the People*, Bangkok: White Lotus, 1987 [1910].

Thompson, Virginia, *Thailand: The New Siam*, New York: MacMillan, 1941.

Thongchai Winichakul, 'The Quest for *"Siwilai"*: A Geographical Discourse of Civilizational Thinking in the Late Nineteenth and Early Twentieth-Century Siam', *Journal of Asian Studies*, 59, 3 (August 2000), pp. 528–49.

——, 'The Changing Landscape of the Past: New Histories in Thailand since 1973', *Journal of Southeast Asian Studies*, 26, 1 (March 1995), pp. 99–120.

——, *Siam Mapped: A History of the Geo-body of a Nation*, Honolulu: University of Hawaii Press, 1994.

Tips, Walter E. J., *Crime and Punishment in King Chulalongkorn's Kingdom: The Special Commission for the Reorganisation of the Provincial Courts of Ayutthaya (1898–1897)*, Bangkok: White Lotus, 1998.

Trocki, Carl A., *Opium, Empire and the Global Political Economy: A Study of the Asian Opium Trade*, London and New York: Routledge, 1999.

Turton, Andrew, 'Thai Institutions of Slavery' in James L. Watson (ed.), *Asian and African Systems of Slavery*, Oxford: Basil Blackwell, 1980, pp. 251–92.

Vella, Walter, 'Thianwan of Siam: A Man Who Fought Giants' in Ronald D. Renard (ed.), *Anuson Walter Vella*, Chiang Mai: W. F. Vella Fund, Payap University; and Honolulu: Center for Asian and Pacific Studies, University of Hawaii at Manoa, 1986, pp. 78–91.

——, *Chaiyo! King Vajiravudh and the Development of Thai Nationalism*, Honolulu: University of Hawaii Press, 1978.

Wakeman Jr., Frederic, *Policing Shanghai, 1927–1937*, Berkeley: University of California Press, 1995.

Warren, James Francis, *Rickshaw Coolie: A People's History of Singapore*, Singapore: Singapore University Press, 2003 [1986].

Wilson, Constance M., 'Revenue Farming, Economic Development and Government Policy during the Early Bangkok Period, 1830–92' in John Butcher and Howard Dick (eds), *The Rise and Fall of Revenue Farming: Business Elites and the Emergence of the Modern State in Southeast Asia*, London: MacMillan, 1993, pp. 142–64.

——, 'Bangkok in 1883: An Economic and Social Profile,' *Journal of the Siam Society*, 77, 2 (1989), pp. 49–58.

——, *Thailand: A Handbook of Historical Statistics*, Boston: G. K. Hall and Co., 1983.

——, 'State and Society in the Reign of Mongkut, 1851–68: Thailand on the Eve of Modernization', PhD dissertation, Cornell University, 1970.

Wood, W. A. R., *Consul in Paradise: Sixty-Nine Years in Siam*, London: Souvenir Press, 1965.

Wright, Arnold and Breakspear, Oliver (eds), *Twentieth Century Impressions of Siam: Its History, People, Commerce, Industries, and Resources*, Bangkok: White Lotus, 1994 [1908].

Wyatt, David K., *Thailand: A Short History*, 2nd ed., New Haven and London: Yale University Press, 2003.

——, *The Politics of Reform in Thailand: Education in the Reign of King Chulalongkorn*, New Haven and London: Yale University Press, 1969.

Young, Ernest, *The Kingdom of the Yellow Robe*, London: Archibald Constable and Co., 1900.

Zimmerman, Carle C., *Siam: Rural Economic Survey, 1930–31*, Bangkok: Bangkok Times Press, 1931.

Index

Abhisit Vejjajiva 185
absolute monarchy 7, 56, 58, 61, 73, 112, 161; criticisms of 60–1, 83, 89, 112–13, 118, 120–1, 125, 126, 132, 135–6, 180, 186; in Thai historiography 8–9, 11
absolutist state 7, 45–6, 51, 64, 66–7, 75, 89
alcohol 18, 20, 21, 32, 70, 77; tax farms on 15, 22, 181
anti-gambling discourse 68–74, 88–9, 137, 179–80; in present-day Thailand 184–7; in the press 122, 123, 136
Anti-Gambling League 10, 141–2
aristocracy *see* nobility *and* royalty
Arkartdamkeung Rapheephat, M. C. 82, 173–4, 178
Athikon Prakat, Phraya 94, 126, 127–8, 134–5
Ayutthaya period 14, 15–16, 17, 74, 111, 149–50

banditry 31, 33, 53, 70–1, 91, 92–3
Bangkok 15, 24, 33, 38, 166, 186; card dens in 80, 84–5; casinos in 2, 66; Chinese in 19–20, 78; comparison with Shanghai 103–4; crime in 32, 70; as gambling centre 31, 36, 55, 181; gambling houses in 28, 49, 50–1, 53–5; motor racing in 58; opium in 149, 154, 165; police force in 90–1; prostitution in 149, 150, 151–2, 154, 158, 169; underground gambling dens in 96, 102–3, 182, 183–4
Bangkok Opium Conference 163
Bhumibol Adulyadej, King 8, 187
billiards 2, 69, 81, 85–6, 122, 130, 146
board games 39, 52
boat races 14, 36, 38, 76

bookmaking 81, 87, 182
Bowring Treaty 18, 23, 73, 152; *see also* unequal treaties
Bradley, Dr Dan Beach 15, 118, 178
Britain/England 2, 49, 53, 101, 102, 152; and colonialism 6–7, 9, 18, 68; gambling in 43, 44, 81, 179; and opium 150, 151, 152, 160, 165
British Malaya 9, 22, 47, 65, 158
Buddhism 7, 133, 139, 147; proscriptions against gambling 69, 88, 137–8, 140, 186–7
bullfighting 38
Bunnag family 18, 44, 46, 48–9, 73, 153
bureaucrats/bureaucracy *see* government officials

card playing 14, 33, 38–9, 41, 80, 109, 110, 144; by the elite 40, 125, 146; at fairs and festivals 60, 76, 139–40; licensing of 36, 52, 53, 84–5
casinos 2, 64–6, 82, 84, 89; illegal 95, 182–3; legalization of 183–7
Chanthaburi, Prince 55–6, 57, 58, 72, 74, 80, 85
Chiang Mai 38, 52, 142
children: and gambling 30, 34, 39, 40; and slavery 71–2, 152; *see also* human trafficking
Chinese in Thailand 9, 14–16, 17, 26, 42; anti-Chinese sentiment 76, 77–8, 123; gambling by 15, 20–2, 28, 30, 41, 65–6, 77–80, 98–9; gambling games of 27, 34–5, 39, 83, 89; immigration 6, 19–20, 162, 164–5, 172; and remittances 74–5; secret societies (*angyi*) 20, 32–3, 47, 48, 92, 150, 152, 183
Chinese New Year *see* festivals

Index

Chulalongkorn, King 1, 8, 48–50, 81, 140, 178, 186–7; abolition of slavery 71, 175; attitude towards women 171; on the Bangkok police force 93; on extraterritoriality 104; policies on gambling 34, 39, 40, 68–9, 70, 72, 74, 78–9, 99, 112, 123; policies on opium 156; reforms of the Thai state 2, 51, 56, 66, 90, 91, 111, 113, 115
civilization *see siwilai*
cockfighting 14, 18, 36–8, 52, 115, 145; prohibition of 69, 76–7, 82, 84, 87, 89
colonialism 6–7, 68, 72, 142; attitudes towards the Chinese 79; semi-colonialism 8, 9–10, 104; Siamese 9–10, 45, 72, 75
commoners 16, 17, 118, 147; in the bureaucracy 7, 113, 178; gambling by 77, 89, 100, 179
constitutionalism 7, 62, 63–4, 67
corvée labour 7, 16–17, 23, 53, 73
crime: definitions of 4–5; gambling as cause of 60, 70–1, 74, 103, 112, 122, 135, 174, 177, 179, 185; and the gambling houses 31–3, 51; levels of 31–2, 70, 91, 175–7
Cultural Mandates *see* State Conventions
currency 22–6, 34, 43

Damrong Rachanuphap, Prince 10, 51, 74, 141, 178; on gambling 11, 40, 46, 53–4, 70, 80, 85; on opium 154
Devawongse, Prince 56, 99, 178
dice games 36, 39, 52, 60, 69, 116; *see also hi-lo*
dominoes 14, 39, 52
drugs 103, 115–16, 158, 159–60, 162; *see also* opium

extraterritoriality 6, 9, 10, 96, 105, 121; effect on policing 101–4

fairs 39, 59, 60, 122, 128–9; temple 41, 87–8, 139–41, 147; Winter 59–60, 61, 131–2
fan-tan *see thua*
farmers 16, 25–6, 61; defence of cockfighting 145; elite attitudes towards 71, 75, 178, 179; gambling by 37, 42–3, 70–1, 96, 100

festivals 39, 41, 52, 76, 87, 98–9, 169
fish fighting 18, 36, 38, 69, 76–7
football gambling 182, 183
France 1, 7, 53, 68, 101–2; gambling in 62, 63, 81, 82, 133

gambling: as conspicuous consumption 17, 39; as a crime 4–5, 96; criminalization of 6, 68, 88, 167–8; definitions of 2–4, 110–11; and economic development 16–18, 22–26, 43, 180–1; folktales and proverbs about 42–3, 142; legalization of 104, 183–7; reasons for 40–3; Thai historiography on 10–11
gambling counters 24–5, 6
gambling houses 2, 14, 15, 16, 20–1, 25, 27–8, 36, 49, 70–1; clientele of 21, 30–1, 40; closures of 33, 50, 52, 53–6, 74, 143; and crime 31, 32–3, 70; as entertainment centres 31, 41, 50; games played inside 28–30; in the press 123, 124; regulations for 50–1, 112–13, 138
Golden Triangle 165
Government Lottery Office (GLO) 63, 184, 185
government officials: criticisms of 125–6, 127, 131–2; gambling by 83, 99–100, 111–15, 133, 144; and opium smuggling 151, 152; popular attitudes towards 145, 146–7
greyhound racing: in Shanghai 103–4, 135

hi-lo 39, 131, 140, 169
horse racing 2, 10, 65, 69, 81–2, 87, 182; and the press 132–5
huai lottery 14, 16, 21, 23, 34–6, 49, 139; abolition of 55–6, 70, 74; in the press 123, 124; regulations for 112, 138; underground *huai* 92, 97, 107, 144, 182, 183, 184
human trafficking 158, 159, 161, 162, 164–5, 171

informers 83, 96, 97, 98, 184
Internet gambling 182, 183

Japan 7–8, 160, 162, 164, 165–6; and extraterritoriality 101, 102–3
judiciary 5, 6, 117, 176; and definitions of gambling 110–11; and sentencing 106–9

Index

kite flying 38

Lawson, Eric St John 51, 91; on causes of crime 31–2, 70, 176–7; on the police force 93–4, 112, 139; on rewards 95; on gambling by royalty 101
League of Nations 158, 160–5
legal system 105, 106, 111, 117
legislation 168; on gambling 2, 52–3, 83–7, 88, 92, 97–8, 111; on human trafficking 162; on opium 150, 158, 162, 163, 170; on prostitution 155–6, 157, 167
licensing: of gambling 4, 52–3, 80, 83–4, 85, 182
lotteries 2, 44, 45, 56–7, 58–9, 61; justifications for 80–1, 82, 123, 179; Liverpool Football Club lottery 184–5; state lotteries 62–4, 66–7, 182, 184, 185–6; *see also huai* lottery

marijuana *see* drugs
middle class 7, 9, 118, 120–1, 135–6, 174, 179–80, 183
missionaries 15, 72, 153, 159, 174, 178
modernity 9, 43, 65, 82, 135, 180, 181
Mongkut, King 18, 23, 68, 91, 178; attitude towards women 153; policies on gambling 23, 39–40, 69; policies on opium 152–3
monkhood/monks 36, 137, 139–41, 147, 153; gambling by 133, 138–9
Monte Carlo 60, 64, 65, 82, 173–4

Nakhon Si Thammarat 21, 54; gambling houses in 52, 71, 79, 142–3
narcotics *see* drugs *and* opium
nation-state 7, 44, 62, 75, 76, 89, 178
nationalism 135–6; Thai 7, 57, 59, 76, 118, 171
newspapers *see* press
nobility 44–5, 46, 48–9, 78; criticisms of 125–6, 133–4; gambling by 39–40, 83, 99–100, 111–12
Nonthisen, Phraya (Maek Siansewi) 58–9, 129–30, 131–2

opium 18–19, 20, 31, 142, 149, 152, 154, 165, 167–8, 169; as cause of crime 32, 70, 154–5; and the Chinese 21–2, 39, 152–3, 170–1, 172; government control efforts 157–8, 162, 163–4; government opium monopoly 156–7; international control efforts 159–61; in prison 115–17; prohibition of 149–50, 166–7; *see also* tax farming
organized crime 10, 183

pawnshops 31–2, 133
penalties 105, 111; for gambling offences 86, 107–10; for government officials 39, 113–14; for opium offences 153; for sexual offences 151
People's Party 7, 61, 62–3, 67
peasantry 7, 55; *see also* farmers
Phao Siyanon 166
Phibun Songkhram, Luang 7, 62, 73, 164, 166, 178; policies on gambling 65, 72–3, 76, 88, 145
Phuket 20, 21–2, 57, 79, 154
pitching coins 4, 111, 169
playing cards 38, 88; *see also* card playing
po pan 14, 27, 28–30, 77; *see also thua*
police 5, 20, 31, 32, 90–1, 93, 104, 112, 176, 179; complicity in illegal gambling 94–6, 113, 144–5, 180, 183–4; press depictions of 119, 120, 126–8; stationed in gambling houses 33, 50; suppression of gambling 87–8, 92–3, 96–7, 99–103, 116, 139
Prajadhipok, King 1, 9, 59, 60–1, 64, 114, 132; on the Bangkok Opium Conference 163; and the press 119, 121–2
press 5, 118–22, 141, 158, 175; criticisms of the absolute monarchy 125, 128–32; criticisms of government officials 112, 125–8; on gambling 60, 64, 66, 108, 122–4, 177, 185; on horse racing 132–5
Pridi Phanomyong 62–3, 65, 66, 81, 178
prisons 107, 115–17, 174, 177
prostitution 149, 150–2, 153–4, 165–6, 168–9, 171–2; demographics of 152, 158, 164–5, 169; and gambling houses 31, 32; international control efforts 159, 164, 165, 166; legislation on 155–6, 157, 167
public opinion 5, 59, 118, 121, 141; on gambling 64, 66, 126, 133, 134, 141–3, 146–8; on prostitution 166, 169, 171–2

Rama I, King 15, 39, 69, 111
Rama III, King 16, 17, 23, 40, 123, 150
Ratchaburi 21, 25, 57, 94; fairs in 60, 122, 128
revenue: from gambling 15, 19, 44, 45, 48, 49, 51–2, 53, 54–5, 80, 168; from opium 153, 154, 156–7, 161, 163, 165, 168; from prostitution 153, 157
rewards 95, 97–8
Royal Bangkok Sports Club (RBSC) *see* horse racing
Royal Turf Club *see* horse racing
royalty 46, 62, 78, 81, 178; gambling by 17, 39–40, 99, 100, 101, 111–12, 186

Sampheng 20, 28, 96, 102, 108, 139; prostitution in 151–2
Sangha *see* monkhood/monks
Sarit Thanarat 166–7
Sem Sumanan 120, 127–8, 130
semi-colonialism *see* colonialism
Shanghai 103–4, 135, 160
Si Suriyawong, Somdet Chaophraya (Chuang Bunnag) 48–50
Siamese Red Cross 57, 61, 62, 63, 81, 130
Singapore 44, 69, 134, 151, 158, 183
siwilai 68–9, 72–4, 75, 81, 82–3, 88–9, 124, 132
slavery 68, 71–2; and gambling 70, 71, 73–4, 77, 174–5; 'white slave trade' 159; and women 150, 151–2, 153
slaves: gambling by 40, 42
Songkran *see* festivals
sport 76, 178–9
state-building 56, 66–7
State Conventions 76–7
sweepstakes *see* horse racing

Taksin, King 15
tax farmers 25–6, 47, 50–1, 90, 92, 126; Chinese 19, 20, 46, 74–5, 77–8, 123
tax farming 16, 18–19, 21–2, 45–8, 49–50, 51, 54, 56, 181; and cockfighting 36–7, 69; and gambling houses 11, 15, 16, 27, 49, 50, 52, 54–6, 124; and the *huai* lottery 11, 16, 34, 49, 56; and opium 18, 46, 50, 51, 152–3, 154, 156; and prostitution 153
taxation 17, 23, 45, 53–5, 56, 61, 63, 65, 66–7, 73; of the Chinese 20–2, 78
Thai boxing 38
Thai identity 7, 45, 63, 75, 145, 153, 159, 187
Thaksin Shinawatra 184–7
Thianwan (T. W. S. Wannapho) 123–4
thua (fan-tan) 14, 15, 28–9, 56, 89; and the Chinese 77, 79–80, 98–9
tote 81–2, 135, 182
tourism 44, 65–6

unequal treaties 6, 18–19, 45, 66, 101, 105, 121; revision of 53–4, 56, 61, 88, 102, 161–2
United Nations (UN) 165, 166
United States (US) 2, 6, 18–19, 72, 101, 166, 172; and opium 150, 159–60, 165

Vajiravudh, King 1, 2, 9, 45, 57, 58, 59, 60, 113, 181; on the Chinese 78, 79; policies on gambling 55–6, 58, 76, 81, 103, 108, 113–14, 139; and the press 119, 121–2, 124, 125, 130, 132; and sport 76, 178–9
venereal disease 155–6, 157, 164–5, 166, 171

Wild Tiger Corps 57, 58, 59, 60, 81, 129–30; lottery scandal 58–9, 61
women 120, 152; attitudes towards 77, 150–1, 153, 155, 164, 171; gambling by 30, 39, 125–6, 133, 143; *see also* human trafficking, prostitution *and* slavery
Wongsanupraphat, Chaophraya (M. R. W. Sathan Sanitwong) 70, 75, 178, 179

Yomarat, Chaophraya (Pan Sukhum) 21, 58, 71, 74, 83, 100, 103, 133